North Carolina Juvenile Defender Manual

2017

David W. Andrews
John Rubin

🏛 UNC | **SCHOOL OF GOVERNMENT**

This manual is part of the North Carolina Indigent Defense Manual Series. Production of the series is made possible by funding from the North Carolina Office of Indigent Defense Services. John Rubin is series editor.

The School of Government at the University of North Carolina at Chapel Hill works to improve the lives of North Carolinians by engaging in practical scholarship that helps public officials and citizens understand and improve state and local government. Established in 1931 as the Institute of Government, the School provides educational, advisory, and research services for state and local governments. The School of Government is also home to a nationally ranked Master of Public Administration program, the North Carolina Judicial College, and specialized centers focused on community and economic development, information technology, and environmental finance.

As the largest university-based local government training, advisory, and research organization in the United States, the School of Government offers up to 200 courses, webinars, and specialized conferences for more than 12,000 public officials each year. In addition, faculty members annually publish approximately 50 books, manuals, reports, articles, bulletins, and other print and online content related to state and local government. The School also produces the Daily Bulletin Online each day the General Assembly is in session, reporting on activities for members of the legislature and others who need to follow the course of legislation.

Operating support for the School of Government's programs and activities comes from many sources, including state appropriations, local government membership dues, private contributions, publication sales, course fees, and service contracts.

Visit sog.unc.edu or call 919.966.5381 for more information on the School's courses, publications, programs, and services.

Michael R. Smith, Dean
Thomas H. Thornburg, Senior Associate Dean
Johnny Burleson, Associate Dean for Development
Michael Vollmer, Associate Dean for Administration
Linda H. Weiner, Associate Dean for Operations
Janet Holston, Director of Strategy and Innovation

FACULTY

Whitney Afonso
Trey Allen
Gregory S. Allison
David N. Ammons
Ann M. Anderson
Maureen Berner
Mark F. Botts
Anita R. Brown-Graham
Peg Carlson
Leisha DeHart-Davis
Shea Riggsbee Denning
Sara DePasquale
James C. Drennan
Richard D. Ducker
Norma Houston
Cheryl Daniels Howell
Jeffrey A. Hughes
Willow S. Jacobson
Robert P. Joyce
Diane M. Juffras
Dona G. Lewandowski
Adam Lovelady

James M. Markham
Christopher B. McLaughlin
Kara A. Millonzi
Jill D. Moore
Jonathan Q. Morgan
Ricardo S. Morse
C. Tyler Mulligan
Kimberly L. Nelson
David W. Owens
LaToya B. Powell
William C. Rivenbark
Dale J. Roenigk
John Rubin
Jessica Smith
Meredith Smith
Carl W. Stenberg III
John B. Stephens
Charles Szypszak
Shannon H. Tufts
Aimee N. Wall
Jeffrey B. Welty
Richard B. Whisnant

© 2017
School of Government
The University of North Carolina at Chapel Hill

First edition 2008. Second edition 2017.

ISBN 978-1-56011-918-0

Contents

Each chapter contains a detailed table of contents.

Appendix A
Juvenile Justice and Medicaid   **A-1**

Preface

We are pleased to release the 2017 edition of the North Carolina Juvenile Defender Manual. The first edition of the manual was written to provide a framework of juvenile delinquency law and proceedings in North Carolina to new juvenile defenders, as well as a review of statutes and case law for attorneys experienced in juvenile court. We hope this second edition of the manual achieves these same goals and that it provides new insights for those who represent juveniles in delinquency proceedings.

This edition of the manual would not have been possible without the support of several institutions and people. Thanks go to the Office of Indigent Defense Services and the UNC School of Government, which recognized the importance of updating and further developing the material in this manual. Thanks also go to Lou Newman, the lead author of the initial edition of this manual, who provided the foundation for our work on this edition. We are grateful to Staples Hughes, the North Carolina Appellate Defender until 2015, and Glenn Gerding, the current North Carolina Appellate Defender, who supported and encouraged our work on the manual. This edition of the manual also benefitted tremendously from the feedback and suggestions of Eric Zogry, the North Carolina Juvenile Defender; LaToya B. Powell, Assistant Professor of Public Law and Government at the UNC School of Government; Austine Long, Program Attorney at the UNC School of Government; and Kim Howes, Assistant Juvenile Defender. Thanks also to Caitlin Little for her careful editing of the citations and other information in this edition of the manual.

The preface to the first edition of this manual began with a quote from *In re Gault*, 387 U.S. 1 (1967), the Supreme Court decision that transformed the practice of law in juvenile delinquency cases. This year, stakeholders in juvenile courts around the country celebrated the 50th anniversary of the *Gault* opinion. Though a half century has passed since *Gault* was issued, the principles at stake—the right to counsel, the right to notice, the right to confrontation, the right against self-incrimination—are as relevant today as they were in 1967. Juveniles—*children*—deserve hearings that "measure up to the essentials of due process and fair treatment." *Id.* at 30 (*quoting Kent v. United States*, 383 U.S. 541, 562 (1966)). With these principles as a guide, we hope this manual gives juvenile defenders the tools they need to defend children who enter the juvenile court system in this state.

Comments and suggestions are welcome. They may be sent to David Andrews at david.w.andrews@nccourts.org or John Rubin at rubin@sog.unc.edu.

David W. Andrews
John Rubin
October 2017

About the North Carolina Indigent Defense Manual Series

The North Carolina Indigent Defense Manual Series is a collection of reference manuals addressing law and practice in areas in which indigent defendants and respondents are entitled to the representation of counsel at state expense. The series was created to address the need for comprehensive reference materials for public defenders and appointed counsel, who devote their time, skill, and effort to representing poor people. In addition to assisting indigent defenders with their responsibilities, the manuals also may be useful to others who work in the court system and who need a reference source on the law. In keeping with the School of Government's commitment to practical scholarship, the manuals are written by authors with subject-matter expertise in their respective fields, experience in developing effective educational materials, and knowledge of how things work in practice. The editor of the series is John Rubin, a member of the School of Government faculty who specializes in indigent defense education. Other manuals in the series can be found on our Indigent Defense Manual Series website. Production of the series is made possible by funding from the North Carolina Office of Indigent Defense Services, which is responsible for overseeing and enhancing the provision of indigent defense representation in North Carolina.

About the Authors of the North Carolina Juvenile Defender Manual (2017 Edition)

David W. Andrews is an assistant appellate defender and the Director of Non-Jury Dispositions at the Office of the Appellate Defender in Durham, North Carolina. There, he represents indigent appellants in criminal, juvenile delinquency, and involuntary commitment appeals in the North Carolina Court of Appeals and the Supreme Court of North Carolina. David has worked extensively on cases involving juvenile defendants subject to sentences of life without parole and serves as the liaison between the Office of the Appellate Defender and attorneys who handle juvenile delinquency and involuntary commitment cases. He earned a B.B.A. from the University of Georgia and J.D. from North Carolina Central University.

John Rubin joined the School of Government faculty in 1991. He specializes in criminal law and procedure and indigent defense education. Before joining the School, he practiced law for nine years in Washington, D.C., and Los Angeles, California. He has written extensively on criminal law and procedure and teaches and consults with indigent defenders, judges, magistrates, prosecutors, and others who work in the court system. He earned a B.A. from the University of California at Berkeley and a J.D. from UNC-Chapel Hill. In 2008, he received the Albert and Gladys Coates Term Award for Faculty Excellence. In 2012, he was named Albert Coates Professor of Public Law and Government.

Chapter 1
Overview of Manual and Juvenile Delinquency Proceedings

1.1 Purpose of Manual

With support from the Office of Indigent Defense Services, which includes the Office of the Juvenile Defender (*see infra* § 1.4, Office of the Juvenile Defender), the School of Government at the University of North Carolina at Chapel Hill has created a series of manuals designed to assist indigent defense attorneys representing defendants and respondents in a variety of proceedings. The purpose of this manual is to provide a thorough review of juvenile delinquency law and proceedings for the attorney new to practice in juvenile court, as well as to serve as a statutory and case law reference for seasoned juvenile defenders. Incorporated in the legal authority, the reader will find practice tips or suggestions for best practices at each stage of the proceedings, which have been provided by experienced juvenile defenders in North Carolina.

This manual contains a discussion of the role of counsel in juvenile proceedings as well as information from the National Juvenile Defender Center on the special challenges and approaches to communicating with a juvenile client. The jurisdiction of juvenile court and the parties and other participants to the proceeding are reviewed. Each stage of a delinquency proceeding is examined, from the intake process, through the filing of a petition, custody hearings, probable cause and transfer hearings, and discovery in juvenile court, to the adjudicatory and dispositional hearings.

Important issues, such as the juvenile's capacity to proceed, motions to suppress statements of the juvenile or evidence seized, probation and violation of probation hearings in juvenile proceedings, and commitment of juveniles to the Division of Adult Correction and Juvenile Justice are addressed in separate chapters. Procedures for appeals of juvenile cases and expunction of juvenile court records are also covered briefly.

Other indigent defense manuals in the series, which may be viewed on the School of Government's <u>defender manuals website</u> at no charge, are sources of more in-depth information in their respective areas of law:

- North Carolina Defender Manual (Vol. 1, Pretrial; Vol. 2, Trial)
- North Carolina Civil Commitment Manual
- North Carolina Guardianship Manual
- Immigration Consequences of a Criminal Conviction in North Carolina
- Raising Issues of Race in North Carolina Criminal Cases

Manuals on other topics, including child support contempt proceedings and abuse, neglect, dependency, and termination of rights proceedings, are also available on that site under the Other Manuals tab.

1.2   Basic Terminology

While juveniles enjoy many of the same rights as adults in the criminal justice system, juvenile delinquency cases have been referred to as civil proceedings in North Carolina case law. The juvenile is referred to as a respondent to the proceeding, not a defendant. A delinquency case is initiated by the filing of a petition and proceeds to an adjudicatory hearing, not a trial, before a district court judge. The judge does not sentence the juvenile who has been adjudicated delinquent, but instead is required to craft a disposition after a dispositional hearing that is carefully tailored to address the unique circumstances of the juvenile. Other terms used in various areas of juvenile law are highlighted at the beginning of each chapter.

1.3   Brief Overview of Juvenile Delinquency Proceedings

Overview. Juvenile law in the United States evolved from the English common law, which held that juveniles under a certain age were not culpable for their acts, and those over that age were tried as adults. Beginning in the early 20th century, many courts followed the doctrine of *parens patriae*. Under this doctrine, courts provided rehabilitation and protective supervision, but few legal rights, for delinquent and dependent children. In 1919, the North Carolina General Assembly enacted the Juvenile Court Act, which reflected many of the goals of the doctrine of *parens patriae* and was upheld in *State v. Burnett*, 179 N.C. 735 (1920). In the 1960s and 1970s, the United States Supreme Court issued several rulings that departed from many of the informal procedures associated with the doctrine of *parens patriae* and extended constitutional rights traditionally associated with adult criminal cases to juveniles alleged to be delinquent. Based on those rulings, the North Carolina General Assembly has incorporated these and other rights in the North Carolina Juvenile Code.

Constitutional milestones. The United States Supreme Court recognized in 1966 that juveniles have the constitutional right to due process in delinquency proceedings. *Kent v.*

U.S., 383 U.S. 541 (1966). This holding was affirmed and expanded in 1967 by *In re Gault*, 387 U.S. 1 (1967), which held that due process required that the juvenile receive notice of the allegations in the petition and due notice of the adjudicatory hearing. The Court further held that juveniles have the right to be represented by counsel and to confront the witnesses against them. Finally, the Court held that the Fifth Amendment right against self-incrimination applied to juveniles in delinquency proceedings. In 1970, the United States Supreme Court held that juveniles have the constitutional right under the Due Process Clause to have delinquency allegations proven beyond a reasonable doubt. *In re Winship*, 397 U.S. 358 (1970). Five years later, the Court held that juveniles have the right to be free from double jeopardy. *Breed v. Jones*, 421 U.S. 519, 541 (1975). Practice in North Carolina juvenile delinquency proceedings is based on these important constitutional holdings and subsequent appellate cases recognizing the rights of juveniles alleged to be delinquent, as well as on the statutory rights and procedures provided by the North Carolina Juvenile Code.

Evolution of the juvenile's right to counsel in North Carolina. Soon after the Supreme Court issued its decision in *Gault*, the North Carolina General Assembly enacted former G.S. 110-29.1 (1967 Cum. Supplement), which guaranteed the right to counsel for juveniles facing the possibility of commitment to a training school, as well as the right to appointed counsel for indigent juveniles. Appellate decisions interpreting *Gault* also required affirmative evidence in the record that the trial court advised both the juvenile and the juvenile's parents of these rights. *In re Garcia*, 9 N.C. App. 691, 694 (1970) (reversing adjudication order because the trial court failed to advise juvenile and his parents of the right to appointed counsel); *In re Stanley*, 17 N.C. App. 370, 371 (1973) (same).

In 1979, the Juvenile Code Revision Committee, part of the former Department of Crime Control and Public Safety, recommended the enactment of a statute guaranteeing juveniles the right to counsel in all proceedings. The committee also recommended requiring the appointment of counsel for juveniles unless counsel was retained or the juvenile voluntarily, knowingly, and intelligently waived the right to counsel. The General Assembly determined that juveniles must have the right to counsel at all stages of delinquency proceedings and that the trial court must appoint counsel in any proceeding in which delinquency is alleged unless counsel was retained for the juvenile. *See* former G.S. 7A-584 (1980). The statute did not contain any provisions permitting juveniles to waive the right to counsel. *Id*. Since 1980, juveniles in North Carolina have automatically been afforded counsel in delinquency cases unless counsel has been retained. G.S. 7B-2000.

The public defender system in North Carolina has played an important role in representing juveniles in delinquency cases. The first two public defender offices, located in Guilford and Cumberland counties, provided representation to juveniles when the offices began operating in 1970. Currently, all but two public defender offices represent juveniles. The Office of the Appellate Defender also provides representation to juveniles who appeal.

The Counsel for Children's Rights (CFCR), a non-profit law firm in Mecklenburg County, has maintained a contract to represent juveniles since 1987, making it one of the oldest indigent defense contracts in the state. CFCR promotes best practices in juvenile defense, including the use of in-house investigators and social workers.

For a further discussion of the evolution of the right to counsel, see LaToya Powell, *Due Process Rights and Children: Fifty Years of In re Gault – Part Two, the Right to Counsel*, ON THE CIVIL SIDE, UNC SCH. OF GOV'T BLOG, (Sep. 14, 2016).

Juvenile court jurisdiction. Juvenile court proceedings are held in district court before a judge sitting without a jury. The juvenile court has jurisdiction over juveniles alleged to be delinquent who are at least six years old and less than 16 years old at the time the alleged offense occurred. Delinquency allegations are generally the same acts described as criminal offenses under the Criminal Code. Jurisdiction over juveniles who are 13, 14, or 15 years old and who are alleged to have committed a felony may be transferred to superior court for trial of the juvenile as an adult.

Juvenile delinquency proceedings. A delinquency case is commenced in juvenile court by the filing of a petition. If a felony is alleged there must be a first appearance hearing as well as a subsequent probable cause hearing. A secure or nonsecure custody hearing must be held if the juvenile is placed in custody pending the adjudicatory hearing. A transfer hearing is held if the juvenile is 13, 14, or 15 years old, is alleged to have committed a felony, and either a party or the court requests that the matter be transferred to superior court for trial.

Adjudication is the evidentiary hearing before a district court judge to determine whether the allegations in the petition have been proven beyond a reasonable doubt. The State is represented by the district attorney, and the juvenile must be represented by counsel. If a juvenile is adjudicated to be delinquent, a dispositional hearing will be held to determine the disposition to be ordered. Post-dispositional hearings include those for alleged violations of probation or post-release supervision, hearings on request for extended commitment, and review hearings.

Legislative note: This chapter reviews the laws in effect at the time of completion of this manual in Fall 2017. During the 2017 legislative session, the General Assembly enacted the Juvenile Justice Reinvestment Act, which expanded the jurisdiction of juvenile court to include crimes committed by 16 and 17-year-olds, except for motor vehicle offenses. Most of the changes apply to offenses committed on or after December 1, 2019. For a discussion of the changes that take effect in 2017, see *infra* Ch. 19, Raise the Age Legislation. For a discussion of the changes that take effect in 2019, see LaToya Powell, *2017 Juvenile Justice Reinvestment Act*.

1.4   Office of the Juvenile Defender

A. Creation of the Office

The Office of the Juvenile Defender (OJD) began operations in January 2005 following a comprehensive study of juvenile representation in North Carolina prepared by the American Bar Association, the National Juvenile Defender Center, and the Southern Juvenile Defender Center. The study identified deficiencies in the North Carolina juvenile justice system and made several recommendations. In response, the North Carolina Commission on Indigent Defense Services formed a Juvenile Committee to review the study. After several meetings, the Juvenile Committee released a report in which it recommended the creation of a statewide Juvenile Defender as a "positive first step" toward improving the representation of juveniles in North Carolina. In July 2004, the North Carolina General Assembly issued a budget authorizing the creation of OJD.

B. Mission

There are four parts of the mission of the OJD, which stem from the report prepared by the Juvenile Committee: (1) to provide services and support to juvenile defense attorneys, (2) to evaluate the current system of representation and make recommendations as needed, (3) to elevate the stature of juvenile delinquency representation, and (4) to work with juvenile justice advocates to promote positive change in the juvenile justice system.

Provide services and support to juvenile defense counsel. The OJD helps organize trainings on introductory, intermediate, and advanced topics for juvenile defense attorneys. The OJD has partnered with the School of Government to establish an annual one-day conference that includes updates on recent case law and new legislation and sessions on specific topics, as well as a biennial three-day intensive program for juvenile defense attorneys. Upcoming training sessions are listed on the OJD website and on the School of Government's indigent defense education website.

The OJD also provides several online resources for juvenile defense attorneys. The OJD website provides case summaries of North Carolina appellate decisions in juvenile delinquency appeals, a motions bank, training materials, a blog, information on recent legislative changes, and links to other agencies and organizations. In addition, the OJD uses a listserv for juvenile defense attorneys across the state. The listserv provides a forum for the OJD to announce relevant appellate decisions and for juvenile defense attorneys to discuss case problems, systemic issues, and other relevant topics. Juvenile defense attorneys can also follow the OJD on Twitter and Facebook.

Finally, the OJD is available to consult with juvenile defense attorneys on individual cases. The OJD often strategizes with attorneys on trial and appellate cases and can provide information on experts and other resources that might assist attorneys in defending juveniles.

Evaluate the current system and make recommendations. The OJD visits judicial districts across the state, gathering information from juvenile defense counsel, judges, and other court officials. Recommendations to improve the quality of juvenile defense representation are made to the Office of Indigent Defense Services (IDS), including recommendations to enter into contracts with local counsel to represent juveniles. In 2006, the OJD issued a statement on the role of defense counsel in juvenile delinquency cases and model qualification standards for juvenile defense attorneys. The model qualification standards are used by IDS and public defender offices to determine whether an attorney has sufficient experience and training to represent juveniles in delinquency cases. In 2007, the OJD, in conjunction with a committee of defense attorneys, judges, and educators, developed performance guidelines for juvenile defense counsel, which are included in Chapter 18 of this manual and are available on the OJD website.

Elevate the stature of juvenile delinquency representation. The OJD promotes juvenile defense representation through presentations at law schools, responses to the media, and participation of staff on boards and committees involved with juvenile delinquency issues. The OJD worked with the North Carolina State Bar Board of Legal Specialization to create a subspecialty in juvenile delinquency law. The first attorneys to earn the subspecialty were certified in 2012. Additionally, the OJD collaborated with the North Carolina Advocates for Justice to create a section of members dedicated to juvenile defense. From 2010 through 2014, the Juvenile Defender acted as Director of the Southern Juvenile Defender Center, providing resources and support for juvenile defense attorneys in seven southeastern states.

Work with juvenile justice advocates to promote positive change. The OJD regularly works to strengthen the rights of juveniles in the juvenile justice system. Since its inception, the OJD has worked with stakeholders to address systemic issues, such as overrepresentation of minorities in the juvenile justice system, overutilization of criminal and juvenile proceedings to address conduct that occurs in schools, and shackling of juveniles during court proceedings. Over the past decade, the OJD has supported efforts to raise the age of juvenile jurisdiction in North Carolina. The OJD worked with the North Carolina Commission on the Administration of Law and Justice on legislation to handle offenses by 16- and 17-year olds in juvenile court.

Chapter 2
Rights and Protections Afforded to Juveniles

2.1 Sources of Juvenile Rights and Protections

The U.S. Supreme Court has recognized that juveniles have many of the constitutional due process rights afforded adult defendants: the right to counsel, the right to notice of the charges against them, the right to confront and cross-examine witnesses, and the right against self-incrimination. *In re Gault*, 387 U.S. 1 (1967). Juveniles also have the right to have the alleged offense proven beyond a reasonable doubt, *In re Winship*, 397 U.S. 358, 368 (1970), and the right to be free from double jeopardy. *Breed v. Jones*, 421 U.S. 519,

541 (1975). The North Carolina Juvenile Code provides additional statutory rights to juveniles, such as the right to have a parent present during in-custody interrogation, the presumption of indigency, and confidentiality of information related to juvenile court proceedings. G.S. 7B-2101(a), (b); 7A-2000(b); 7A-3000(b). The principal rights are discussed in this chapter, although it is not intended to be exhaustive.

2.2   Constitutional Rights Not Afforded to Juveniles

The U.S. Supreme Court has held that juveniles are not afforded the right to trial by jury. *McKeiver v. Pennsylvania*, 403 U.S. 528, 545 (1971). The Supreme Court has not ruled on whether juveniles have the right to bail, the right to a speedy trial, or the right to self-representation under the United States Constitution, and the North Carolina General Assembly did not extend those rights to juveniles as part of the Juvenile Code. G.S. 7B-2405.

Each of these rights attaches on transfer of a juvenile case to superior court for trial as an adult. If the prosecutor requests transfer of the case to superior court, counsel should advise the juvenile of these differences.

Transfer of a juvenile case to superior court is almost always detrimental to the juvenile in the long term. Some juveniles may believe that transfer is a good alternative—for example, a juvenile who is in secure custody pending hearing and who would probably be released on bail in superior court, or a juvenile who faces commitment to a youth development center and who might get probation in superior court. Counsel should advise the juvenile of the potentially harsh consequences of transfer, such as having a criminal record or being sentenced to prison. *See infra* § 9.8, Transfer of Jurisdiction to Superior Court.

2.3   Right to Counsel

The juvenile's constitutional right to counsel was first recognized by the U.S. Supreme Court in *In re Gault*, 387 U.S. 1, 41 (1967). This right is codified in G.S. 7B-2000, which states that the juvenile has the right to be represented by counsel in all delinquency proceedings. The right to counsel extends to hearings on revocation of post-release supervision, G.S. 7B-2516, but not to the juvenile court counselor's decision to file a juvenile petition. Nevertheless, if counsel is retained or appointed to represent the juvenile on another case, counsel could assist the juvenile while the court counselor screens the case. *See infra* § 5.1B, Importance to Juvenile's Counsel.

In addition, all juveniles are conclusively presumed to be indigent and must be appointed counsel in any proceeding in which the juvenile is alleged to be delinquent unless counsel is retained for the juvenile. Although the right to an appointed attorney extends to appeals, juveniles are not entitled to an appointed attorney in expunction proceedings. *See* G.S. 7A-451 (defining the scope of the entitlement to appointment of counsel).

By statute, the juvenile also must be advised during any custodial interrogation of the "right to consult with an attorney and that one will be appointed . . . if the juvenile is not represented and wants representation." G.S. 7B-2101(a)(4). Questioning must cease once the juvenile has invoked the right to consult an attorney. *See* G.S. 7B-2101(c) (questioning must cease if juvenile indicates wish not to be questioned further). Under G.S. 7B-1501(17), "[w]herever the term 'juvenile' is used with reference to rights and privileges, that term encompasses the attorney for the juvenile as well."

Counsel for the juvenile serves as the juvenile's "voice to the court, representing the expressed interests of the juvenile at every stage of the proceedings." IDS Performance Guidelines for Appointed Counsel in Juvenile Delinquency Proceedings at the Trial Level, Performance Guideline 2.1(a) (2007); *see also infra* Appendix 3-1, Role of Defense Counsel in Juvenile Delinquency Proceedings (stating that the juvenile's attorney "is bound to advocate the expressed interests of the juvenile"). Counsel does not seek to advance the juvenile's best interests, as defined by the juvenile's parents or guardian, the prosecutor, or the trial court. Instead, the role of the juvenile defense attorney is to seek the juvenile's input, understand the juvenile's perspective, and enable the juvenile, to the greatest extent possible, to decide how to proceed. If counsel does not serve the juvenile's expressed interests, "the juvenile would be subjected to a pre-*Gault* proceeding in which protecting the juvenile's due process rights are relegated to a mere technicality." Robin Walker Sterling, *Role of Juvenile Defense Counsel in Delinquency Court* at 8 (National Juvenile Defender Center 2009).

2.4   Right Against Self-Incrimination

This section briefly reviews a juvenile's right against self-incrimination. For a more in-depth review, see *infra* § 11.3, Bases for Motions to Suppress Statement or Admission of Juvenile, and § 11.4, Case Law: Motions to Suppress In-Custody Statements of Juveniles.

A. Constitutional Right

The constitutional right against self-incrimination guaranteed by the Fifth Amendment has been held applicable to juvenile proceedings by the U.S. Supreme Court. *In re Gault*, 387 U.S. 1, 55 (1967). A juvenile cannot be compelled to give information that could later be used against the juvenile in an adjudicatory hearing and cannot be compelled to testify. *Id.*

B. Statutory Rights

A juvenile in custody is entitled to statutory protections that include and go beyond the requirements of *Miranda* warnings. G.S. 7B-2101. The Juvenile Code provides that any juvenile in custody must be advised before questioning of the following: the right to remain silent; that any statement the juvenile chooses to make may be used against the juvenile; that the juvenile has the right to have a parent, guardian, or custodian present during the questioning; and that the juvenile has a right to an attorney and that one will be appointed on request. G.S. 7B-2101(a); *see infra* § 11.3, Bases for Motions to Suppress Statement or Admission of Juvenile.

Additionally, a juvenile under 16 years of age cannot waive the presence of a parent, guardian, or custodian during interrogation. G.S. 7B-2101(b). If an attorney is not present, interrogating officers must also advise the juvenile's parent, guardian, or custodian of the juvenile's rights. However, the juvenile's rights may not be waived by the juvenile's parent, guardian, or custodian. *Id.*

If the requirements of G.S. 7B-2101(b) are satisfied, the juvenile may waive the right against self-incrimination. *State v. Flowers*, 128 N.C. App. 697, 701-02 (1998). The State bears the burden of proving by a preponderance of the evidence that the waiver is knowing and intelligent. *Id.* The court must then determine, based on the "specific facts and circumstances of each case, including background, experience, and conduct" of the juvenile," whether the waiver was knowing and intelligent. *State v. Johnson*, 136 N.C. App. 683, 693 (2000).

C. Admission to Juvenile Court Counselor at Intake

A statement made by the juvenile to the juvenile court counselor during the intake process is not admissible before the dispositional hearing. G.S. 7B-2408. There is no provision for the juvenile's waiver of this protection. Counsel should object to admission at the adjudicatory hearing of any inculpatory statements made by the juvenile to the juvenile court counselor during the intake process.

2.5   Right to Standard of Proof Beyond a Reasonable Doubt

Juveniles have the constitutional right under the Due Process Clause of the 14th Amendment to be adjudicated under the standard of proof of beyond a reasonable doubt. *In re Winship*, 397 U.S. 358, 368 (1970). In *Winship*, the U.S. Supreme Court recognized that although important differences exist between juvenile proceedings and criminal trials, the potential for the juvenile's loss of liberty requires that the standard of proof of beyond a reasonable doubt be applied in juvenile delinquency proceedings. *Id.* at 366–68. This right is codified in G.S. 7B-2409. *See infra* § 12.5D, Burden of Proof.

2.6   Right to Be Free from Double Jeopardy

Juveniles have the right to be free from double jeopardy. *Breed v. Jones*, 421 U.S. 519, 541 (1975). Jeopardy attaches in juvenile cases when the trial court begins to hear evidence. *In re Hunt and In re Dowd*, 46 N.C. App. 732, 735 (1980). Based on double jeopardy principles, a court may not adjudicate the juvenile delinquent for an offense and then transfer the juvenile to adult court for prosecution of the same offense. *Breed*, 421 U.S. at 541; *In re J.L.W.*, 136 N.C. App. 596, 598 (2000). Additionally, if the court dismisses a petition based on the lack of sufficient evidence, the State may not prosecute the juvenile based on a new petition for the same offense or a greater or lesser offense. *See also In re Drakeford*, 32 N.C. App. 113, 119 (1977) (vacating adjudication for affray because the trial court had previously dismissed a petition for assault, which arose out of the same incident as the affray, and jeopardy had attached on the assault petition before it was dismissed).

A juvenile's right to double jeopardy is ordinarily not violated when the trial court continues an adjudication hearing for the State to subpoena witnesses. *See Hunt and Dowd*, 46 N.C. App. at 735 (in two related appeals, trial court did not violate the respondents' right to be free from double jeopardy by continuing the cases so the State could present the testimony of additional witnesses). But, a mid-adjudication continuance may violate double jeopardy in limited circumstances, such as when the adjudication begins anew. *See State v. Coats,* 17 N.C. App. 407 (1973); *see also* 1 NORTH CAROLINA DEFENDER MANUAL § 10.8D, Extending Session to Compete Trial (2d ed. 2013) (discussing other circumstances in which double jeopardy may be violated by mid-trial continuance).

2.7   Right to an Open Hearing

Juvenile hearings are open by statute, although a hearing may be closed to the public for good cause on motion of a party or the court *unless* the juvenile requests that it be open. In ruling on a motion to close a hearing, the court must consider the allegations against the juvenile, the age and maturity of the juvenile, the benefit of confidentiality to the juvenile, and the possibility of breach of confidentiality of the juvenile court file and weigh these factors against the benefit to the public of an open hearing. G.S. 7B-2402. It is within the court's discretion whether to close the hearing, and the court's ruling must be upheld unless it is shown to be arbitrary or manifestly unsupported by reason. *In re K.T.L.*, 177 N.C. App. 365, 370 (2006) (court did not abuse discretion in denying motions of State and juvenile for hearing to be closed where testimony, findings of fact, and conclusions of law supported court's decision). Important factors in *K.T.L.* were the publicity the case had already received and the widespread knowledge within the community of the allegations and the juvenile's identity. *Id.* at 370–71.

The juvenile's interest is most often served by closing the hearing to the public, thereby preserving the confidentiality of the proceedings. For instance, confidentiality would particularly benefit the juvenile in cases involving allegations of sexual activity or discussions of the juvenile's mental health. When the hearing is closed, the juvenile is not subjected to potential emotional or psychological damage resulting from public knowledge of the allegations and evidence. The juvenile may also feel more at ease without additional people in the courtroom. A closed hearing may also be important in cases that draw the attention of the media or that involve gang-related activities, as the juvenile might be subjected to unwanted public reaction or reprisals. Counsel should consult with the juvenile before determining whether to move for a closed hearing.

In some districts, delinquency cases may be heard in a court session that includes other kinds of cases. In these instances, counsel must make a motion to close the hearing before it starts. If the motion is granted, the court must issue an order closing the hearing, requiring all persons not directly involved in the case to leave the courtroom. Counsel should request that a deputy be stationed at the courtroom door, or that a sign be posted stating that the court is in closed session, to prevent others from entering during the proceeding.

2.8   Right to Confidentiality

This section briefly reviews a juvenile's right to confidentiality of information related to juvenile court proceedings. For a more in-depth discussion of this topic, see Janet Mason, *Confidentiality in Juvenile Delinquency Proceedings,* ADMINISTRATION OF JUSTICE BULLETIN No. 2011/01 (May 2011).

A. Juvenile Court Records

Juvenile court records generally closed to public. The clerk of superior court must maintain a complete record that includes every document filed in a juvenile case. G.S. 7B-3000(a). This record is not open to the public except by court order. G.S. 7B-3000(b). The juvenile court record is accessible to the following people without an order: the juvenile or the juvenile's attorney; the juvenile's parent, guardian, or custodian; the prosecutor; court counselors; and probation officers (as provided in subsection (e)(1) of G.S. 7B-3000 for the purpose of assessing risk related to supervision). The prosecutor has discretion to share information from the court file with magistrates and law enforcement officers sworn in this state, but may not provide a photocopy of any part of the record. G.S. 7B-3000(b).

The clerk's records for juvenile cases include both paper files and electronic files maintained in JWise, the electronic records management system for juvenile courts. As part of the Juvenile Justice Reinvestment Act of 2017, the General Assembly mandated that the Administrative Office of the Courts expand access to JWise to prosecutors and juvenile defense attorneys by July 1, 2018. For a further discussion of access to JWise, see *infra* § 19.2, Changes Effective in 2017.

If a court issues an order under G.S. 7B-3000(b) allowing access to a juvenile record, it may concurrently issue a protective order preventing further dissemination of the information. *See generally Doe 1 v. Swannanoa Valley Youth Development Center*, 163 N.C. App. 136, 142 (2004) (court issued protective order prohibiting disclosure of information from juvenile record beyond those directly involved in case and allowed parties to submit confidential information under seal).

The court may direct the clerk to seal any part of the court record, which can then be examined or copied only on court order. G.S. 7B-3000(c). This order extends to all people, including those that ordinarily have access to the juvenile court record. Counsel should move to seal especially sensitive information in the file, such as mental health records or a psychological or sex offender evaluation, to provide additional protection to the juvenile. A sample motion and order to seal records is available on the Juvenile Defender website.

Statutory exceptions for use in limited criminal court proceedings. If a defendant is charged in an adult criminal proceeding for a Class A1 misdemeanor or a felony and he or she was less than 21 years of age at the time of the offense, law enforcement officers, magistrates, courts, and prosecutors may examine the defendant's juvenile court records under G.S. 7B-3000(e). The following additional criteria must be met:

- the records involve adjudications for offenses that would be a Class A1 misdemeanor or felony if committed by an adult,
- the adjudications occurred after the defendant reached 13 years of age, and
- the records are only used for pretrial release, plea negotiation recommendations, and plea acceptance decisions.

If these criteria are met and the defendant's juvenile court record is used, the records must remain confidential and must not be placed in any public record. G.S. 7B-3000(e).

An adjudication of delinquency for an offense that would be a Class A, B1, B2, C, D, or E felony if committed by an adult may be used in other ways against the juvenile in a subsequent criminal prosecution. The adjudication can be used to show "proof of motive, opportunity, intent, preparation, plan, knowledge, identity, or absence of mistake, entrapment or accident" under N.C. Evidence Rule 404(b). G.S. 7B-3000(f). It may also be used to prove an aggravating factor for felonies and capital cases on order of the criminal court after an in camera hearing to determine admissibility. *Id.* Counsel should explain these possible consequences to the juvenile if the juvenile is alleged to have committed one of the specified felonies, especially if there is an offer to plead to a misdemeanor or a lesser felony.

Impeachment exception in limited circumstances. Under Rule 609(d) of the North Carolina Rules of Evidence, evidence of an adjudication of delinquency is not generally admissible for impeachment purposes. In a criminal case, however, witnesses other than the defendant may be impeached with adjudications "if conviction of the offense would be admissible to attack the credibility of an adult and the court is satisfied that admission in evidence is necessary for a fair determination of the issue of guilt or innocence." *Id.*

In a 1972 opinion, the North Carolina Supreme Court held that adjudications could be used to impeach a criminal defendant who is under the age of 18. *State v. Miller*, 281 N.C. 70, 80 (1972). However, *Miller* appears to be superseded by Rule 609.

School exception for offenses that would be felonies if committed by an adult. A statutory exception exists for information in the juvenile court file that *must* be released to the juvenile's school if the case concerns an offense that would be a felony if committed by an adult. G.S. 7B-3101(a). The juvenile court counselor must notify the school principal if a petition is filed alleging that the juvenile committed a felony, other than a Chapter 20 (motor vehicle) offense. G.S. 7B-3101(a)(1). If the court dismisses the petition after an adjudicatory hearing, the school must be informed of the dismissal. G.S. 7B-3101(a)(3).

The school must be notified if the court modifies or vacates any order or disposition regarding a juvenile alleged or found to be delinquent for such an offense, or if jurisdiction is transferred to superior court. G.S. 7B-3101(a)(2), (5). The principal also must be notified of any dispositional order, including an order that requires school attendance as a condition of probation. G.S. 7B-3101(a)(4).

Counsel should advise the juvenile that the school will receive this information. The principal will know if school attendance has been ordered as a condition of probation and will be expected to report unauthorized absences. The juvenile should also be informed that any school that is a member of the North Carolina High School Athletic Association prohibits a student who is adjudicated delinquent for an offense that would be a felony if committed by an adult from participating in sports. This might be an important factor for some juveniles in plea negotiations.

B. Juvenile Court Counselor's Records

The juvenile court counselor's records are not open to public inspection but may be examined by the juvenile or the juvenile's attorney without a motion or court order. G.S. 7B-3001(c). Counsel should obtain these records and review them to develop potential defenses during the adjudicatory hearing or alternative dispositional plans for the juvenile. The court counselor's records include "family background information; reports of social, medical, psychiatric, or psychological information concerning a juvenile or the juvenile's family; probation reports; interviews with the juvenile's family; or other information the court finds should be protected from public inspection in the best interests of the juvenile." G.S. 7B-3001(a).

As part of the Juvenile Justice Reinvestment Act of 2017, the General Assembly amended G.S. 7B-3001 to provide that the court counselor must, on request, share information with a law enforcement officer about a juvenile if the officer is investigating a matter that could result in the filing of a complaint. The court counselor may not provide the officer with copies of any part of the court counselor's record, and any information shared with the officer must remain confidential. The change is effective October 1, 2017. *See infra* § 19.2, Changes Effective in 2017.

C. Law Enforcement Records and Files

Law enforcement records and files of a juvenile case must be kept separate from those of adults and are not open to public inspection except on a court order. The following people may examine law enforcement records without a court order: the juvenile or the juvenile's attorney; the juvenile's parent, guardian, custodian, or authorized representative thereof; the prosecutor; juvenile court counselors; and law enforcement officers sworn in this state. G.S. 7B-3001(b).

D. Division of Adult Correction and Juvenile Justice Records

Generally. Records of the Division of Adult Correction and Juvenile Justice include both records of the local court counselor and of facilities to which the juvenile has been committed. Those who may access and obtain copies of Division records about a juvenile without a court order are the juvenile, the juvenile's attorney, and the juvenile's parent, guardian, or custodian, or authorized representative of one of those people. G.S. 7B-3001(c). Additionally, professionals within the Division who are directly involved in the juvenile's case and juvenile court counselors may access the records without a court order. Otherwise, records maintained by the Division may only be disclosed pursuant to a court order. *Id.; see also Doe 1 v. Swannanoa Valley Youth Development Center*, 163 N.C. App. 136, 139 (2004) (deputy commissioner of Industrial Commission had authority to order discovery of records in a tort claims action).

Escape. If a juvenile who has been adjudicated delinquent escapes from secure custody, a detention facility, or a youth development center, the Division must release the following information to the public within 24 hours of the escape:

- the juvenile's first name and last initial,
- the juvenile's photograph, and
- the name and location of the facility from which the juvenile escaped or, if the juvenile's escape was not from a facility, the circumstances and location of the escape.

G.S. 7B-3102(a). If deemed appropriate, the Division must also release a statement, based on the juvenile's record, of the level of concern of the Division as to the threat the juvenile poses to himself, herself, or others. *Id.*

When a juvenile who is alleged to have committed a felony escapes from a detention facility or secure custody before adjudication, the Division is not required to release any information. However, the Division may release the same information described above within 24 hours after the escape if it determines, based on the juvenile's record, that the juvenile presents a danger to himself, herself, or others. G.S. 7B-3102(b).

Before the Division releases information about the juvenile to the public, it must make a reasonable effort to notify the juvenile's parent, guardian, or custodian. G.S. 7B-3102(e). If the juvenile is returned to custody before the information is released, the Division is prohibited from releasing it. G.S. 7B-3102(c).

E. Nontestimonial Identification Records

Limited authority to conduct nontestimonial identification procedures. A law enforcement officer must obtain a court order before conducting nontestimonial identification procedures on a juvenile unless the juvenile has been charged as an adult or has been transferred to superior court for trial as an adult. G.S. 7B-2103. There are limited exceptions for fingerprints and photographs, discussed below.

Retention and destruction of nontestimonial identification records. Nontestimonial identification records of a juvenile 13 years of age or older who is adjudicated delinquent for an offense that would be a felony if committed by an adult may be kept in the juvenile court file. G.S. 7B-2108(3). *But see* G.S. 7B-2102(d), (e) (regarding retention and destruction of fingerprints). The records can be used by law enforcement officers only for comparison purposes in the investigation of a crime. "Special precautions," which are not defined, must be taken to ensure that the nontestimonial identification records are "maintained in a manner and under sufficient safeguards" to ensure that they are accessible only to law enforcement officers for this purpose. G.S. 7B-2108(3).

All nontestimonial identification records must be destroyed if a juvenile petition is not filed, the juvenile is not adjudicated delinquent or convicted in superior court, or a juvenile under the age of 13 is adjudicated for an offense that would be less than a felony if committed by an adult. G.S. 7B-2108(1), (2).

Fingerprints and photographs. A law enforcement officer must take fingerprints and photographs without a court order in the following limited circumstances:

(1) the juvenile was 10 years of age or older at the time of allegedly committing a nondivertible offense (*see infra* "Nondivertible and divertible offenses" in § 5.3A, Preliminary Inquiry), a petition is to be filed, and the juvenile is in the physical custody of law enforcement or the Division of Adult Correction and Juvenile Justice;
(2) the juvenile has been adjudicated delinquent for an offense that would be a felony if committed by an adult and was 10 years of age or older at the time the offense was committed; or
(3) the juvenile has been committed to a county juvenile detention facility.

G.S. 7B-2102(a), (a1), (b). Exception (1) applies to a juvenile in custody for a nondivertible offense *before* adjudication, while exception (2) applies *after* adjudication of an offense that would be a felony if committed by an adult. Exception (3) applies when a juvenile has been committed to a detention facility. There is no provision for fingerprints and photographs to be taken without a court order under any other circumstances.

Destruction of fingerprints and photographs. Counsel should file a motion to destroy fingerprints and photographs taken in violation of the provisions of G.S. 7B-2102. A sample motion and order to destroy fingerprints and photographs is available on the Juvenile Defender website. For example, there is no statutory provision for a juvenile charged with a *divertible* offense to be fingerprinted or photographed unless later adjudicated for an offense that would be a felony if committed by an adult. There is also no provision for photographing a juvenile who is adjudicated delinquent for an offense that would be less than a felony if committed by an adult.

Fingerprints and photographs taken pursuant to G.S. 7B-2102(a) must be destroyed if a petition is not filed within one year, the court does not find probable cause, or the juvenile is not adjudicated delinquent of an offense that would be a felony or misdemeanor if committed by an adult. G.S. 7B-2102(e). It is the responsibility of the chief court counselor to notify the local custodian of records, and the local custodian of records must notify any other record-holding agencies, when any of the above conditions are met. *Id.* A motion should be filed if the evidence is not destroyed according to statutory provisions.

F. Exception for Designated Local Agencies

The Division of Adult Correction and Juvenile Justice is authorized by statute to designate local agencies that must share information on request concerning a juvenile who is the subject of a petition alleging abuse, neglect, dependency, delinquency, or undisciplined behavior. Designated agencies may include the local mental health facilities, health department, Department of Social Services, school, district attorney's office, and Office of Guardian ad Litem Services. The Division is also included as an agency that may be a designated agency. Shared information is to be used "only for the protection of the juvenile and others or to improve the educational opportunities of the juvenile . . ." and must remain confidential and not open to public inspection. G.S. 7B-3100(a). Counsel should learn whether any local rule or order adds a local agency that is required to share information concerning a juvenile. *See* 14B North Carolina Administrative Code 11A.0301(j) (chief district court judge may designate a local agency as an agency authorized to share information), 11A.0302 (governing information sharing among agencies).

G. Confidentiality on Appeal

If a juvenile appeals, the juvenile's right to confidentiality continues in the appellate division. The juvenile's appellate attorney typically prepares the record on appeal, which is a compilation of documents and filings from the juvenile court file in the trial division. Under N.C. R. App. P. 3.1(b), the cover of the record on appeal must contain a notice stating that the record is not subject to public inspection. In addition, the contents of the record may only be disclosed with permission of a court of the appellate division. Transcripts for juvenile delinquency appeals must include the same notice and may not be disclosed to the public without permission of an appellate court. *Id.*

Attorneys assigned to the appeal may only refer to the juvenile in briefs and petitions through the use of initials or a pseudonym. *Id.* The attorneys must also redact the juvenile's name from any appendices or exhibits submitted with a brief or petition.

The courts of the appellate division release opinions for juvenile delinquency appeals to the public along with opinions in civil and criminal appeals. However, the caption of the opinion in a juvenile delinquency appeal only lists the juvenile's initials. The juvenile is also referred to in the body of the opinion through initials or a pseudonym.

Transcripts in juvenile delinquency cases are usually prepared by court reporters who listen to audio recordings of the hearings. In other words, court reporters are not present in court taking contemporaneous notes of the proceedings. Court clerks retain the recordings in their records of juvenile delinquency cases. If a juvenile does not appeal, the trial court may enter an order directing the clerk to destroy any recordings of the proceedings that occurred in the case. G.S. 7B-3000(d).

2.9   Right to Appointment of Guardian

Generally. The Juvenile Code provides under Article 20, "Basic Rights," that a guardian of the person *may* be appointed for the juvenile if no parent, guardian, or custodian appears at a hearing with the juvenile or if the court finds that it would be in the juvenile's best interest. G.S. 7B-2001 (emphasis added). The guardian is given custody of the juvenile or the discretion to arrange placement, authority to consent to necessary remedial, psychological, medical, or surgical treatment, and authority to represent the juvenile in legal actions before any court. The guardian also may stand *in loco parentis* to consent to marriage, enlistment in the armed forces, and enrollment in school. *Id.*

Although this statute is listed under basic rights of the juvenile and is intended to safeguard the juvenile, it does not specify procedural protections in the appointment of a guardian for either the parent or the juvenile. It does not specifically provide for notice and a hearing regarding the proposed appointment, and it does not specify the standard for a judicial decision other than "best interests of the juvenile" or that the parent is absent from a hearing. G.S. 7B-2001. The juvenile statute may conflict with Chapter 35A, which applies specifically to guardianships and provides greater protections, as well as due process requirements.

Considerations if parent, guardian, or custodian not present. The presence of a parent, guardian, or custodian is mandated for any hearing for which the parent, guardian, or custodian receives notice. G.S. 7B-1805. If the parent, guardian, or custodian does not appear at a hearing after proper notice, counsel should consider the juvenile's circumstances and wishes, as well as possible consequences, in deciding whether to request that the court appoint a guardian or compel the presence of the parent.

A supportive parent can be a positive factor in the outcome of a delinquency case by advocating for the juvenile, providing supervision, participating in treatment, and providing transportation. Conversely, the compelled presence of a parent adverse to the juvenile's position may have a harmful effect.

An interested and active guardian may fill the role served by a supportive parent. Appointment of a guardian without notice to the parent and juvenile and without a hearing, however, could result in the appointment of an inappropriate guardian or a guardian to whom the juvenile objects, such as a disliked relative or the Department of Social Services.

Guardian ad litem distinguished. A guardian ad litem is a person who is appointed in a legal proceeding, often pursuant to Rule 17 of the Rules of Civil Procedure, to represent the interests of a party who is under a legal disability, such as minority or incompetence. *See infra* § 3.5J, Guardian ad Litem. For example, courts are required to appoint guardians ad litem to represent children in cases involving allegations of abuse or neglect. G.S. 7B-601. The duties of a guardian ad litem appointed under G.S. 7B-601 are primarily to investigate and determine the needs of the child. *Id.* In an incompetency case, a guardian ad litem is appointed to determine the respondent's wishes regarding the proceedings and any proposed guardianship. G.S. 35A-1107(b).

Chapter 3
Juvenile Court Jurisdiction and Parties to Juvenile Proceedings

3.1   Jurisdictional Overview

The district court has exclusive, original jurisdiction over all juveniles alleged to be delinquent as well as their parents, guardians, or custodians, on the proper filing and service of a petition and summons. Jurisdiction is initially determined by the juvenile's age at the time of the alleged offense. Statutory provisions mandate when a juvenile ages out of the jurisdiction of the juvenile court or when a juvenile case is otherwise closed. *See infra* § 3.3, Jurisdiction.

3.2   Terminology Used in this Chapter

Custodian is a "person or agency that has been awarded legal custody of a juvenile by a court." G.S. 7B-1501(6).

Division is the Division of Adult Correction and Juvenile Justice. The Division is charged with far-reaching duties, which include responsibility for operating State juvenile facilities and youth development centers, appointment of the chief court counselor in each district, establishment of community-based treatment and prevention services, and developing training plans for juvenile court counselors and other personnel responsible for the care, supervision, and treatment of juveniles. *See* G.S. 143B-806(b)(1)–(19).

Guardian is a person with legal authority to make decisions for another person. The court may appoint a guardian of the person for a juvenile who is the subject of a petition alleging delinquency. G.S. 7B-2001. Under Chapter 35A, "Incompetency and Guardianship," a guardian of the person can be appointed for a minor only if there is no "natural guardian." G.S. 35A-1224(a). The term "natural guardian" includes biological parents. *Valles de Portillo v. D.H. Griffin Wrecking Co.*, 134 N.C. App. 714 (1999).

Guardian ad Litem is a person who is appointed in a legal proceeding to represent the interest of a party who is under a legal disability, including minority and incompetence.

Jurisdiction is the legal authority of a tribunal to adjudicate and determine the subject matter before the court.

Juvenile court counselor is a "person responsible for intake services and court supervision services to juveniles under the supervision of the chief court counselor." G.S. 7B-1501(18a). The juvenile court counselor is also responsible for preparing a predisposition report with an attached risk and needs assessment of the juvenile that is presented to the court at disposition pursuant to G.S. 7B-2413.

Venue is the judicial district within the state in which a juvenile case is properly heard.

Youth development center is a "secure residential facility authorized to provide long-term treatment, education, and rehabilitative services for delinquent juveniles committed by the court to the Division," often referred to as training school. G.S. 7B-1501(29).

3.3   Jurisdiction

A. Jurisdictional Age Limits

Minimum age. A juvenile must be at least six years of age to come under the jurisdiction of the juvenile court on allegations of delinquency. G.S. 7B-1501(7).

Maximum age. A juvenile must have been less than 16 years of age at the time the alleged offense occurred. G.S. 7B-1501(7). The juvenile court has no jurisdiction to adjudicate a matter if the defendant was 16 years or older at the time of the alleged offense.

Legislative note: This chapter reviews the statutes in effect at the time of completion of this manual in Fall 2017. During the 2017 legislative session, the General Assembly enacted the Juvenile Justice Reinvestment Act, which expanded the jurisdiction of juvenile court to include crimes committed by 16 and 17-year-olds, except for motor vehicle offenses. Most of the changes apply to offenses committed on or after December 1, 2019. For a discussion of the changes that take effect in 2017, see *infra* Ch. 19, Raise the Age Legislation. For a discussion of the changes that take effect in 2019, see LaToya Powell, 2017 Juvenile Justice Reinvestment Act.

Special circumstances. When a delinquency proceeding has been initiated but is not concluded before the juvenile's 18th birthday, the juvenile court retains limited jurisdiction to determine whether the juvenile petition will be dismissed or the case will be transferred to superior court for trial as an adult. G.S. 7B-1601(c). If the juvenile is subject to this provision, counsel should endeavor to conclude the case before the juvenile's 18th birthday so that the juvenile is not exposed to the risk of transfer to superior court.

When a person over the age of 18 is charged with a felony and any related misdemeanors alleged to have been committed when the person was at least 13 but less than 16 years of age, the juvenile court has limited jurisdiction to determine whether the juvenile petition will be dismissed or the case will be transferred to superior court for trial as an adult. G.S. 7B-1601(d).

G.S. 7B-1601(c) and (d) are applied most often in cases where allegations of sexual assault are reported years after the alleged act or acts. Counsel should calculate the ages of both the juvenile and the victim at the time of the alleged offense to determine whether there is a defense to an allegation of statutory rape under G.S. 14-27.4 or statutory sexual offense under G.S. 14-27.29.

B. Termination of Jurisdiction

After the court has obtained jurisdiction over the juvenile, jurisdiction generally continues until terminated by order of the court or until the juvenile reaches the age of 18.

G.S. 7B-1601(b). Jurisdiction of the court continues if the court has extended jurisdiction, discussed below. Counsel should request an order terminating jurisdiction when court-ordered supervision ends.

C. Extended Jurisdiction

Until age 21. Jurisdiction may continue until the age of 21 for certain juveniles who were adjudicated delinquent and are in the custody of the Division for placement in a youth development center. The juvenile must have been adjudicated delinquent for an offense that would constitute one of the following crimes if committed by an adult: first degree murder pursuant to G.S. 14-17; first-degree rape pursuant to G.S. 14-27.21 or first-degree sexual offense pursuant to G.S. 14-27.26. In these cases, jurisdiction continues until terminated by order of the court or the juvenile reaches the age of 21, whichever first occurs. G.S. 7B-1602(a).

Until age 19. Jurisdiction may continue until the age of 19 for certain juveniles who were adjudicated delinquent and are in the custody of the Division for placement in a youth development center. The juvenile must have been adjudicated delinquent for an offense that would constitute a Class B1, B2, C, D, or E felony if committed by an adult. In these cases jurisdiction continues until terminated by order of the court or the juvenile reaches the age of 19, whichever first occurs. G.S. 7B-1602(b).

D. Jurisdiction over Parent

Upon proper service of the summons and petition, the court has jurisdiction over the parent, guardian, or custodian of a juvenile who is under the jurisdiction of the court as a result of allegations of delinquency. G.S. 7B-1601(g); *see infra* § 3.5E, Parent, Guardian, or Custodian. For example, a parent may be ordered to attend parental responsibility classes, obtain an evaluation and receive any recommended treatment, participate in the juvenile's evaluation and treatment, or pay the costs of the juvenile's treatment, support, or appointed attorney's fees. *See* G.S. 7B-2700 through 7B-2706 (Article 27, Authority over Parents of Juveniles Adjudicated Delinquent or Undisciplined).

E. Transfer of Jurisdiction to Superior Court

A juvenile who is at least 13 years of age at the time of an alleged offense that would be a felony if committed by an adult is subject to transfer of jurisdiction to superior court for trial as an adult. The case *must* be transferred if the alleged offense would be a Class A felony and the juvenile court judge finds probable cause. G.S. 7B-2200; *see infra* § 9.8, Transfer of Jurisdiction to Superior Court.

SIGNIFICANT AGES UNDER STATUTES	
6	Earliest age one can be alleged or adjudicated to be a delinquent or undisciplined juvenile
10	Youngest age an alleged delinquent juvenile may be fingerprinted or photographed
10	Youngest age a delinquent juvenile may be committed to a youth development center
11	Youngest age a delinquent juvenile may be required to register as a juvenile sex offender
13	Youngest age an alleged delinquent juvenile may be transferred to superior court for trial
Under 14	Age at which an alleged delinquent juvenile's admission or confession must be excluded if the juvenile's parent/guardian or attorney was not present during an in-custody interrogation
14-18	Age at which an alleged delinquent juvenile must be notified of the right to have a parent or guardian present, as well as an attorney, before an admission or confession may be used against the juvenile
Under 16	Maximum age at which a juvenile may be adjudicated an undisciplined juvenile solely for truancy
16	Age at which a juvenile is charged as an adult
17	Maximum age at which a juvenile may be adjudicated an undisciplined juvenile for acts other than truancy
18	Age at which juvenile court jurisdiction must end, unless under extended jurisdiction
19	Maximum age for extended jurisdiction over delinquent juveniles committed to a youth development center pursuant to adjudication of delinquency for a B1 through E offense
21	Maximum age for extended jurisdiction over delinquent juveniles committed to a youth development center pursuant to adjudication of delinquency for first-degree murder, first-degree rape, or first-degree sex offense

3.4   Venue

Venue is the judicial district within the state in which a juvenile case is properly heard. A juvenile proceeding may be bifurcated, with adjudication entered in one judicial district and the case transferred to another judicial district for disposition. G.S. 7B-1800.

Adjudication. A juvenile petition must be filed and the matter adjudicated in the judicial district where the offense is alleged to have occurred. G.S. 7B-1800(a).

Disposition. Disposition is typically held in the judicial district in which the juvenile legally resides. If the adjudication occurs in a district where the juvenile is in placement but does not have legal residence, the dispositional hearing is usually not transferred. The case is transferred for disposition only if the court "enters an order, supported by findings of fact, that a transfer would serve the ends of justice or is in the best interests of the juvenile." G.S. 7B-1800(a).

> Example: A juvenile who legally resides in Mecklenburg County is in a residential treatment facility in Wake County. If the juvenile is alleged to have committed an offense in Wake County, both the adjudicatory and dispositional hearings will usually be in Wake County. The court may transfer the dispositional hearing to Mecklenburg County only by order setting forth reasons that disposition should occur in the juvenile's home county. Reasons for transfer might include availability of the juvenile's treatment providers and records or a prior history with the juvenile court in Mecklenburg County.

If the juvenile does not legally reside in the district where the matter was adjudicated and is not in placement there, the juvenile has the right, upon motion, to have the matter transferred for disposition to the district of residence. Additionally, the chief district court judge in the district of residence must be given notice of the proceeding and may, by timely request, have venue transferred for disposition to that district. Otherwise, it is in the discretion of the adjudicating court whether to transfer venue to the district of residence. G.S. 7B-1800(b).

When the case is transferred for disposition, an attorney in the receiving district is ordinarily appointed to represent the juvenile at the dispositional hearing. The attorney for the dispositional hearing should confer with counsel who represented the juvenile at adjudication and should request information that could be presented in support of a favorable disposition.

3.5　Parties and Other Participants

A. Overview

There are two primary parties in a delinquency case, the juvenile and the State. The juvenile is the subject of the petition and the State bears the burden of proving the allegations beyond a reasonable doubt. At some stages of the proceeding the juvenile's parent, guardian, or custodian has statutory rights and responsibilities. The juvenile court counselor and the law enforcement officer also have statutory mandates. Other participants may have a substantial role in the proceeding.

B. State

The State is a party to the proceedings through the authority and responsibilities given its agents at various stages of the proceedings. The prosecutor must represent the State in all probable cause hearings and at *contested* delinquency hearings, including first appearance, detention, transfer, adjudicatory, dispositional, probation revocation, post-release supervision, and extended jurisdiction hearings. G.S. 7B-2404; 7B-2202(b)(1). Neither statute nor case law has defined "contested" for the purpose of this statute. It is commonly assumed that a contested hearing is one that is adversarial—that is, there is an issue that must be decided by the court that is not the subject of an admission or agreement between the parties. Because there is a question of who other than the prosecutor would present the State's position in an uncontested matter, the better practice is for the prosecutor to represent the State in all delinquency hearings.

In practice, at uncontested hearings and sometimes at contested hearings, the juvenile court counselor assumes the role of representing the State's interest because the court counselor is typically more familiar with the facts of the case and the juvenile's background than the prosecutor. Such an expanded role by the court counselor tends to make the proceedings less formal and may pose a threat to the juvenile's due process rights by making it easier for inadmissible evidence to be allowed and harder for the juvenile's attorney to object and to be heard. Counsel should consider objecting if this occurs.

The State's right to appeal is limited to any order that terminates the case by: upholding the defense of double jeopardy; holding that a cause of action is not stated under a statute; granting a motion to suppress; or finding a State statute unconstitutional. G.S. 7B-2604(b); *see infra* Ch. 16, Appeals.

Interaction with the prosecutor is necessary for counsel to represent the juvenile effectively. A professional relationship may facilitate various procedures, including discovery and plea negotiations. Although a written motion for discovery should always be filed, counsel may also contact the prosecutor to make arrangements for discovery as well as to negotiate an admission, when appropriate, and to discuss proposals for disposition.

C. Juvenile

The juvenile alleged to be delinquent is the subject of the petition and, as such, is the respondent. The juvenile must be personally served with a summons directing the juvenile to appear at a hearing at a specified place and time, along with a copy of the petition setting forth the delinquent acts that the juvenile is alleged to have committed. G.S. 7B-1802, 7B-1805(a), 7B-1806. Counsel should check the juvenile court file for proper service of the petition and summons, particularly if the juvenile does not appear at the hearing and the court is considering issuing a secure custody order. *See infra* Ch. 6, Petition and Summons.

The juvenile has the right to be represented by counsel and must be present at all proceedings; there is no provision for waiver of counsel or appearance. G.S. 7B-2000, 7B-1805. The juvenile is a party at all stages of the proceeding, including pre-adjudicatory hearings, discovery, adjudication, and disposition. At adjudication, the juvenile has the right to confront and cross-examine witnesses and to decide whether or not to testify. G.S. 7B-2405. At the dispositional hearing, the juvenile may present evidence and argument for a specific disposition. G.S. 7B-2501.

D. Attorney for Juvenile

Statutory provisions. Although not a party, the juvenile's attorney is a participant in every court proceeding and has statutory rights as well as ethical obligations. The statutory definition of "juvenile" provides that "[w]herever the term 'juvenile' is used with reference to rights and privileges, that term encompasses the attorney for the juvenile as well." G.S. 7B-1501(17). Because the juvenile does not have the right to self-representation, counsel will be involved in every aspect of the delinquency proceeding. *See generally infra* Appendix 3-1, Role of Defense Counsel in Juvenile Delinquency Proceedings; *compare* 1 NORTH CAROLINA DEFENDER MANUAL § 12.8, Attorney-Client Relationship (2d ed. 2013).

Repayment of attorney's fees. While the juvenile cannot be held liable for attorney's fees, the court may require payment of attorney's fees from a person other than the juvenile, such as a parent, guardian, or trustee. G.S. 7B-2002; G.S. 7A-450.1, 7A-450.2, 7A-450.3. The court determines at the dispositional hearing whether the parent, guardian, or trustee should be held responsible for attorney's fees. G.S. 7A-450.3.

E. Parent, Guardian, or Custodian

Role of parent, guardian, or custodian. The parent, guardian, or custodian (hereinafter the parent) plays an integral role throughout the proceedings, from participation in the intake process and appearance at all scheduled hearings to involvement in dispositional and post-dispositional plans. Parental support, or lack thereof, can make a difference in the outcome of the case and may require ongoing interaction with the parent. Counsel should represent the expressed wishes of the juvenile, however, which sometimes may conflict with those of the parent. *See generally infra* Appendix 3-1, Role of Defense Counsel in Juvenile Delinquency Proceedings; *see also* 1 NORTH CAROLINA DEFENDER MANUAL § 12.8A, Control and Direction of Case (2d ed. 2013).

There is no duty for the juvenile's attorney to talk with the parent, although doing so will generally be necessary as a part of case preparation. Generally, the parent should not be allowed to sit in on counsel's interview with the juvenile. Because there is no parent-child privilege, the parent is subject to being called as a witness and must be excluded to maintain attorney-client confidentiality. Counsel should explain to the parent the need for a private meeting with the juvenile to prevent hurt or angry feelings.

Intake. The juvenile court counselor who conducts the intake evaluation usually sends a letter to the parent requesting that the juvenile be brought in for an appointment. If the parent brings the juvenile to the appointment and is cooperative, depending on the circumstances of the case, the complaint is more likely to be diverted. Conversely, the case is less likely to be diverted if the appointment is missed or if the parent is uncooperative.

Petition, summons, and notice. The parent's name and last known address must be included on the petition, which must be personally served along with a summons issued to the parent. G.S. 7B-1802, 7B-1805(a), 7B-1806. A statement must be included in the summons advising that jurisdiction is obtained over the parent upon service of the summons and petition. G.S. 7B-1805(c). Notice of all scheduled hearings must be given "to all parties, including both parents of the juvenile. . . ." G.S. 7B-1807. The parent is required to appear at and bring the juvenile to scheduled hearings and to comply with orders of the court. A parent may be held in criminal contempt for failure to follow these mandates. G.S. 7B-1805, 7B-2700.

Secure custody hearing. At a secure custody hearing, the parent is allowed to examine witnesses, present evidence, and testify on the parent's own behalf. G.S. 7B-1906(d). Counsel for the juvenile should be prepared to respond, if necessary, to the parent's presentation to the court.

The parent's position at a secure custody hearing is crucial. A parent who is willing to have the child back home and enforce any court-imposed conditions might persuade the court to release the juvenile from secure custody. Conversely, a parent who insists that the juvenile cannot come home will harm the juvenile's chances for release.

Counsel should talk with the parent about the juvenile's release from secure custody and discuss possible options. For example, if the parent wants the juvenile to come home, counsel could help the parent formulate a plan for care at home. Possible conditions of release might include after-school supervision, a curfew, counseling, or other treatment.

If the parent is against release from secure custody, counsel should try to ascertain the parent's underlying concerns. Counsel can then discuss with the juvenile the parent's objections to release. If the juvenile is willing to make changes in behavior and to follow conditions set out by the court, counsel can relay that information to the parent. Counsel may also explain to the parent the possible consequences of continued secure custody, such as extended out-of-home placement, a referral to the department of social services, or a more restrictive disposition for the juvenile if found delinquent. If the parent remains opposed to the wishes of the juvenile, counsel should present evidence and argument to counter the parent's position at the dispositional hearing.

Discovery. The parent may be able to provide information to counsel that will assist in discovery, such as statements made by or actions of a law enforcement officer during the investigation, or the existence of prior evaluations or treatment of the juvenile. The parent may also provide names and addresses of potential witnesses. Consultation with the parent may be required for counsel to understand fully the information received through discovery.

Adjudication. Although the statute provides that the parent has the same rights that the juvenile has in an adjudication hearing (G.S. 7B-2405), the general practice is not to include the parent as a party during the adjudicatory hearing.

The juvenile may want to consult the parent regarding terms of admission or "plea negotiations," and may ask counsel to explain any offer to the parent. Counsel must make clear to the juvenile and the parent, however, that the decision whether to accept a plea offer is ultimately the juvenile's.

Disposition. The parent is allowed to offer evidence in rebuttal to the predisposition report and to present evidence and recommendations at the dispositional hearing. G.S. 7B-2413, 7B-2501(b). Usually the court will ask if the parent wishes to make a statement during the hearing. *Cf. In re M.J.G.*, 234 N.C. App. 350 (2014) (assuming arguendo that trial court erred by failing to give the juvenile's mother an opportunity to make a statement before entering a disposition, any error was harmless given that the juvenile's mother did not object to the disposition when the court ultimately permitted her to speak); *In re Powers*, 144 N.C. App. 140 (2001) (parents' rights to present evidence and make recommendations at dispositional hearing were not violated when trial court did not address parents and record did not show any attempt by parents to make statement). The court may also explain the parent's duties while the juvenile is on probation or otherwise under the court's jurisdiction. As part of a dispositional order, the parent may be ordered to undergo psychiatric, psychological or other treatment, attend parental responsibility classes, or pay the cost of the juvenile's treatment or placement. G.S. 7B-2502(b), 7B-2701, 7B-2702(c).

The parent's presentation at the dispositional hearing may have a determinative effect in persuading the court to adopt the juvenile's proposed plan. If the parent's position is contrary to that of the juvenile, counsel should try to resolve the conflict but otherwise be prepared to argue against the parent's position at the hearing.

If the parent's position on the disposition of the case is consistent with the juvenile's, counsel may consider calling the parent as a witness at disposition. Counsel should observe the parent's demeanor when talking about the juvenile, discuss possible questions with the parent, and review the testimony that the parent would present. After this discussion, counsel must decide whether the parent's testimony will be beneficial or detrimental to the juvenile.

Post-disposition. The parent can play a key role in the success or failure of the juvenile's compliance with the dispositional order. Among other things, the parent can provide encouragement, supervision, and reminders of and transportation to appointments. Counsel should talk with the parent as well as the juvenile about the requirements of the dispositional order and the consequences of failure to follow the order. If the juvenile is placed outside the home as part of the disposition, the parent can offer support through visits, letters, and telephone calls. If the juvenile is committed to a youth development center, the parent should also participate in post-release planning and assist the juvenile in following post-release conditions. *See infra* § 15.9, Revocation of Post-Release Supervision.

Appeal. A parent has the right to appeal an order of the court. G.S. 7B-2604(a). *See infra* Ch. 16, Appeals. A parent presumably can appeal the adjudicatory or dispositional order in addition to orders directed only to the parent. *See In re Powers*, 144 N.C. App. 140 (2001) (parents appealed dispositional order committing juvenile to a residential facility). Orders directed solely to the parent include those requiring the parent to attend parental responsibility classes or undergo medical, psychiatric, or psychological treatment or counseling, contempt orders, and orders requiring the parent to pay the juvenile's attorney's fees. G.S. 7B-2002, 7B-2700 to 7B-2706.

Civil restitution. A person who has suffered physical injury or damage to real or personal property as a result of the malicious or willful actions of a minor may sue to recover monetary damages in civil court from the parent of the minor. The parent is strictly liable for monetary damages up to $2000 under the statute. G.S. 1-538.1. However, parents are not liable if the minor was removed from their custody by court order or contract prior to the act. *Id.* Although a civil suit is a separate proceeding, the payment of damages to an alleged victim by a parent may be helpful in reaching a satisfactory resolution in the juvenile case.

A parent may also be civilly liable for losses resulting from larceny, shoplifting, theft by employee, embezzlement, or obtaining property by false pretenses by an unemancipated minor. Civil liability arises if the parent knew or should have known that the child was likely to commit such an act and failed to make reasonable efforts to control the child despite having had the opportunity to do so. Compensatory and consequential damages are limited to not less than $150 and not more than $1000. G.S. 1-538.2.

Educational entities are entitled to recover much more substantial sums from a parent of an unemancipated minor who commits certain offenses specified by statute. These offenses include those occurring on "educational property" involving explosives or incendiary devices, a hoax using a false bomb, a false report of a destructive device, or use of a firearm. Civil liability arises if the parent knew or should have known that the child was likely to commit such an act and failed to make reasonable efforts to control the child despite having had the opportunity to do so. G.S. 1-538.3 (Negligent supervision of minor).

Repayment of attorney's fees. The court may require payment of attorney's fees from a person other than the juvenile, such as a parent, guardian, or trustee. G.S. 7B-2002; G.S. 7A-450.1, 7A-450.2, 7A-450.3. The court determines at the dispositional hearing whether the parent, guardian, or trustee should be held responsible for attorney's fees. G.S. 7A-450.3.

F. Foster Parents and Other Caretakers

Foster parents and other caregivers who have "assumed the status and obligation of a parent without being awarded legal custody of the juvenile by a court" are entitled to receive notice of juvenile hearings. G.S. 7B-1807. They are not otherwise given statutory rights as a party or participant in the proceeding because they are not a parent, custodian, or guardian. In practice, however, they play an important role. For example, although a juvenile may be in the legal custody of the department of social services, the foster parent is the person who provides day-to-day care. The foster parent may be the person who brings the juvenile to appointments with the court counselor and the juvenile's attorney, and accompanies the juvenile to court. Likewise, the juvenile may live with a relative or friend who has no legal authority but who serves as a parental figure.

A caretaker may be called as a witness by the State or by the juvenile at the adjudicatory or dispositional hearing. The court counselor's dispositional recommendations and the feasibility of a dispositional plan may be greatly influenced by the caretaker. A caretaker should be consulted by counsel just as a parent would be. For a discussion of whether a caretaker may be considered a guardian for purposes of interrogation, see *infra* § 11.4E, Right to Have Parent, Custodian, or Guardian Present.

G. Juvenile Court Counselor

Overview. The juvenile court counselor (hereinafter court counselor), although not a party, has important statutory duties throughout the juvenile proceeding, from receiving and evaluating complaints during the intake process to preparing a predisposition report and risk and needs assessment to be submitted if the case progresses to disposition. Counsel for the juvenile should endeavor to establish a good working relationship with the court counselor to facilitate access to records and other information. The counselor may also be more inclined to review information provided by counsel on the juvenile's behalf.

Historically, the court counselor has played an important role in the courtroom. In some instances, counselors have acted outside statutorily defined duties and assumed the role of prosecutor, making remarks in open court that are, in effect, testimony without having been sworn as a witness. This practice may minimize the role of the juvenile's attorney by making it more difficult to cross-examine the court counselor or make objections. Counsel should be well acquainted with the statutory responsibilities of the court counselor and should object as necessary if the counselor exceeds that role.

Statutory role. The court counselor has the statutory duty to decide whether a complaint should or must be filed as a petition or whether it will be diverted. G.S. 7B-1701, 7B-1702; *see infra* § 5.3, Intake. Thus, the court counselor has the power to determine that a divertible offense will never come to court. *See infra* § 5.4, Diversion.

Secure custody. A secure custody order is often issued based on information from the court counselor. In addition, the chief district court judge may delegate authority by administrative order to the chief court counselor or the chief court counselor's counseling staff to issue a secure custody order. G.S. 7B-1902. The court may not, however, delegate the authority for the juvenile to be detained or housed in a holdover facility. *Id.* Counsel should contact the court counselor when the juvenile is in secure custody to obtain information concerning the issuance of the secure custody order.

Adjudication. Other than at a probable cause hearing, the prosecutor is *required* by statute to represent the State at contested hearings only. G.S. 7B-2202(b)(1), 7B-2404. Therefore, the court counselor may step in to present the State's evidence in an uncontested adjudication. This practice, however, may constitute the unauthorized practice of law as well as conflict with the court counselor's duty to present an unbiased report and recommendations at the dispositional hearing.

Disposition. At disposition, the court counselor has a prominent role mandated by statute. The court counselor submits a predisposition report, also called a dispositional report, with a risk and needs assessment of the juvenile. The report must include information regarding the juvenile's "social, medical, psychiatric, psychological, and educational history, as well as any factors indicating the probability of the juvenile committing further delinquent acts. . . ." G.S. 7B-2413. The report containing the risk and needs assessment is not to be undertaken before adjudication without the written consent of the juvenile, the juvenile's parent, guardian, or custodian, or the juvenile's attorney. *Id.* Counsel should obtain or provide this consent if a delay in disposition might be detrimental to the juvenile.

The dispositional hearing cannot proceed until the court receives the predisposition report containing the dispositional recommendations unless the court makes a written finding that one is not needed. Counsel for the juvenile is entitled to have and to review the report before the dispositional hearing. G.S. 7B-2413. In practice, the court may proceed on an oral presentation by the court counselor. Counsel should object if lack of a written report is detrimental to the juvenile. Because the court often gives great weight to the report of the court counselor, juvenile's counsel should work with the counselor, if possible, to arrive at recommendations acceptable to the juvenile. Otherwise counsel should be prepared to respond to the dispositional report and offer alternatives that further the juvenile's objectives. Counsel should be alert for the need to cross-examine the court counselor regarding the report and recommendations, or to move to strike portions of the report that contradict or are not supported by evidence presented at adjudication.

Counsel for the juvenile is entitled to review the court counselor's records. G.S. 7B-2413. Reviewing the records and contacting the court counselor are an important part of counsel's investigation. Counsel should request a copy of the predisposition report in advance and be prepared to counter any information contained in the predisposition report.

H. Law Enforcement Officer

A law enforcement officer is often the petitioner or a witness in a delinquency proceeding. There are statutory guidelines that a law enforcement officer must follow in interrogating, fingerprinting, and photographing a juvenile or obtaining other nontestimonial identification of a juvenile. G.S. 7B-2100 to 7B-2109; *see infra* § 2.8E, Nontestimonial Identification Records. If a law enforcement officer is involved with the juvenile's case, counsel should request all law enforcement records in order to determine whether:

- statutory and constitutional guidelines were followed in investigating the case;
- any physical evidence is in the possession of law enforcement;
- the juvenile made an in-custody statement or admission;
- the juvenile made an out-of-custody statement or admission to anyone; or
- statements were taken from potential witnesses.

Many juvenile cases are based on an admission of the juvenile, so it is important to review any admissions made by the juvenile and evaluate the circumstances surrounding the admissions. Counsel should be alert for violations of the juvenile's statutory and constitutional rights and should be prepared to move to suppress admissions that result from such violations. A careful review of law enforcement records may also reveal potential witnesses for the juvenile, as well as assist counsel in making objections during the adjudicatory hearing.

I. Guardian ad Litem

A guardian ad litem is a person who is appointed in a legal proceeding to represent the interests of a party who is under a legal disability, including minority and incompetence, often pursuant to Rule 17 of the North Carolina Rules of Civil Procedure. The guardian ad litem stands in place of the real party in interest—the person for whom the appointment was made—and makes decisions as required for the case.

Even though all juveniles are minors, appointment of a guardian ad litem for an alleged delinquent is neither required, as in cases alleging neglect or abuse, nor provided for in the court's discretion, as in cases alleging dependency. *See* G.S. 7B-601. A guardian ad litem might arguably be appointed pursuant to Rule 17 of the Rules of Civil Procedure, but there is no statutory provision authorizing payment of the guardian ad litem from State funds. A juvenile unable to make decisions and assist counsel in formulating a defense, however, would generally be considered incapable of proceeding and therefore subject to the provisions of G.S. 15A-1001 through 15A-1003 of the North Carolina Criminal Procedure Act. One who is incapable of proceeding cannot be subject to an adjudication of delinquency. *See infra* Chapter 7, Capacity to Proceed; *see also* Janet Mason, *Minors as Parties in Civil Actions,* JUVENILE LAW BULLETIN No. 2007/02, at 12–13 (June 2007).

If a parent or a sibling is the alleged victim, the juvenile might benefit from appointment of a guardian ad litem to advocate for the best interests of the juvenile, which is ordinarily the role of the parent. In these cases, the parent might have divided loyalties or even hostility toward the juvenile resulting from the alleged offense.

J. Other Participants

Department of Social Services. The juvenile may be the subject of an investigation by or be in the custody of the local department of social services (hereinafter DSS) because of abuse, neglect, or dependency allegations. This could affect many aspects of the delinquency proceeding, including disposition, in that the juvenile may be unable to return home as a result of a juvenile order in a DSS proceeding. Counsel should contact the DSS social worker to determine the juvenile's status.

If the juvenile is not in DSS custody and is in need of treatment or is ordered at disposition in the juvenile delinquency case to comply with conditions, the juvenile court counselor will be responsible for supervising the juvenile's compliance with those conditions. As an alternative to the court counselor supervising the juvenile, the delinquency court can also place the juvenile in DSS custody. G.S. 7B-2503(1)c., 7B-2506(1)c. The director of DSS would then be permitted to arrange for treatment for the juvenile and assign a social worker to assist the juvenile in complying with treatment.

Mental health service providers. The juvenile may have received or may be receiving mental health services. If so, there are records that include progress notes, medication history, and evaluations of the juvenile. Counsel should obtain the standard release form used by the provider involved and have the juvenile and the juvenile's parent sign for release of the records to counsel. This will allow counsel to receive copies of the juvenile's records and to discuss the juvenile's history and needs with the treatment providers. The counselor or therapist may be more likely than others to promote treatment and may be a potential witness and ally for the juvenile at disposition.

School personnel. Counsel should obtain a release of information and investigate the juvenile's current school status, academic and disciplinary history, and special education needs, if any. School personnel are often involved in the juvenile's case, both in and out of court, because of the allegations or other school issues. The juvenile's attorney should contact school personnel to determine the school's objectives, which may conflict with those of the juvenile. Counsel should be prepared to respond to information provided to the court by school personnel.

Counsel should ask whether the juvenile has an Individualized Education Plan (IEP). IEP is the unique plan developed for each public school child with a disability who needs special education and related services. The IEP is developed by a team of qualified professionals and the child's parents to address the specific needs of the child within the school setting. *See* A Guide to the Individualized Education Program, U.S. Department of Education (July 2000).

Appendix 3-1: Role of Defense Counsel in Juvenile Delinquency Proceedings[1]
Prepared by the North Carolina Office of the Juvenile Defender

An attorney in a juvenile delinquency proceeding shall be the juvenile's voice to the court, representing the expressed interests of the juvenile at every stage of the proceedings. The attorney owes the same duties to the juvenile under the Rules of Professional Conduct, including the duties of loyalty and confidentiality, as an attorney owes to an adult criminal defendant.

The attorney for a juvenile is bound to advocate the expressed interests of the juvenile. In addition, the attorney has a responsibility to counsel the juvenile, recommend to the juvenile actions consistent with the juvenile's interest, and advise the juvenile as to potential outcomes of various courses of action.

The attorney for a juvenile shall meet with the juvenile as soon as practical; communicate with the juvenile in a manner that will be effective, considering the juvenile's maturity, physical, mental and/or emotional health, intellectual abilities, language, educational level, special education needs, cultural background and gender; educate the juvenile as to the nature of the proceedings; determine the objectives of the juvenile; and keep the juvenile informed of the status of the proceedings. The attorney should move the court for appointment of an interpreter if the primary language of the juvenile or the juvenile's parents or guardian is other than English and the attorney has difficulty communicating with them.

If the attorney determines that the juvenile is unable to understand the proceedings or otherwise cannot assist the attorney in representing the juvenile, the attorney shall move the court for an evaluation of the juvenile's capacity to proceed and otherwise proceed according to Rule 1.14 of the Rules of Professional Conduct.

The attorney for a juvenile should consider moving the court to appoint a guardian if it appears to the attorney that the juvenile does not have a parent or other adult to provide assistance in making decisions outside the scope of the attorney's representation.

---

1. This statement of the role of defense counsel in juvenile delinquency proceedings was derived from a number of sources. *See, e.g.*, National Council of Juvenile and Family Court Judges, Juvenile Delinquency Guidelines: Improving Court Practice in Juvenile Delinquency Cases (2005); American Council of Chief Defenders, National Juvenile Defender Center, Ten Core Principles for Providing Quality Delinquency Representation Through Indigent Defense Delivery Systems (2005); Amy Howell & Brook Silverthorn, Southern Juvenile Defender Center, Representing the Whole Child: A Juvenile Defender Training Manual, § IV (2004); California Administrative Office of the Courts, Effective Representation of Children in Juvenile Delinquency Court (2004); Juvenile Justice Bulletin, Office of Juvenile Justice and Delinquency Prevention, U.S. Department of Justice, Access to Counsel (2004); Katherine R. Kruse, Washington University Journal of Law and Policy, Lawyers Should be Lawyers, But What does that Mean? A Response to Aiken & Wizer & Smith (2004); Frank E. Vandervort, Michigan Bar Journal, When Minors Face Major Consequences: What Attorneys in Representing Children in Delinquency, Designation, and Waiver Proceedings Need to Know (2001); National Association of Counsel for Children, Recommendations for Representation of Children in Abuse and Neglect Cases, Part IV (2001); Barbara Butterworth, Will Rhee & Mary Ann Scali, American Bar Association Juvenile Justice Center, Juvenile Defender Delinquency Notebook, Chapter 2, § 2.2 (2000); Massachusetts Committee for Public Counsel Services, Assigned Counsel Manual: Policies and Procedures, Parts III. A.4 & J 1.2 (2000); Kentucky Department of Public Advocacy, Juvenile Law Manual, Chapters 1 & 3 (1999); IJA/ABA Juvenile Justice Standards, Standards Relating to Private Parties, Standard 3.1 (1996); Stephen Wizner, 4 Columbia Human Rights Law Review 389, The Child and the State: Adversaries in the Juvenile Justice System (1972).

Decisions whether to admit to allegations of a petition and whether to testify are those of the juvenile, after consultation with the attorney. Decisions regarding the method and manner of conducting the defense are those of the attorney, after consultation with the juvenile.

An attorney for the juvenile should be knowledgeable of dispositional alternatives available to the court. The attorney should inform the juvenile and the juvenile's parents or guardian of those alternatives, of possible recommendations to the court, and of the possible outcome of the hearing. At the dispositional hearing, the attorney shall provide the court with reasonable dispositional alternatives, if desired by the juvenile.

Chapter 4
Communicating with the Juvenile Client

Appendix 4-1: Initiating the Attorney-Client Relationship

Communicating effectively with the client is essential to representation in juvenile delinquency proceedings. The National Juvenile Defender Center (NJDC) has prepared an excellent treatment of attorney-client communications in Chapter 2, "Initiating the Attorney-Client Relationship," of the Juvenile Defender Delinquency Notebook (2d ed. Spring 2006), which is reprinted here with permission.

Initiating the Attorney-Client Relationship

Your relationship with your client is central to effective representation. Make every effort, from your first meeting on, to ensure that it is strong. Do not expect your client to trust you immediately; it is more likely that rapport will build over time as you demonstrate commitment to her case and respect her wishes. The recommendations in this chapter are meant to help you think about building a relationship with your client as you collect vital information during your early meetings with her. Take into account your personality and interpersonal style as you develop a method of getting to know your clients.

What to consider before your first case

- *Your client's neighborhood, environment, and background.* Each client will be unique, but there will most likely be commonalities among youth who end up in court in your jurisdiction. Think about how your client's upbringing— such as the sort of neighborhood she grew up in and the school she attends—affects how she thinks, speaks, and acts as well as how she relates to you.

- *How to communicate with your client.* Educate yourself about child and adolescent development. Books like the *Handbook on Questioning Children* and continuing legal education programs, such as the MacArthur Foundation's *Understanding Adolescents: A Juvenile Court Training Curriculum* (available at http://www.njdc.info/macarthur.php), are great places to start.[25]

[I]t is the obligation of juvenile defense counsel to maximize each client's participation in his or her own case in order to ensure that the client understands the court process and to facilitate the most informed decision making by the client.

—ACCD-NJDC *Ten Core Principles for Providing Quality Delinquency Representation Through Indigent Defense Delivery Systems,* Preamble

CONTENTS

I. ETHICAL CONSIDERATIONS

A. Legal advocacy vs. "best interests"

The rehabilitative focus of juvenile court can create confusion about the role of defense counsel. Defenders will find themselves tempted to focus on the perceived "best interest" of the child rather than on legal advocacy. You are obligated to keep in mind, though, that it is through counsel that the child exercises the most fundamental due process guarantee: the opportunity to be heard. In delinquency cases, all other perspectives are accounted for: community safety is represented by the prosecution, the parent's interests by him or his counsel, and the view of "best interests" by probation and child care agencies. Defense counsel's function is to articulate and advocate as zealously as possible for the expressed legal position and desires of the child, your *client*. The best decisions are made when all positions are fully articulated and tested via the adversarial court process.

The *Institute of Judicial Administration-American Bar Association Juvenile Justice Standards* state that the defense counsel's principal duty is to advocate, within the bounds of law, for the best outcome available under the circumstances, *according to the client's view of the matter*.[26] Similarly, the ABA *Model Rules of Professional Conduct* provide that so long as your client is not so incompetent as to be unable to adequately act in her own interest, your client must be accorded the prerogative of making decisions concerning the objectives of representation.[27] In that the *Model Rules* contemplate application to children as young as ages five or six,[28] delinquency clientele are conclusively within these critical decision-making guidelines.

In practice, advocating for your client's expressed interests, as opposed to your view of her best interests, means that you must allow her to make decisions. Although, you have the expertise required to navigate the court process, predict possible outcomes of choices your client must make, give advice based on your evaluation of your client's situation, and speak for your client, she has fundamental control of her defense. At each and every stage of the case, you will use your knowledge to help her make informed decisions, but you must confer with her and abide by her decisions concerning the objective of representation.[29] In this regard, representing a child client is just like representing an adult. For example, sometimes a client will feel a strong desire to testify so she has had a chance to explain herself to the judge. Even if you think she will hurt rather than help her case, you must put her on the stand. Your role is to provide counsel and ensure that she understands the possible legal consequences of testifying in a particular case. Once she has decided to testify, regardless of how you feel about the decision, your role shifts and you must assist her in presenting herself well on the stand.

Juvenile Justice Standards

The IJA/ABA Juvenile Justice Standards and rules of professional conduct provide guidelines for control and direction of the case.

As long as she is competent, the client has control over key decisions relating to the goals of the representation. The lawyer is responsible for determining and pursuing the legal strategies to achieve these goals.

The following guidelines are from the IJA/ABA Juvenile Justice Standards:

The client, after full consultation with counsel, is ordinarily responsible for determining:
- *the plea to be entered at adjudication;*
- *whether to cooperate in consent judgment or early disposition plans;*
- *whether to be tried as a juvenile or an adult, where the client has that choice;*
- *whether to waive jury trial; and*
- *whether to testify on his [or her] own behalf.*

Decisions within the exclusive province of the lawyer, after full consultation with the client, include:
- *what witnesses to call,*
- *whether and how to conduct cross-examination,*
- *what jurors to accept and strike,*
- *what trial motions should be made, and*
- *any other strategic and tactical decisions not inconsistent with determinations ultimately the responsibility of and made by the client.[30]*

B. Conflicts of interest

Zealous advocacy includes giving each client your undivided loyalty. It is a violation of ethical rules to represent a client if you have a conflict of interest in her case. The ABA *Model Rules of Professional Conduct* state: "A lawyer shall not represent a client if … the representation would be directly adverse to another client or there is a significant risk that the representation of a client would be materially limited by the lawyer's responsibilities to another client, a former client, or a third person, or by a personal interest of the lawyer."[31] As you are considering taking on a new case, ask yourself if you have learned anything from any previous or current client that could be useful in preparing the defense of this new client. If the answer is yes, then you have a conflict of interest and you should decline the new case. Common examples of conflicts of interest include: representing more than one person charged in relation to the same events, or representing a respondent in one case and her complaining witness or other witness in a different case. Even if you think that a conflict is more apparent than real, the mere appearance of a conflict is problematic because adolescents are quick to notice and react to perceived unfairness. For this reason, you should also consider whether you have a personal or professional relationship with someone that will compromise your zealousness on behalf of your client or inhibit your client's trust in you. Discuss concerns with your client openly and directly so that she can decide whether she still wants you to represent her.

If you perceive a conflict of interest between two potential clients, do not discuss the facts of the case with either client until you have tried to eliminate the conflict. Immediately seek the judge's permission to withdraw from the conflicting case. If there are few lawyers available, you may be pressured to represent co-respondents in the same proceeding. This is extremely problematic because one client's best defense may lie in suggesting that the other client committed the alleged offense. All jurisdictions have ethical rules addressing conflicts of interest. Cite these rules in arguing to the judge that another attorney should be appointed to represent the co-respondent. Remind the judge that a conflict of interest could be a reason for the case to be overturned on appeal. Research the procedures in your jurisdiction for appointing counsel so that you can help secure another attorney for the child. If the judge grants your request to withdraw, your ethical obligations include turning over any case files and information promptly to the child's new attorney.

Even if the judge declines your request to withdraw, you can proceed with representation *only* if you reasonably believe that you can provide competent counsel to each of your clients and if both clients give their informed, written consent to the shared representation.[32] If you proceed without informed consent, you risk disciplinary action for violation of ethical rules. Explain the nature of the conflict to each child in an individual conversation. Allow each child to ask questions of you confidentially. If both clients grant their informed consent and you proceed with representation, make sure that the conflict and its resolution are reflected in the case record.

II. TIPS FOR QUESTIONING CHILDREN

Before you focus on the content of your early conversations with your client, think about how you will approach your meetings with her. Take her age, background, and abilities or disabilities into account when you speak to her and ask her questions. Adolescents process and use language differently than adults. Adolescents, especially if they are under-educated or have mental disabilities, are prone to becoming confused by linguistic ambiguities or lengthy questions, have an immature understanding of time, and may have difficulty constructing narratives. They may also interpret language literally and be unable to handle abstractions well. Whenever you speak with children and adolescents, phrase your questions with care in order to elicit accurate information. Specific suggestions adapted from Anne Graffam Walker's *Handbook on Questioning Children* follow.[33]

Suggestions for questioning children

> **General precepts:**
>
> > • *Aim for simplicity and clarity in your questions.* If the child uses simple words and short sentences, so should you.
> >
> > • *Be alert for possible miscommunication.* If a child's answer seems inconsistent with prior answers or doesn't make sense to you, investigate the possibility that there is some problem 1) with the way the question was phrased or ordered, 2) with a literal interpretation on the part of the child, or 3) with assumptions the question makes about the child's linguistic/cognitive development or knowledge of the adult world.
> >
> > • *Make sure you understand the child.* You cannot be embarrassed to ask your client to define slang terms. Very few adults are fully fluent in street slang, and it is important to know what the terms a child is using mean. Do not guess.

Some specifics:

- Break long sentences/questions into shorter ones that have one main idea each.

- Choose easy words over hard ones: use simple expressions like "show," "tell me about," or "said" instead of more formal words like "depict," "describe," or "indicated."

- Avoid legal jargon like "What if anything" or "Did there come a time."

- It is important that you and the children use words to mean the same thing, so run a check now and then on what a word means to each child. Although children generally are not good at definitions, you can still ask something like, "Tell me what you think a ___ is," or "What do you do with a ___?" or "What does a ___ do?" Do not expect an adult-like answer, however, even if the word is well known. The inability to define, for example, "wind" does not mean that the person does not know what wind is. Definitions require a linguistic skill.

- Avoid asking children directly about abstract concepts like what constitutes truth or what the difference is between the truth and a lie. In seeking to judge a young (under nine or ten) child's knowledge of truth and lies, ask simple, concrete questions that make use of a child's experience. E.g., "I forgot: how old are you?" (Pause.) "So if someone said you are ___, is that the truth, or a lie?" Young children equate truth with fact, lies with non-fact.

- Avoid the question of belief entirely ("Do you believe that to be true?").

- Avoid using the word "story." ("Tell me your story in your own words.") "Story" means both "narrative account of a happening" and "fiction." Adults listening to adults take both meanings into consideration. Children listening to adults, however, might well hear "story" as only the latter. "Story" is not only an ambiguous concept, it can be prejudicial.

- With children, redundancy in questions is a useful thing. Repeat names and places often instead of using strings of (often ambiguous) pronouns. Avoid unanchored "that's" and "there's." Give verbs all of their appropriate nouns (subjects and objects), as in "I want you to promise me that you will tell me the truth," instead of "Promise me to tell the truth."

- Watch your pronouns carefully (including "that"). Be sure they refer either to something you can physically point at or to something in the very immediate (spoken) past, such as in the same sentence, or in the last few seconds.

- In a related caution, be very careful about words whose meanings depend on their relation to the speaker and the immediate situation, such as personal pronouns (I, you, we), locatives (here, there), objects (this, that), and verbs of motion (come/go; bring/take).

- Avoid tag questions (e.g., "You did it, didn't you?"). They are confusing to children because a youth may lose track of what the subject is. Avoid also Yes/No questions that are packed with lots of propositions. (Example of a bad simple-sounding question, with propositions numbered: "[1] Do you remember [2] when Mary asked you [3] if you knew [4] what color Mark's shirt was, and [5] you said, [6] 'Blue'?" What would a "Yes" or "No" answer tell you here?) It does not help the fact-finder to rely on an answer if it's not clear what the question was.

- See that the child stays firmly grounded in the appropriate questioning time frame and situation. If you are asking about the past, be sure the child understands that. If you shift to the present, make that clear too. If it is necessary to have the child recall a specific time/date/place in which an event occurred, remind the child of the context of the questions. Do not use phrases like, "Let me direct your attention to." Try instead, "I want you to think back to...," or "Make a picture in your mind of when...," or "I'm going to ask you some questions about..."

- Explain to children why they are being asked the same questions more than once by more than one person. Repeated questioning is often interpreted to mean that the first answer was regarded as a lie or was not the answer that was desired.

- Be alert to the tendency of young children to be very literal and concrete in their language. "Did you have your clothes on?" might get a "No" answer; "Did you have your p.j.'s on?" might get a "Yes."

- Do not expect children under about age 9 or 10 to give "reliable" estimates of time, speed, distance, size, height, weight, color, or to have mastered any relational concept, including kinship. (Adults' ability to give many of these estimates is also commonly overrated.)

- Do not tell a child, "Just answer my question(s) yes or no." With their literal view of language, children can interpret this to mean that only a Yes or a No answer (or even "Yes or No"!) is permitted—period, whether or not such answers are appropriate. Under such an interpretation, children might think that answers like "I do not know/remember" and detailed explanations would be forbidden.

Sentence-building principles for talking to children

Vocabulary:

- Use words that are short (1-2 syllables) and common. For example, call it a "house" instead of "residence."

- Translate difficult words into easy phrases. Use "what happened to you" instead of "what you experienced."

- Use proper names and places instead of pronouns, e.g., "what did Marcy do?" instead of "what did she do?"; "in the house" instead of "in there."

- Use concrete nouns that can be visualized ("backyard") instead of abstract ones ("area").

- Use verbs that are action-oriented, such as "point to," "tell me about," instead of "describe."

- Substitute simple, short verb forms for multi-word phrases when possible. Try, for example, "if you went" instead of "if you were to have gone."

- Use active voice for verbs instead of the passive. For example, ask "Did you see a doctor?" instead of "Were you seen by a doctor?" Note: One exception is the use of the passive "get" ("Did you get hurt?"), which children acquire very early and is easier to process than "Were you hurt?"

Putting the words together:

- Aim for one main idea per question/sentence.

- When combining ideas, introduce no more than one new idea at a time.

- Avoid interrupting an idea with a descriptive phrase. Put the phrase (known as a relative clause) at the end of the idea instead. For example, "Please tell me about the man who had the red hat on" instead of "The man who had the red hat on is the one I'd like you to tell me about."

- Avoid difficult-to-process connectives like "while" and "during."

- Avoid negatives whenever possible.

- Avoid questions that give a child only two choices. Add an open-end choice at the end. "Was the hat red, or blue, or some other color?"

The bottom line: Keep it short and simple.

III. INTERACTIONS WITH YOUR CLIENT

A. Initial meeting and interview

Ideally, your initial meeting with your client (and possibly her parent) will take place in your office with ample time to get to know each other. In reality, you are more likely to meet your client just before a court appearance, with little time or privacy in which to hold a productive conversation—for your purposes or hers. You must be prepared to conduct a quick yet efficient initial interview with your client, remembering that establishing a good relationship with her is as important as collecting vital information about the case. Document A1 in Appendix A is a sample form that can help you collect the critical information you will need prior to a detention hearing. Please feel free to adapt this form for your own use. As you interview her, maintain a calm, even tone so as not to make your client feel anxious or rushed. You will conduct a more extensive interview later, during which you will have more time to gather additional information.

If you are truly rushed or there are complex issues you need time to address before you can adequately represent your client, *you should request a delay from the court*. If the judge will not grant a later call or continuance, state repeatedly for the record that you are not prepared and cannot effectively represent your client. See Chapter 7, page 133, for more detail. Of course, when considering whether to request a delay, always take into account the need to prevent your client from being detained any longer than is absolutely necessary.

If you get cases in advance of court proceedings, your first conversation should cover the same crucial areas as if you were rushed, but you will have time to address each issue thoroughly and ask more questions on additional topics. It is also a good practice to send a letter to each client when you are assigned to her case. Many attorneys use a form or standard letter to introduce themselves and their job, as well as to request that the client call to schedule a first meeting. Document A2 in Appendix A is a sample introductory letter you can use as a starting point.

Your first in-person conversation with your client is significant to the entire case. It will lay the foundation for a strong attorney-client relationship and, therefore, effective representation. Be sure to include these crucial steps:

1. Introduce yourself and your role to your client

Tell your client who you are and what your job is, emphasizing that you work for her (and not her parent or the judge), are on her side, and will keep your conversations between just the two of you. Explain the attorney-client privilege and emphasize how serious it is in the law and to you. Give her your card and tell her she can call you anytime. The encounter might open along these lines:

> *Hi, my name is _____. I'm your attorney. How are you doing?* [Pause, listen.] *Have you ever had an attorney before? No? Let me tell you a couple of things about having an attorney. First, our relationship will be different than any other you've had with an adult. I work for you, not your mom, not your dad, not the court — nobody but you. My job is to help you understand what's going on in court and help you decide what you want to do on this case. Then, I'll work in court and outside of court to help take care of this case. I don't tell you what to do, and I will only do what you want me to do. Do you have any questions about that?* [Pause, listen.] *The second thing I want to let you know is that everything you tell me is confidential, it's secret. Do you know what I mean by that? Would you tell me what you think it means in your own words?* [Pause, listen.] *Yeah, that's right. And there is a law that says no one can make me tell what you've said to me. That makes it so you and I can talk about anything, and you don't have to worry, it is just between us. I will not repeat it to anyone without your permission. Does this make sense?* [Pause, listen.] *Do you have any questions about what I just said?* [Pause, listen.] [At this point, hand your business card to your client. Document A12 in Appendix A is a camera-ready sample of an assertion of *Miranda* rights you can have printed on the back of your cards; if you choose to do so, you will want to explain its purpose.]

Your individual style will dictate the exact language you use, but the point is to convey absolute loyalty to your client. Your clients will often have poor self-esteem and come from low-income families. They may also be untrusting of adults as a result of many unfortunate experiences. The extra effort to build rapport will pay off in innumerable ways, not the least of which is avoiding eliciting mistruths or half truths which can waste time and lead into unproductive defense theories. Furthermore, the benefits of a demoralized child experiencing camaraderie and trust with a non-threatening adult may be enormous.

2. Ask about your client

Asking about your client's grade in school, likes and dislikes, favorite activities, and home situation gives her a chance to get comfortable talking to you. It also provides you with a chance to collect valuable information and to assess her cognitive level.   (For example, she might mention a teacher she likes who will be a useful ally later.) Use her answers to tailor your language, explanations, and questions to her capabilities. (For example, high school students who have studied government should know that the Constitution provides rights, which can help introduce your explanation of the right to counsel.) If you are pressed for time in your initial meeting, you may have no choice but to skip this step, but be sure to remember it when you next have a conversation with your client.

3. Explain what is going on

Your client probably understands little about the court process—even if she has been through it before. Part of gaining her trust is showing her that you care about her questions and concerns. Before you begin asking case-related questions of her, take a minute or two to briefly explain her situation and what you need to accomplish in this quick meeting. You may say something like:

> We are about to go into court so the judge can decide whether you can stay at home between now and when he listens to longer arguments about your case. We will have more time later to talk about everything that happened to you and for me to answer all of your questions, but right now I have to get some information from you pretty quickly so I can explain things to the judge at this first hearing.

4. Ask for written permission for access to confidential information

A central goal of your first meeting is to get written consent for the release of confidential information to you. The release is crucial to your investigation. School files, medical records, mental health evaluations, and other documents will help you not only in defending against the charges, but also in creating a disposition plan (see Chapter 11). It is important to send for these records as soon as possible because it can take time for other agencies to send the documents to you. For the information to be useful, you will need it as soon as possible. Because these documents contain confidential information, in most cases you will need written consent for the information to be released to you.

The rules vary as to whether it is the parent, the child, or both who have to sign a release of information, so you need to know the laws in your jurisdiction. Find out when it is necessary to have a parent's signature and when it is not, so you will be prepared if your client's parent is uncooperative or absent. Determine if your state takes into consideration the age of a child and the subject matter of the records. For example, a state may give a 16-year-old the authority to release school records or a 13-year-old the ability to consent to release of mental health information but require a parent's consent for collecting other documents.

A sample release of information form is included as Document A3 in Appendix A. Adapt that form to your state's laws and explain to the child and parent at your first meeting why it is important for you to get these records. You can reiterate the strength of the attorney-client privilege if they express concerns about how the information will be used. Give your client a copy of the release she has signed. (Note that the release of information form gives you permission to collect records but not necessarily to share them with others; see page 231 in Chapter 11 for information about laws governing sharing educational and medical records.)

5. Conduct an interview about the case, in as much detail as you have time for

If the parent has been present up to now, this is the time to ask him to give you and your client privacy. Explain that attorney-client confidentiality extends only to you and your client. Describe the risk of the parent being called to testify about this conversation. Tell him it is better for everyone if you talk to your client alone for a few minutes.

Begin this part of the conversation by asking your client's permission to take notes, explaining that you want to write things down to help you remember all the important information she tells you. Tell her specifically that you will not share your notes with anyone. As you listen, pay close attention to your client's personality, intelligence, and communication ability, as well as the facts she provides. These observations will help you recognize possible educational disabilities, mental health problems, and/or other issues addressed in later chapters of this guide.

If you have time, try letting your client tell her whole story first, without interruption, and then start over by asking questions about each part of her explanation. Ask questions while keeping in mind your time constraints, immediate concerns, and the tips for framing questions from earlier in this chapter. Begin with the crucial issues, such as:

- *What happened in this case?* Where did the incident take place, when did it happen, who was there, why was she arrested? If the client claims she was not present for the alleged incident, where was she, and how can she prove it? Reading through the police report with your client may help her articulate her version of the events.

- *Does your client have a prior record or any pending cases?* If so, what can she tell you about them? What were the offenses? What was the disposition? Is your client now on probation or parole? What are the conditions of probation or parole? Who is her probation/parole officer? Does the probation/parole officer know about the current charge yet? How does your client think the probation/parole officer will react to the most recent charge?

- *Where is your client staying right now, and is the situation there okay?* Is there assaultive behavior at home, a current family crisis, lack of supervision, narcotics dealing by family members, etc.? Did the offense occur at home or while your client was on the run from home? If she does not want to stay where she is, does she have another place to stay? What about other family members or friends? Are there adults who could help supervise her, such as someone whose house she could go to after school? Can that person come to court to say he will take your client in, and will your client's parent agree to that arrangement?

- *Who does your client think will testify against and for her?* Make suggestions to help her think of possibilities and keep track of her answers in a witness chart, where you can keep—and readily relocate—contact and other information about each person as you collect it.

There are, of course, many more questions you will want to ask, some depending on the nature of the case and others as a result of your client's answers to these questions. Again, use your time wisely, reminding yourself and your client that you will have more time later. If you have time, ask:

- *Is the police report right about what happened?* Is anything missing? Is there other information that explains why the incident happened?

- *Will your client's parent come to this hearing?* If not, why? How can you contact the parent? Are there other relatives or adults who might be able to come if asked? Who are they, and how can they be reached?

- *Where does your client go to school?* Does she miss class? How often? Has she been in trouble at school? What are her grades? Is she receiving special education services? Does she participate in any extracurricular activities? Has she won any awards? Are there any teachers or administrators there who would say good things about her?

- *Does your client have a job?* Is it full-time or part-time? Has she ever worked before? When did she work? Are there any employers who can act as references?

- *Is there any other social information that can be used to support pre-adjudication release?* Does she participate in clubs, sports, or religious activities? How can she show that she is responsible (e.g., does she babysit for her siblings while her parent is at work)? Does she have any hobbies?

- *Does your client have any substance abuse or medical problems?* Will a parent, probation officer, or detention center employee bring up these problems in court? Has your client ever been in treatment? Did she successfully complete treatment (even if now using drugs)? If treatment is incomplete, what supplemental services might be suggested?

- *Has your client participated in any counseling programs?* Is there a counselor who could serve as a reference?

- *What are your client's dreams/hopes for herself?* What does she want to do when she is an adult? Where does she see herself in five years? Ten? Twenty?

More detailed questions regarding particular situations appear below.

6. Explain your client's proactive role during the case

Take a couple of minutes to convey to your client how her future conduct will affect the outcome of her case, for better or for much worse. Initially, you can get that message across with a simple, generic description focused on the most important areas: 1) avoiding any further trouble with the police, 2) going to school, and 3) behaving well at home. This part of the conversation may be more productive if you include the parent; you can quickly surmise whether bringing in a parent could reduce your client's trust in you at this point. (Note that you may also want to consider having a private conversation with the parent; see Section IV of this chapter.) Find out what you can about your client's home situation and social behavior, but most importantly, emphasize the implications of your client's actions outside the courtroom. Again, while expressing these ideas in your own style, you may say something like:

> *Let's talk a few minutes about what you can do to help your case. Do you have any ideas about that? What kind of things do you think you could be doing that could help things out at this point? What do you think the judge will be watching for now?* [Pause, listen. Respond positively to her ideas. Build on and refer back to her ideas as you move forward.]

> *I think there are three main things that the judge looks at. First is your record. I see you have XX charges. It's really important that you don't get in trouble while this case is going on. If you do, the judge will take that as a sign that you think court is just a big joke, nothing important. And this will tick off the judge in a big way and make him decide to lock you up in detention. Getting in*

trouble right now, while this case is going on, is a much bigger deal than getting in trouble when you don't have a case going on—Tell me you'll be careful...[Pause, listen.] It's going to mean that you're going have to watch not only what you are doing, but be careful about who you are hanging out with. Can you be careful about what your friends are doing, too? [Pause, listen.] Like, if you are at the mall and a friend starts shoplifting, you need to just get out of there. Right away. If you're out with friends and someone pulls out a blunt, you gotta leave, immediately. Don't try to talk them out of it, don't bother explaining things, just leave. If the guys roll up in a car and you're not sure it's their car, say no thanks to a ride. You just can't risk being near people who are doing something wrong, even if you weren't doing anything wrong. I know that is unfair, but it's the situation you're in at this point. What do you think will be the hardest thing about this? [Pause, listen.]

Second, judges look at school. You can't be messing up in school. Prosecutors go out of their way to find out about school problems because they know if a judge hears about it he'll want to lock you up. So, be on time. Don't miss any classes. No fights, no talking back to teachers — just don't get into trouble at school. We're going to talk in a few minutes about how things are going in school, but the main thing now is remember that you need to keep school as your focus.

Third, judges watch what is happening at home. Basically, if you're not doing what your parent says, a judge thinks, "Well, okay, I guess if home isn't working out then detention is where you should be staying." Try to follow the rules at home, help around the house, get along with your brother and sister. Your parent loves you, but when the judge asks him how you are doing, he has to tell the truth. Make it easy on him so he can say you're doing well, and that since this case you've been really getting it together. When a judge hears that, he's likely to think, "Okay now, I guess we don't need to think about detention if things can turn around like this at home."

You should be listening for your client's good qualities, as well as red flags. Focus your client on her strengths and her positive potential, emphasizing how doing well in these three ways can make a huge impact on the outcome of the case. Discuss strategies for addressing any problems in these three areas and review the status of those remediation plans at each subsequent meeting with your client. She has to understand how important her behavior is while her case is in progress, and you should be prepared to work with her to find viable solutions as problems continue or arise. It may be easier to convince her of the significance of her role if you ask her to think about how her behavior must look to the judge. (Using this reasoning also helps make clear that what seems like criticism does not come from you, but from concerns about the judge's perception.) Your assistance may include helping her obtain special education school services, family counseling, medical or social services, or other assistance. The many benefits of these strategies will become clear as the case progresses.

7. Listen to your client and find out what she wants

You must act on your client's expressed interests at every stage of the case. Before you enter the courtroom and speak on her behalf about anything, find out what her goals are for the hearing. Explain the possibilities for what you will say as well as how you will present the arguments and let her determine the best course of action.

B. Further conversations

As early as possible, you will want to gather as much information as you can from your client. Depending on what you know—from her, the police report, or other sources—about the circumstances of the offense and arrest, you will engage your client in different lines of questioning. Your goals in gathering this information are to begin to determine what legal defense is appropriate in the case, consider the potential for meritorious suppression and other pre-adjudication motions, and identify possible witnesses for the prosecution and defense. (An explanation of how to process and consolidate this information appears in Chapter 6.) Remember to take time to explain to your client why you are asking questions and how her answers may help her case. See Chapter 6 for an overview of possible grounds for suppression and suggested questions associated with each legal issue. In any situation, ask whether your client was ill or under the influence of medication, drugs, or alcohol; if she was, her decision-making capabilities may have been compromised. (In the event that illegal drugs or alcohol caused the impairment, weigh the benefits and risks of introducing that information in court.) Then, research applicable law to determine whether there are grounds to exclude harmful evidence from court.

C. Continued contact

It is very important that you maintain regular contact with your client. After your initial client interviews are complete, you should still meet with or talk to your client regularly, at least once every two weeks if the child is in the community and at least once every week if the child is detained. Regular contact with your client allows you to maintain your rapport and helps provide you and your client with deadlines for performing specific tasks. It also reminds your client of the pending case and her pre-adjudication obligations to the court.

It is a good policy to meet your client on her turf and preferably in her home, as long as you can meet in private when necessary. This strategy provides insight into your client's home situation and alleviates concerns about how or if she will come to meetings at your office. Be aware of any safety concerns related to traveling to an unfamiliar neighborhood and plan accordingly.

Though the substance of each conversation will differ, the fundamentals remain the same. Always:

- Show your client that you care about what she thinks and what happens to her,

- Keep your client informed about developments in her case,

- Let your client know of work you are doing on her case,

- Answer your client's questions plainly and clearly,

- Be timely and responsive to all your client's inquiries, and

- Keep your promises.[34]

I learn more from spending one hour in a child's home than by spending five hours taking a social history from the child.

—Juvenile defender

Be careful not to promise your client anything you are not absolutely sure you can deliver; you risk losing her trust if you fail her. In general, if you always keep in mind that you work for your client and act upon her expressed interests, these displays of respect and frequent consultations will become a natural part of the development of each case.

IV. YOUR CLIENT'S PARENT

Interacting with your client's parent is a complicated issue unique to juvenile court. You must be clear at all times that you work for the child, but at the same time, you need to cultivate the parent's cooperation. Do what you can to work with or around the parent.

Ideally, the parent wants to be an ally. In some cases, though, he will be the complainant, or you will discover troubling information about his relationship with his child. Regardless of his willingness to help your client's case, be clear about how he can be involved and how he cannot. You have to be able to talk to your client alone, so you can be sure she is not altering anything she tells you for the parent's benefit. Similarly, you should talk to the parent alone so you can collect information free from any distortions designed to influence the child. You can also use these individual interviews to frame things for the benefit of each party. (For example, you could explain to the parent that your client's behavior, though unacceptable, is typical for adolescents or explain to the child that her parent's nagging is a sign of concern for her.)

It will often become apparent during these interviews that there is a significant parent-child conflict. It could be a typical disagreement over curfew, sibling rivalry or perceived favoritism, or privacy boundaries and/or a more serious problem, such as neglect, abuse, or desire on the part of one or both parties to stop living together. Smoothing over relatively minor problems, on your own or with the help of a social worker, will benefit your client and her case. Encouraging a parent to enroll in counseling with her child or to enroll her child in desired counseling alone can also be helpful. If the parent was the complainant and counseling is successful, you may be able to bring a statement to the prosecutor that the parent no longer wants the case pursued, which could earn a dismissal or *nolle prosequi* (see Chapter 6, page 107). (Handling serious parent-child issues is more complicated and transferring a case to dependency court, for example, can be a significant step to a more appropriate resolution.)

> One of the ways I let my clients know they are in charge is by asking them for permission before sharing information or case documents, like a police report, with their parents. Whatever the client says, the point is made.
>
> —Juvenile defender

Let the parent know what impact his statements to the court, probation officer, and others will have. A parent may try to get help for his child by relating to the judge the details of difficulties at home without realizing he is actually encouraging the judge to order detention. Understand that the parent may be justifiably frustrated and let him vent to you, but help him figure out how to convey what he means to others in a way that is less harmful to his child. Do not advise the parent to lie, of course, but assist with framing the complaint: "There are some curfew problems" sounds much better than "She stays out all night. I don't know where she goes, who she's with, or what she's doing."

Further thoughts about dealing with parents at various points in the case, including strategies for winning over an uncooperative parent , are provided in Chapter 7 on page 137, as well as in other sections in which they are relevant.

Remember that you must continuously assess the child's comprehension of what you say and her ability to articulate her thoughts to you. If you are having trouble communicating with a client, consider whether that difficulty is indicative of a mental health problem or disability and whether these issues could mean she is incompetent to face adjudication. Chapter 3 addresses these difficult and complex issues.

DOCUMENT A1: SAMPLE INTERVIEW FORM

DETENTION INTERVIEW FORM
TO BE ADMINISTERED BY JUVENILE DEFENDER

Explanation for youth of attorney-client relationship:

- I am your lawyer. That means my job is to help you to understand what is happening in your case. I also speak for you in court.

- I work for you. I do not work for the judge or the prosecutor. I do not work for your parent(s).

- Anything you tell me will be confidential. This means that I cannot tell anyone else what you say to me unless you say that I can. I cannot tell the judge anything you tell me unless you say it is okay.

- If anyone else asks you for information about your case, do not answer their questions. Just say that your lawyer told you not to talk about the case. I am going to give you a card that you can show to people to explain that you do not want to talk.

Client Information:

With whom does client live?_____

Does the guardian know about the hearing today?   YES   NO   NOT SURE

Does client think the guardian will come to court today?   YES   NO   NOT SURE

IF YES, what the guardian will probably say about the client in court today:

_____
_____
_____

Will the guardian agree to take client home tonight?   YES   NO   NOT SURE

DOCUMENT A1

Alternate Supervision:

Is there any one else client can stay with?   YES   NO   NOT SURE

IF YES, what is this person's name: _____

Relationship to client: _____

Does client think this person can come to court today?   YES   NO   NOT SURE

Does client know how to contact this person?   YES   NO

Home phone: _____   Cell phone: _____
Address:_____

Delinquency History (if there is no court file):

Has client ever been arrested before?   YES   NO   NOT SURE

IF YES, about how many times has client been arrested?   1 2 3 4 5 or more

When? _____

Has client ever been to court before?   YES   NO   NOT SURE

IF YES,

(1) When: _____   Why_____

What happened in that case?

_____
_____

(2) When: _____   Why_____

What happened in that case?

_____
_____

DOCUMENT A1

(3) When: _____ Why_____

What happened in that case?

_____

_____

Has client had a probation officer before?   YES   NO   NOT SURE

IF YES, does client remember name of probation officer?_____

Does client remember what officer did:
☐ release conditions: _____
☐ health treatment: _____
☐ mental health treatment: _____
☐ education: _____
☐ supervision: _____
☐ OTHER: _____

Running Away:

About how long has client lived in this community:_____

Has client ever run away from home?   YES   NO

IF YES, client has run away about how many times: 1   2   3   4   5
or more

Last time client ran away: _____

About how long client stayed away from home: _____

Can client tell interviewer why s/he ran away?

_____

_____

_____

_____

DOCUMENT A1

Education and Truancy:

Is client in school now?   YES   NO

IF NOT IN SCHOOL, did s/he get GED or drop out?   GED   DROPPED OUT

    Was client in regular classes or special classes?   REGULAR   SPECIAL

IF IN SCHOOL, is client in regular classes or special classes?   REGULAR   SPECIAL

IF IN SPECIAL CLASSES, what kind?
☐ for kids who have trouble learning (special education)
☐ for kids who have trouble paying attention (attention deficit/hyperactivity disorder)
☐ OTHER: _____

Does client go to school all the time?   YES   NO

How many days does client go to school per week?   1   2   3   4   5

Is there anything happening at school that makes client not want to go there?

YES   NO

Can client tell interviewer about it? _____
_____
_____

Employment and Activities:

Does client have a job?   YES   NO

IF YES, what is the job? _____

Is there anything else that the client does every week that he/she enjoys?
☐ sports team
☐ religious group
☐ volunteering/public service
☐ extra class (art, music, etc.)
☐ OTHER: _____

DOCUMENT A1

Health and Mental Health:

Has the client ever talked to a counselor or doctor to get help with emotional or mental problems?

YES   NO   NOT SURE

Has the client ever been in a hospital or sent to stay someplace in order to feel better emotionally?

YES   NO   NOT SURE

IF YES, when?
☐ Doesn't remember
☐ Thinks it was: _____
Does the client remember where? _____

At this time, is the client taking any medicine regularly?   YES   NO   NOT SURE

IF YES, what is it for?
☐ Doesn't know
☐ Thinks it is for:
_____
_____

Vulnerability to Harm:

Has client ever been in detention before?   YES   NO   NOT SURE

Did client feel safe when in detention?   YES   NO   NOT SURE

In detention, did anyone hurt or try to hurt client?   YES   NO   NOT SURE

IF YES, what happened?
_____
_____
_____
_____

DOCUMENT A1

If the child needs medical or psychotropic drugs, when in detention, did the client get his/her medicine:

NEVER   SOMETIMES   ALWAYS

IF NEVER OR SOMETIMES, what happened?

_____
_____
_____
_____

Anything else client wants to tell the judge:

_____
_____
_____
_____

DOCUMENT A2: INTRODUCTORY LETTER TO CLIENT

June 20, 2005

Client Name
Street
City, ST 40569

Dear Ms. Name,

My name is Your Attorney. I am a lawyer, and I have been appointed by the Public Defender office in Our City to represent you in juvenile court. You are my client, which means that I work for you. You and your family do not have to pay me.

You are accused of petit larceny, which means taking someone else's property. Your next court date is May 3, 2005 at 10:30am in the City Juvenile Court.

It is important for us to meet as soon as possible so we can talk about your case and figure out how I can help you in court. Please bring with you the names, addresses, and telephone numbers of anyone who you think can help with your case.

Please call my secretary at (222) 333-4444, extension 55, so you can schedule a meeting with me. I am looking forward to meeting you.

Sincerely,

Your Attorney
Public Defender

DOCUMENT A3: AUTHORIZATION TO RELEASE INFORMATION

Authorization to Release Information

I hereby authorize [Your Name] of [Your Office], or any person or persons duly authorized by [him/her] to:

- Verify all financial information pertaining to me with employers, banks, credit unions, loan companies or any other source.

- Obtain all necessary medical information, evaluations, or memoranda from doctors, psychologists, social workers clinics and hospitals concerning my and my child's examinations, diagnoses, treatment or hospitalization. Obtain information from any school, counseling, labor department, welfare or other agency that has rendered its services to me or my child.

I hereby authorize all proper officials of all such organizations to forward to [Your Name], [his/her] employees, or any persons duly authorized by [him/her], such requested information for one year from this date for use in regard to legal proceedings.

I understand that the information disclosed may be from records whose confidentiality is protected by state and/or federal law and may contain information pertaining to psychiatric, HIV/AIDS, drug and/or alcohol diagnosis and treatment and that this authorization may be revoked by me at any time except to the extent that action has been taken in compliance with this request.

Client: _____   Parent: _____

_____   _____

Child/Witness Signature   Parent/Guardian Signature

Client's DOB:

Date:

DOCUMENT A12: ASSERTION OF *MIRANDA* RIGHTS CARD

Assertion of *Miranda* rights
(front of card / back of business card)

Notice to Police and Prosecutors

I will not waive my constitutional rights to remain silent and to have my attorney present.

I do not wish to answer any questions without speaking to my attorney first.

I will not consent to participate in any search until I have spoken to my attorney.

Signed: _____

Contact information
(back of card / unused)

My name: _____
My parent(s) name(s): _____
_____
Their phone number(s): _____
_____
My address: _____
_____
My phone number: _____
My date of birth: _____
My attorney's name: _____
My attorney's phone number: _____
My attorney's registration number: _____

Chapter 5
Intake and Diversion

5.1   Overview

A. Role of the Juvenile Court Counselor

A juvenile court counselor must evaluate each complaint received alleging that a juvenile has committed a delinquent act. The juvenile court counselor then decides whether the complaint will be filed as a juvenile court petition or will be diverted from the court system. Because there is no magistrate or district attorney involved in this initial determination, the juvenile court counselor serves as the gatekeeper to the juvenile justice system.

The juvenile court counselor first evaluates the complaint to determine whether the allegations, if true, would constitute a delinquent act. If the allegations are not legally sufficient, the counselor should not approve the filing of a juvenile court petition. If the allegations are legally sufficient and constitute a *nondivertible* offense, a juvenile court petition must be filed. *See infra* "Nondivertible and divertible offenses" in § 5.3A, Preliminary Inquiry. If the allegations are legally sufficient but constitute a *divertible* offense, the juvenile court counselor decides whether a juvenile petition should be filed or whether the matter can be diverted from the juvenile court system through referral to community services.

B. Importance to Juvenile's Counsel

Although the decision whether to file a juvenile petition is crucial, the juvenile has no right to an attorney at this stage of the process. An understanding of intake and diversion, however, is often necessary for the juvenile's attorney to provide effective representation. Because only the juvenile court counselor has the authority to divert cases from court, counsel should be prepared to use any opportunity that might lead to diversion and a non-judicial resolution of the case.

First, counsel might be involved at the intake stage if privately retained or through prior appointment for the juvenile on another case. Counsel should advise the client on strategies most likely to lead to diversion and should participate in the intake interview if allowed. Second, if intake did not occur because of a missed appointment or similar circumstance, counsel should try to convince the juvenile court counselor or the court that the juvenile should have an intake evaluation that could lead to diversion. Finally, an offense initially deemed nondivertible by the juvenile court counselor might actually be divertible and the juvenile may still be eligible for an intake evaluation. *See infra* "Nondivertible and divertible offenses" in § 5.3A, Preliminary Inquiry.

5.2   Terminology Used in this Chapter

Complaint is the report from a law enforcement officer or from a member of the community made to the juvenile court counselor alleging delinquent acts committed by a juvenile. The complaint is typically recorded on the AOC juvenile petition form. *See* Form AOC-J-310 (Juvenile Petition (Delinquent)) (Oct. 2008).

Delinquent juvenile is a person who, "while less than 16 years of age but at least 6 years of age, commits a crime or infraction under State law or under an ordinance of local government, including violation of the motor vehicle laws, or who commits indirect contempt by a juvenile as defined in G.S. 5A-31." G.S. 7B-1501(7).

Diversion is the decision of the juvenile court counselor not to authorize the filing of a petition in juvenile court even though the allegations, if true, would constitute a crime if committed by an adult. A diversion plan may consist of referral to community resources and may include a diversion contract between the juvenile court counselor, the juvenile, and the juvenile's parent, guardian, or custodian containing specific statutory requirements. G.S. 7B-1706(a), (b).

Intake is the "process of screening and evaluating a complaint alleging that a juvenile is delinquent or undisciplined to determine whether the complaint should be filed as a petition." G.S. 7B-1501(13).

Juvenile court counselor is the "person responsible for intake services and court supervision services to juveniles under the supervision of the chief court counselor." G.S.

7B-1501(18a). In some jurisdictions the juvenile court counselor who primarily provides intake services is referred to as the "intake counselor."

Petition is the document filed in the office of the Clerk of Superior Court initiating a juvenile court proceeding. The petition is analogous to a warrant filed against an adult in criminal court.

5.3   Intake

A. Preliminary Inquiry

Screening of complaint. A juvenile court counselor determines whether a complaint alleges a matter within the jurisdiction of the juvenile court. The juvenile must have been at least age 6 and less than age 16 when the act was allegedly committed, and the allegations, if proven, must constitute a crime or infraction if committed by an adult. The court counselor should not file a petition if the complaint is not legally sufficient or is frivolous. G.S. 7B-1701.

Nondivertible and divertible offenses. The juvenile court counselor must authorize the filing of a petition if there are "reasonable grounds to believe that a juvenile has committed" one of the specified offenses. The following offenses are nondivertible because, if supported by sufficient evidence, they cannot be diverted by the juvenile court counselor:

1. murder;
2. first-degree rape or second degree rape;
3. first-degree sexual offense or second degree sexual offense;
4. arson;
5. any violation of Article 5, Chapter 90 of the General Statutes [North Carolina Controlled Substances Act] that would constitute a felony if committed by an adult;
6. first degree burglary;
7. crime against nature; or
8. any felony that involves the willful infliction of serious bodily injury on another or that was committed by use of a deadly weapon.

G.S. 7B-1701.

"Serious bodily injury" is not defined in the delinquency statutes, but is defined in criminal statutes as "bodily injury that creates a substantial risk of death, or that causes serious permanent disfigurement, coma, a permanent or protracted condition that causes extreme pain, or permanent or protracted loss or impairment of the function of any bodily member or organ, or that results in prolonged hospitalization." G.S. 14-32.4(a) (assault inflicting serious bodily injury); *see also* G.S. 14-318.4 (using an identical definition of serious bodily injury for felony child abuse). The term is also defined in motor vehicle statutes as "bodily injury that involves a substantial risk of death, extreme physical pain, protracted and obvious disfigurement, or protracted loss or impairment of the function of a bodily member, organ, or mental faculty." G.S. 20-160.1(b) (failure to yield causing serious bodily injury).

Divertible offenses include felonies not listed above as well as any act that would constitute a misdemeanor if committed by an adult.

Ordinarily, a juvenile court counselor will meet with the juvenile at the beginning of a divertible case in order to conduct a background investigation and determine whether the case should be diverted. However, some court counselors decide not to meet with juveniles charged with nondivertible offenses before the adjudication hearing. This could result in the dispositional hearing being delayed so that the counselor can complete a background investigation for the case. If the dispositional hearing is delayed, the juvenile may suffer adverse consequences, such as being held in secure custody pending disposition. Counsel should consider consenting to or requesting the preparation of a predisposition report after the filing of a nondivertible petition in order to avoid a delay in disposition if the juvenile is adjudicated delinquent.

B. Evaluation by Juvenile Court Counselor

Statutory requirements. If the complaint is legally sufficient, the juvenile court counselor must perform an evaluation to decide whether the complaint will be filed as a petition, the matter will be diverted, or no further action will be taken. G.S. 7B-1702. The evaluation must be based on criteria developed by the Division of Adult Correction and Juvenile Justice. The Division's criteria for diversion can be found in Section 14B N.C. Admin. Code 11D .0102 and include the following seven factors:

- protection of the community;
- seriousness of the offense;
- juvenile's previous record of involvement in the legal system, including previous diversions;
- ability of the juvenile and the juvenile's family to use community resources;
- consideration of the victim;
- juvenile's age; and
- juvenile's culpability in the alleged complaint.

If practicable, the evaluation must include the following:

- interviews with the complainant and the victim if someone other than the complainant;
- interviews with the juvenile and the juvenile's parent, guardian, or custodian; and
- interviews with people known to have relevant information about the juvenile or the juvenile's family.

G.S. 7B-1702. The Court of Appeals has construed G.S. 7B-1702 to mean that the juvenile court counselor must conduct interviews "only when additional evidence is needed to evaluate the factors provided by" the Division of Juvenile Justice. *In re T.H.*, 218 N.C. App. 123, 130 (2012). The evaluation decision still must be based on an individual assessment of the juvenile and the offense alleged. *See In re Register*, 84 N.C. App. 336, 348 (1987) (diversion decision in matter involving multiple juveniles could not be based solely on a juvenile's ability or willingness to pay restitution).

Intake meeting with juvenile and parent. As part of the intake process, the juvenile court counselor usually sends a letter to the juvenile's parent, guardian, or custodian requesting a meeting with the parent and juvenile. The juvenile and the parent sometimes miss the intake meeting for a number of reasons, including the parent's work obligations, a change in residence, or reluctance to respond. If this occurs, defense counsel should still seek to convince the juvenile court counselor to divert the case or arrange another intake meeting if there is a possibility that the intake counselor might recommend entering into a diversion plan, reducing the charges, or continuing the case indefinitely.

Note: Any statement made by the juvenile to the court counselor during intake is not admissible at the adjudicatory hearing but may be admitted at disposition. G.S. 7B-2408.

C. Evaluation Decision by Juvenile Court Counselor

Time limits. The juvenile court counselor must complete the intake evaluation within 15 days of receipt of the complaint unless the chief court counselor grants an extension of up to 15 additional days. G.S. 7B-1703(a). If the court counselor approves the filing of a petition, the counselor must file the petition within the evaluation period. G.S. 7B-1703(b). Defense counsel should check each petition to see if it was timely filed. *See infra* 6.3C, Timeliness of Filing. There is no such time limit on when a *complaint* must be filed with the juvenile court counselor.

Assistance to complainant if petition approved. Upon approval of the complaint for filing, the statute directs the juvenile court counselor to assist the complainant in preparing and filing the petition if assistance is needed. G.S. 7B-1703(b). In practice, the juvenile court counselor or a law enforcement officer will usually draft the petition. The juvenile court counselor must then mark the petition "Approved for Filing" and sign and date it. *See In re Register*, 84 N.C. App. 336, 346–47 (1987) (record must affirmatively disclose that either the intake counselor or district attorney approved the filing of the petition). It is the responsibility of the juvenile court counselor to transmit the petition to the clerk of superior court for filing. G.S. 7B-1703(b).

Notice to complainant if petition not approved. Upon determination that a petition should not be filed, the juvenile court counselor must immediately notify the complainant of the decision. The notice must be in writing and must contain an explanation of the reasons for denial. In addition, the notice must inform the complainant of the right to have the decision of the juvenile court counselor reviewed by the prosecutor. G.S. 7B-1703(c).

Processing of denied complaints. In addition to notifying the complainant of the decision not to approve a petition, the juvenile court counselor must mark the complaint "Not Approved for Filing," and either "Closed" or "Diverted and Retained" (that is, diverted, discussed *infra* in § 5.4, Diversion). G.S. 7B-1703(c). The juvenile court counselor must sign and date the decision on the complaint. If the case is closed and not diverted, the juvenile court counselor must destroy the complaint after the time has elapsed for review of the decision by the prosecutor. *Id.*

D. Review by Prosecutor of Denial of Petition

Request for review. The complainant may appeal the decision of the juvenile court counselor to the prosecutor. The complainant must request review with the juvenile court counselor within five days of receiving notice of the juvenile court counselor's decision not to file a petition. The juvenile court counselor must immediately notify the prosecutor of the request and forward a copy of the complaint to the prosecutor. G.S. 7B-1704.

Review by prosecutor. The prosecutor must review the decision to deny the petition within 20 days of the notice to the complainant and must provide notice of the review to the juvenile court counselor and the complainant. The prosecutor is required to hold conferences with both the juvenile court counselor and the complainant. A decision must be rendered at the conclusion of the review either affirming the denial or directing the filing of a petition. G.S. 7B-1704, 7B-1705.

Victim's rights under the Juvenile Justice Reinvestment Act of 2017. As part of the Juvenile Justice Reinvestment Act of 2017, the General Assembly amended G.S. 7B-1703(c) to provide that if the court counselor decides not to file a petition, the court counselor must notify not only the complainant, but also the alleged victim. The court counselor must inform both the complainant and the alleged victim of the right to request review by a prosecutor of the decision. The prosecutor must hold conferences with the complainant, the alleged victim, and the court counselor about the decision. The change applies to complaints filed on or after October 1, 2017. *See infra* §19.2, Changes Effective in 2017.

5.4   Diversion

A. Diversion Plan

Discretion of juvenile court counselor. Diversion is the determination by a juvenile court counselor that a petition will not be filed in juvenile court even though the complaint is legally sufficient to allege a delinquent act. The juvenile court counselor has discretion to divert any complaint unless the alleged offense is nondivertible. G.S. 7B-1706(a); *see supra* "Nondivertible and divertible offenses" in § 5.3A, Preliminary Inquiry. Because discretion to divert a case rests primarily with the juvenile court counselor, the court counselor has significant influence over the outcome of individual cases.

In some judicial districts, juvenile court counselors require an admission from a juvenile as a condition for diverting a case. Although this compels the juvenile to incriminate him or herself, there is no clear redress. The Juvenile Code grants juvenile court counselors wide discretion over the decision to divert cases, and there is no statutory authority for a court to review a court counselor's exercise of that discretion. If the decision to divert a case is contingent on the juvenile admitting responsibility, counsel should advise the juvenile of the consequences of an admission.

Terms of plan. The juvenile court counselor may formulate a plan of diversion that includes referral to community resources. Referral to the following resources may be included in a diversion plan:

- an appropriate public or private resource;
- a program to help the juvenile earn funds to pay restitution;
- a community service program;
- victim-offender mediation;
- regimented physical training;
- counseling; and
- a teen court program

G.S. 7B-1706(a).

In the discretion of the juvenile court counselor, a diversion plan may be incorporated into a formal diversion contract, which has more extensive requirements. G.S. 1706(a), (b); *see infra* § 5.4B, Diversion Contract.

A public or private resource might include mental health counseling, an after-school program, a tutoring program, or substance abuse counseling. The diversion plan should address any underlying problems of the juvenile or the juvenile's family and seek to prevent future involvement with the juvenile or the criminal justice system.

Many counties have restitution, community service, mediation, counseling, and teen court programs. As of the writing of this manual there is no regimented physical training program offered in North Carolina.

B. Diversion Contract

Contract requirements. A juvenile court counselor may enter into a diversion contract with the juvenile and the juvenile's parent, guardian, or custodian with their consent. The juvenile court counselor must provide copies of the diversion contract to the juvenile and the juvenile's parent, guardian, or custodian after signing.

The diversion contract must set forth: the conditions agreed to by the juvenile and parent; the responsibilities of the juvenile court counselor; the length of the contract, which is not to exceed six months; and an explanation that violation of the contract by the juvenile may result in the filing of a petition, while successful completion will preclude the filing of a petition. G.S. 7B-1706(b). If the diversion contract includes a referral to local programs, defense counsel should advise the juvenile and the juvenile's parent, guardian, or custodian to comply with any rules or instructions issued by the programs because the failure to do so could result in the termination of the diversion contract and the filing of a petition.

If a diversion contract is executed, the statute directs the juvenile court counselor to mark the *complaint* "Not Approved for Filing" as well as "Diverted and Retained." G.S. 7B-1703(c). In practice, this information is written on the juvenile petition form provided by the North Carolina Administrative Office of the Courts, also used by the juvenile court counselors to record the complaint. *See* Form AOC-J-310 (Juvenile Petition (Delinquent)) (Oct. 2008). The form also provides a section labeled "Post-Diversion Approval for Filing of Petition." This means that if a petition is later filed, the district court judge will know before adjudication that the juvenile violated a diversion contract. Nevertheless, defense counsel should object if the State presents evidence during the adjudication hearing about alleged violations of the diversion contract on the ground that such evidence is irrelevant to determining whether the juvenile committed the offense described in the petition.

Determination of compliance. Within 60 days of diversion, the juvenile court counselor must determine whether the juvenile and the juvenile's parent, guardian, or custodian have complied with the terms of the diversion plan or contract. G.S. 7B-1706(e). The juvenile court counselor must contact referral resources to determine whether there has been compliance with their recommendations for treatment or services. *Id.* If there has not been compliance, the juvenile court counselor may authorize the filing of a petition within 10 days of the determination of non-compliance. *Id.* If a petition is not authorized, the juvenile court counselor may continue the diversion plan or contract for up to six months from the date of diversion. *Id.* Failure to comply at any point during the continuance may result in the filing of a petition.

If a petition is filed because of non-compliance, defense counsel should investigate the nature of the violation of the diversion plan. This information should be accessible to the attorney through the juvenile court file. Counsel might be able to persuade the juvenile court counselor to reconsider going forward with the petition by providing information that explains or excuses the violation. A sincere recommitment to the terms of the diversion plan by the juvenile and parent may also convince the juvenile court counselor not to go forward with the filing of the petition.

Termination. A plan or contract for diversion ends upon the filing of a petition, upon the expiration of the term of the plan or contract, or six months after the date of diversion if no petition has been filed. G.S. 7B-1706(b), (e).

C. Court Counselor's Records of Diversion Plans and Contracts

The juvenile court counselor is required to maintain a file of diversion plans and contracts for determining whether a complaint has been previously diverted. These are not public records and are not to be included in any juvenile court record maintained by the clerk of superior court. The plans and contracts must be destroyed when the juvenile reaches the age of 18 or is no longer under the jurisdiction of the juvenile court, whichever is longer. G.S. 7B-1706(d).

In some circumstances, a court may be able to consider a diversion plan or contract at disposition. In an unpublished decision, a juvenile court counselor recommended a higher dispositional level because, among other things, the juvenile had entered into two previous diversion plans for past offenses. *In re T.P.*, 194 N.C. App. 200 (2008) (unpublished). The Court of Appeals held that it was permissible for the trial court to take the court counselor's recommendation into consideration. *Id.* The decision does not address the extent to which a court may rely on diversion plans or on allegations about how the juvenile violated the terms of the plans. Counsel should object if the State presents inadmissible evidence at disposition about a diversion plan or the juvenile's alleged non-compliance. Although the trial court is permitted to consider reliable hearsay during a dispositional hearing, G.S. 7B-2501(a), out-of-court statements that led to the termination of a diversion contact may be too unreliable to support a dispositional order or even be considered. For example, statements about the juvenile's non-compliance likely occurred outside court and might involve multiple layers of unreliable hearsay. Further, statements the juvenile made when entering the diversion contract or during the period of the contract may have occurred while the juvenile was not represented by counsel and might implicate constitutional or statutory rights.

Chapter 6
Petition and Summons

6.1   Overview

A juvenile delinquency proceeding is initiated by the filing of a petition with the clerk of superior court. The court obtains jurisdiction over the case through the petition. The court then obtains jurisdiction over the person by service of the summons and petition on the juvenile and on the juvenile's parent, guardian, or custodian.

6.2   Terminology Used in this Chapter

Complainant is the person who files a complaint with the juvenile court counselor. It is also the term used for the person who signs the petition that is filed with the clerk of superior court. The person who signs the petition can be someone other than the person who originally filed the complaint. In either instance it is not required that the alleged victim be the complainant.

Complaint is the report from a law enforcement officer or from a member of the community made to the juvenile court counselor's office alleging delinquent acts committed by a juvenile. The complaint is typically recorded on the Administrative Office of the Courts (AOC) juvenile petition form.

Petition is the document filed in the office of the clerk of superior court initiating a juvenile court proceeding. The petition is analogous to a pleading such as a warrant or indictment against an adult in criminal court. *See* AOC-J-310 through AOC-J-337 (juvenile delinquency petition forms).

Summons is the document issued by the clerk of superior court after the petition has been filed. The juvenile must be personally served with the summons and the petition for the court to obtain personal jurisdiction over the juvenile. The parent, guardian, or custodian of the juvenile must also be personally served unless they cannot be found through diligent effort, in which case the court may authorize summons by mail or publication. G.S. 7B-1806. In most jurisdictions the summons will include the name and telephone number of the attorney appointed to represent the juvenile. *See* AOC-J-340 (Juvenile Summons and Notice of Hearing (Undisciplined/Delinquent)) (May 2014).

6.3   Petition

A. Contents

The petition must contain the name, date of birth, and address of the juvenile, and the name and last known address of the juvenile's parent, guardian, or custodian. G.S. 7B-1802. There must be a plain and concise statement of the facts supporting each element of the criminal offense the juvenile is alleged to have committed. *Id.* The information in the petition must be sufficient to inform the juvenile of the alleged delinquent act. *See In re Gault*, 387 U.S. 1, 33 (1967) (Due Process requires that juvenile be notified in writing of the specific charge or factual allegations to be considered at hearing); *see also infra* § 6.3F, Defects and Variances.

B. Filing of the Petition

There are three ways a petition can be filed. First, and most often, the petition is filed by the juvenile court counselor. The court counselor must file a petition if the counselor finds reasonable grounds to believe the juvenile committed a nondivertible offense. G.S. 7B-1701. The court counselor also has discretion to file a petition if the complaint alleges a divertible offense. G.S. 7B-1702. However, the court counselor must first consider the criteria for diversion established by the Division of Adult Correction and Juvenile Justice and, if practicable, conduct interviews about the juvenile and the events giving rise to the complaint. *Id.* In either scenario, the petition must then be drafted by the juvenile court counselor or the clerk of superior court, signed by the complainant, and verified before an official authorized to administer oaths. G.S. 7B-1803(a). The petition also must include the words "Approved for Filing" and be signed by the juvenile court counselor. G.S. 7B-1703(b).

Second, if the court counselor declines to file a petition, but the prosecutor believes a petition should be filed, the prosecutor prepares the petition. G.S. 7B-1803(b).

Third, a magistrate is allowed to draft, verify, and accept a petition for filing if the clerk's office is closed and the juvenile court counselor wants to file an emergency petition in order to request a secure custody order. G.S. 7B-1804(b).

C. Timeliness of Filing

According to G.S. 7B-1703(b), the juvenile court counselor must file the petition within 15 days of receipt of the complaint unless the chief court counselor grants an extension of up to 15 additional days. G.S. 7B-1703(b). In 2006, the Court of Appeals held that a petition filed outside of the time limits described in G.S. 7B-1703(b) deprived the trial court of jurisdiction over the case. *In re L.O.*, 178 N.C. App. 562 (2006) (unpublished). The Court of Appeals then issued several decisions with similar reasoning. *See In re J.B.*, 186 N.C. App. 301 (2007) (court lacked subject matter jurisdiction where petition filed more than 30 days after complaint received); *In re K.W.*, 191 N.C. App. 812 (2008) (court lacked subject matter jurisdiction where petition filed 16 days after complaint received and there was no evidence of an extension); *In re U.V.M.*, 195 N.C. App. 325 (2009) (unpublished) (same).

In 2010, the Supreme Court considered the time limits under G.S. 7B-1703(b) and held that they were not jurisdictional. *In re D.S.*, 364 N.C. 184, 193 (2010). The Court of Appeals has expressed concern that the Supreme Court's interpretation of G.S. 7B-1703(b) disregards the best interests of juveniles, but has recognized that it is binding. *In re J.A.G.*, 206 N.C. App. 318, 322 (2010).

If the juvenile court counselor files a petition significantly outside the time limits in G.S. 7B-1703(b), counsel should still consider filing a motion to dismiss the petition. As part of the motion, counsel should describe any prejudice to the juvenile or the juvenile's defense from the delay. For example, if there is a considerable delay in filing the petition, the juvenile might not have an adequate memory of the events that gave rise to the petition and, thus, might be unable to assist counsel in defending the case. Counsel should assert in the motion to dismiss that proceeding with an adjudication hearing after the delay would violate the juvenile's right to due process under Article I, § 19 of the North Carolina Constitution and the Fourteenth Amendment to the United States Constitution. *See generally* 1 NORTH CAROLINA DEFENDER MANUAL §7.2A, Constitutional Basis of Right (2d ed. 2013).

D. Amendment of Petition

The petition may be amended with the permission of the court if the amendment does not change the nature of the offense alleged. If the court allows the amendment, it must give the juvenile reasonable time to prepare a defense to the petition as amended. G.S. 7B-2400. The court should deny an amendment if it changes the nature of the offense. *In re Davis*, 114 N.C. App. 253, 255–56 (1994) (juvenile could not be adjudicated delinquent for burning *personal property* in a public building when petition alleged burning a *public building*; court improperly allowed amendment, even with consent of juvenile's counsel, because amended allegation constituted separate offense from that alleged in the petition); *State v. Moore*, 162 N.C. App. 268, 273 (2004) (motion to amend indictment alleging possession of drug paraphernalia described as "can designed as a smoking device" to "brown paper container" improperly granted). Counsel should move to dismiss when an amendment that would change the nature of the offense alleged is denied and the State is unable to prove the offense as alleged. *Moore*, 162 N.C. App. at 273. Counsel should also object to any amendment proposed by the State after the juvenile gives notice of appeal on the ground that the court has no jurisdiction to entertain such an amendment. *See In re B.D.W.*, 175 N.C. App. 760, 764–65 (2006) (order allowing amendment of petition at hearing regarding juvenile's continued detention after juvenile perfected appeal was a nullity as trial court lacked jurisdiction to amend petition).

Counsel should object to evidence that is not relevant to the specific offense alleged in the petition. This will prevent the court from hearing evidence involving conduct that is not described in the petition and that could prejudice the juvenile, both at adjudication and, if the case proceeds, disposition.

If the court denies a motion to amend the petition, the State might file a new petition concerning the offense that was the subject of the proposed amendment. Counsel should consider filing a motion to dismiss if the new petition is filed significantly outside of the statutory time limits for filing the petition. *See* G.S. 7B-1703(b); *see also supra* § 6.3C, Timeliness of Filing.

E. Pleading Defects: North Carolina Defender Manual

The North Carolina Defender Manual contains a comprehensive discussion of pleading defects under criminal law, which generally applies to juvenile court petitions. *See* 1 NORTH CAROLINA DEFENDER MANUAL § 8.2F, Common Pleading Defects in District Court, and § 8.5, Common Pleading Defects in Superior Court (2d ed. 2013); *see also* Jessica Smith, *The Criminal Indictment: Fatal Defect, Fatal Variance, and Amendment*, Administration of Justice Bulletin No. 2008/03 (July 2008).

F. Defects and Variances

Pleadings may be defective in two general ways. A facial defect is apparent on the face of the document. A variance is a defect that becomes apparent only after the State begins presenting evidence. These defects may be fatal, depriving the court of jurisdiction, or they may be non-fatal, allowing the court to proceed. This chapter primarily discusses fatal defects and variances.

G. Fatal Defects in Petitions

Lack of the complainant's signature. The petition must be signed by the complainant and verified before an official authorized to administer oaths. G.S. 7B-1803(a). A lack of signature or verification renders the petition defective and insufficient to vest jurisdiction with the court. *See In re T.R.P.*, 360 N.C. 588, 593 (2006) (court lacked subject matter jurisdiction where juvenile petition alleging neglect not signed and verified as required by statute). Any person with knowledge of the alleged offense may sign the complaint; it is not required that the alleged victim be the complainant. *See In re Stowe*, 118 N.C. App. 662, 665 (1995) (prosecutor with knowledge of allegations may be complainant).

Counsel should examine each petition to determine if it has been properly signed and verified. If not, counsel should consider moving to dismiss the petition for lack of jurisdiction pursuant to *In re Green,* 67 N.C. App. 501 (1984). *See infra* § 6.3H, Defects in Petition: Timing of Motion.

Lack of the court counselor's signature and the words "Approved for Filing." The petition must be signed by the court counselor and include the words "Approved for Filing." G.S. 7B-1703(b). In *In re T.K.*, ___ N.C. App. ___, 800 S.E.2d 463 (2017), the juvenile was adjudicated delinquent for disorderly conduct. The Court of Appeals vacated the adjudication order because the petition was not signed by the court counselor or marked as "Approved for Filing." The court declined to extend *In re D.S.*, 364 N.C. 184 (2010), which held that the timelines under G.S. 7B-1703(b) were non-jurisdictional, to the case. The court reasoned that applying *D.S.* to the case would conflict with one of the purposes of the Juvenile Code—"to provide an effective system of intake services for the screening and evaluation of complaints." G.S. 7B-1500(3). According to the court, the court counselor's role in signing and approving a petition for filing is the only indication on the face of a petition that a complaint has been properly screened and evaluated.

Insufficient allegations. The petition must set forth a "plain and concise statement . . . asserting facts supporting every element of a criminal offense. . . ." G.S. 7B-1802. The Court of Appeals has stated that juvenile petitions are "generally held to the standards of a criminal indictment" and that failure to allege each essential element of an offense renders the petition "inoperative" to invoke the jurisdiction of the court. *In re J.F.M.*, 168 N.C. App. 143, 150 (2005); *see also In re Griffin*, 162 N.C. App. 487, 493 (2004) (holding that a petition in juvenile delinquency case serves the same function as an indictment in apprising the defendant of the conduct for which he is being charged).

Petitions that do not meet these requirements are fatally defective and must be dismissed. In applying the standards required for criminal pleadings, the Court of Appeals has found the allegations of the juvenile petition to be deficient in several cases. *See In re B.D.W.*, 175 N.C. App. 760, 762 (2006) (petitions alleging second-degree kidnapping were fatally defective because of failure to allege one of the improper purposes of the confinement as required by statute); *In re R.P.M.*, 172 N.C. App. 782, 787-89 (2005) (petition alleging assault with deadly weapon *with intent to inflict* serious injury failed to allege offense under North Carolina statutes and did not give the juvenile proper notice of offense State attempted to prove); *In re Jones*, 135 N.C. App. 400, 409 (1999) (petitions purporting to allege age-related first-degree sex offenses were fatally defective because they failed to allege ages of victim and juvenile respondent).

The Court of Appeals has also held that a petition, like an indictment, need only give sufficient notice of the allegations and "should not be subjected to hyper technical scrutiny with respect to form." *In re S.R.S.*, 180 N.C. App. 151, 153 (2006). Cases upholding petitions containing technical errors include: *In re S.R.S.*, 180 N.C. App. at 155 (petition that alleged offense of communicating threats was not fatally defective as it cited the correct statute and alleged facts supporting each element of offense; under the totality of the circumstances the juvenile had sufficient notice of offense charged and specific misconduct alleged); *In re J.F.M.*, 168 N.C. App. 143, 151 (2005) (petitions were sufficient to apprise juvenile of each element of assault on a public officer and resisting, delaying, and obstructing a public officer because they cited the correct statutes and alleged facts supporting each element of the offenses).

In felony prosecutions, the State is permitted to use short-form indictments for homicides and some sex crimes. *See* G.S. 15-144, 15-144.1, and 15-144.2. Short-form indictments are "special instruments" that relax the requirements for criminal pleadings. *State v. Hunt*, 357 N.C. 257, 272 (2003). In some published decisions, the Court of Appeals has presumed that the State was permitted to use short-form petitions in juvenile delinquency cases. *See, e.g., In re K.R.B.*, 134 N.C. App. 328, 331–32 (1999) (upholding a first-degree murder petition couched in the language of G.S. 15-144, the short-form indictment statute for murder). In *In re K.H.*, 196 N.C. App. 176 (2009) (unpublished), the Court of Appeals specifically held that it was proper to apply G.S. 15-144.2 to a petition charging the juvenile with first-degree sex offense. However, there is no provision in the Juvenile Code that authorizes the use of short-form petitions. In addition, the Supreme Court has held that courts may not read into the Juvenile Code "provisions that were not included by the legislature." *In re D.L.H.*, 364 N.C. 214, 216 (2010) (refusing to apply the jail credit provisions of G.S. 15-196.1 to a juvenile delinquency case). If the State files a petition that follows the form set forth in G.S. 15-144, 15-144.1, or 15-144.2, counsel should consider filing a motion to dismiss asserting that a petition drafted according to short-form indictment standards is insufficient to confer jurisdiction on the juvenile court.

H. Defects in Petition: Timing of Motion

Jurisdictional defects. A motion to dismiss based on a jurisdictional defect in the pleadings may be made at any time in the proceeding. *In re S.R.S.*, 180 N.C. App. 151, 153 (2006) ("it is well established that fatal defects in an indictment or a juvenile petition are jurisdictional, and thus may be raised at any time"); *State v. Wallace*, 351 N.C. 481, 503 (2000). Dismissal of a petition for a jurisdictional defect, however, generally allows a corrected petition to be re-filed if it is not otherwise barred by time limits or other grounds.

A motion to dismiss is sometimes made at a first appearance, which may include other petitions in addition to the one that is the subject of the motion. Some attorneys move to dismiss after adjudication has begun because the State has prepared the case for hearing and may be more amenable to a plea negotiation on all allegations. Although the issue may be raised at any time, the court may be more reluctant to grant a motion to dismiss after hearing a substantial amount of evidence against the juvenile.

Counsel should advise the juvenile of the possibility of a petition being re-filed before moving for a dismissal and explain the possible benefits and risks. Even if a new petition could be filed, dismissal could nevertheless benefit the juvenile. For example, in the interim the juvenile could increase chances for diversion or a more favorable disposition by making improvements in behavior or school performance or by making restitution. In addition, the State might simply decline to re-file the petition because of the sheer passage of time. The primary risk of dismissal is that the case will be re-filed and the juvenile may be in the same position as if the petition had not been dismissed.

If the juvenile court counselor files a new petition alleging the same offense or another offense related to the same incident and a significant amount of time has passed since the court counselor filed the original petition, counsel should consider filing a motion to dismiss for failure to meet the 30-day deadline following receipt of the complaint (*see supra* § 6.3C, Timeliness of Filing) and for failure to follow the stated purposes of the Juvenile Code in providing "swift, effective dispositions" and to proceed "with all possible speed in making and implementing determinations required . . ." G.S. 7B-1500(2)a. and (4).

Non-jurisdictional defects. If a pleading defect is not jurisdictional, failure to object before the State begins its case may constitute a waiver. *See generally* G.S. 15A-952 (certain challenges to indictment in criminal case must be made before arraignment or they are waived). Even if counsel objects to a non-jurisdictional defect, the defect may be considered technical and, therefore, subject to amendment. It may be difficult to determine whether a defect in a pleading is jurisdictional and justifies dismissal, or is merely technical and subject to amendment. *See generally* 1 NORTH CAROLINA DEFENDER MANUAL § 8.5J, Timing of Motions to Challenge Indictment Defects (2d ed. 2013).

Counsel should always carefully review the petition and identify any defects that might warrant dismissal.

I.   Fatal Variance between Allegations and Proof

Generally. A fatal variance occurs when a petition alleges all the necessary elements of an offense but the State proves an offense not alleged in the petition. Even though the State proves all of the elements of a criminal offense, the petition must be dismissed if it does not allege each element of the proven offense. *In re Griffin*, 162 N.C. App. 487, 494–95 (2004) (juvenile improperly adjudicated delinquent of first-degree sex offense based on respective ages of juvenile and victim, but petition alleged sex offense by force against victim's will and failed to allege either victim's age or difference in age between juvenile and victim); *State v. Loudner*, 77 N.C. App. 453, 454 (1985) (fatal variance existed where indictment alleged sex offense of "performing oral sex" on person in defendant's custody, but evidence showed defendant placed finger in vagina).

A fatal variance also exists if the State presents evidence of every element of the offense alleged, but the evidence does not conform to the allegations in the petition. *See State v. Call*, 349 N.C. 382, 424 (1998) (indictment charging assault on "Gabriel Hernandez Gervacio" constituted fatal variance where evidence showed victim was "Gabriel Gonzalez"); *State v. Eppley*, 282 N.C. 249, 259 (1972) (fatal variance exists where evidence shows stolen property is not owned by person alleged as owner in indictment). There can be some variation between the pleading and proof, however, without the variance being fatal. *See State v. Pickens*, 346 N.C. 628, 646 (1997) (variance involving description of a gun did not warrant reversal of discharging a weapon into occupied property conviction).

There is no fatal variance if the State proves all the essential elements of a lesser-included offense of the offense alleged in the petition. *In re J.H.*, 177 N.C. App. 776 (2006) (petition alleged felonious possession of stolen goods, but State proved all elements of misdemeanor possession of stolen goods; remanded for entry of adjudication on lesser charge); *In re B.D.W.*, 175 N.C. App. 760, 764 (2006) (petition alleged second-degree kidnapping, but State proved all elements of false imprisonment; case remanded for entry of adjudication on lesser charge).

Timing of variance argument. The proper time to raise a variance argument is when counsel moves to dismiss the petition at the end of the State's evidence. *State v. Bell*, 270 N.C. 25, 29 (1967). If counsel then presents evidence, counsel must renew the motion to dismiss, including the variance argument, at the end of all the evidence. *State v. Broome*, 136 N.C. App. 82, 85 (1999). If counsel fails to raise a variance argument at the end of the State's evidence or at the end of all the evidence, the argument will be deemed waived on appeal. *State v. Curry*, 203 N.C. App. 375, 385 (2010).

When moving to dismiss, counsel should specifically allege a fatal variance between the allegations in the petition and the proof to alert the judge to the nature of the problem. For example, if the petition charges assault on an officer, and the proof shows resisting an officer but not an assault, counsel should move to dismiss for insufficient evidence of assault and for fatal variance between the offense alleged in the petition and the State's evidence. In adult criminal actions in superior court, the failure to specifically assert fatal variance when moving to dismiss has been found to waive the error on appeal. *See State v. Mason*, 222 N.C. App. 223 (2012) (by failing to assert fatal variance as a basis for his motion to dismiss in superior court, defendant failed to preserve the argument for appellate review).

6.4   Summons

A. Issuance of Summons

Upon the filing of a delinquency petition, the clerk of superior court must issue a summons to the juvenile and to the juvenile's parent, guardian, or custodian requiring them to appear for a hearing at a stated place and time. G.S. 7B-1805(a). A copy of the juvenile petition must be attached to each summons. *Id.* Counsel should review the juvenile court file to ensure that the summons contains the correct information, that it was properly issued, and that the "Return of Service" reflects proper and timely service on both the juvenile and the juvenile's parents, particularly if the juvenile or parent is not present.

Issuance and service of a summons involve the court's personal jurisdiction over the juvenile. *In re K.J.L.*, 363 N.C. 343, 347 (2009). Errors on the face of a summons or in the service of a summons "are examples of insufficiency of process and insufficiency of service of process," which can be waived by the juvenile. *In re J.T.*, 363 N.C. 1, 4 (2009); *see also In re D.S.B.*, 179 N.C. App. 577, 579 (2006) (juvenile could not challenge summons on appeal because juvenile, through counsel, made general appearance in the case and never objected to the summons). If there is a defect in the summons or in the service of the summons, counsel should consider asserting that the court lacks personal jurisdiction over the juvenile. A challenge to the court's personal jurisdiction must be made in the first motion or pleading that counsel files or during the first appearance in court. *Swenson v. Thibaut*, 39 N.C. App. 77, 89 (1978). If counsel files a pleading or makes an appearance in court without contesting the court's personal jurisdiction over the juvenile, the juvenile will be deemed to have made a general appearance, which waives any objection to the lack of personal jurisdiction. *Id.* However, if counsel includes a challenge to the court's personal jurisdiction in the first pleading or asserts the lack of personal jurisdiction before raising any other argument during the first appearance, the issue of personal jurisdiction will be preserved. *Draughon v. Harnett County Bd. of Educ.*, 166 N.C. App. 449, 452 (2004). As courts are "very liberal" in construing statements of counsel as a general appearance, *In re Hodge*, 153 N.C. App. 102, 106 (2002), the better practice is to file a written motion asserting the lack of personal jurisdiction over the juvenile. *Hall v. Hall*, 65 N.C. App. 797, 799 (1984) (defendant's initial action was filing motion to dismiss for lack of personal jurisdiction; nothing else appearing, subsequent general appearance would not have waived right to challenge personal jurisdiction).

B. Requirements for Summons

A summons must be printed on the form prepared by the Administrative Office of the Courts. G.S. 7B-1805(b); *see* Form AOC-J-340 (Juvenile Summons and Notice of Hearing (undisciplined/delinquent)) (May 2014). Pursuant to G.S. 7B-1805(b)(1)–(5), the juvenile summons must include notice of the following:

- nature of the proceeding and the purpose of the scheduled hearing;
- right to counsel and information on how to have counsel appointed before the hearing;
- that if the court finds at the hearing that the allegations are true, the court will hold a dispositional hearing with the authority to enter orders affecting substantial rights of the juvenile and the juvenile's parent, guardian, or custodian;
- that the parent, guardian, or custodian is required to attend scheduled hearings and that failure to attend without reasonable cause may result in proceedings for contempt of court; and
- that the parent, guardian, or custodian must bring the juvenile to court for all scheduled hearings and that failure to do so without reasonable cause may result in proceedings for contempt of court.

The summons must also notify the juvenile and the juvenile's parent, guardian, or custodian that dispositional orders affecting substantial rights may include those that affect the juvenile's custody; impose conditions on the juvenile; require that the juvenile receive medical, psychiatric, psychological, or other treatment and that the parent participate in the treatment; require the parent to undergo psychiatric, psychological, or other treatment or counseling; order the parent to pay for treatment that is ordered for the juvenile or the parent; order the parent to pay support for the juvenile for any period the juvenile does not reside with the parent; and order the parent to pay attorney's fees or other fees or expenses as determined by the court. G.S. 7B-1805(b)(3)a.–f.

Counsel should check the summons to make sure that the statutory information is included and the appropriate boxes on the form have been checked. If the summons is not in proper form, counsel should consider filing a motion to dismiss based on lack of personal jurisdiction over the juvenile.

C. Service

The juvenile and the parent, guardian, or custodian must be personally served with the summons and petition not less than five days before the date of a scheduled hearing. G.S. 7B-1806. The court has discretion to waive the time requirements for service; however, the statute provides no criteria for exercising that discretion. *Id.* A law enforcement officer is responsible for service of the summons and petition. G.S. 15A-301(c). If the officer fails to serve the summons and petition, the officer must return them to the clerk within 30 days with a reason for the failure of service. G.S. 7B-1806, G.S. 15A-301(d)(2). If the officer cannot find the parent, guardian, or custodian through diligent effort, the court may authorize service of the summons by mail or publication. G.S. 7B-1806. The court may also issue a show cause order to a parent, guardian, or custodian who is personally served, but fails without reasonable cause to appear and bring the juvenile to the scheduled hearing. *Id.*

Counsel should examine the court file to determine whether the summons was properly served. If there was a defect in the service of the summons, counsel should consider filing a motion to dismiss based on the lack of personal jurisdiction over the juvenile.

6.5   Notice of Hearing

The clerk must give all parties, including both parents, the juvenile's guardian or custodian, and any other person standing in loco parentis five days written notice of the date and time of all scheduled hearings. G.S. 7B-1807. Written notice is required unless the parties receive notice in open court or the court orders otherwise. *Id.* In some districts it is customary for court counselors to give oral notice of hearing. Counsel should consider objecting as this notice does not satisfy the requirements of G.S. 7B-1807.

Chapter 7
Capacity to Proceed

7.1   Overview

A juvenile who lacks the mental capacity to proceed may not be subjected to an adjudicatory or dispositional proceeding in juvenile court. Several provisions of the Criminal Procedure Act, "Incapacity to Proceed," apply to the court's determination of whether a juvenile is capable of proceeding. G.S. 7B-2401. These statutes are G.S. 15A-1001, providing that proceedings cannot go forward when the juvenile is incapacitated; G.S. 15A-1002, setting forth procedures for determination of incapacity; and G.S. 15A-1003, containing procedures for the court to determine whether civil commitment proceedings should be instituted if the juvenile is found incapable of proceeding.

In practice, evaluation of a juvenile's capacity to proceed may be quite different from that of an adult client. A juvenile may be functioning at a lower level than an adult simply by virtue of age or immaturity. It can be difficult to determine if the juvenile is simply immature or lacks the capacity to proceed, although extreme immaturity could be grounds for a finding of lack of capacity. *See infra* 7.5B, Test of Capacity.

This chapter will review the standard for capacity to proceed, the test for capacity, judicial procedures for a hearing on capacity, and considerations for counsel in representing a juvenile whose capacity may be in question.

7.2   Resources on Juvenile Capacity Issues

The North Carolina Defender Manual, published by the School of Government, explores in detail the issue of capacity to proceed in criminal cases. *See* 1 NORTH CAROLINA DEFENDER MANUAL Ch. 2, Capacity to Proceed (2d ed. 2013). The issues and case law discussed there generally apply to juvenile proceedings, as capacity to proceed in delinquency cases is determined pursuant to the designated statutes in the Criminal Procedure Act, G.S. 15A-1001, 15A-1002, and 15A-1003, and constitutional requirements.

This chapter is largely based on Chapter 2 of the Defender Manual, "Capacity to Proceed," which has been adapted to take into account the juvenile court context and vocabulary. Most of the citations from the Defender Manual are to criminal cases and thus use the terms employed in criminal proceedings. These cases are applicable to juvenile cases to the extent that they involve the three relevant provisions of Chapter 15A and applicable constitutional considerations.

For a discussion of capacity in the context of delinquency proceedings, see LaToya Powell, Incapacity to Proceed and Juveniles, ON THE CIVIL SIDE, UNC SCH. OF GOV'T BLOG (Oct. 13, 2017), and her forthcoming Juvenile Law Bulletin on juvenile capacity.

7.3   Terminology Used in this Chapter

Incapacity to proceed is defined under North Carolina's statutes to mean a juvenile who "by reason of mental illness or defect . . . is unable to understand the nature and object of the proceedings against him, to comprehend his own situation in reference to the proceedings, or to assist in his defense in a rational or reasonable manner." G.S. 15A-1001(a). The term "incapable of proceeding" is used interchangeably. The term "incompetent" (see definition below) has a separate and distinct legal definition under current North Carolina law and is not interchangeable with "capacity," but is sometimes used as such. Older North Carolina cases, as well as opinions from federal court and courts of other states, may also use the terms interchangeably.

Incompetent refers to an individual who has been adjudicated incompetent to make or communicate important decisions concerning one's person, family, or property pursuant to the procedures of Chapter 35A, "Incompetency and Guardianship," and who has been appointed a guardian pursuant to that chapter. *See* G.S. 35A-1101(7), (8).

Individualized education program (IEP) is the unique plan developed for each public school child with a disability who needs special education and related services. The IEP is developed by a team of qualified professionals and the child's parents to address the specific needs of the child within the school setting. The IEP must be designed to meet the requirements of the Individuals with Disabilities Education Act (IDEA), Part B. *See* A Guide to the Individualized Education Program, U.S. Department of Education (July 2000).

7.4   Motions Pending Capacity Proceedings

G.S. 15A-1001(b) permits the court to go forward with any motions that the juvenile's counsel can handle without the assistance of the juvenile pending determination of capacity to proceed. *See also Jackson v. Indiana*, 406 U.S. 715, 740–41 (1972) (indicating that counsel may proceed even with dispositive motions that do not require the defendant's assistance, such as a motion challenging the sufficiency of the indictment).

7.5   Standard for Capacity to Proceed to Adjudication

A. Requirement of Capacity

Due process and North Carolina law prohibit the trial or punishment of a person who is legally incapable of proceeding. *See Drope v. Missouri*, 420 U.S. 162, 171–72 (1975); G.S. Ch. 15A, art. 56 Official Commentary (recognizing that North Carolina statutes on capacity to proceed codify the principle of law that a criminal defendant may not be tried or punished when he or she lacks mental capacity to proceed). The requirement of capacity to proceed applies to all phases of a juvenile proceeding. A juvenile may not be "tried, convicted, sentenced, or punished" if mentally incapacitated as defined by statute. G.S. 15A-1001(a); G.S. 7B-2401.

B. Test of Capacity

Generally. G.S. 15A-1001(a) sets forth the general standard of capacity to proceed. Under the statute, a juvenile lacks capacity to proceed if, by reason of mental illness or defect, the juvenile is unable to:

- understand the nature and object of the proceedings;
- comprehend his or her situation in reference to the proceedings; or
- assist in the defense in a rational or reasonable manner.

Mental illness or defect. The above test has two parts. First, the juvenile must have a mental illness or defect. Conditions that do not constitute a mental illness or defect generally do not support a finding that a person is incapable to proceed. *See State v. Brown*, 339 N.C. 426 (1994) (holding that trial court properly concluded defendant was capable of proceeding where capacity examination indicated that defendant's attitude, not a mental illness or defect, prevented him from assisting in his own defense); *State v. Aytche*, 98 N.C. App. 358 (1990) (upholding finding that the defendant was capable to stand trial despite evidence that the defendant experienced some back pain during trial).

If the juvenile has not been diagnosed with a specific mental illness but is unable to help defend the case because of age or immaturity, counsel should consider arguing that the juvenile's age or immaturity are essentially a "mental defect" for the purpose of determining capacity to proceed. *See generally Timothy J. v. Superior Court*, 150 Cal.

App. 4th 847, 862 (2007) (holding that the juvenile's developmental immaturity could result in incapacity to proceed despite lack of a specific mental illness or defect); *Tate v. State*, 864 So. 2d 44, 48 (Fla. Dist. Ct. App. 2003) (holding that a capacity evaluation was required due to the juvenile's "extremely young age and lack of previous exposure to the judicial system").

In the alternative, counsel should argue that the court can find the juvenile incapable to proceed without determining that the juvenile has a mental illness or defect because the standard for capacity under the Due Process Clause of the United States Constitution does not require a specific mental illness or defect. Instead, the standard is whether the juvenile has "sufficient present ability to consult with his lawyer with a reasonable degree of rational understanding" and has "a rational as well as factual understanding of the proceedings against him." *Dusky v. United States*, 362 U.S. 402, 402 (1960) (per curiam). The California Court in *Timothy J.* found that in determining whether the juvenile was capable "of understanding the proceedings and of cooperating with counsel," the developmental immaturity of the juvenile could be considered without proof of a mental disorder or developmental disability. 150 Cal. App. 4th at 862. The Court discussed at length testimony presented concerning the developmental stage of the juvenile's brain and thinking processes. *Id.* at 853–54.

Capabilities. Second, the mental condition must render the juvenile unable to perform at least one of the functions specified in G.S. 15A-1001(a). The existence of a mental condition alone does not necessarily mean that the juvenile lacks the capacity to proceed. *See State v. Willard*, 292 N.C. 567, 576–77 (1977) (amnesia does not per se render defendant incapable, although temporary amnesia may warrant continuance of trial); *In re I.R.T.*, 184 N.C. App. 579, 582–83 (2007) (although one evaluation noted "progressive decline in intellectual abilities," both reports indicated juvenile could understand legal terms and procedures if explained in concrete terms); *In re Robinson*, 151 N.C. App. 733 (2002) (evidence sufficient to support court's finding of capacity to proceed although private psychologist found moderate mental retardation and schizophreniform disorder).

The three functions listed in G.S. 15A-1001(a) are written in the disjunctive, which means that a juvenile's inability to perform any individual function bars further proceedings. *See State v. Shytle*, 323 N.C. 684, 688 (1989); *State v. Jenkins*, 300 N.C. 578, 582–83 (1980). The Supreme Court and the Court of Appeals sometimes refer to a fourth condition of capacity: the ability to cooperate with counsel to the end that any available defense may be interposed. *See, e.g., State v. Jackson*, 302 N.C. 101, 104 (1981); *State v. O'Neal*, 116 N.C. App. 390, 395 (1994). The Supreme Court has held that trial courts need not make a specific finding on this fourth condition. *See Jenkins*, 300 N.C. at 583. Nevertheless, the court still appears to consider the condition to be a requirement of capacity, treating it as a subset of the statutory test. *See, e.g., Shytle*, 323 N.C. at 688–89.

C. Medication

North Carolina courts have upheld rulings finding defendants who were on medication to be capable to proceed. *See State v. Buie*, 297 N.C. 159, 161 (1979) (upholding finding that defendant was capable of proceeding and stating that the "fact that defendant was competent only as a result of receiving medication does not require a different result"); *State v. Cooper*, 286 N.C. 549, 566 (1975) (medication was necessary to prevent exacerbation of mental illness and did not dull defendant's mind), *disapproved on other grounds in State v. Leonard*, 300 N.C. 223 (1980); *State v. McRae*, 163 N.C. App. 359, 368 (2004) (trial court properly found defendant capable where there was evidence that he took antipsychotic medication during the trial).

It is less clear when the State can use forcible medication to render defendants and juveniles capable to proceed. North Carolina statutes do not specifically authorize treatment or medication to restore capacity. *See, e.g.,* G.S. 122C-54(b) (statute states that forensic examiner must provide treatment recommendation after completing capacity evaluation, but it does not specifically authorize treatment or medication to restore capacity); *see also* 1 NORTH CAROLINA DEFENDER MANUAL § 2.1C, Medication (2d ed. 2013).

In addition, the United States Supreme Court has set constitutional limits on forcible medication. The use of forcible medication to render an adult defendant capable to proceed violates the defendant's right to due process unless it is (1) medically appropriate, (2) substantially unlikely to have side effects that might undermine a trial's fairness, (3) is done only after considering less intrusive alternatives, and (4) is necessary to further important government trial-related issues. *Sell v. United States*, 539 U.S. 166, 179 (2003). The Court held that the use of forcible medication should be "rare" and occur only in "limited circumstances." *Id.* at 169, 180. Applying the criteria in *Sell*, the Fourth Circuit held that the government could not use forcible medication to render the defendant capable to proceed because, among other things, the alleged crimes were non-violent and the defendant had already been confined for a significant amount of time as compared to her possible sentence. *United States v. White*, 620 F.3d 401, 413–14 (4th Cir. 2010). The Fourth Circuit also vacated an order permitting the State to forcibly medicate the defendant where the trial court failed to consider less intrusive means for administering medication, such as a court order backed by contempt sanctions. *United States v. Chatmon*, 718 F.3d 369, 376 (4th Cir. 2013).

D. Time of Determination

The juvenile's capacity to proceed is evaluated as of the time of the adjudicatory hearing or other proceeding. The question of capacity may be raised at any time by the juvenile, the court, or the prosecutor. *See* G.S. 15A-1002(a); *Drope v. Missouri*, 420 U.S. 162 (1975) (capacity issues may arise during trial). When the question of capacity arises before the adjudicatory hearing, the court should determine the question before proceeding with the hearing. *See State v. Silvers*, 323 N.C. 646, 653 (1989); *State v. Propst*, 274 N.C. 62, 69 (1968).

Because capacity to proceed is measured as of the time of the proceeding, more recent examinations or observations of the juvenile tend to carry more weight. *See State v. Silvers*, 323 N.C. 646, 654–55 (1989) (conviction vacated where trial judge based finding of capacity entirely on psychiatric examinations conducted three to five months before trial and excluded more recent observations by lay witnesses); *State v. Robinson*, 221 N.C. App. 509, 516 (2012) (trial judge erred in denying motion for capacity examination at beginning of trial; earlier evaluations finding defendant capable indicated that his condition could deteriorate, and defense counsel's evidence in support of current motion for examination indicated that defendant's mental condition had significantly declined); *State v. Reid*, 38 N.C. App. 547, 549–50 (1978) (trial court's finding of capacity *not* supported by evidence where State's expert testified as follows: defendant was suffering from chronic paranoid schizophrenia; defendant was capable at time of examination two to three months earlier, but condition could worsen without medication; and State's expert had not reexamined defendant and had no opinion on defendant's capacity at time of capacity hearing).

E. Compared to Other Standards

Insanity. Incapacity to proceed refers to the juvenile's ability to understand and participate in the adjudicatory hearing and other proceedings. The question of whether the juvenile is capable to proceed is determined after a juvenile has been alleged to have committed a delinquent act and before or during the adjudicatory hearing on the allegations. In contrast, an insanity defense relates to the juvenile's state of mind at the time the alleged delinquent act occurred. A juvenile who is "insane" at the time of hearing might be found incapable of proceeding. An insanity defense cannot be raised, however, unless the juvenile is capable of proceeding to the adjudicatory hearing. *See State v. Propst*, 274 N.C. 62, 69–70 (1968) (comparing capacity to proceed with insanity).

Admission by the juvenile. The standard of capacity for entering an admission to the allegations is the same as the standard of capacity to proceed to the adjudication hearing with the added proviso that the juvenile also must act knowingly and voluntarily in making any admission. *See Godinez v. Moran*, 509 U.S. 389, 398–99 (1993) (holding that the standard of capacity for a defendant to plead guilty is the same as the standard to stand trial); G.S. 7B-2407 (When admissions by juvenile may be accepted).

F. Burden of Proof

The juvenile has the burden of proof to show incapacity to proceed. *See In re H.D.*, 184 N.C. App. 188 (2007) (unpublished) (*citing State v. O'Neal*, 116 N.C. App. 390, 395 (1994)); *see also Medina v. California*, 505 U.S. 437, 450–51 (1992) (burden of proof to show incapacity to proceed may be placed on defendant). The burden may not be higher than by the preponderance of the evidence. *See Cooper v. Oklahoma*, 517 U.S. 348, 366–67 (1996).

G. Retrospective Capacity Determination

If an appellate court finds that the trial court erroneously failed to determine the juvenile's capacity to proceed, the appellate court has two main options. First, the appellate court can remand the case for a new adjudication hearing. *State v. Robinson*, 221 N.C. App. 509, 516 (2012) (finding that the "proper remedy" where trial court proceeds to trial notwithstanding evidence that the defendant was incapable of proceeding is to vacate the judgment and remand for a new trial if and when defendant is capable of proceeding). Second, the appellate court can remand the case to the trial court to determine whether a retrospective capacity hearing is possible and, if so, determine whether the juvenile was capable of proceeding to trial. *State v. McRae (McRae I)*, 139 N.C. App. 387, 392 (2000) (first North Carolina case on issue authorizing such a hearing, but stating that such a hearing may be conducted "only if a meaningful hearing on the issue of the competency of the defendant at the prior proceedings is still possible"); *see also State v. Whitted*, 209 N.C. App. 522 (2011) (remanding to trial court to determine whether retrospective capacity hearing was possible). This remedy is disfavored. *See State v. McRae (McRae II)*, 163 N.C. App. 359, 367 (2004) (recognizing "the inherent difficulty in making such *nunc pro tunc* evaluations"). In the few cases in which retrospective capacity hearings were held and the results appealed, the court upheld the procedure. *See id.*; *State v. Blancher*, 170 N.C. App. 171, 174 (2005).

7.6   Investigating Capacity to Proceed

A. Duty to Investigate

Counsel has a duty to make a "reasonable investigation" into the juvenile's capacity to proceed to an adjudicatory hearing. *See Becton v. Barnett*, 920 F.2d 1190, 1192–93 (4th Cir. 1990) (counsel must make reasonable investigation into defendant's capacity to proceed and must use reasonable diligence in investigating capacity; counsel may not rely on own belief that defendant was incapable of proceeding). Counsel should first try to discuss with the juvenile the issue of raising capacity and its consequences. However, when counsel has a "good faith doubt" as to the juvenile's capacity to proceed, counsel should file an ex parte motion for a mental health expert or a motion for a capacity hearing. *See* ABA Criminal Justice Standards, Standard 7-4.2(c) (Responsibility for raising the issue of incapacity to stand trial) and Commentary; *see also infra* Appendix 7-1: Practical Tips for Attorneys on Using Capacity; *see generally* 1 NORTH CAROLINA DEFENDER MANUAL § 2.3A, Ethical Considerations (2d ed. 2013). For a further discussion of moving for funds for an expert or for a capacity hearing, see *infra* § 7.8, Obtaining an Expert Evaluation.

B. Sources of Information

Personal interview. A face-to-face meeting—at which counsel can observe the juvenile's speech, thinking, appearance, mannerisms, and other behavior—provides the best opportunity to assess the juvenile's condition and its potential effect on capacity to proceed. Counsel may observe unusual or inappropriate behavior while interacting with the juvenile. The juvenile's inability to understand a simple explanation of the proceedings, repeatedly asking the same questions, responding to internal stimuli, giddiness, or extreme sadness may be signs of an underlying condition affecting capacity to proceed. Counsel should obtain permission from the juvenile during the meeting to talk with parents or other people who may have information about the juvenile's condition.

Medical history. Counsel should obtain the juvenile's medical history, including any history of mental health treatment, and ask that the juvenile and the parent, guardian, or custodian authorize the release of medical and other records for the juvenile. If the hospital or facility has its own release form, counsel should have the juvenile and the parent, guardian, or custodian sign that form. A sample release form is available on the Juvenile Defender website. Parents and other caretakers may be able to provide more specific information concerning past treatment and diagnoses.

Witnesses. The juvenile's family and friends may have helpful information about the juvenile's condition. Other people who see the juvenile daily, including staff at the detention center if the juvenile is in secure custody, teachers, foster parents, group home staff, and social workers, may have observations relevant to the issue of capacity to proceed.

School records. School records that reflect poor academic performance, repeated suspensions, or an expulsion may be indicative of mental illness or other disability. Past or continuing concerns about the juvenile's level of functioning may be disclosed in school records. Counsel should review report cards, disciplinary records, and other school records that describe the juvenile's behavior. Under the Family Educational Rights and Privacy Act (FERPA), the school can release such records with the written consent of the juvenile's parent or guardian. 20 U.S.C. § 1232g. A sample release form is available on the Juvenile Defender website. The school can also release the records in response to a subpoena or court order. *See* 1 NORTH CAROLINA DEFENDER MANUAL § 4.7F, Specific Types of Confidential Records (2d ed. 2013). For additional information on obtaining school records, see Jason B. Langberg & Barbara A. Fedders, *How Juvenile Defenders Can Help Dismantle the School-to-Prison Pipeline: A Primer on Educational Advocacy and Incorporating Clients' Education Histories and Records into Delinquency Representation*, 42 J. L. & EDUC. 653 (2013).

Individualized education program. School records are a particularly good source of information if the juvenile has an Individualized Education Program (IEP), mandated by the federal government for each child in public school who has been identified as having a disability requiring a special education plan. The IEP must be tailored to the juvenile's needs as determined by evaluations and assessments by qualified professionals. As with other school records, the school can release records related to the juvenile's IEP with the written consent of the juvenile's parent or guardian or in response to a subpoena or court order.

Commitment proceedings. The juvenile may have been voluntarily admitted or involuntarily committed in the past. To obtain court records from prior proceedings, counsel may make a motion to the district court that heard the case. *See* G.S. 122C-54(d). For medical records not in the court file, the juvenile and the parent, guardian, or custodian can authorize the appropriate hospital or other facility to release those records. Counsel also may make a motion to the juvenile court to compel production of records from other court proceedings or medical records in the possession of a nonparty. *See generally* 1 NORTH CAROLINA DEFENDER MANUAL § 4.6A, Evidence in Possession of Third Parties (2d ed. 2013).

Other records. Several other types of records may contain relevant information. For example, counsel should review any prior juvenile court records for the juvenile. Similarly, counsel should ask whether the juvenile's parent receives a monthly payment from the Social Security Administration as a result of the juvenile's disability. If so, counsel should review any available records related to the disability payments.

7.7   Consequences of Questioning Capacity

While counsel has a good faith duty to ensure that the juvenile is legally capable of proceeding, counsel should be aware of the potential repercussions, positive and negative, of questioning capacity.

A. Potential Benefits

Some of the benefits of questioning capacity to proceed include the following:

- The petition may be dismissed by the prosecutor.
- The examination may lead to needed treatment.
- A juvenile found incapable of proceeding cannot be adjudicated delinquent, precluding both an adjudication and dispositional order.
- Even if the juvenile is found capable to proceed, the examination and hearing may generate evidence in support of a mental health defense, a favorable disposition, or a motion to suppress a confession on the ground that the juvenile did not knowingly and voluntarily waive *Miranda* or statutory rights.
- Information about the juvenile's mental condition may have a positive impact on discussions with the prosecutor and the juvenile court counselor.

B. Potential Adverse Consequences

Some of the adverse consequences that result from questioning capacity include the following:

- The evaluation may result in disclosure of information that is damaging to the juvenile at disposition and could potentially be admitted during the adjudicatory hearing. Counsel may be able to reduce this risk by moving for an *in camera* review of the evaluation and for an order limiting the use of the evaluation. *See infra* § 7.9E, Limiting Scope and Use of Examination.

- An evaluation on capacity to proceed before the juvenile makes a motion for funds for an expert (*see infra* § 7.8A, Procedures to Obtain Expert Evaluation) may hurt the juvenile's chance for success on a motion for an expert.

- If found incapable of proceeding and involuntarily committed, the juvenile will be confined for some period, even though there might have been no confinement if adjudicated delinquent, or the confinement might be for a longer period than under a dispositional order, particularly if the underlying offense is a misdemeanor or the juvenile does not have a significant history of delinquency.

- The juvenile may be confined while proceedings to determine capacity are pending. *See* G.S. 15A-1002(b)(2) (court may place defendant in state hospital for up to 60 days for capacity evaluation, although the stay is ordinarily shorter); G.S. 15A-1002(c) (court may order defendant confined after evaluation and pending hearing). It is not uncommon for a juvenile to be placed in a detention facility pending an evaluation. Counsel should request a hearing to review secure custody and argue for release if the juvenile does not meet the statutory criteria. *See infra* § 8.6C, Criteria for Secure Custody Pending Adjudication.

- A finding of incapacity to proceed and subsequent involuntary commitment may stigmatize the juvenile.

7.8   Obtaining an Expert Evaluation

A. Procedures to Obtain Expert Evaluation

There are three ways that counsel may obtain expert assistance to evaluate capacity.

Ex parte motion. Counsel may obtain the assistance of a mental health expert for the juvenile by filing an ex parte motion with the court. *See* 1 NORTH CAROLINA DEFENDER MANUAL § 5.5, Obtaining an Expert Ex Parte in Noncapital Cases (2d ed. 2013). The motion does not ask the court to determine the defendant's capacity. Rather, it seeks funds for counsel to hire an expert of counsel's choosing to provide assistance on all applicable mental health issues. Once the expert has evaluated the juvenile, counsel will be in a better position to determine whether there are grounds for questioning capacity to proceed. Moving for funds for an expert affords counsel the best opportunity to obtain an expert who is well versed in evaluating, diagnosing, and treating children and adolescents. Counsel should include in the ex parte motion the amount necessary to pay for expert's services. A sample ex parte motion and order for funds for an expert is available on the Juvenile Defender website.

One of the principal benefits of the above procedure is greater confidentiality. Because the motion is ex parte, it does not reveal to the prosecution that counsel has a question about the juvenile's mental condition. Also, if counsel decides not to raise lack of capacity or call the expert as a witness, the prosecution generally does not have a right to the results of the examination. *See* 1 NORTH CAROLINA DEFENDER MANUAL § 4.8C,

Results of Examinations and Tests (2d ed. 2013) (discussing general prohibition in criminal cases on disclosure to State of nontestifying expert's report and circumstances in which disclosure may be allowed).

Motion requesting court to appoint a particular expert. Typically, courts use state facilities or local mental health centers to perform evaluations of capacity to proceed, discussed next, but counsel may request appointment of a specific expert as part of a motion questioning the juvenile's capacity to proceed. *See* G.S. 15A-1002(b)(1a) (court may appoint one or more impartial medical experts). While uncommon in adult criminal cases, in juvenile cases such an appointment may help ensure that the examiner has the necessary qualifications to evaluate children and adolescents.

Motion for examination by local examiner or state facility. Counsel may begin the evaluation of the juvenile's capacity to proceed by obtaining an examination of the juvenile at a state or local mental health facility rather than moving for funds for an expert. *See infra* § 7.9, Examination by Local Examiner or State Facility. Examination by a local examiner or state facility may be the only means of obtaining an expert's assistance in some cases. Counsel should ask if the local examiners use testing designed to evaluate children and adolescents and request that testing and techniques designed especially for children and adolescents be employed.

B. Choosing which Motion to Make

In appropriate cases, counsel should consider obtaining an evaluation of the juvenile by moving ex parte for funds for an expert rather than moving initially for an examination at a state or local mental health facility. In determining whether to seek funds for the juvenile's own expert, counsel should consider factors such as the seriousness of the charges, the presence of other mental health issues, the importance of keeping the juvenile's statements confidential, the likelihood that the case will proceed to adjudication, and the opportunity to obtain an examiner who employs tools and techniques specifically tailored to evaluate children and adolescents.

C. Choosing an Expert

Most examiners have much more experience evaluating the capacity to proceed of adult defendants. Counsel should consider using an evaluator who employs tools and techniques specifically tailored to evaluate children and adolescents. *See* THOMAS GRISSO, *What is Different about Evaluating Youths' Competence to Stand Trial?,* in CLINICAL EVALUATION FOR JUVENILES' COMPETENCE TO STAND TRIAL: A GUIDE FOR LEGAL PROFESSIONALS 15 (2005). When searching for an examiner, counsel should consider the database of experts compiled by the Forensic Resource Counsel at the Office of Indigent Defense Services. Counsel can use the database to identify psychiatric or psychological experts who have experience working with juveniles. The Forensic Resource Counsel cannot guarantee that any individual expert is qualified or is the appropriate expert for a specific case. Consequently, if the database includes an expert who has experience working with juveniles, counsel should independently evaluate the expert to determine whether he or she is appropriate for conducting a capacity evaluation of the juvenile.

D. Basis for Motion

Counsel should detail the specific conduct or information that warrants funds for an expert or a capacity examination at a state or local facility, including observations of counsel. If the showing for a capacity examination contains confidential information, including information obtained in the course of privileged attorney-client communications, counsel may ask the court to review the information in camera. *See infra* "Contents of motion" in § 7.9A, Moving for Examination. If the motion is for funds for an expert, the motion and accompanying showing should always be made ex parte. *See* 1 NORTH CAROLINA DEFENDER MANUAL Ch. 5, Experts and Other Assistance (2d ed. 2013).

7.9   Examination by Local Examiner or State Facility

Counsel may begin the evaluation of capacity to proceed by obtaining an examination of the juvenile at a state or local mental health facility (rather than moving for funds for an expert, discussed *supra* in § 7.8, Obtaining an Expert Evaluation).

A. Moving for Examination

Time limit. There is no formal time limit on a motion questioning the juvenile's capacity and requesting an examination. Lack of capacity may be raised at any time. *See* G.S. 15A-1002(a). A court may be less receptive, however, to a last-minute motion. *See, e.g., State v. Washington,* 283 N.C. 175, 185 (1973) (characterizing as "belated" a motion for initial examination two weeks before trial).

Contents of motion. Counsel may obtain a state or local examination by filing a motion questioning the juvenile's capacity to proceed and asking that the juvenile be evaluated. A sample motion and order is available on the Juvenile Defender website. *See also* Form AOC-CR-207B, "Motion and Order Appointing Local Certified Forensic Evaluator" (Dec. 2013); and Form AOC-CR-208B, "Motion and Order Committing Defendant to Central Regional Hospital – Butner Campus for Examination on Capacity to Proceed" (Dec. 2013). Counsel should provide sufficient information to the court in support of the request for an examination, particularly if counsel anticipates resistance to the request. *See* G.S. 15A-1002(a) (requiring moving party to detail conduct in support of motion); *State v. Grooms,* 353 N.C. 50, 78 (2000) (where defendant demonstrates or matters indicate there is a significant possibility that defendant is incapable of proceeding, trial court must appoint expert to inquire into defendant's mental health); *State v. Taylor,* 298 N.C. 405, 409–10 (1979) (motion must contain sufficient detail to cause "prudent judge" to call for psychiatric examination before determining capacity); *State v. Robinson,* 221 N.C. App. 509, 516 (2012) (trial court erred by denying motion for capacity examination where defense counsel provided an affidavit detailing his observation that the defendant's mental condition had significantly declined during the week before trial).

If the showing contains confidential information, such as information obtained in the course of privileged attorney-client communications, counsel should ask the court to review that information in camera.

Subsequent examinations. The juvenile may be able to obtain additional examinations if the report from the first examination has become stale or the juvenile's condition has changed. *See supra* § 7.5D, Time of Determination.

Motion by prosecutor or court for examination. The prosecutor may request an evaluation of capacity to proceed. As with a motion by the juvenile for an examination, the prosecutor must detail the specific conduct warranting an examination. *See* G.S. 15A-1002(a). The prosecutor should give counsel for the juvenile notice of the motion. *See State v. Jackson,* 77 N.C. App. 491, 496–97 (1985) (disapproving of entry of order for examination without notice to defendant); *see also infra* § 7.12B, Fifth and Sixth Amendment Protections (discussing Sixth Amendment right to notice of examination).

Practice note: If the trial court grants a motion by the prosecutor for a capacity examination, defense counsel should consider requesting that the court limit the scope of the examination. *See infra* § 7.9E, Limiting Scope and Use of Examination.

The trial court has the power on its own motion to order an evaluation of the juvenile's capacity to proceed. *State v. Grooms,* 353 N.C. 50, 78 (2000). Further, the court is obligated to inquire into capacity, even in the absence of a request by defense counsel, if there is a bona fide doubt about the juvenile's capacity to proceed. *State v. Staten,* 172 N.C. App. 673, 678 (2005).

B. Who Does Examination

Misdemeanors. On a motion for a capacity examination when the underlying offense alleged is a misdemeanor, the juvenile is evaluated by a local forensic examiner. G.S. 15A-1002(b)(1a). An earlier version of G.S. 15A-1002 permitted the court to refer a juvenile charged with a misdemeanor to a State facility for evaluation after the local examination was completed. However, the General Assembly amended G.S. 15A-1002, effective for offenses committed on or after December 1, 2013, to remove the court's authority to order examinations at State facilities in misdemeanor cases. 2013 N.C. Sess. Laws Ch. 18 (S 45). Local examinations tend to be brief.

Felonies. If the underlying offense alleged is a felony, the court may order a local evaluation or may order the juvenile to a State psychiatric facility. G.S. 15A-1002(b)(1a), (2). To order the juvenile to a State facility without ordering a local evaluation first, the court must find that a state facility examination is more appropriate. G.S. 15A-1002(b)(2). Examinations at state facilities may take longer than local examinations.

There are three state psychiatric hospitals in North Carolina: Central Regional Hospital in Butner, Cherry Hospital in Goldsboro, and Broughton Hospital in Morganton. Of those three facilities, only Central Regional Hospital provides capacity evaluations for juveniles. Juveniles referred to Central Regional Hospital are placed in a separate unit, which complies with the provision in G.S. 7B-2401 prohibiting courts from referring juveniles to facilities where they will come into contact with adults.

C. Providing Information to Examiner

Counsel should ensure that the examiner has access to relevant information concerning the juvenile's mental health. Counsel may relate his or her observations of the juvenile, identify people knowledgeable of the juvenile's condition, transmit copies of relevant records, and provide other relevant information. The National Juvenile Defender Center also recommends that counsel submit a written request to the examiner outlining the specific areas to be addressed in the evaluation. *See* National Juvenile Defender Center, Juvenile Defender Delinquency Notebook at 51–55 (2d ed. Spring 2006).

D. Confidentiality

Subject to certain exceptions, an examination at a state or local mental health facility is confidential. *See* G.S. 122C-52 (Right to confidentiality). According to G.S. 122C-53, disclosure is allowed to a "client," which is defined by statute as "an individual who is admitted to and receiving service from, or who in the past had been admitted to and received services from, a facility." G.S. 122C-3(6). Disclosure is also allowed pursuant to a written consent to release of information to a specific person, in certain court proceedings, and for treatment and research. G.S. 122C-54 through 122C-56. For juvenile court purposes, the most significant of these exceptions are as follows:

- The facility may provide a report of the examination to the court and prosecutor in the circumstances described in subsection F., below. *See* G.S. 122C-54(b).
- The results of the examination, including statements by the juvenile, could be admissible at subsequent court proceedings. *See infra* § 7.11, Hearing on Capacity to Proceed, § 7.12, Admissibility at Adjudication of Results of Capacity Evaluation; *see also* G.S. 122C-54(a1) (use in involuntary commitment proceedings).
- The facility may disclose otherwise confidential information if a court of competent jurisdiction orders disclosure. *See* G.S. 122C-54(a).

E. Limiting Scope and Use of Examination

A central part of any court-ordered examination is the interview of the juvenile. The interview will likely cover the alleged offense, as the juvenile's understanding of the allegations may bear on capacity to proceed. For recommendations on statutory changes creating greater protections for juveniles, see Lourdes M. Rosado and Riya S. Shah, *Protecting Youth from Self-Incrimination when Undergoing Screening, Assessment and Treatment within the Juvenile Justice System* (2007). Discussed below are options for limiting the scope of an examination. For a discussion of the admissibility of the examination results, see *infra* § 7.12, Admissibility at Adjudication of Results of Capacity Evaluation.

Refusal to discuss offense. North Carolina courts have not addressed the question of whether the juvenile may refuse to discuss the alleged offense when the examination concerns only capacity to proceed. The juvenile's refusal may result in an incomplete report, however, and may make it difficult to show incapacity.

Presence of counsel. There is no constitutional right to the presence of counsel during an examination concerning capacity to proceed. *State v. Davis*, 349 N.C. 1, 20 (1998). There is no prohibition on counsel attending the examination, however. Thus, counsel may request that the examiner allow counsel to be present during the interview portion of the evaluation. If the examiner refuses, counsel may ask the court to exercise its discretion to order that counsel be permitted to attend the interview portion of the examination. *But see Estelle v. Smith*, 451 U.S. 454, 470 n.14 (1981) (noting that presence of counsel during psychiatric interview may be disruptive in some instances).

Court order. Counsel for the juvenile may request a court order limiting the scope and use of the evaluation. Such an order might provide that the examiner is to report to the court on the issue of capacity to proceed only and is not to inquire into any area not necessary to that determination; that the results are to be used for the determination of capacity only and for no other purpose; and that information obtained during the evaluation regarding the alleged offense may not be divulged to the prosecution. Additionally, counsel should request that the evaluation be submitted and remain under seal in the juvenile court file, to be disclosed only pursuant to further order of the court. *See infra* § 7.9F, Report of Examination.

F. Report of Examination

Time of report. Examination reports must be completed within the following time limits, which are described in G.S. 15A-1002(b2). The statute does not set time limits on the holding of the examination, however, except in the last circumstance.

- If the juvenile was charged with a misdemeanor and was in custody at the time of the examination, the report must be completed no later than 10 days after the examination.
- If the juvenile was charged with a misdemeanor and was not in custody at the time of the examination, the report must be completed no later than 20 days after the examination.
- If the juvenile was charged with a felony, the report must be completed no later than 30 days after the examination.
- If the juvenile challenges the determination of the local screener or state facility and the court orders an independent psychiatric examination, that examination and report to the court must be completed no later than 60 days after entry of the order.

The statute allows the court to grant extensions for the preparation of the report of up to 120 days beyond the limits described in G.S. 15A-1002(b2). The statute does not specify a remedy for the failure to complete a report within the statutory time limits.

Limiting disclosure of the report. A copy of the examination report is to be provided to the clerk of court in a sealed envelope addressed to the attention of the presiding judge with a covering statement to the clerk of the fact of the examination and any conclusion as to whether the juvenile has or lacks capacity to proceed. G.S. 15A-1002(d). Additionally, a copy of the report must be provided to defense counsel or to the defendant if not represented by counsel. *Id.* G.S. 15A-1002(d) then states that "if the question of the defendant's capacity to proceed is raised at any time, a copy of the full report must be forwarded to the district attorney." This statutory scheme appears to contemplate that the court and the defense are to get a copy of the report automatically after a capacity examination, but that the prosecutor is to get a copy of the report only if capacity is questioned after the examination and further court proceedings are necessary.

The above-quoted provision of G.S. 15A-1002(d) was added by the General Assembly to limit the prosecution's access to capacity evaluations. Previously, the statute provided for reports to be sent automatically to the defense and the prosecution. 1979 N.C. Sess. Laws Ch. 1313 (S 941). In 1985, the General Assembly added the current language of the statute as part of a bill entitled: "An act to provide that an indigent defendant's competency evaluation report will not be forwarded to the district attorney." 1985 N.C. Sess. Laws Ch. 588 (S 696). Therefore, the statute appears to allow a prosecutor to receive a copy of the evaluation only if capacity continues to be an issue and a hearing is necessary.

In 2003, the General Assembly amended G.S. 122C-54(b) to require facilities to disclose a capacity examination as provided in G.S. 15A-1002(d). 2003 N.C. Sess. Laws Ch. 313 (H 826). This change was part of a larger act dealing with mental health system reform. *Id.* Previously, G.S. 122C-54(b) stated that a facility "may" send the capacity report to the specified persons as provided in G.S. 15A-1002(d). Now, G.S. 122C-54(b) provides that the facility "shall" send the report as provided in G.S. 15A-1002(d). Thus, the disclosure provisions in G.S. 122C-54(b) continue to be linked to the requirements of G.S. 15A-1002(d), authorizing the facility to disclose a capacity examination report only to the extent provided in G.S. 15A-1002(d). As discussed above, G.S. 15A-1002(d) appears to authorize disclosure to the prosecutor only if the defendant's capacity is questioned after the examination and further court proceedings are necessary.

Practice note: State psychiatric facilities have interpreted the 2003 change to G.S. 122C-54(b) as authorizing automatic disclosure of capacity evaluations to the prosecutor. Some local examiners may follow the same practice. Therefore, when requesting a capacity evaluation, defense counsel should ask the court to enter an order prohibiting the facility and evaluators from disclosing the evaluation to the prosecutor except on further order of the court. Counsel should also ensure that the order is transmitted to the facility and the examiner.

7.10 Post-Examination Procedure

A. Reviewing the Examination Report

Counsel should carefully review the examination report once it is completed. For a helpful resource for understanding examination reports, see THOMAS GRISSO, CLINICAL EVALUATIONS FOR JUVENILES' COMPETENCE TO STAND TRIAL: A GUIDE FOR LEGAL PROFESSIONALS (Professional Resource Press, 2005). The book describes some of the clinical and psychological factors that are relevant to the question of the juvenile's capacity and explains what attorneys should expect to see in examination reports.

B. After Examination Finding Juvenile Capable of Proceeding

G.S. 15A-1002(b) states that the court "shall" hold a hearing to determine the juvenile's capacity to proceed after the capacity examination. However, the court might decline to hold a hearing if the evaluation report states that the juvenile is capable of proceeding and counsel does not request a hearing.

If defense counsel fails to request a hearing after the examination and the court fails to hold one, the juvenile's statutory right to a hearing will likely be deemed waived. *See State v. Young,* 291 N.C. 562, 568 (1977) (defendant waived right to a capacity hearing "by his failure to assert that right"). Nevertheless, as a constitutional matter the trial court must hold a hearing, even when defense counsel fails to request one, when the evidence raises a bona fide doubt as to the juvenile's capacity. *State v. McRae,* 139 N.C. App. 387, 391 (2000).

C. After Examination Finding Juvenile Incapable of Proceeding

The provisions of Chapter 15A-1004 through 15A-1008, which list the options available for resolution of a criminal case when the defendant is found incapable of proceeding, are not incorporated into the Juvenile Code. *See* G.S. 7B-2401. Counsel may consider the following alternatives.

Dismissal. Counsel may advocate to the prosecutor that dismissal is the appropriate resolution of the case when the juvenile lacks capacity to proceed. Arrangement for treatment or other plans to address the juvenile's underlying problems will bolster this argument. Dismissal is most appropriate if the juvenile's incapacitating condition is permanent or long-term or if the juvenile is in ongoing or residential treatment. *See also* 1 NORTH CAROLINA DEFENDER MANUAL § 2.8A, Constitutional Backdrop (2d ed. 2013) (discussing constitutional grounds for dismissal of charges against defendant who is unlikely to gain capacity to proceed). Under earlier versions of the Juvenile Code, there was no provision that specifically authorized the State to dismiss a case. In 2015, the General Assembly amended G.S. 7B-2404 to include language expressly permitting prosecutors to dismiss juvenile petitions. 2015 N.C. Sess. Laws Ch. 58 (H 879). The new law, which is effective for offenses committed on or after December 1, 2015, does not provide any limitations on the grounds for dismissing a case. Thus, dismissal under G.S. 7B-2404 would be an appropriate alternative if the juvenile is incapable to proceed.

Hearing on capacity to proceed. If the prosecutor or court are unwilling to dismiss the case and counsel believes that the client is incapable of proceeding, counsel must request a formal hearing on the juvenile's capacity to proceed. G.S. 15A-1002(b). The statute now bars the parties from stipulating that the juvenile lacks capacity. The statute allows the parties to stipulate that the juvenile has the capacity to proceed, but a court may be unwilling to accept a stipulation if it has a bona fide doubt about capacity. *See supra* § 7.10B, After Examination Finding Juvenile Capable of Proceeding.

7.11   Hearing on Capacity to Proceed

A. Request for Hearing

A hearing on capacity is typically calendared on receipt of the examiner's report, but if one has not been calendared, counsel should specifically request a hearing on capacity to proceed. *See also supra* § 7.10B, After Examination Finding Defendant Capable to Proceed.

B. Nature of Hearing

In practice, a hearing on the juvenile's capacity may be somewhat informal. Nevertheless, a capacity hearing must, at a minimum, afford the juvenile the opportunity to present any evidence relevant to the question of the juvenile's capacity to proceed. *State v. Gates*, 65 N.C. App. 277, 283 (1983).

Although no appellate court has yet addressed the question of whether the North Carolina Rules of Evidence apply at capacity hearings, the operation of Rules of Evidence 101 and 1101 indicate that they apply. *See, e.g., State v. Foster*, 222 N.C. App. 199, 202–03 (2012) (holding that the Rules of Evidence apply to post-conviction DNA testing proceedings because such proceedings are not listed as excluded under N.C. R. Evid. 1101(b) and no statute bars their application to the proceedings). At the least, the courts have stated that the "safer practice" is for the courts to follow the rules of evidence because they may not base findings on inadmissible evidence. *State v. Willard*, 292 N.C. 567, 592 (1977).

G.S. 15A-1002(b1) mandates that the trial court make findings of fact, based on evidence presented at the hearing, to support its determination of the juvenile's capacity to proceed. G.S. 15A-1002(b1). Previously, findings were recommended but not required. *See State v. O'Neal*, 116 N.C. App. 390, 395–96 (1994) (the "better practice" is for judge to make findings).

C. Evidentiary Issues

Examination results. Either party may call the examiner from a court-ordered examination, and the examiner's report is admissible. G.S. 15A-1002(b)(1a), (b)(2).

Opinion testimony. Both lay and expert witnesses may give opinions about whether the juvenile is able to perform the functions listed in G.S. 15A-1001(a). *State v. Silvers,* 323 N.C. 646, 654 (1989). However, neither lay nor expert witnesses may testify that the juvenile is or is not capable to proceed because such testimony involves a legal conclusion. *Id.* If the trial court prevents counsel from presenting proper opinion testimony on the question of the juvenile's capacity to proceed, counsel must make an offer of proof to preserve the testimony in the event of an appeal. *State v. Simpson,* 314 N.C. 359, 370 (1985); *In re H.D.,* 184 N.C. App. 188 (2007) (unpublished).

Testimony by lay witnesses may support or even override expert testimony. In addition to testifying about the functions in G.S. 15A-1001(a), lay witnesses may be in a good position to relate their observations of and dealings with the juvenile. *See State v. Silvers,* 323 N.C. 646 (1989) (vacating conviction and remanding case for failure to allow defendant to present testimony of lay witnesses); *State v. Willard,* 292 N.C. 567 (1977) (upholding finding of capacity based in part on testimony of lay witnesses).

Counsel's observations and opinion. Defense attorneys may offer their own observations and opinions about the juvenile's capacity, but such statements without more may be unpersuasive and may not even be permitted. *See State v. Gates,* 65 N.C. App. 277 (1983) (upholding capacity finding where counsel offered own observations of defendant's behavior but presented no medical evidence); *In re H.D.,* 184 N.C. App. 188 (2007) (unpublished) (counsel's statement that he felt juvenile lacked capacity was not competent evidence and did not provide basis for reversing finding of capacity; court also found no error in trial court's ruling that counsel could not testify about his juvenile client's capacity unless he withdrew from representation). *But see State v. McRae,* 163 N.C. App. 359 (2004) ("Because defense counsel is usually in the best position to determine that the defendant is able to understand the proceedings and assist in his defense, it is well established that significant weight is afforded to a defense counsel's representation that his client is competent"); N.C. Rules of Professional Conduct, Rule 3.7(a)(3) (lawyer may act as advocate at trial in which lawyer is likely to be necessary witness if disqualification of lawyer would work substantial hardship on client), Rule 1.14(c) (lawyer is impliedly authorized to reveal confidential information about client with diminished capacity to extent reasonably necessary to protect client's interest).

D. Objection to Finding of Capacity

If the trial court enters an order finding the juvenile capable to proceed, counsel should object at the conclusion of the capacity hearing and again at the beginning of the adjudicatory hearing to ensure the issue is preserved for appeal. The failure to object waives the issue. *State v. Robertson,* 161 N.C. App. 288, 290 (2003) (requiring that the defendant make a capacity objection at the beginning of trial); *In re Pope,* 151 N.C. App.

117, 119 (2002) (noting lack of objection to capacity at the capacity or adjudication hearing). Counsel should also assert that the finding would violate the juvenile's right to due process. The failure to specify due process as a ground for objection waives the argument on appeal. *State v. Wiley*, 355 N.C. 592, 624 (2002). *But see* 1 NORTH CAROLINA DEFENDER MANUAL § 2.7E, Objection to Finding of Capacity (2d ed. 2013) (suggesting that failure to object may not waive issue).

E. Effect of Finding of Incapacity by Court

When the court finds a juvenile incapable of proceeding, it is authorized by G.S. 15A-1003 to initiate commitment proceedings under Part 7 of Article 5 of Chapter 122C of the General Statutes. *See* G.S. 7B-2401 (stating that G.S. 15A-1003 applies). For a discussion of commitment procedures, see NORTH CAROLINA CIVIL COMMITMENT MANUAL Ch. 2, Involuntary Commitment of Adults and Minors for Mental Health Treatment (2d ed. 2011).

G.S. 15A-1006 and 15A-1007 permit a court to hold supplemental hearings to determine if the defendant in a criminal case has gained capacity to proceed and calendar the criminal case for trial. However, the General Assembly did not make these statutes applicable to juvenile delinquency cases. G.S. 7B-2401. The procedure for bringing a juvenile back to court if he or she later becomes capable is therefore uncertain. Rather than leave the case pending while the juvenile is incapable, some prosecutors may choose to dismiss the case and refile the petition later if the juvenile appears to have gained capacity. Language recently added to G.S. 7B-2404 authorizes a prosecutor to take a voluntary dismissal of a juvenile petition. *See* 2015 N.C. Sess. Laws Ch. 58 (H 879). The statute is unclear about the circumstances in which the prosecutor may refile.

7.12 Admissibility at Adjudication of Results of Capacity Evaluation

The admissibility at the adjudicatory hearing of the results of a court-ordered capacity examination is a complicated topic, reviewed only briefly here. Several arguments, legal and factual, exist for excluding or at least limiting the use of the examination, including the juvenile's statements to and the opinions formed by the examiners. Nevertheless, counsel should anticipate the possibility that the results of a court-ordered examination of capacity to proceed may be admitted. *See supra* § 7.9E, Limiting Scope and Use of Examination.

A. Doctor-Patient Privilege

The doctor-patient privilege does not protect the results of a court-ordered evaluation of capacity to proceed. *See State v. Williams*, 350 N.C. 1, 20–21 (1999); *State v. Mayhand*, 298 N.C. 418, 429 (1979).

B. Fifth and Sixth Amendment Protections

Subject to certain key exceptions (discussed in C., below), the Fifth Amendment privilege against self-incrimination generally applies to capacity evaluations and precludes the admission of evaluation results during the guilt and sentencing phases of criminal trials. *See Estelle v. Smith*, 451 U.S. 454, 468 (1981). The Sixth Amendment right to counsel also precludes the admission of evaluation results during criminal trials if the defendant's counsel does not have notice of the scope and nature of the examination. *Estelle* relied on this additional ground in holding that the results of a capacity examination were inadmissible at trial, reasoning that the defendant was denied the assistance of an attorney in deciding whether to submit to the examination. 451 U.S. at 471. This protection is also subject to certain key exceptions (discussed in C., below).

C. Rebuttal of Mental Health Defense

If the juvenile presents a mental status defense and introduces expert testimony in support of the defense, the results of a capacity evaluation are not protected by the Fifth Amendment and may be admitted to rebut the expert testimony. *Buchanan v. Kentucky*, 483 U.S. 402, 422–23 (1987); *State v. Huff*, 325 N.C. 1, 44 (1989), *vacated on other grounds*, 497 U.S. 1021 (1990); *State v. Atkins*, 349 N.C. 62, 107–08 (1998). A mental status defense includes not only a mental disease or defect, but also an inability to form the requisite intent to commit a crime, which includes the defense of voluntary intoxication. *Kansas v. Cheever*, ___ U.S. ___, ___, 134 S. Ct. 596, 602 (2013). In addition, the Sixth Amendment does not bar the use of the evaluation results because counsel should have anticipated and advised the client that the examination could be used to rebut a mental health defense. *Buchanan v. Kentucky*, 483 U.S. at 425; *State v. Davis*, 349 N.C. 1, 43–44 (1998); *State v. McClary*, 157 N.C. App. 70, 79 (2003). *But see Delguidice v. Singletary*, 84 F.3d 1359 (11th Cir. 1996) (defense counsel did not have notice that an evaluation report from a separate case against the defendant would be used to rebut an insanity defense to unrelated charges).

Under the reasoning of the above decisions, the Fifth Amendment may protect the examination results if the juvenile relies on a mental status defense but does not introduce expert testimony. For example, the U.S. Supreme Court held in *Cheever* that the State may present psychiatric evidence when a defense expert "testifies" or the defendant "presents evidence through a psychological expert . . . ." 134 S. Ct. at 601.

D. Waiver

The U.S. Supreme Court suggested in dicta in *Estelle* that the State might be able to obtain, through *Miranda* warnings, a waiver of the defendant's Fifth Amendment rights for statements made during a capacity evaluation. *Estelle*, 451 U.S. at 469. However, a review of federal and state case law indicates that such waivers are uncommon and, even if obtained, are not a basis for admitting evidence from a capacity evaluation. *See* 1 NORTH CAROLINA DEFENDER MANUAL § 2.9F, Waiver (2d ed. 2013).

Appendix 7-1: Practical Tips for Attorneys on Using Capacity
Prepared by Valerie Pearce

1. Meet with client as soon as possible after appointment to case.
2. Take time to get to know client, establish rapport and trust. (See interview tips and information about what information to look for in the interview)
3. Observe client and family members.
4. After talking with client, interview family and other interested parties and obtain as much detailed information as possible.
5. Get releases signed for records.
6. Obtain and review discovery, including written statements and audio/video recordings of statements.
7. Decide if there is capacity to proceed or capacity limited to suppression issue.
8. If so, file appropriate motions for evaluations.
    -   Evaluations should be completed by a competent, experienced evaluator knowledgeable about juvenile capacity. The evaluator must be skilled at doing culturally sensitive assessments of adolescent development. Mental health professionals qualified to diagnose mental disorders in adults are not necessarily qualified to identify adolescent developmental disabilities or mental illness. Be particularly attentive to qualifications of mental health examiners and the quality of their evaluations. You may need to obtain an order for the court to pay for a specific examiner who is qualified to do these types of evaluations in children. An expert witness will be helpful in explaining the research and its implications in juvenile court.
9. Gather complete records from the Department of Social Services, Schools, Medical records, Mental Health and Developmental Disability records, Substance Abuse records, Department of Juvenile Justice records, any psychological or psychiatric testing, including IQ tests, Special education records and IEP's, any written or oral statements made by the juvenile, any audio or video recording of interviews, investigator notes of all officers involved in interviewing, investigating, or transporting the juvenile, detention records, case management records, and any other agency or program involved with the juvenile that may be relevant.
10. You may need court orders to obtain some records.
11. Provide records to the evaluator.
12. Go over the statements and any audio or video recordings with a fine tooth comb, paying close attention to the interrogation environment, tone of voice, verbal and non-verbal communication between the juvenile and the officers, terms used, and observations of the juvenile's reactions.
13. File a written motion to suppress with an affidavit and request that a pre-trial hearing be set.
14. Consider putting together a memorandum of law to provide to the court, as well as copies of case law and research articles on this issue.

15. Be specific and detailed in laying out the circumstances for the judge that show that this was NOT a voluntary, knowing, or intelligent waiver.

16. Prepare for the hearing and subpoena witnesses. Use records and have copies for the court when helpful

17. Prepare your expert. The expert will need to be able to explain the research in simple layman terms and how it applies in this particular case.

18. Decide whether or not you will put the juvenile on the stand and if so, prepare him for what to expect in the courtroom.

19. Be prepared for adverse reactions from the Court and from court personnel. Be prepared to hear such comments as:
     -   "If you do this, you will open up the floodgates."
     -   "Are you going to raise capacity in every case?"
     -   "This is just juvenile court, this court is about treatment and not punitive."
     -   "The child needs to accept consequences for his actions and this is a door to services"
     -   "Why are you trying to make this court like adult court?"
     -   "This is just a delay tactic."
     -   "This is a waste of court time and money."
     Some suggested responses:
     -   "It is our job as juvenile defenders to ensure that the most vulnerable in our society are given every protection allowed under the Constitution."
     -   "Justice naturally requires that we assure accuracy. It would be unfair to the alleged victims and to the courts if this child made statements that were inaccurate and the real suspects went unpunished because we assumed that the statements were true."
     Keep the court focused on this individual child and their individual circumstances.

20. Just because a child says they understand does not make it true.

21. The ability to read does not equal understanding.

22. The law presumes that children under the age of 18 are not capable of deciding about medical treatment, entering into binding legal contracts, or operating automobiles. Why then do we assume that they are capable of understanding complicated legal concepts and waive their constitutional rights?

23. When involved in the suppression hearing, be sure to flesh out all of the details that add up to the totality of the circumstances. Most officers have not been trained on how to interview children. They are focused on obtaining a confession in order to prove their theory of the case and are trained in using adult tactics. Focus on what they did not pick up on and what they did not do as well as what they said and did in the interrogation of the child. Keep the focus on the fact that this was a "child" and not an adult.

24. If the juvenile client takes the witness stand, keep the child focused on how they felt and what their perception was of the interrogation. You want the judge to see through the eyes of the child.

25. If the judge denies the motion to suppress, continue to object for the record so that you do not waive the issue at trial and preserve the issue for appeal.

Chapter 8
Custody and Custody Hearings

8.1   Overview of Custody in Delinquency Proceedings

Juveniles alleged to be delinquent usually remain in their own residences pending both the adjudicatory and dispositional hearings. The Juvenile Code provides for a juvenile to be placed in custody only in specific circumstances, discussed in this chapter. Because there is no right to bail in juvenile court, statutory restrictions on the use of secure custody are important. Counsel must be prepared to argue against an order for secure custody. *See infra* § 8.6A, Overview. Custody is not intended to be punishment under the Code; counsel has a crucial role in ensuring that its use is limited.

There are three types of custody in juvenile delinquency proceedings:

- Temporary custody means taking physical custody of a juvenile until a court order for secure or nonsecure custody can be obtained, such as where a law enforcement officer arrests a juvenile based on reasonable grounds to believe the juvenile is an absconder or has committed a crime for which arrest would be lawful.
- Secure custody is the placement of a juvenile in an approved locked facility after a petition has been filed and pending an adjudicatory or dispositional hearing, or pending placement pursuant to a dispositional order.
- Nonsecure custody is the placement of a juvenile without restriction on the juvenile's freedom of movement in the custody of the Department of Social Services or a person designated by the court. The juvenile may be placed in nonsecure custody after a petition has been filed and pending an adjudicatory or dispositional hearing, or pending placement pursuant to a dispositional order.

8.2   Terminology Used in this Chapter

Absconder is a juvenile who has been ordered into secure custody at an approved detention center or who is in the custody of the Division for placement in a residential facility who has unlawfully left the detention center or residential facility. *See* G.S. 7B-1900(3).

Division is the Division of Adult Correction and Juvenile Justice. The Division is charged with far-reaching duties, including responsibility for operating State juvenile facilities and youth development centers, appointment of the chief court counselor in each district, establishment of community-based treatment and prevention services, and developing training plans for juvenile court counselors and other personnel responsible for the care, supervision, and treatment of juveniles. *See* G.S. 143B-806(b)(1)–(19).

Detention facility is a "facility approved to provide secure confinement and care for juveniles. Detention facilities include both State and locally administered detention homes, centers, and facilities." G.S. 7B-1501(9). These locked facilities are commonly referred to as "detention centers." *See infra* Appendix 8-1: Juvenile Detention Centers in North Carolina.

Holdover facility is a separate space in a jail that has been approved for the detention of juveniles in secure custody. The holdover facility must not allow the juvenile to converse with, see, or be seen by the adult inmates, and must provide close supervision of the juvenile. G.S. 7B-1501(11). Use of the holdover facility is limited to detention for no more than 72 hours of juveniles who are alleged to have committed an offense that would be a Class A, B1, B2, C, D, or E felony if committed by an adult. The court must determine that there is no acceptable alternative placement and that the juvenile must be detained in a holdover facility for the protection of the public. G.S. 7B-1905(c).

Nonsecure custody is placement of a juvenile without restriction on the juvenile's freedom of movement in the custody of the Department of Social Services or a person other than the juvenile's parent, guardian, or custodian.

Secure custody is the detention of a juvenile alleged to be delinquent or adjudicated to be delinquent in an approved locked facility pursuant to a secure custody order.

Temporary custody is the "taking of physical custody [of a juvenile] and providing personal care and supervision until a court order for secure or nonsecure custody can be obtained." G.S. 7B-1900. Temporary custody may be assumed only under specified conditions and is limited to 12 hours or, if any of the 12 hours falls on a weekend or legal holiday, to 24 hours. *Id.*; G.S. 7B-1901(b).

8.3 Temporary Custody

Temporary custody is the assumption of physical custody of a juvenile by a law enforcement officer or other authorized person under specified criteria without a court order until a secure or nonsecure custody order can be obtained. G.S. 7B-1900; *see infra* § 8.5, Authority to Issue Custody Orders.

Criteria for temporary custody. Temporary custody of a juvenile may be assumed by a law enforcement officer if grounds would exist for arrest under G.S. 15A-401(b) (Arrest by Officer without a Warrant) if the juvenile were an adult. G.S. 7B-1900(1). If there are reasonable grounds to believe that the juvenile is an absconder from a residential facility operated by the Division, temporary custody may be assumed by a law enforcement officer or by personnel authorized by statute. G.S. 7B-1900(3).

Duties of temporary custodian. A law enforcement officer who takes a juvenile other than an absconder into temporary custody must notify the juvenile's parent, guardian, or custodian (hereinafter the parent) that the juvenile is in temporary custody. The parent must be advised of the right to stay with the juvenile until it is determined whether the juvenile will be placed in secure or nonsecure custody. Failure to notify the parent that the juvenile is in temporary custody is not grounds for release of the juvenile. G.S. 7B-1901(a)(1). Except for an alleged absconder, the law enforcement officer may release the juvenile to the parent if the officer decides that continued custody is not necessary. G.S. 7B-1901(a)(2).

If the juvenile is not released, the law enforcement officer must request that a juvenile court counselor file a petition alleging delinquency unless the juvenile is an alleged absconder. G.S. 7B-1901(a)(3). On the filing of a petition, a district court judge or a juvenile court counselor with delegated authority pursuant to G.S. 7B-1902 must determine the need for continued custody. *Id.* If the juvenile court counselor does not approve the petition, or if the judge or juvenile court counselor decides that continued custody is not warranted after a petition is filed, the juvenile must be released.

Limits on temporary custody. A juvenile may not be held in temporary custody for more than 12 hours or, if the time falls on a Saturday, Sunday, or legal holiday, more than 24 hours. A petition or motion for review must be filed and an order for secure or nonsecure custody must be issued to continue custody beyond these limits. G.S. 7B-1901(b).

Remedies for violations of temporary custody requirements. Counsel should move to suppress any statements made by the juvenile while held in custody in violation of the juvenile's constitutional and statutory rights. *See infra* § 11.3, Bases for Motions to Suppress Statement or Admission of Juvenile; § 11.4, Case Law: Motions to Suppress In-Custody Statements of Juveniles. The violations also may bolster an argument for release of the juvenile from secure custody because of the failure to follow statutory procedure. *But cf.* G.S. 7B-1901(a)(1) (failure to notify parent that the juvenile is in temporary custody is not grounds for release of the juvenile).

8.4　Release

Many juveniles are released into the custody of parents soon after the initiation of delinquency proceedings. If the court releases the juvenile, it may impose the following conditions:

1. release on the written promise of the juvenile's parent, guardian, or custodian to produce the juvenile in court for subsequent proceedings;
2. release into the care of a responsible person or organization;
3. release conditioned on restrictions on activities, associations, residence, or travel if reasonably related to securing the juvenile's presence in court; or
4. any other conditions reasonably related to securing the juvenile's presence in court.

G.S. 7B-1906(f). Some judges will impose electronic house arrest or curfew as conditions of release. If the court imposes conditions, counsel should object to any conditions that are not reasonably related to securing the juvenile's presence in court.

Sometimes the juvenile's parent may refuse to take custody of the juvenile out of frustration with the juvenile's behavior. If the parent is unwilling to take custody of the juvenile, the court may release the juvenile into the custody of a "responsible adult." G.S. 7B-1903(a). Counsel should determine whether the parent is willing to take custody of the juvenile. If the parent is not willing to take custody of the juvenile, counsel should determine whether another adult would be willing to do so and be prepared to offer the court an alternative adult to whom it can release the juvenile. Counsel should also ensure that the person who is willing to accept custody of the juvenile appears in court in order for the judge to confirm that the adult is ready, willing, and able to take custody of the juvenile.

8.5   Authority to Issue Custody Orders

Any district court judge may issue an order for secure or nonsecure custody if the criteria set forth in G.S. 7B-1903 are met. G.S. 7B-1902; *see infra* § 8.6, Secure Custody; § 8.7 Nonsecure Custody. Some judges might decline to modify a secure custody order issued by another judge. However, the court of appeals has held that any judge has the authority to review and modify a secure custody order even if it was issued by a different judge. *In re D.L.H.*, 198 N.C. App. 286, 294 (2009), *overruled on other grounds*, 364 N.C. 214 (2010).

The chief district court judge may delegate the authority to issue secure or nonsecure custody orders to the chief court counselor or the chief court counselor's counseling staff by administrative order filed in the office of the clerk of superior court. G.S. 7B-1902. The authority of the court to issue custody orders is routinely delegated in some districts, giving significant authority to the juvenile court counselor at the initial stage of the juvenile proceeding. If juvenile court counselors are issuing secure custody orders, counsel should determine whether there is a properly filed administrative order delegating this authority. Counsel should object and move for release from custody if there is not.

8.6   Secure Custody

A. Overview

A juvenile may be held in secure custody during three stages of the proceeding: pre-adjudication; post-adjudication/pre-disposition; and post-disposition. G.S. 7B-1903(b), (c). A secure custody order provides for detention of a juvenile in a secure, or locked, facility. G.S. 7B-1501(8), (9); 7B-1905(b), (c). Secure custody entails significant restriction on the juvenile's freedom of movement because the facility is locked and juveniles do not have the right to bail. The statutes provide procedural protection to ensure that a juvenile is not held in secure custody except under specified circumstances. *See infra* § 8.6C, Criteria for Secure Custody Pending Adjudication. Counsel should be prepared to offer alternatives to the court that provide both protection and supervision for the juvenile and protection of the public.

B. Shackling

Requiring the juvenile to be shackled and wear jail attire during court proceedings may cause the juvenile humiliation and may prejudice the judge against releasing the juvenile from secure custody. Shackling also may impede the ability of juveniles to communicate with counsel and assist in their defense. *See generally Deck v. Missouri*, 544 U.S. 622, 630–31 (2005) (discussing reasons U.S. Constitution prohibits routine shackling in adult criminal cases). Counsel should make prior contact with the detention facility to determine the facility's plans for transporting the juvenile to court and request that the juvenile be attired in appropriate clothing and be free of shackles when brought into the courtroom.

G.S. 7B-2402.1 was enacted in 2007 to protect a juvenile from unnecessary shackling, allowing the court to order shackling only if "reasonably necessary to maintain order, prevent the juvenile's escape, or provide for the safety of the courtroom." *Id.* The court must give the juvenile and the juvenile's attorney an opportunity to be heard, if practical, and make findings of fact in support of any order. *Id.* If shackling will be an issue, counsel should make a motion for removal of restraints before the proceeding begins and be prepared to argue that the statutory criteria for restraints are not met.

C. Criteria for Secure Custody Pending Adjudication

When a petition has been filed, the court may enter an order for secure custody pending adjudication if it determines that there is a "reasonable factual basis to believe that the juvenile committed the offense as alleged in the petition" *and* that the juvenile:

- is charged with a felony and is a danger to property or persons;
- is a danger to others and is charged with either a misdemeanor having assault as an element of the offense, or is charged with a misdemeanor alleging that the juvenile used, threatened to use, or displayed a firearm or other deadly weapon;
- has demonstrated that the juvenile is a danger to persons and is charged with a violation of G.S. 20-138.1 (impaired driving) or G.S. 20-138.3 (driving by person less than 21 years old after consuming alcohol or drugs);
- willfully failed to appear on a pending delinquency charge or on charges of violation of probation or post-release supervision after receiving proper notice;
- has a pending delinquency charge and there is reasonable cause to believe that the juvenile will not appear in court;
- is an absconder from a residential facility operated by the Division or a comparable facility in another state; or
- should be detained for the juvenile's own protection because of recent attempted or actual self-inflicted injury. (The juvenile must have been refused admission by an appropriate hospital. Secure custody is then limited to 24 hours for determination of the need for inpatient hospitalization. Continuous supervision must be provided and a physician must be notified immediately.)

G.S. 7B-1903(b)(1)–(6).

The statute does not give the court discretion to order secure custody for any reasons other than those listed.

D. Initial Order for Secure Custody

The secure custody order must be in writing and direct a law enforcement officer or other authorized person to take the juvenile into custody for transportation to the detention or holdover facility. G.S. 7B-1904. The officer who takes the juvenile into custody must give a copy of the secure custody order to the juvenile's parent, guardian, or custodian. *Id.* The officer must also give a copy of the petition and secure custody order to the facility. *Id.* Alternatively, the detention facility is authorized to detain the juvenile upon notification by the Department of Public Safety that the petition and secure custody order are on file in the county. *Id.* The petition and secure custody order must then be transmitted to the detention facility within 72 hours of the initial detention of the juvenile. *Id.*

All communications, orders, authorizations, and requests regarding secure custody may be by telephone if other means of communication are "impractical." G.S. 7B-1907. Any resulting written order must indicate the name and title of the person communicating by telephone, the signature and title of the official entering the order, and the hour and date of the authorization. *Id.*

E. Place of Secure Custody

A juvenile meeting the criteria for secure custody may be detained in an approved detention facility. G.S. 7B-1905(b). The detention facility must be separate from any jail, lockup, prison, or other adult penal institution unless the juvenile is alleged to have committed an offense that would constitute a Class A, B1, B2, C, D, or E felony if committed by an adult. In that circumstance, the juvenile may be held in a holdover facility for up to 72 hours if the court finds, based on information provided by the juvenile court counselor, that there is no acceptable alternative placement and the protection of the public requires that the juvenile be detained. G.S. 7B-1905(b), (c).

F. Secure Custody Hearing

Time limits. A juvenile may not be held under a secure custody order for more than five calendar days without either an adjudicatory hearing or an initial hearing to determine the need for continued custody. G.S. 7B-1906(a). If the order was entered by a court counselor pursuant to authority delegated by administrative order of the court, a hearing to review secure custody must be held at the next regularly scheduled court session if it precedes the five-day limit. *Id.* There are no provisions for waiver of the initial secure custody review hearing or of the juvenile's appearance.

Further hearings to review secure custody must be held at intervals of no more than 10 calendar days. G.S. 7B-1906(b). Counsel should continue to work with the juvenile and others to devise an alternative to secure custody.

After the initial secure custody review hearing, further hearings may be waived by the juvenile through counsel. *Id.* Waiver should occur only with the consent of the juvenile and may provide a basis for a concession by the State, such as an earlier date for adjudication or a plea agreement.

Counsel for the juvenile. The court must determine whether the juvenile has retained or been appointed counsel. If the juvenile is not represented, the court must appoint counsel in accordance with the rules of the Office of Indigent Defense Services. G.S. 7B-1906(c); 7B-2000. The juvenile is entitled to representation of counsel at the initial secure custody hearing as well as at subsequent hearings. *Id.*

Conduct of hearing. The court must first determine whether there is a "reasonable factual basis to believe that the juvenile committed the offense as alleged in the petition . . . ." G.S. 7B-1903(b). The statute does not define the term "factual basis" or specify the evidence required in support. If the court finds that there is a reasonable factual basis, the State bears the burden of proving by clear and convincing evidence that secure custody is necessary and that there is "no less intrusive alternative." G.S. 7B-1906(d). The court must allow the juvenile and the juvenile's parent, guardian, or custodian to present evidence, testify, and examine witnesses, although the usual rules of evidence do not apply. *Id.*; *see also* "Advocating for release from secure custody," below. After hearing from all participants, the court must determine whether continued secure custody is warranted based on the criteria in G.S. 7B-1903. G.S. 7B-1906(e). If the court orders the juvenile to remain in secure custody, it must issue a written order with findings that include "the evidence relied upon in reaching the decision and the purposes which continued custody is to achieve." G.S. 7B-1906(g).

It is permissible for the court to conduct a secure custody hearing by audio and video transmission approved by the Administrative Office of the Courts. G.S. 7B-1906(h). The equipment must enable the juvenile and the court to see and hear each other. *Id.* In addition, the juvenile and the juvenile's attorney must be able to communicate "fully and confidentially" during the hearing. *Id.* If the court uses audio and video equipment at the custody hearing, counsel should make sure that communication between counsel and the juvenile is confidential.

There is no requirement that the secure custody hearing be recorded. The only hearings that must be recorded are adjudication and dispositional hearings and hearings on probable cause and transfer to superior court. G.S. 7B-2410. However, the court may order that other hearings be recorded. *Id.* Counsel should consider requesting that the proceeding be recorded so that a court reporter can prepare a transcript if one is needed at a later time.

Advocating for release from secure custody. Counsel for the juvenile should counter the State's evidence by demonstrating to the court that either: no legal basis exists for secure custody under G.S. 7B-1903(b)(1)–(6) (criteria for secure custody); or a "less intrusive alternative" to secure custody is available to address the underlying reason secure custody has been requested. G.S. 7B-1906(d). For example, if the juvenile is charged with a felony and the prosecutor asserts that the juvenile is a danger to person or property under G.S. 7B-1903(b)(1), counsel should determine whether there is a demonstrated danger based on the nature of the felony described in the petition. A felony that is not inherently dangerous should not be the basis of a secure custody order. In addition, if the juvenile has failed to appear at past hearings, the court might nevertheless be willing to release the juvenile if counsel presents the testimony of a dependable adult willing to be responsible for the juvenile's appearance or reasons why the juvenile did not previously appear.

Counsel should discuss alternatives to detention with both the juvenile and the parent before the hearing. The court is unlikely to release a juvenile to the parent unless the parent is willing and able to supervise the juvenile and wants the juvenile to return home. If the parent is resistant, counsel should explain that the court may be less likely to release the juvenile later if the parent argues against release at the initial hearing. Counsel can also ask the parent if there are conditions under which the juvenile could return home, such as a court-ordered curfew, day program, or house arrest.

Counsel should offer the court additional alternatives to secure custody if placement with a parent would be unsuitable. For example, placement with a relative or other responsible adult, or in a temporary shelter, may be a viable alternative to secure custody. Conditions on placement also may make release viable. Electronic house arrest is available in some districts. Some districts also have "alternatives to detention" (ATD) programs that involve daily contact with the juvenile by the juvenile court counselor. If an ATD program is not available, counsel could propose a plan to the court that has those features. *See* "Release from secure custody," below.

Counsel should take advantage of the relaxed rules of evidence to present positive aspects of the juvenile's life. Such information might include little or no prior juvenile court involvement, strong family support or other support in the community, good school attendance or grades, and the availability of services. It may be important to inform the court if the juvenile is receiving services such as special school assistance, mental health treatment, or services through the Department of Social Services that negate the need for secure custody.

Release from secure custody. The court must release the juvenile if the criteria for secure custody are not met. "Appropriate restrictions" to ensure the juvenile's appearance at subsequent hearings may be imposed by the order of release from secure custody. G.S. 7B-1906(f). *See supra* § 8.4, Release.

Continuation of secure custody. If the court does not allow release, it must enter a written order finding that there is a reasonable factual basis to believe that the allegations in the petition are true and stating the grounds for secure custody under G.S. 7B-1903(b) (criteria for secure custody). G.S. 7B-1906(g). The findings of fact must set forth the evidence supporting the decision and the purposes of continuing secure custody. *Id.*

Subsequent hearings to review secure custody must be held every 10 calendar days. G.S. 7B-1906(b). Counsel should continue to confer with the juvenile and others in pursuit of an alternative to secure custody.

After the initial hearing to review secure custody, the juvenile may waive further custody hearings. *Id.* The waiver must be made through the juvenile's attorney and may be conditioned on a concession by the State, such as an earlier date for adjudication or a plea agreement.

Credit for time served. In 2010, the Supreme Court of North Carolina held that juveniles are not entitled to credit for time served in secure custody. *In re D.L.H.*, 364 N.C. 214, 216 (2010). The decision overruled older decisions issued by the court of appeals, such as *In re R.T.L.*, 183 N.C. App. 299 (2007) (unpublished), and *In re Allison*, 143 N.C. App. 586 (2001), in which the court held that it was proper for trial courts to give juveniles credit for time served. Although juveniles are no longer entitled to credit for time spent in secure custody, there is no bar to the court taking such time into account at the dispositional hearing. The court has a great deal of latitude at the dispositional hearing. *See* G.S. 7B-2501 (granting the court authority to select the "most appropriate disposition" for the juvenile). In addition, according to G.S. 7B-2500, a dispositional order should promote public safety, emphasize accountability and responsibility, and provide the appropriate consequences, treatment, training, and rehabilitation to assist the juvenile toward becoming a responsible and productive member of the community. If the juvenile has spent a significant amount of time in secure custody or received services while in secure custody, counsel should argue that many of the purposes of disposition have already been met.

G. Secure Custody Following Adjudication of Delinquency

When secure custody may be ordered. After an adjudication of delinquency, the court may continue the dispositional hearing pursuant to G.S. 7B-2406 and order that the juvenile be held in secure custody pending the dispositional hearing. G.S. 7B-1903(c). The most common reason judges continue dispositional hearings is because the juvenile court counselor has not completed the predisposition report and risks and needs assessment. However, the judge might also grant a continuance to permit the juvenile to obtain an evaluation or gather other evidence for the hearing.

Criteria for secure custody. Secure custody orders issued after an adjudication of delinquency are governed by a less stringent standard than secure custody orders issued after the initial accusation. The court of appeals has held that G.S. 7B-1906(g), which requires the court to specify the evidence on which it bases an order of secure custody after the initial accusation, does not apply to secure custody orders issued after the juvenile has been adjudicated delinquent. *In re Z.T.W.*, 238 N.C. App. 365, 374 (2014). Rather, G.S. 7B-1903(c) allows the court to hold a juvenile in secure custody pending disposition or placement when "the juvenile has been adjudicated delinquent." The decision is reviewed for abuse of discretion. *See id.* at 374–75 (holding that trial court was justified in ordering secure custody pending out-of-home placement based on various aspects of court counselor's report); *see also In re R.D.R.*, 175 N.C. App. 397, 401 (2006) (upholding post-adjudication secure custody under G.S. 7B-1903(c) based on trial court's finding that juvenile had been adjudicated delinquent on three different charges and should be in secure custody pending disposition hearing a week later).

Advocating for release from secure custody. After adjudication, the court may proceed without a predisposition report if one is not available and the court makes a written finding that one is not needed. G.S. 7B-2413. If the prosecutor or court counselor requests a continuance and an order for secure custody even though a predisposition report is not needed, counsel should object and ask the court to deny the continuance and make a finding that a predisposition report is not needed. Counsel should determine the highest permissible period of confinement, if any, allowed at disposition for the offense adjudicated and the juvenile's delinquency history. If continued secure custody would exceed the amount of time the juvenile could be confined pursuant to a dispositional order, counsel should argue for reduction or termination of secure custody.

Review of secure custody following adjudication. For several years, there was some confusion about whether judges should hold review hearings after the juvenile was adjudicated delinquent. Although G.S. 7B-1906(b) stated that review hearings were required "[a]s long as the juvenile remains in secure or nonsecure custody," some judges declined to hold review hearings. In 2009, the court of appeals held that juveniles are entitled to review hearings after adjudication. *In re D.L.H.*, 198 N.C. App. 286, 294 (2009), *overruled on other grounds*, 364 N.C. 214 (2010). The General Assembly amended G.S. 7B-1903 in 2015 to codify the holding in *D.L.H. See* 2015 N.C. Sess. Laws Ch. 58 (H 879). Under current G.S. 7B-1903(c), the court must hold review hearings every 10 calendar days for juveniles in secure custody after adjudication. The juvenile may waive further hearings for no more than 30 calendar days. *Id.*

If the court places the juvenile in secure custody after the adjudication hearing, counsel should monitor the progress toward completion of the predisposition report, risk and needs assessment, and any evaluations needed for disposition, and argue for release from secure custody if there are unreasonable delays. Counsel should offer the court alternatives to detention and reasons supporting release at each review.

H. Secure Custody Pending Placement Pursuant to Dispositional Order

The court may order secure custody following the dispositional hearing but before placement pursuant to the dispositional order. G.S. 7B-1903(c). The period between the dispositional hearing and the juvenile's placement may be lengthy if the placement facility has a long waiting list. This period may also be harmful to the juvenile if the juvenile lacks necessary services or counseling that might occur once the placement begins. The juvenile retains the same right to review hearings and release from secure custody as in other stages of the case. G.S. 7B-1906(b). Counsel should present the court with alternatives to detention and reasons for release at each hearing.

8.7 Nonsecure Custody

Definition. Nonsecure custody is the granting of legal and physical custody without restriction on the juvenile's freedom of movement to the Department of Social Services (DSS) or to a person other than the juvenile's parent, guardian, or custodian. G.S. 7B-1903(a). The juvenile cannot be placed in a locked facility pursuant to a nonsecure custody order. Nonsecure custody is more often ordered in cases involving undisciplined juveniles but is sometimes ordered in delinquency cases.

Criteria. Before entering a nonsecure custody order, the court must first consider releasing the juvenile to the juvenile's parent, guardian, custodian, or other responsible adult. G.S. 7B-1903(a). If the court places the juvenile in nonsecure custody, it must find that the juvenile meets one or more criteria for secure custody but that it is in the juvenile's best interest to be in a nonsecure placement. G.S. 7B-1903(a)(2); *see supra* § 8.6C, Criteria for Secure Custody Pending Adjudication. If the court orders nonsecure custody, the court must give preference to a relative who is "willing and able to provide proper care and supervision of the juvenile" unless such placement is not in the juvenile's best interest. G.S. 7B-1905(a). Otherwise, a juvenile must be placed in nonsecure custody with DSS, or a person designated by the court, for temporary residential placement in a licensed foster home or a home authorized to provide such care, a facility operated by DSS, or any other home or facility approved by the court and designated in the order. G.S. 7B-1905(a)(1)–(3).

Nonsecure custody with the Department of Social Services. Placement of the juvenile in nonsecure custody with DSS is rare. Nevertheless, if the court places the juvenile in the custody of DSS, counsel should determine the length and location of the placement and the name and contact information of the person responsible for the juvenile. Counsel should also discuss the placement with the juvenile. If the juvenile opposes the placement, counsel should present alternatives to the court at the next custody review hearing.

In some cases, DSS will file a petition under Subchapter I of the Juvenile Code alleging that the juvenile is abused or neglected. These cases are sometimes referred to as "dual jurisdiction or cross-over cases." *See* Janet Mason, *Dual Jurisdiction or Cross-Over Cases in Juvenile Court* (District Court Judges' Summer Conference, June 23, 2010). If DSS files a petition alleging abuse or neglect, the court must appoint a guardian ad litem and, if the guardian ad litem is not an attorney, an attorney advocate for the juvenile. G.S. 7B-601. The court will also hold proceedings to adjudicate the allegations in the petition. *See* G.S. 7B-800 through G.S. 7B-808 (Hearing Procedures). Counsel for the juvenile in the delinquency case does not represent the juvenile in the proceedings against the juvenile's parent. *See* G.S. 7B-601(a) (stating that the guardian ad litem and attorney advocate "have standing to represent the juvenile in all actions under" Subchapter I of the Juvenile Code). Counsel should therefore maintain contact with the guardian ad litem and attorney advocate in order to stay informed about the location of the juvenile, what services the juvenile is receiving, and other information that may bear on delinquency proceedings.

Advocating for nonsecure custody. Counsel for the juvenile might request nonsecure custody as an alternative to secure custody, particularly if there is a suitable relative with whom the juvenile would agree to live. The court also might be willing to place the juvenile in nonsecure custody with a responsible adult. Some juveniles, however, prefer to remain in secure custody rather than be in DSS placement. Counsel should discuss the alternatives with the juvenile before making a request to the court.

Initial order for nonsecure custody. A nonsecure custody order must be in writing and must direct the law enforcement officer or other authorized person to assume custody of the juvenile. G.S. 7B-1904. The juvenile should be in the officer's custody only for transportation to a DSS placement or to the person granted nonsecure custody by the court.

Review hearings. Hearings pursuant to a nonsecure custody order follow the procedures for a secure custody hearing except that the initial review hearing must be within seven calendar days of the court's placing the juvenile in nonsecure custody, a subsequent review hearing must be within seven business days, and further reviews must occur at intervals of no more than 30 calendar days. G.S. 7B-1906(b). The court must find that the juvenile meets the criteria for nonsecure custody under G.S. 7B-1903(a)(2). *See supra* § 8.6F, Secure Custody Hearing.

Continuation of nonsecure custody. The court must enter a written order finding that the juvenile meets one or more criteria for secure custody but that it is in the best interest of the juvenile to continue in nonsecure custody. G.S. 7B-1906(g). The findings of fact must set forth the evidence supporting the decision and the purposes of continuing nonsecure custody.

8.8   Custody Pending Appeal

If the juvenile appeals the case, the court must release the juvenile, with or without conditions, unless it enters a temporary order affecting custody or placement. Such an order must be in writing and must state "compelling reasons" that the placement or custody is in the best interests of the juvenile or the State. G.S. 7B-2605; *In re J.J., Jr.*, 216 N.C. App. 366, 376 (2011). The court of appeals has held that findings included in a dispositional order can support a custody order under G.S. 7B-2506. *In re R.A.S.*, 166 N.C. App. 515 (2004) (unpublished). However, a finding that no placement is available for the juvenile during the appeal is "clearly insufficient." *In re W.G.C.*, 166 N.C. App. 516 (2004) (unpublished).

If counsel gives oral notice of appeal from a dispositional order imposing a period of confinement, counsel should ask the court to release the juvenile pursuant to G.S. 7B-2605. If counsel gives written notice of appeal after the dispositional hearing, counsel should include a request for release under G.S. 7B-2605 in the notice of appeal or in a separate motion. A sample notice of appeal and a sample motion for release pending appeal are available on the Juvenile Defender website.

For a discussion of appeals in juvenile delinquency cases, see *infra* Ch. 16, Appeals.

Appendix 8-1: Juvenile Detention Centers in North Carolina

State Detention Centers

ALEXANDER
928 NC HIGHWAY 16 S.
TAYLORSVILLE, NC 28681
Manager: KIMBERLY COWART
Telephone: 828.632.1141
Attorney Visiting Hours: Anytime (call first)
Regular Visiting Hours: Tuesday and Thursday (6:30-7:30 p.m.)
Saturday-Sunday (1:30-3:00 p.m.)
Available to Visit: Parents, Grandparents, Legal Guardian

CUMBERLAND
1911 COLISEUM DRIVE
FAYETTEVILLE, NC 28306
Director: EUGENE S. HALLOCK
Telephone: 910.486.1399
Attorney Visiting Hours: Anytime (call first)
Regular Visiting Hours: Monday (7:30-8:30 p.m.)
Saturday and Sunday (1:00-2:00 p.m.)
Available to Visit: Parents, Grandparents, Legal Guardian

CABARRUS
822 McWHORTER ROAD
CONCORD, NC 28027
Director: ANGELA WILSON
Telephone: 704.720.0807
Attorney Visiting Hours: Anytime (call first)
Regular Visiting Hours: Wednesday (5:30-6:30 p.m.)
Saturday (12:30-3:30 p.m.) and Sunday (12:30-1:30 p.m.)
Available to Visit: Parents, Grandparents, Legal Guardian

NEW HANOVER
3830 JUVENILE CENTER ROAD
CASTLE HAYNE, NC 28429
Director: JIM SPEIGHT
Telephone: 910.675.0594
Attorney Visiting Hours: Anytime (call first)
Regular Visiting Hours: Wednesday (6:30-7:30 p.m.)
Saturday and Sunday (1:00-3:30 p.m.)
Available to Visit: Parents, Grandparents, Legal Guardian

PITT
451 BELVOIR ROAD
GREENVILLE, NC 27834
Director: STANLEY MELVIN
Telephone: 252.830.6590
Attorney Visiting Hours: Anytime (call first)
Regular Visiting Hours: Wednesdays (7:00-8:00 p.m.)
Saturday and Sunday (2:00-4:00 p.m.)
Available to Visit: Parents, Grandparents, Legal Guardian

WAKE
700 BEACON LAKE DRIVE
RALEIGH, NC 27610
Director: SHEILA L. DAVIS
Telephone: 919.212.3104
Attorney Visiting Hours: Anytime (call first)
Regular Visiting Hours: Tuesday and Wednesday (5:30 -6:30 p.m.)
Saturday and Sunday (2:00-4:00 p.m.)
Available to Visit: Parents, Grandparents, Legal Guardian

County Detention Centers

DURHAM COUNTY YOUTH HOME
2432 BROAD STREET
DURHAM, NC 27704
Director: ANGELA NUNN
Telephone: 919.560.0840
Attorney Visiting Hours: Anytime (call first)
Regular Visiting Hours: Wednesday, Saturday, and Sunday (6:00-8:00 p.m.)
Available to Visit: Parents and any other visitor who is 18-years old or older and approved by the juvenile court counselor

GUILFORD COUNTY
15 LOCKHEED COURT
GREENSBORO, NC 27409
Director: DOUG LOGAN
Telephone: 336.641.2600
Attorney Visiting Hours: Anytime (call first)
Regular Visiting Hours: Wednesday (5:30-8:00 p.m.)
Saturday (10:00-12:30 p.m.)
Available to Visit: Parents, Grandparents, Other Relatives (21-years old or older), Legal Guardian

Chapter 9
Probable Cause and Transfer Hearings

9.1   Overview

A probable cause hearing is required if a juvenile who is 13 years of age or older is alleged to have committed an offense that would be a felony if committed by an adult. The court must determine that there is probable cause before the case can proceed to adjudication. The probable cause hearing affords the juvenile an opportunity to assess the strength of the State's case, to challenge the sufficiency of the evidence, and to discover information for the adjudicatory hearing if probable cause is found. If there is no finding of probable cause, the petition must be dismissed.

If the court finds probable cause and the offense alleged would be a Class A felony (first degree murder), the case must be transferred to superior court for trial of the juvenile as an adult. If probable cause is found for a felony that is less than a Class A felony, the court may hold a transfer hearing on motion of the prosecutor, the juvenile's attorney, or its own motion to determine whether to transfer jurisdiction to superior court. A discretionary order transferring jurisdiction must be immediately appealed to superior court to preserve the issue for appellate review by the North Carolina Court of Appeals.

Legislative note: This chapter reviews the laws in effect at the time of release of this manual in Fall 2017. During the 2017 legislative session, the General Assembly enacted the Juvenile Justice Reinvestment Act, which expanded the jurisdiction of juvenile court to include crimes committed by 16 and 17-year-olds, except for motor vehicle offenses. Most of the changes apply to offenses committed on or after December 1, 2019. For a discussion of the changes that take effect in 2017, see *infra* Ch. 19, Raise the Age Legislation. For a discussion of the changes that take effect in 2019, see LaToya Powell, 2017 Juvenile Justice Reinvestment Act.

9.2   Terminology Used in this Chapter

Probable cause is a finding by the court that a juvenile who is 13 years of age or older is alleged to have committed an offense that would be a felony if committed by an adult and that there is "probable cause to believe that the offense charged has been committed and that there is probable cause to believe that the juvenile committed it. . . ." G.S. 7B-2202(a), (c).

Transfer is the removal of a juvenile proceeding from district court to superior court for trial of the juvenile as an adult. *See infra* § 9.8, Transfer of Jurisdiction to Superior Court.

9.3   First Appearance

A first appearance is an initial hearing that must be held if a petition alleges that a juvenile committed an offense that would be a felony if committed by an adult. The first appearance must occur within 10 days of the filing of the petition or at the secure custody review hearing if the juvenile is in secure or nonsecure custody. A continuance may be granted for "good cause" if the juvenile is not in custody. G.S. 7B-1808(a).

At the juvenile's first appearance, the court must inform the juvenile of the allegations in the petition and the date of the probable cause hearing, if applicable, and determine whether counsel has been retained or appointed. Additionally, the court must inform the juvenile's parents that they must attend all scheduled hearings. G.S. 7B-1808(b)(1)–(4). There is no statutory provision for the court to make other determinations or to set conditions, such as to impose a curfew or to restrict with whom the juvenile may associate, at the first appearance. Counsel should object if the court attempts to go beyond the statutory requirements.

9.4   Probable Cause Hearing

A. When Required

A probable cause hearing must be conducted in any proceeding in which a juvenile is alleged to have committed an offense that would be a felony if committed by an adult and the juvenile was 13 years of age or older at the time of the alleged offense. G.S. 7B-2202(a).

Although the statute requires a hearing if the criteria are met, in some districts a probable cause hearing is not routinely held unless the prosecution is moving for transfer to superior court. In other districts, probable cause hearings are held for all felony allegations. Counsel should consider the merits of requesting a probable cause hearing if one is not routinely scheduled within the statutory time limits. *See infra* § 9.4B, Waiver of Probable Cause Hearing. For instance, the court may dismiss the petition if the State has a weak case, or it may find probable cause for a lesser included offense only. If the court does not dismiss the petition, information obtained during the probable cause hearing may assist counsel in plea negotiations or in preparing for adjudication.

B. Waiver of Probable Cause Hearing

The juvenile, through counsel, may waive by written notice the right to a probable cause hearing. If the hearing is waived, the juvenile must stipulate to probable cause. G.S. 7B-2202(d). Counsel should consider several factors in advising the juvenile whether to waive the probable cause hearing. These factors are discussed below.

Reasons for the hearing.

- If the State's evidence is marginal, the court may be willing to dismiss for lack of probable cause or find probable cause for a lesser-included misdemeanor, which would preclude transfer of the case to superior court.

- A probable cause hearing may provide counsel with an opportunity to obtain discovery, observe the demeanor of witnesses, and develop impeachment material for the adjudicatory hearing.
- A probable cause hearing may give the juvenile and prosecutor a more realistic view of the case and encourage a plea agreement.

Reasons against the hearing.

- The prosecutor may be willing to make some concession in exchange for a waiver of the hearing, such as a favorable plea agreement either in juvenile or superior court or an agreement not to seek transfer.
- The court may decide to transfer the case to superior court on its own motion if the evidence presented at the probable cause hearing is sufficiently compelling.
- On occasion, a probable cause hearing may alert the prosecutor to additional charges.
- If a witness from a probable cause hearing is unavailable at the adjudicatory hearing, the State may argue that the juvenile had an adequate opportunity to cross-examine the witness at the probable cause hearing and, therefore, that the Confrontation Clause does not bar the State from introducing the witness's testimony or other out-of-court statements. *See* 1 NORTH CAROLINA DEFENDER MANUAL § 3.4C, Impact of *Crawford* (2d ed. 2013).

Generally, the opportunity to test the State's evidence outweighs the potential drawbacks of having a hearing.

C. Time Limits

The probable cause hearing must be held within 15 days of the juvenile's first appearance. The court may continue the hearing for good cause. G.S. 7B-2202(a).

D. Hearing Procedures

Defender Manual. The North Carolina Defender Manual contains a chapter on probable cause hearings in criminal court that includes information generally applicable to juvenile court proceedings. *See* 1 NORTH CAROLINA DEFENDER MANUAL, Ch. 3, Probable Cause Hearings (2d ed. 2013).

Representation. The prosecutor must represent the State at a probable cause hearing. G.S. 7B-2202(b)(1); *cf.* G.S. 7B-2404 (prosecutor must represent State in contested delinquency proceedings, including probable cause). Counsel should object if the prosecutor is not present for the probable cause hearing.

The juvenile must be represented by counsel at the probable cause hearing. G.S. 7B-2202(b)(2).

Evidence and hearsay exceptions. Subject to limited exceptions, discussed below, the State must establish, by nonhearsay evidence or evidence within a hearsay exception, probable cause that the juvenile committed the charged offense. G.S. 7B-2202(c). Each witness must be under oath and subject to cross-examination. G.S. 7B-2202(b)(4).

In addition to the restriction on hearsay, other requirements of the North Carolina Rules of Evidence may apply at a probable cause hearing in juvenile cases. *See In re Ford*, 49 N.C. App. 680, 683 (1980) (observing that evidentiary questions at a probable cause hearing "may well merit" the court's attention in a juvenile delinquency appeal). Rule 1101(b) states that the Rules of Evidence do not apply at probable cause hearings "in criminal cases." There is no comparable provision for probable cause hearings in juvenile cases. However, counsel may not want to object if the evidence provides useful discovery. Even if the rules of evidence are relaxed in juvenile cases and inadmissible evidence is permissible, the State still must establish probable cause by admissible evidence pursuant to G.S. 7B-2202(c).

There is a statutory exception to the hearsay rule at a probable cause hearing allowing the court to receive a report by a physicist, chemist, firearms identification expert, fingerprint technician, or expert or technician in another scientific, professional, or medical field. The report must contain the result of any examination, comparison, or test performed regarding the case. G.S. 7B- 2202(c)(1). "Reliable hearsay" as to value, ownership of property, possession of property by a person other than the juvenile, lack of consent of the owner, possessor, or custodian of property to the breaking and entering of the premises, chain of custody, and authenticity of signature is also admissible if there is "no serious contest." G.S. 7B-2202(c)(2).

Counsel may object to hearsay that does not fall within an exception. Requiring the State to present non-hearsay evidence may provide an opportunity to evaluate the strength of the State's evidence and could lead to a finding of no probable cause and dismissal of the petition.

Counsel must determine whether there is a benefit to presenting evidence at the probable cause hearing. Because the State's burden of proof is relatively low, it is generally disadvantageous to present evidence, as it might establish probable cause or reveal the defense strategy for the adjudicatory hearing.

Confrontation Clause. Although North Carolina law restricts the use of out-of-court statements at probable cause hearings that do not satisfy hearsay rules, the Confrontation Clause may not apply at this stage of the proceedings and may not bar on constitutional grounds out-of-court statements that would be inadmissible at trial. *See Peterson v. California*, 604 F.3d 1166 (9th Cir. 2010) (holding that the Confrontation Clause does not apply to preliminary hearings); *State v. Lopez*, 314 P.3d 236, 239 (N.M. 2013) (same); *Sheriff v. Witzenburg*, 145 P.3d 1002, 1005 (Nev. 2006) (same). *But see Curry v. State*, 228 S.W.3d 292, 296–98 (Tex. App. 2007) (holding that the Confrontation Clause applies at pretrial suppression hearings).

Burden of proof. The State must show that there is "probable cause to believe that the offense charged has been committed and that there is probable cause to believe that the juvenile committed it. . . . " G.S. 7B-2202(c). North Carolina courts have not defined the standard of probable cause for probable cause hearings in juvenile court. However, some commentators suggest that the standard for probable cause hearings in adult cases is higher than for a lawful arrest—that it is closer to the prima facie evidence requirement for submission of an offense to the jury. *See* 4 WAYNE R. LAFAVE ET AL., CRIMINAL PROCEDURE § 14.3(a), at 321-22 (3d ed. 2007) (probable cause standard for arrest tolerates "considerable uncertainty" because of need for officers to take immediate action; however, standard for probable cause hearing "should require a higher and different degree of probability" than standard for arrest); CHARLES H. WHITEBREAD & CHRISTOPHER SLOBOGIN, CRIMINAL PROCEDURE: AN ANALYSIS OF CASES AND CONCEPTS § 22.03, at 517 (6th ed. 2015) (standard for probable cause hearing in a growing number of states requires prosecutor to present enough evidence to overcome directed verdict for defendant).

E. Advocacy at Probable Cause Hearing

Preparation. Counsel should prepare to challenge the State to meet its burden of proof and should move for dismissal if the State fails to present evidence of each element of the offense alleged and of identification of the juvenile as the perpetrator. Preparation for the hearing includes becoming familiar with the elements of each offense alleged as well as lesser included offenses. If advantageous to the juvenile, counsel should argue for a finding of probable cause for a lesser included offense. Counsel should also prepare case law or legal memoranda to support a motion to dismiss.

Cross-examination. Because the court may not allow counsel a great deal of latitude, cross-examination should be structured to elicit the most important information first. Sample probable cause questions appear at the end of this chapter. *See infra* Appendix 9-1: Sample Questions for Probable Cause and Preliminary Hearings.

Questions on cross-examination will vary depending on counsel's goal for the hearing. If the desired result is dismissal for lack of probable cause, counsel may want to limit cross-examination, as extensive cross-examination could lead the witness to supply information that supports a finding of probable cause. Closed-ended questions, requiring a yes or no answer, typically provide counsel more control over the witness and are therefore desirable when counsel is seeking dismissal for lack of probable cause. Aggressive cross-examination can be risky, however, as it may cause the witness to refuse to cooperate later or harden his or her resolve for prosecution. Questions may also alert witnesses to problem areas in their testimony that can be addressed at the adjudicatory hearing.

Extensive cross-examination may be desirable where counsel's goal is to elicit answers that can be used to impeach any inconsistent testimony by the witness at a subsequent hearing or to obtain additional information. Open-ended questions may elicit the most information, with follow-up questions as needed. Obtaining information has been recognized as a legitimate purpose of a probable cause hearing in criminal proceedings. *Coleman v. Alabama*, 399 U.S. 1, 9 (1970) (recognizing constitutional right to counsel at probable cause hearing based on counsel's ability to obtain discovery and develop impeachment evidence); *Vance v. North Carolina*, 432 F.2d 984, 988–89 (4th Cir. 1970) (to same effect). Other cases state that the purpose of a probable cause hearing is for the court to determine whether there is probable cause but still recognize that the opportunity for discovery is incidental to that purpose. *State v. Hudson*, 295 N.C. 427, 430 (1978); *cf. In re Bass*, 77 N.C. App. 110, 114 (1985) (stating that a probable cause hearing is not conducted for the purpose of discovery). Counsel should therefore be prepared to explain how questions relate to the issue of probable cause.

Juvenile's evidence. Under G.S. 7B-2202(b)(3), the juvenile may testify and call other witnesses at the probable cause hearing. Presenting witnesses on the juvenile's behalf is not usually beneficial, however, as they may reveal the defense strategy for adjudication and may assist the State in meeting its burden of proving probable cause. Potential defense witnesses should ordinarily not be present at the probable cause hearing because the State could call them to testify. Counsel might want to subpoena witnesses for the prosecution if they are unwilling to be interviewed.

Record of the hearing. Counsel should ensure that the probable cause hearing is recorded as required pursuant to G.S. 7B-2410. This may aid in impeachment of a witness at the adjudicatory hearing or trial or support a claim of error on appeal. If the courtroom does not have recording equipment, counsel should request that a court reporter attend the hearing and take transcription notes. Counsel could also have an investigator or other person working on behalf of the juvenile be present to make notes of the testimony. That person could then be called to impeach a witness who subsequently gives inconsistent testimony. Finally, counsel could bring their own recording equipment to record the testimony at the hearing.

9.5   Finding of No Probable Cause

The petition must be dismissed if the court finds that the State has failed to show probable cause that the juvenile committed the alleged felony unless the court finds probable cause that the juvenile committed a lesser included misdemeanor offense. G.S. 7B-2202(f)(1)–(2). Because jeopardy does not attach at a probable cause hearing, a subsequent petition is not barred by double jeopardy. *See In re Bullard*, 22 N.C. App. 245, 249 (1974) (determination of probable cause does not place the juvenile in jeopardy). There may be a defense, however, if there is a significant delay in the filing of a new petition. *See supra* § 6.3C, Timeliness of Filing.

If the court finds probable cause to believe that the juvenile committed a lesser included misdemeanor offense, the court may either proceed to adjudication or set a date for an adjudicatory hearing. G.S. 7B-2202(f)(2). If the court proceeds to adjudication, the adjudication must be a separate hearing. *Id.* The juvenile may request a continuance if needed. G.S. 7B-2406.

9.6   Finding of Probable Cause

Mandatory transfer to superior court. If the court finds probable cause to believe that the juvenile committed an offense that would constitute a Class A felony if committed by an adult, the court *must* transfer the case to superior court for the juvenile to be tried as an adult. G.S. 7B-2200.

Discretionary transfer to superior court. On a finding of probable cause to believe that the juvenile committed a felony that would be less than a Class A felony if committed by an adult, the prosecutor, the juvenile, or the court may move for a hearing on transfer to superior court. G.S. 7B-2200. If the juvenile has not had at least five days notice of the intent to seek transfer, the court must continue the transfer hearing at the juvenile's request. G.S. 7B-2202(e).

If the matter proceeds to adjudication in juvenile court in front of the judge who presided over the probable cause hearing, counsel may consider moving for recusal. The judge has ruled on probable cause and might have heard prejudicial hearsay testimony or other evidence that would be inadmissible at the adjudicatory hearing.

9.7   Appeal of Finding of Probable Cause

A finding of probable cause is not a final order and is therefore not immediately reviewable; errors relating to a determination of probable cause may, however, be the subject of an appeal following entry of the dispositional order. *In re K.R.B.*, 134 N.C. App. 328, 331 (1999) (dismissing the juvenile's appeal from the order finding probable cause as it was not properly before the court on appeal). In the case of *In re Ford*, 49 N.C. App. 680, 683 (1980), the Court stated that evidentiary rulings of the trial court during the probable cause hearing "may well merit our attention upon his appeal from a trial resulting in a disposition unfavorable to him. They are not properly before us, however, in relation to a finding of probable cause, which is not a 'final order.'"

9.8   Transfer of Jurisdiction to Superior Court

Jurisdiction over a juvenile *may* be transferred to superior court if the juvenile was at least 13 years old at the time of allegedly committing an offense that would be a felony, other than a Class A felony, if committed by an adult. There must be a motion, notice, hearing, and finding of probable cause before the court may consider transfer. G.S. 7B-2200.

Jurisdiction over a juvenile *must* be transferred to superior court if the juvenile was at least 13 years old at the time of allegedly committing an offense that would be a Class A felony (first-degree murder) and the court finds probable cause. *Id.*

Following transfer, all further proceedings in the matter occur in superior court; generally, adult criminal law and procedure apply. The juvenile must be fingerprinted and the fingerprints sent to the State Bureau of Investigation. G.S. 7B-2201(a). The juvenile must also provide a DNA sample if any of the offenses for which the juvenile is transferred are included in the provisions of G.S. 15A-266.3A. G.S. 7B-2201(b). If the juvenile is convicted in superior court, any subsequent charges will be heard in criminal rather than juvenile court, even if the juvenile has not yet reached the age of 16. G.S. 7B-1604(b).

The juvenile may request transfer to superior court, although transfer rarely benefits the juvenile. The confidentiality of juvenile court proceedings is lost, and the juvenile is exposed to the adult criminal and penal system. The juvenile is also subject to the collateral consequences of conviction in superior court, which could include bars to employment and professional licensure, voting disenfranchisement, and the loss of public benefits. For a description of collateral consequences for North Carolina offenses, see the Collateral Consequences Assessment Tool (C-CAT). Juveniles who are not citizens risk deportation or harm to their immigration status if convicted as an adult. *Compare* IMMIGRATION CONSEQUENCES OF A CRIMINAL CONVICTION IN NORTH CAROLINA § 4.2F, Juvenile Delinquency Adjudication (Sept. 2017); *see also infra* § 12.7, Collateral Effects of Adjudication. While counsel should advise clients of the adverse consequences of transfer, ultimately it is the juvenile's decision whether to request transfer.

9.9   Procedures for Transfer Hearing

A. Evidence

The prosecutor and juvenile may be heard and offer evidence at the transfer hearing. Counsel for the juvenile is allowed to examine probation or court records that may be considered as evidence by the court. G.S. 7B-2203(a). Counsel should request to review any such records immediately after being appointed to a case subject to transfer.

Although no appellate court has yet addressed the question of whether the North Carolina Rules of Evidence apply at transfer hearings, the operation of Rules of Evidence 101 and 1101 indicate that they apply. *See, e.g., State v. Foster*, 222 N.C. App. 199, 202–03 (2012) (holding that the Rules of Evidence apply to post-conviction DNA testing proceedings because such proceedings are not listed as excluded under N.C. R. Evid. 1101(b) and no statute bars their application to the proceedings). Counsel should therefore object to evidence presented by the State that would be inadmissible under the Rules of Evidence.

Counsel should request other records pertaining to the juvenile's level of maturity, mental and emotional status, educational and service needs, or any other factors that might bolster the argument for retaining the matter in juvenile court. Counsel should also consider filing an *ex parte* motion for funds to hire an expert to examine the juvenile in order to develop evidence supporting retention of the case in juvenile court. Sample release forms and a sample motion for an expert witness are available on the Juvenile Defender website.

Unless the juvenile directs counsel to seek transfer, counsel should present evidence against transfer to superior court. Evidence may include the juvenile's record, performance on court supervision, educational history, mental and emotional state, intellectual functioning, developmental issues, and family history. Witnesses who can provide helpful insight into the juvenile's character, such as teachers, counselors, psychologists, members of the juvenile's religious community, family, friends, employers, or other people with a positive personal or professional opinion of the juvenile, may be called to testify.

Community services should also be explored. Counsel should be prepared to offer alternatives for disposition that would not be available if the matter were transferred to superior court.

B. Criteria for Determination

The court must decide whether "the protection of the public and the needs of the juvenile will be served by transfer of the case to superior court . . . . " G.S. 7B-2203(b). The statute lists eight criteria for making this determination:

- the age of the juvenile;
- the maturity of the juvenile;
- the intellectual functioning of the juvenile;
- the prior record of the juvenile;
- prior attempts to rehabilitate the juvenile;
- facilities or programs available to the court before the expiration of the court's jurisdiction and the likelihood that the juvenile would benefit from treatment or rehabilitative efforts;
- whether the alleged offense was committed in an aggressive, violent, premeditated, or willful manner; and
- the seriousness of the offense and whether the protection of the public requires that the juvenile be prosecuted as an adult.

G.S. 7B-2203(b)(1)–(8).

The eight statutory criteria are neither weighted nor listed in order of importance for consideration by the court. Counsel should be prepared to argue those factors that support retention of the case in juvenile court as well as to counter the factors most likely to be relied on by the State in seeking transfer. Objections should be raised if the court considers any factors not listed under the statute.

C. Transfer Order

If the court determines that the case should be transferred to superior court, it must enter an order specifying the reasons for transfer. G.S. 7B-2203(c). A transfer of a felony offense also confers jurisdiction on the superior court to try any other offenses arising out of the underlying act or any greater or lesser included offense of that felony. *Id.*; *see also State v. Jackson*, 165 N.C. App. 763, 774 (2004) (superior court had jurisdiction over conspiracy charge that was never filed in district court because the charge was part of transaction that gave rise to other charges properly transferred from district court).

If the court determines that under the statutory criteria the case should be retained in district court, the court must either proceed to an adjudicatory hearing or set a date for adjudication. G.S. 7B-2203(d). If the court proceeds to adjudication, the adjudication must be a separate hearing. *Id.*

9.10 Appeal of Order of Transfer

Appeal to superior court. If the court issues an order transferring the case to superior court, the juvenile may appeal the order to superior court for a "hearing on the record." G.S. 7B-2603(a). The juvenile must give notice of appeal in open court or in writing within 10 days after entry of the transfer order. The date of entry of the order is determined in the same manner as under Rule 58 of the Rules of Civil Procedure—that is, an order is entered when it is "reduced to writing, signed by the judge, and filed with the clerk of court." The transfer order must be properly appealed to the superior court to preserve the issue for appeal to the Court of Appeals. If the juvenile fails to properly appeal the order to superior court, any arguments about the transfer order are subject to dismissal. *See State v. Wilson*, 151 N.C. App. 219, 223 (2002) (transfer order not reviewable because juvenile appealed directly to the Court of Appeals instead of appealing to superior court as required by G.S. 7B-2603).

The superior court must review the decision to transfer the case "within a reasonable time" after the juvenile gives notice of appeal. G.S. 7B-2603(a). There are no explicit statutory procedures for the review in superior court, although the use of the term "hearing on the record" indicates that the superior court will review the transcript of the transfer hearing and the juvenile court file. Counsel should be allowed to appear and make arguments based on the record.

The superior court may not reweigh the evidence that the district court considered. *In re E.S.*, 191 N.C. App. 568, 574 (2008). Instead, the superior court must determine whether the district court properly exercised its discretion in transferring the case to superior court. Under an older version of the Juvenile Code, the superior court could only reverse an order transferring a case to superior court for "gross abuse of discretion." *State v. Green*, 348 N.C. 588, 595 (1998). In contrast, the superior court may reverse a transfer order under the current version of the Juvenile Code "for abuse of discretion" by the district court, which on its face is a less deferential standard. G.S. 7B-2603(a). Cases have held that a court abuses its discretion when it makes an "error of law," *State v. Rhodes*, 366 N.C. 532, 535 (2013), or when it "refuses to exercise its discretion in the erroneous belief that it has no discretion as to the question presented." *State v. Lang*, 301 N.C. 508, 510 (1980).

The superior court has two alternatives after the hearing on the record. It may either remand the case to district court for adjudication or uphold the transfer order. G.S. 7B-2603(c).

Appeal to Court of Appeals. If the superior court upholds the transfer order, the order may be appealed to the Court of Appeals only if the juvenile is subsequently found guilty in superior court. G.S. 7B-2603(d); *State v. Wilson,* 151 N.C. App. 219, 222 (2002) (juvenile may appeal order of transfer to Court of Appeals only after conviction in superior court and only if issue was preserved by proper appeal of issue to superior court); *State v. Hatchett,* 177 N.C. App. 812 (2006) (unpublished) (citing *Wilson*).

In addition, G.S. 15A-1444 provides strict limitations on appeals from guilty pleas. Based on those limitations, a juvenile may not challenge a transfer order on direct appeal if the juvenile pled guilty in superior court. *State v. Evans*, 184 N.C. App. 736, 739 (2007) (dismissing appeal because defendant had no right to challenge transfer order under G.S. 15A-1444). To ensure appellate review of a transfer order, the juvenile must take the case to trial.

Although a juvenile does not have the right to direct appeal of a transfer order after pleading guilty in superior court, a juvenile who pleads guilty may challenge the transfer order in a petition for writ of certiorari. In contrast to direct appeals, review by writ of certiorari is "discretionary." *State v. Hammonds*, 218 N.C. App. 158, 162–63 (2012).

Under Rule 21 of the Rules of Appellate Procedure, review by writ of certiorari is limited and does not include transfer orders. However, Rule 21 "cannot take away jurisdiction given to [the appellate court] by the General Assembly in accordance with the North Carolina Constitution." *State v. Stubbs*, 368 N.C. 40, 44 (2015). According to G.S. 15A-1444(e), a defendant who has pled guilty and seeks review of issues that are not appealable as of right "may petition the appellate division for review by writ of certiorari." Consequently, a juvenile may be able to obtain reversal of a transfer order even if the juvenile lost the right to direct appeal of the order by pleading guilty.

9.11 Right to Pretrial Release on Transfer

Once an order of transfer has been entered, a juvenile has the same right to pretrial release as an adult under G.S. 15A-533 and 15A-534. G.S. 7B-2204, 7B-2603(b). After entering the transfer order, the district court judge must determine the conditions under which the juvenile may obtain release, as provided in G.S. 15A-533 and 15A-534 (i.e., written promise to appear, unsecured bond, custody release, secured bond, or electronic house arrest with a secured bond). An order of release also must specify the person or people to whom the juvenile may be released. G.S. 7B-2204, 7B-2603(b).

When transfer to superior court is a possibility, counsel should work with the juvenile and the juvenile's family to have a plan for pretrial release to present to the court.

9.12 Detention Following Transfer

If the juvenile does not meet pretrial release conditions, the court must order that the juvenile be held in a detention center while awaiting trial. G.S. 7B-2204, 7B-2603(b). The court may order that the juvenile be held in a holdover facility when the juvenile is required to be in court for pretrial hearings or for trial, if the court finds that it would be inconvenient to return the juvenile to the detention center. *Id*. For more information about detention centers and holdover facilities, see *supra* § 8.6, Secure Custody.

Appendix 9-1: Sample Questions for Probable Cause and Preliminary Hearings

The following is reprinted with permission from CRIMINAL PRACTICE INSTITUTE: PRACTICE MANUAL, Chapter 2 Appendix C (Public Defender Service for the District of Columbia, 2011 Edition). The sample questions were created for probable cause hearings in criminal cases, but they may be useful for such hearings in juvenile cases.

The following questions are very basic and include only some aspects of certain offenses. The questions are not designed to replace the specific, detailed questioning of witnesses necessary to elicit the unique facts in a particular case.

I. Identification

A. Questions about the Event Itself

1. Get a detailed narrative of what happened, including where the witness was coming from, what the witness was doing prior to the incident, and where the witness was going.
2. Who was the witness with?
3. What was the witness paying attention to just before the witness noticed the perpetrator for the first time?
4. From which direction did the perpetrator approach (front, rear, side, don't know)?
5. What was the exact location of the confrontation? (Get this in words and try to have the witness draw a diagram of the scene.)
6. Exactly what happened? Was there more than one person involved? (Get the exact and relative roles of the persons involved.)
7. If there was more than one perpetrator, find out which one is supposed to be the defendant. (Where was the defendant at all times, in absolute terms and in relation to the other perpetrators and witnesses?)
8. Which perpetrator made contact with the witness?
9. When did the witness first notice the perpetrator(s)? How far away were they? What drew the witness's attention to the perpetrator(s)?
10. Was anything taken from the witness? What was done with it after it was taken?
11. In which direction or to where did the perpetrator(s) flee? For how long after the incident did the witness keep the perpetrator(s) in sight?

B. Opportunity to Observe

Witness's state of mind

1. What had the witness been doing prior to the incident?
2. Had the witness been drinking or using any drugs?
3. Where was the witness going at the time of the incident?
4. How much sleep had the witness had the night before?
5. Was the witness tired? Preoccupied?

6. Was the witness frightened?
7. Was the witness focusing on a weapon during the incident, or on another individual?

Physical conditions of observation

1. What was the distance between the witness and the perpetrator when the witness first noticed the perpetrator?
2. What was the distance between the two of them during the majority of the incident?
3. What was the duration of the incident? (If it was a long time, split it up into parts. The witness may not have had a good opportunity to view during some of the segments or may have been focusing on one particular item or person.)
4. What was the angle of observation between the witness and the perpetrator?
5. What is the witness's hearing like? Vision?
6. How long did the incident take? (Note: Time is **very** important. Most witnesses will say that an event took minutes when it actually took seconds. Demonstrate how long a minute is—the time may be cut considerably.)
7. What were the weather conditions like? (Sunny, rainy, overcast, stars out, etc.)
8. What were the lighting conditions? Were there streetlights, house lights, car lights, etc.? Was any of the lighting filtered or obstructed? Get exact locations of all lights. Were the streetlights high or low intensity? Were there any lights available that were not turned on?
9. Were there any physical barriers or obstructions between the witness and the perpetrator, e.g., cars, trees, or other witnesses?

C. Reporting the Incident

Police

1. How was the incident reported to the police? (Call made? Flagging down a car?)
2. Who reported the incident?
3. How soon after the event was it reported?
4. With whom was the incident discussed?
5. Exactly what did the witness say in giving the report?
6. Did the person to whom the report was made make any statements or say anything?
7. Were there other witnesses who talked to the police?
8. Were there other witnesses who did not talk to the police?
9. Did the police read back to the witness what had been written down? Did the witness change anything or adopt it?
10. Did the witness forget to tell the police anything that the witness is now telling you?
11. What was the initial description the witness gave to the police?
12. Did the witness make a written statement?
13. Was the witness under the influence of any drugs or alcohol when speaking with the police?
14. Has the witness spoken with anyone else about the incident?

Prosecutor

1. Has the witness been to the grand jury? Did the witness testify or only meet with a prosecutor? What questions were asked by the prosecutor and the grand jurors?
2. What was the witness's testimony?
3. Did the prosecutor take notes of the meeting?
4. Who else has met with the prosecutor?
5. Is there anything the witness told the grand jury or the prosecutor that the witness has not told you?
6. Is there anything the witness told you that the witness did not tell the grand jury or the prosecutor?

D. Description of the Perpetrator

1. Age
2. Height (relative to witness or another object)
3. Weight
4. Skin color and complexion
5. Nose (shape)
6. Mouth (shape, especially lips)
7. Teeth—color, missing, crooked, straight, crowded, gaps, unusual shape, noticeable crowns
8. Eyes (color, shape, and positioning)
9. Shape of face (broad, narrow, type of forehead, etc.)
10. Glasses?
11. Facial hair (type, style, color, amount)
12. Hair (style, amount, color)
13. Clothing description (style, color, distinguishing features)
    a. Coat
    b. Hat
    c. Pants
    d. Shirt
    e. Shoes
    f. Any other articles?
14. Any distinguishing or unusual features?
15. Was the perpetrator carrying any object? (Get full descriptions of any weapons: style, type, color, size, where the item came from.)
16. Was there anything distinctive about the perpetrator's voice, the way the perpetrator walked, or any unusual mannerisms?
17. Does the description that the witness gave to you differ in any way from that which the witness gave to the police? Did the witness add anything or leave anything out?

E. Evaluation of the Witness—Background

1. Has the witness ever been a victim of a crime before?
2. Has the witness ever been a witness to a crime before?

3. How articulate is the witness?
4. How certain or sure does the witness appear to be?
5. How anxious is the witness to pursue this case?

F. Making an Identification

1. How was the identification made—show-up, photo array, line-up, caught on the scene, second sighting?
2. What did the police say to the witness before the identification? Did the witness overhear anything being said?
3. What did the police say during the identification?
4. What did the witness say in making the identification? (Exact words.)
5. What did the police say after the identification?
6. Did the police write down what the witness said?
7. Were there any other witnesses around during the identification? How close were they to this witness?
8. Were there other identifications made?
9. What did any other witness say about an identification?
10. Was the witness asked to identify anyone but was unable to do so? (Get full details.)
11. On what did the witness base the identification—clothes, face, relative size, body build?
12. How soon after the incident was the identification made?
13. Did the person the witness identified appear to be different in any way from the perpetrator? (Was there different facial hair? Different clothes?)
14. If there was more than one perpetrator, how was each one identified? (Brought out together in a show-up? Pictures together in one photo array? Together in a line-up?)
15. How certain is the witness of this identification? Did police ask this? What was witness's response?
16. Is the witness more certain now than at the time of the original identification? Have there been multiple identifications that now make the person more certain?
17. If there is more than one person, is the witness more certain of one than the other?

G. Show-up Identification

1. Was the witness taken to the suspect, or was the suspect transported to the witness?
2. Was this show-up at the scene of the crime or at another location?
3. Where was the witness at the time of the identification? (Actual position on a diagram or in detailed words, and relative to the perpetrator.) Could the suspect see the witness? Could the suspect hear the witness?
4. What was said by the police before, during, and after the identification?
5. What did the witness tell the police at all stages (before, during, and after the identification)?
6. What description had the witness given to the police? What description did the police have from other witnesses?
7. Were there police around the suspect when the suspect was brought back? Was the suspect handcuffed? In a police car?

8. Who else was present during the identification? Could other witnesses hear what this witness said? Could this witness hear what other witnesses said?

9. Did the suspect have to do anything during the show-up (e.g., say anything, put on or take off an article of clothing)?

10. What were the viewing conditions at the time of the show-up in terms of lighting, distance from the subject, and general opportunity to observe the person being shown?

11. Note: Ask all the questions in Making an Identification, above.

H. Second Sighting

1. Did the witness ever see the suspect again on the street? (When? Where? Under what circumstances?)

2. What did the witness do after seeing the suspect again?

3. Was anyone else present?

4. What was the witness paying attention to just before seeing the person again?

5. What was the lighting?

6. Was anything said to or by the suspect?

7. Note: Ask all the questions in Making an Identification, above.

I. Photo Identification

1. Was this the first identification?

2. Were there any identifications or failures to identify at the scene?

3. Where were the photos shown?

4. Were the pictures loose or in a book? What kind of photos were they?

5. Did the police say anything to the witness about the pictures (e.g., that the pictures were all of known rapists, that they suspected someone in the pictures or book, etc.)?

6. How did the police handle the pictures? Did they let the witness look through the pictures on his or her own? Did they sit there with the witness? Did they show the witness the pictures one at a time? How did they lay the pictures out—in a row, in a stack, in two rows? In what order?

7. How many pictures were there?

8. Were all the pictures the same? Same size, same color?

9. What did the police say before showing the pictures?

10. Did the police say anything while showing the pictures?

11. Did the police say anything after the viewing? After the identification?

12. What exactly did the witness do? Did the witness look through all of them and then pick out one? Did the witness stop at one picture and make an identification? After identifying one picture, did the witness go through the pictures again or finish going through them? Did the witness ever turn the pictures over and see the back? Was anything on the back?

13. Was the witness aware of any dates on the pictures?

14. Did the witness write anything on any picture?

15. What exactly did the witness say in picking a picture?

16. Was more than one picture picked?

17. How sure is the witness that the identification is correct?
18. Did the picture differ in any way from the witness's memory of the perpetrator?
19. Did the police write anything down at any time?
20. Where in the stack or book was the person whom the witness identified?
21. What drew the witness to the identified picture?
22. How long did the showing take? Who else was present? If there were other witnesses present, did they view the photos together or separately?
23. What other identifications were made?
24. Note: Ask all the questions in Making an Identification, above.

J. Line-up Identification

1. Did the witness go to the line-up? Did the witness identify anyone there?
2. What was the witness told before going to the line-up? Was the witness shown photos before the line-up?
3. How did the witness get to the line-up? (Picked up by the police? With other witnesses?)
4. What was the witness told by the police outside the line-up room?
5. Did the witness ask the police any questions?
6. Did the witness talk to other witnesses while waiting outside the line-up room?
7. How many people were in the line-up room?
8. In what position in the line-up was the suspect standing?
9. Did the witness identify the suspect in the presence of other witnesses?
10. What exactly did the witness say in making the identification?
11. What did the police say to the witness outside the line-up room?
12. What did the witness say to other witnesses, or what did the witnesses say to him or her?
13. What did the witness tell the police? (Especially find out the witness's degree of certainty about the identification.)
14. How sure is the witness of the identification?
15. On what basis was the identification made? (Face, clothes, relative body build?)
16. Was there anyone else in the line-up who resembled the person whom the witness identified?
17. Was there anything different between the person the witness identified and the perpetrator?
18. Did the witness look down the line and then identify someone or did the witness just center on one person?
19. Had the witness ever made another identification in this case? When and how? (Get full details.)
20. Had the witness been shown any pictures recently? (When, how many, by whom, what other witnesses, what was said?)
21. Did the witness ask anyone in the line to do anything, say something, turn a particular way?
22. Note: Ask all the questions in Making an Identification, above.

II. Alibi Witness

1. Was the defendant with you on [date]?
2. How do you recall that specific day?
3. How do you recall the specific time?
4. When did the defendant arrive?
5. When did you first see the defendant?
6. Where did you first see the defendant (address, exact place, etc.)?
7. Was the defendant alone or with someone else?
8. Who was the defendant with?
9. Where does that person live?
10. Did anyone else see you and the defendant together?
11. Who?
12. Where does that person live?
13. How long was defendant with you?
14. How do you know it was this long?
15. What exactly did defendant do or say? (As specific and detailed as possible.)
16. Did defendant ever leave your presence during this period of time?
    a. When?
    b. How many times?
    c. How long was defendant gone each time?
    d. When did defendant return?
17. When did defendant finally leave?
18. How do you know?
19. Who, if anyone, left with defendant?
20. Where did defendant go?
21. How do you know?
22. How did the defendant act during the period of time the defendant was with you? (As specific as possible.)
    a. Intoxicated? Drugged?
    b. Nervous?
    c. Excited? Calm?
    d. Normal?
    e. Angry? Happy? Sad?
23. What is your relationship with the defendant?
    a. Close friend? Casual friend? Know to speak of?
    b. Relative by blood? Relative by marriage?
    c. Employer?
24. How long have you known the defendant?
25. When was the last time you saw the defendant before [date in question]?
26. Where? What was the defendant doing, etc.?
27. Have you seen the defendant since [date in question]?
28. Where? What was the defendant doing?
29. Are you aware that the defendant is charged with [offense]?
30. How did you learn this?
31. What exactly do you know about the offense?

32. Have you ever talked about the offense with the defendant? (If yes, details.)
33. Have you ever talked with police about the offense? (If yes, details as to when, where, what said, etc.)
34. Have you ever talked with the Assistant United States Attorney about this case? (If yes, details as to when, what said, etc.)
35. Have you testified before the grand jury about this case? (If yes, details as to when, what said, etc.)
36. Have you spoken to anyone else about the offense? (If yes, details as to when, what said, by whom, etc.)
37. Did you ever tell the police, the grand jury, or the prosecutor that the defendant was with you on [date of offense]?
38. Have you previously testified as an alibi witness for the defendant?
39. Have you ever been convicted of an offense? (When, where, disposition.)
40. Where do you now live? Phone number? Length of time?
41. Where did you live before that? Length of time?
42. Where do you work? (If unemployed, how long?)
43. What is your position?
44. How long have you been employed there?
45. Where did you work before that? How long? Position?

III. Self-defense

All the following questions should be asked of all witnesses (the complainant, eyewitnesses, complainant's friends and relatives, defendant's friends and relatives, police officers). They **must** be asked in cases where the defense may be self-defense—i.e., all homicides, ADWs, assaults, etc. These questions are not exhaustive, but merely guidelines. Additional questions should be asked and tailored to the particular fact situation involved. The investigator must try to elicit specific instances rather than general impressions, e.g., he's a bad guy, always fighting.

A. Evidence of Complainant's Aggressive or Bad Character to Show Propensity for Violence

1. Was the complainant a violent, aggressive person? Always getting into fights, arguments, altercations with people? Threatening people? (Specify details as to when, where, with whom, persons present, outcome, etc.)
2. Did the complainant associate with people with a reputation for assaultive behavior toward others? If so, who were these other people and where do they live?
3. Have you ever known the complainant to carry any type of weapon?
4. What kind of weapon?
5. Did the complainant always carry it? Frequently? Occasionally? (Specify.) Who would know the complainant carried a weapon?
6. Has the complainant ever used a weapon on anyone other than the defendant? (If yes, specify details as to when, where, on whom, injuries, persons present, outcome, etc.)
7. Do you know of the above from personal observation or from what others have told you? (If others, specify details as to who, when, where, etc.)
8. Was the complainant violent, aggressive when sober, or violent only when intoxicated or drinking?

9. Was the complainant known to drink to excess? Use narcotics?
10. Was the complainant ever charged, arrested, or tried for any assaultive behavior against anyone? (If so, details as to date, jurisdiction, result.) (Also find out the details of any non-violent charges.)

B. Defendant's Knowledge of Complainant's Violent, Aggressive, or Bad Character

1. Determine whether the defendant was aware of any of the above factors pertaining to the complainant. If the defendant was aware, obtain the specific details as to how the defendant knew, who told the defendant, when the defendant became aware, etc.
2. Had the complainant ever made threats against the defendant in the past?
   a. To the defendant personally? (When, where, who was present, etc.)
   b. To other people concerning the defendant? (When, where, who was present, etc.)
   c. Did the defendant know of these threats? (How? When? Where? What was defendant's reaction?)
   d. Was the defendant ever present when the complainant made threats to others?
3. Did the defendant know of the complainant's reputation for carrying a weapon?
   a. Does the defendant know this from personal observation?
   b. Does the defendant know this from other people?

C. Prior Relationship Between Defendant and Complainant

1. Have the defendant and the complainant had any difficulty with each other in the past?
   a. When—day, date, time?
   b. Where? (Precise place.)
   c. Who else present? (Full names, addresses, telephone numbers.)
   d. Cause of dispute or altercation?
   e. Who spoke first and what exactly was said?
   f. Any challenges or threats made? What and by whom and response?
   g. Who committed first overt act? What was it? Response?
   h. Did defendant attempt to withdraw?
   i. Were any weapons involved? What type? Who had them? How used?
   j. Anyone injured? Nature and what extent?
   k. Why did the defendant do what he or she did?
2. Did the witness ever tell police and/or prosecutor any of the above? If so, what and when?

Note: These questions do not attempt to explore the details of the altercation giving rise to the instant offense, an area that of course must be covered in great detail. Specific questions concerning this area are suggested below.

IV. Crimes against Persons

A. Where

1. Where did offense take place (address)?
2. Where at this address was the exact location of the offense?
3. Where exactly were the participants when the altercation began?
4. Where exactly were the participants immediately prior to the blow being struck?
5. Where exactly were the participants at the time of the (fatal) blow?
6. Where exactly was the witness during all of the above?
7. Where exactly were all other witnesses during all of above?
8. (Homicide case:) Where at this address was the exact place of death?

B. When

1. When did the altercation begin?
2. When did the defendant arrive on the scene?
3. When did the complainant arrive on the scene?
4. When did the witness being interviewed arrive on the scene?
5. When did the other witnesses arrive on the scene?
6. (Homicide case:) When was the fatal blow struck?
7. When was the offense reported?
8. (Homicide case:) When did the decedent die?

C. What

1. What was the cause of the altercation?
2. What exactly took place and what was said and done by the defendant and the complainant during the course of the altercation?
   a. Who spoke first and what was said? Done?
   b. Any challenge or threats made? What? By whom? Response?
   c. Who committed the first physical act?
   d. What was it?
   e. What was the response?
   f. Did defendant try to withdraw or wade in?
   g. Did the complainant retreat?
3. Were any weapons involved?
   a. Who had them?
   b. Where were they?
   c. What type?
   d. Who used them?
   e. Was the weapon used by defendant visible to the complainant?
   f. Was the weapon used by complainant visible to the defendant?
   g. Were any weapons recovered by the police on or near the decedent? By anyone? Turned over to police?
   h. Did the police recover any weapon from the defendant?

4. What, in your opinion, caused defendant to do what he or she did?
5. (Homicide case:) What if anything did defendant say or do immediately after inflicting the fatal blow?
6. (Homicide case:) What if anything did decedent say or do immediately after receiving the fatal blow?
7. (Homicide case:) Did decedent say anything to police after the fatal blow was struck? What? Where? When?
8. (Homicide case:) Did the decedent say anything to anyone else after the fatal blow was struck? What? When? Where?
9. What, if anything, did the witness being interviewed tell the police? Prosecutor?
   a. When?
   b. Where?
   c. To whom?
   d. Sign statements?
   e. Testify at preliminary hearing? Grand jury?
10. What did other witnesses tell the police? Prosecutor?
11. What did the witness being interviewed do during the entire incident?
12. What did the other witnesses do during the entire incident?

D. How

1. How did defendant, complainant, witness, and other witnesses arrive and leave?
2. How long did entire incident last?
3. How were the weapons used?
   a. By defendant?
   b. By complainant?
   c. By anyone else?
4. How were the injuries inflicted on complainant/defendant?
   a. Where?
   b. How severe?
   c. How many?
   d. Where was person treated?
   e. How did person get there?
5. How many times, if any, did the defendant tell the complainant to leave him or her alone? What was said? Did complainant hear it?
6. How far from complainant was defendant when incident began?
7. How far from decedent was defendant immediately before the (fatal) blow was struck?
8. How many times did the complainant tell the defendant to leave him or her alone? What was said? Did the defendant hear it?
9. How far from the complainant and the defendant was the witness during all of the above?
10. How many people participated in the altercation? Who? What did they do?

V. Crimes against Property

A. Where

1. Where did the offense take place (address)?
2. Where specifically did entry into the premises occur?
3. Where specifically did the taking occur?
4. Where specifically was the perpetrator during entire incident?
5. Where specifically were any witnesses during incident?
6. Where specifically were any occupants during incident?
7. What locations did police dust for fingerprints?
8. What items did police dust for fingerprints?
9. Where on the premises or items were prints lifted?
10. Where was the property stolen from or from where to where was it moved?

B. When

1. When did the offenses occur—date, time?
2. When did the perpetrator first arrive? Leave?
3. When was the offense discovered? By whom?
4. When was the offense reported? By whom?
5. When was the offense recovered—date, time?
6. When was property purchased? Where? Price paid? Is there a receipt? Estimate of value at time of taking? Basis of estimate?

C. What

1. What exactly occurred during entire incident?
2. What exactly was said by perpetrator during entire incident?
3. What exactly was said by each of the witnesses during entire incident?
4. What property was taken by perpetrator?
   a. Complete detailed description.
   b. Unusual characteristics?
   c. How was item identified?
5. What tools were used to gain entrance? How used? Marks left on premises? Any recovered?
6. What weapon, if any, did perpetrator use? (Describe weapon and use.)
7. What items, if any, did perpetrator leave at premises? Where are they now?
8. What information was reported to police?
9. What information was reported to insurance company? When? Where? What company? Result?
10. Was the complainant told by the insurance company that no recovery was possible unless a report was first made to the police?

D. How

1. How did the perpetrator arrive? Depart? (Mode of transportation.)
2. How did perpetrator gain entrance to premises where the property was? How did the perpetrator depart the house? (Detail each.)
   a. Breaking?
   b. Jimmying?
   c. Picking locks?
   d. Slipping locks?
   e. Unlocked entrance?
   f. Let in by occupant?
3. How was any property removed from the premises?
4. How was the property recovered?

E. Who

Answers to questions contained in General Identification section should be obtained, if applicable.

VI. Unauthorized Use of Motor Vehicle

A. Where

1. Where was car taken from? Address? Exact location at this address?
2. Where was the car's driver? Address?
3. Where was the car recovered? Address? Exact location at this address?

B. When

1. When was the car taken—date, time? Basis for estimate?
2. When was the car discovered missing—date, time? Basis for estimate?
3. When was the car reported missing—date, time?
4. When was the car driven after the theft—date, time? Duration?
5. When was the car recovered—date, time?
6. When was the defendant arrested—date, time? Statements? Others with defendant? Who was driving? Where in the car was defendant?

C. What

1. What kind of car—make, model, year, color, license plate number, manufacturer's number, mileage at time of taking and recovery, condition at time of taking and recovery.
2. What items, if any, were removed from the car by the user?
3. What items, if any, belonging to user were left in the car?
4. What portion of the car was dusted for prints?
5. From what portion of the car were prints lifted?

6. What prior relationship, if any, existed between the owner of vehicle and the defendant?
7. What police officers were involved in the case?

D. How

1. How was car taken?
    a. Keys in car?
    b. Car jumped?
    c. Another key used?
    d. Ignition locked/unlocked?
    e. Windows/door jimmied/broken?
    f. Slashed top?
    g. Tools used? Describe how.
    h. Permission to drive given to anyone?
2. How did participants arrive on scene? Depart?

E. Who

1. Who witnessed the removal? Recovery? (Details, names, addresses, and what seen.)
2. Who was in car at time of recovery? (Details, names, addresses, positions in car.)
3. Who reported vehicle stolen?
4. Who else participated in removal of vehicle? Use of vehicle?

VII. False Pretenses, Forgery, and Uttering

A. Where

1. Where did the offense take place (address)?
2. Where specifically did the exchange occur at this address?
3. Where specifically was the defendant during the entire incident?
4. Where specifically were all witnesses located during the entire incident?

B. When

1. When did offense occur—date, time?
2. When did the forger/utterer first arrive?
3. When did the forger/utterer leave?
4. When was the offense reported?
5. When was the property recovered?

C. What

1. What exactly occurred during the entire incident?
2. What exactly was said by forger/utterer during the entire incident?
3. What exactly was said by all witnesses to the incident?

4. What type of identification did forger/utterer use?
5. What type of instrument was used by forger/utterer (check, credit card, etc.)?
6. What property and/or money did forger/utterer get?
    a. Complete detailed description?
    b. When purchased?
    c. Value (at time of purchase and at time of taking)?
    d. How is item identified?
    e. Any unusual characteristics?
    f. Condition at time of purchase and time of recovery?
7. What names were on the instrument?
    a. Payee?
    b. Maker?
    c. Endorser?
8. What exactly did forger/utterer write?
    a. When?
    b. Where?
    c. In whose presence?

D. Who

1. Who else was with forger/utterer? (Detail everything they said and did during entire incident.)
2. Who reported incident?
3. Who responded (MPD, FBI, Secret Service)? Detail everything that transpired thereafter.

E. Photograph

Was photograph of forger/utterer taken when the instrument was passed? If so, where was camera, where was forger/utterer at the time of picture, where is picture now?

F. Handwriting Analysis

This is generally applicable if interviewing the arresting or investigating officer. Probe all the details surrounding the taking of a handwriting sample from the defendant: when, where, who was present, what was written, what was said by all, waiver obtained, etc.

Chapter 10
Discovery

10.1   Overview

Generally. The parties to a juvenile proceeding have rights to obtain evidence and information from each other through the process of discovery. A juvenile has the right to discovery in all cases, regardless of whether the underlying offense alleged is a misdemeanor or felony. This chapter discusses grounds and procedures for obtaining discovery, including statutory rights to discovery of each party under the Juvenile Code and constitutional rights of the juvenile to obtain information from the State. Discovery is essential to development of a strong defense for the juvenile and evaluation of the State's case.

Statutory rights. The parties' statutory rights to discovery are set forth in Article 23 of the Juvenile Code. G.S. 7B-2300 through 7B-2303. Counsel must file a motion and obtain an order for disclosure of specific information or materials. G.S. 7B-2300(a).

The State's statutory right to discovery depends largely on the juvenile's exercise of rights under G.S. 7B-2300 and is limited to evidence that the juvenile intends to introduce at hearing. G.S. 7B-2301.

Constitutional rights. Disclosure by the State of exculpatory evidence that is material to the defense, commonly known as *Brady* material, has been recognized by the U.S. Supreme Court as essential under the Due Process Clause of the Fourteenth Amendment to ensuring fairness in a criminal case. The constitutional requirements of due process under the 14th Amendment are applicable to juvenile cases under *In re Gault*, 387 U.S. 1 (1967). *See infra* § 10.5, Juvenile's Constitutional Right to Disclosure of Exculpatory Evidence.

Local rules governing discovery. Some districts have adopted local rules of discovery that may include deadlines for filing discovery motions and for producing discovery.

Other bases for disclosure. There are several other means of obtaining information in juvenile proceedings. Voluntary disclosure by the State is specifically allowed by statute. G.S. 7B-2300(f). G.S. 7B-2901 and 7B-3001 give the juvenile access to records concerning the juvenile maintained by the clerk in abuse, neglect, and dependency cases under Subchapter I of the Juvenile Code, by the Department of Social Services (DSS), by law enforcement, and by the Division of Adult Correction and Juvenile Justice. Rule

3.8(d) of the North Carolina Rules of Professional Conduct requires disclosure by the prosecutor of exculpatory or mitigating information in criminal cases and may be applicable to juvenile proceedings. In addition, counsel may use a subpoena to require a witness to appear and produce documents or may move for production of documents from a non-party witness. *See* 1 NORTH CAROLINA DEFENDER MANUAL § 4.6A, Evidence in Possession of Third Parties; § 4.7, Subpoenas (2d ed. 2013).Counsel also may make a request to inspect and examine public records under Chapter 132 of the North Carolina General Statutes. These alternative means of discovery are discussed in more detail *infra* in §§ 10.6–10.9.

10.2   Terminology Used in this Chapter

Brady material is evidence or information that is favorable to the defense and material to the outcome of either the guilt-innocence or sentencing phase of a trial. This evidence must be disclosed by the State in a criminal case under the Due Process Clause of the 14th Amendment pursuant to *Brady v. Maryland*, 373 U.S. 83 (1963), and its progeny. *See infra* § 10.5A, *Brady* Material.

Petitioner is "the individual who initiates court action by the filing of a petition or a motion for review alleging the matter for adjudication." G.S. 7B-1501(20). The discovery statutes describe the obligation of the "petitioner" to provide discovery to the juvenile (and vice versa). *See, e.g.*, G.S. 7B-2300. As used in the discovery statutes, the term "petitioner" appears to be broader. It essentially refers to agents of the State acting on behalf of the petitioner, including the prosecutor, law enforcement officers, and juvenile court counselors—that is, the State.

10.3   Procedures for Obtaining Discovery

A. Motion and Order Required

The categories of information that each party is statutorily entitled to obtain are set forth in G.S. 7B-2300. *See infra* § 10.4, Juvenile's Statutory Right to Discovery, and § 10.10, State's Statutory Right to Discovery. Each statutory section providing for discovery requires that a motion be filed and an order obtained. G.S. 7B-2300. It is common practice to file a single motion identifying all the categories of information sought. A sample discovery motion is available on the Office of the Juvenile Defender website. Counsel should ask that discovery be produced by a specific date and request a hearing on the motion, if necessary.

In some districts the prosecutor has an open file policy or the juvenile court counselor routinely provides discovery materials to the juvenile's counsel. Even if discovery materials are voluntarily provided, counsel should file a discovery motion to protect the juvenile's rights to discoverable information that might not have been provided by the State. In criminal cases in which the defendant has failed to make a formal request for discovery from the State pursuant to the statutory requirements, the courts have held that the defendant has no remedy if the State fails to produce the information voluntarily. *See State v. Abbott*, 320 N.C. 475, 483 (1987) (prosecutor not barred from using defendant's statement at trial even though it was discoverable under statute and was not produced before trial; open-file discovery policy was no substitute for formal request and motion).

Counsel should therefore file a motion for discovery and secure an order compelling discovery to protect the juvenile's rights in all cases. Although G.S. 7B-2300 does not require the court to enter a written discovery order, counsel should request a written order so the requirements of the order are clearly documented and preserved.

G.S. 15A-902(b), a part of the Criminal Procedure Act, requires an adult criminal defendant to make a written request for discovery before making a discovery motion. If the prosecutor voluntarily agrees to provide discovery in response to an adult defendant's written request, the agreement is binding without an order of the court. There is not a specific provision to that effect in the Juvenile Code. The absence of such a provision further underscores the need for counsel to prepare and file a written, comprehensive motion for discovery in juvenile cases and obtain a court order.

B. When to File Motion

The Juvenile Code does not specify a deadline for moving for discovery. A motion for discovery should be filed early in the proceeding, however, so that counsel will have as much time as possible to review the information and evidence produced, investigate the evidence, and make additional motions if necessary. Discovery material may also be important for a probable cause hearing. Because adjudicatory hearings are usually set for hearing soon after the filing of the petition, discovery must proceed in a timely manner so that counsel will be prepared for the hearing. It is particularly important to act expeditiously with discovery and avoid unnecessary continuances when the juvenile is in secure custody pending adjudication.

C. Contents of Motion

A discovery motion should be broad enough to include all evidence and information covered by statute. Although cases after *Brady* have held that a specific request is not required, the motion should also ask for all exculpatory information to put the State on notice of the information it should produce and to strengthen the record in the event of an appeal. *See infra* § 10.4, Juvenile's Statutory Right to Discovery, and § 10.5, Juvenile's Constitutional Right to Disclosure of Exculpatory Evidence.

The motion for discovery should also request any other information believed to be helpful to the juvenile's case regardless of whether the information is specified by statute. The duty to advocate zealously for the juvenile requires that counsel seek all evidence necessary to mount an effective defense.

Although the Juvenile Code does not set a deadline for production of discovery, counsel should request that the court specify a deadline in its order. Local rules in some districts provide deadlines for production of discovery. Counsel should be familiar with these rules to protect the juvenile's rights.

D. Hearing on Motion for Discovery

The discovery statute does not specify that a hearing is required, as the wording is mandatory that "upon motion" the court "shall order" disclosure of the information. G.S. 7B-2300(a)–(d). It may be necessary to schedule a hearing and give notice, however, if required by the court, local rules or custom, or the State objects to entry of an order for discovery. Also, a hearing may be beneficial to obtain an order setting a deadline for production of discovery or if the State has not produced requested information in a timely manner.

At the hearing, counsel should be prepared to cite the statutory bases for disclosure of the material, as well as the constitutional bases for exculpatory material requested under *Brady*. *See infra* § 10.5, Juvenile's Constitutional Right to Disclosure of Exculpatory Evidence.

E. Continuing Duty to Disclose

Each party who has been ordered to disclose information or evidence is under a continuing duty to disclose newly-discovered evidence that is subject to discovery. The other party must be given prompt notice of the new or additional evidence. G.S. 7B-2303. The State has an additional continuing duty under *Brady* and related cases to disclose evidence that is favorable to the juvenile and is material to the outcome of the case. *See infra* § 10.5, Juvenile's Constitutional Right to Disclosure of Exculpatory Evidence.

F. Continuances and Sanctions

Counsel may need additional time to review evidence that has just been disclosed by the State. In some instances, the failure of the State to disclose evidence under a discovery order in a timely manner may justify a continuance or other remedy for violation of the juvenile's statutory or constitutional rights. *See In re A.M.*, 220 N.C. App. 136, 138 (2012) (trial court erred by depriving juvenile of any remedy, such as granting a motion in limine or continuing the case, for the State's failure to disclose the name of a witness during discovery).

Likewise, counsel for the juvenile should promptly turn over required information to avoid a request for a continuance by the State or sanctions.

10.4   Juvenile's Statutory Right to Discovery

A.   Statement of the Juvenile and Co-Respondents

The State must provide information regarding both written and oral statements made by the juvenile or by any co-respondents. G.S. 7B-2300(a). Specifically, on motion and order, the State must:

- allow the juvenile to inspect *and* copy any relevant written or recorded statements within the possession, custody, or control of the petitioner made by the juvenile or any other party charged in the same action; and
- divulge, in written or recorded form, the substance of any oral statement made by the juvenile or any other party charged in the same action.

G.S. 7B-2300(a)(1), (2).

Counsel should also include in the discovery motion a request for copies of any waiver forms read to or signed by the juvenile during questioning. Counsel should then review the waiver forms to determine whether the juvenile's constitutional or statutory rights were violated. If an adult waiver form was used, it is likely that the juvenile did not receive adequate information regarding statutory rights, such as the right to have a parent or guardian present during questioning. *See infra* § 11.4I, Knowing, Willing, and Understanding Waiver of Rights.

B.   Within the Possession, Custody, or Control

The State is required to produce the statements described above if they are "within the possession, custody, or control" of the State. G.S. 7B-2300(a). Thus, any information subject to discovery received by the State must be disclosed to the juvenile. These materials could include statements within DSS reports, psychological evaluations, or reports of school resource officers. *See, e.g.,* G.S. 7B-307(a) (DSS must report to the district attorney evidence of child abuse, and law enforcement must coordinate its investigation with the protective services investigation). The phrase "possession, custody, or control" has been construed to mean "within the possession, custody, or control of the prosecutor *or those working in conjunction with him and his office.*" *State v. Pigott*, 320 N.C. 96, 102 (1987) (emphasis in original). The State is therefore obligated to produce the required materials and information, such as information in the possession of law enforcement, whether or not contained in the prosecutor's files.

C.   Names of Witnesses

The State must provide, on motion and order, the names of all people to be called as witnesses. If the juvenile files a motion under G.S. 7B-2300 requesting disclosure of the State's witness list, the trial court must grant the motion. *See In re A.M.*, 220 N.C. App. 136, 138 (2012) (holding that the trial court erred by "failing to allow [the juvenile's] motion in limine, continue the case, or find another way to remedy a situation created by the petitioner's failure to comply with the plain mandate of N.C. Gen. Stat. § 7B-2300(b).”). Counsel should include in the motion a request for the records of any witnesses under the age of 16, which must be provided “if accessible to the petitioner.” G.S. 7B-2300(b). The requirement that the State provide the records of juvenile witnesses implies that they may be used to impeach the credibility of a juvenile witness. *See also infra* § 12.5C, Rules of Evidence (prior adjudication of delinquency may be used to impeach juvenile or juvenile witness). Impeachment by a juvenile record may be particularly important if a co-respondent is testifying against the juvenile.

D. Documents and Tangible Objects

The State must allow the juvenile, on motion and order, to inspect *and* copy books, papers, documents, photographs, motion pictures, mechanical or electronic recordings, and tangible objects. G.S. 7B-2300(c). These materials must meet two conditions:

- First, the information must be within the possession, custody, or control of the petitioner, prosecutor, or an investigating law enforcement officer. This language reinforces the obligation of the prosecutor to turn over discoverable information even if it is not in the immediate possession of the prosecutor. *See supra* § 10.4B, Within the Possession, Custody, or Control.
- Second, the information must be material to the preparation of the defense, *or* intended for use by the State as evidence, *or* obtained from or belonging to the juvenile.

G.S. 7B-2300(c)(1), (2).

Counsel should include in the motion a request for any documents or tangible objects obtained from the scene of the offense or from the alleged victim. The motion may include a request for such items as videotapes of the alleged victim or the scene of the offense, which may have to be copied from a computer hard drive, as well as any audio recordings describing the scene of the offense, of a call to 911, or of the alleged victim's statement. In some instances it may be easier for counsel to obtain information directly from the source. For example, counsel may be able to obtain copies of 911 calls directly from law enforcement under G.S. 7B-3001. *See infra* § 10.8, Other Sources of Information. It may be necessary to file a motion to preserve evidence that law enforcement may routinely destroy after a certain amount of time has elapsed. A sample motion to preserve rough notes of investigators is available on the <u>Office of the Juvenile Defender website</u>.

E. Reports and Examinations

Tests. The State must allow the juvenile, on motion and order, to inspect and copy the results of tests and examinations within its possession, custody, or control. Results of physical or mental examinations, and tests, measurements, or experiments made in connection with the case, as well as underlying data, must be disclosed. G.S. 7B-2300(d); *see State v. Cunningham*, 108 N.C. App. 185 (1992) (defendant entitled to data underlying lab report based on language in the version of G.S. 15A-903 in effect at the time, which is similar to the language that currently exists in G.S. 7B-2300(d)). Counsel should request copies of any physical or mental examinations of the alleged victim, the juvenile, or witnesses. Further, the data underlying tests, experiments, and measurements should be specifically requested in the motion, particularly regarding evidence obtained from the alleged victim or scene of the offense.

Physical evidence. Physical evidence that the State intends to offer at the adjudication hearing is discoverable by the juvenile. On motion of the juvenile, the court must order the State to allow the juvenile access to the physical evidence, or a sample of it, for the juvenile to inspect, examine, and test under appropriate safeguards. G.S. 7B-2300(d).

F. "Work Product" Exception

The State is not required under Article 23 of the Juvenile Code to produce "reports, memoranda, or other internal documents made by the petitioner, law enforcement officers, or other persons acting on behalf of the petitioner" in the investigation or prosecution of the case unless required pursuant to G.S. 7B-2300(a)–(d). G.S. 7B-2300(e). Additionally, there is no requirement under Article 23 that the State produce statements made by witnesses, the petitioner, or anyone acting on behalf of the petitioner unless otherwise required by the statute. *Id.* This type of information is sometimes referred to as "work product." This provision does not override other rights to obtain information, however.

Information that falls within the discovery statute, or that must be disclosed pursuant to constitutional mandates, must be produced. Statutory and constitutional disclosure requirements override any work product exception. *See infra* § 10.5, Juvenile's Constitutional Right to Disclosure of Exculpatory Evidence.

Further, according to G.S. 7B-3001(b), which appears in a separate article of the Juvenile Code, a juvenile is entitled to "examine and obtain copies" of law enforcement records and files concerning the juvenile. *See infra* § 10.8, Other Sources of Information. Counsel should therefore request copies of law enforcement files concerning the juvenile under the authority in G.S. 7B-3001(b) to obtain information that would normally be protected from disclosure under the work production exception in G.S. 7B-2300(e).

In addition, if the witness has reviewed the material before testifying—for example, an officer may review his or her report or a witness his or her statement—the juvenile should request disclosure under Rule 612 of the North Carolina Rules of Evidence, which authorizes the court to order disclosure.

G. Consequences of Juvenile Obtaining a Discovery Order

Except for the names of the juvenile's witnesses, the State's statutory right to discovery depends on the juvenile's exercise of statutory rights under G.S. 7B-2300 and is limited to evidence that the juvenile intends to introduce at the hearing. G.S. 7B-2301. If the juvenile obtains an order for *any* discovery under the statute, the State may obtain information from the juvenile as allowed by statute. G.S. 7B-2301(b), (c); *see infra* § 10.10, State's Statutory Right to Discovery.

In most cases, the State has more information than the juvenile, so the benefits of obtaining information from the State outweigh the risks of disclosing evidence. It is therefore generally best to file a broad request for discovery as early as possible in the proceeding.

H. Local Discovery Rules

Some districts have adopted local rules governing discovery. Local rules are authorized by G.S. 7A-34 and Rule 2(d) of the General Rules of Practice for the Superior and District Courts Supplemental to the Rules of Civil Procedure, if they are supplemental to and not inconsistent with acts of the General Assembly. These rules may expand the information available to the juvenile or set deadlines for requesting and producing discovery. It is vital for counsel to be familiar with any local rules to ensure that all discoverable information is requested and obtained in a timely manner. Local rules for each district are available on the Administrative Office of the Courts website.

10.5   Juvenile's Constitutional Right to Disclosure of Exculpatory Evidence

A. *Brady* Material

The U.S. Supreme Court recognized the constitutional right of a criminal defendant under the Due Process Clause of the 14th Amendment to disclosure by the State of evidence that is:

- favorable to the defense, *and*
- material to the outcome of either the guilt-innocence or the sentencing phase of the trial.

Brady v. Maryland, 373 U.S. 83, 87 (1963). Subsequent cases have clarified that the right to disclosure does not depend on a request by the defendant for the exculpatory information. *Kyles v. Whitley*, 514 U.S. 419, 433 (1995); *United States v. Bagley*, 473 U.S. 667, 676 (1985). Citing *Brady*, the North Carolina Court of Appeals has stated in a juvenile appeal that "it is true that suppression of evidence favorable to an accused upon request violates due process where the evidence is material to guilt." *In re Coleman*, 55 N.C. App. 673, 674 (1982).

Although not required by *Kyles* and *Bagley*, it is good practice to file a motion requesting that the State produce exculpatory evidence and specifying to the extent known the evidence that counsel wants the State to produce. This will put the State on notice and will strengthen the record in the event of an appeal.

B. Evidence Required to be Disclosed under *Brady*

Defender Manual. The North Carolina Defender Manual contains a more complete discussion of information required to be disclosed under *Brady* and related cases. *See* 1 NORTH CAROLINA DEFENDER MANUAL § 4.5, *Brady* Material (2d ed. 2013).

Favorable to the defense. Categories of evidence that must be disclosed as favorable to the defense are discussed, with case citations, in 1 NORTH CAROLINA DEFENDER MANUAL § 4.5C, Favorable to Defense (2d ed. 2013). Favorable evidence includes evidence that tends to negate guilt, mitigate an offense or sentence, or impeach the truthfulness of a witness or reliability of evidence. Examples of favorable evidence include:

- impeachment evidence, such as:
  - false statements of a witness
  - prior inconsistent statements
  - bias of a witness
  - witness's capacity to observe, perceive, or recollect
  - psychiatric evaluations of a witness
  - prior convictions and other misconduct
- evidence discrediting police investigation and credibility
- other favorable evidence, such as:
  - evidence undermining identification of defendant
  - evidence tending to show guilt of another
  - physical evidence
  - "negative" exculpatory evidence (e.g., defendant not mentioned in statement regarding crime)
  - identity of favorable witnesses

Material to outcome. Under *Brady,* evidence must be material to the outcome of either the guilt-innocence or the sentencing phase of the case, in addition to being favorable to the defense. *Brady v. Maryland,* 373 U.S. 83, 87 (1963). The U.S. Supreme Court, in *Kyles v. Whitley*, 514 U.S. 419 (1995), provided further guidance regarding when evidence is material to the outcome of the case and must be disclosed. In *Kyles,* the Court stated four aspects of materiality under *Brady*:

- The standard of review for constitutional error for failure to disclose by the State is a "reasonable probability" that the outcome of the trial would have been different.
- The test is not the sufficiency of the evidence presented, but rather whether the favorable evidence might have cast a different light on the evidence presented, thereby undermining confidence in the verdict.
- If the appellate court finds constitutional error, the defendant is entitled to a new trial; the harmless error standard is not applicable.
- Materiality is determined by the cumulative effect of all undisclosed evidence, not on an item-by-item basis.

Kyles v. Whitley, 514 U.S. 419, 434–37 (1995).

10.6   North Carolina Rules of Professional Conduct

Rule 3.8(d) of the Rules of Professional Conduct requires that the prosecutor in a criminal case disclose evidence that "tends to negate the guilt of the accused or mitigates the offense" and information that might mitigate at sentencing. Although this rule does not specifically apply to juvenile cases, the reasons underlying the duty to disclose are equally applicable. The rule requires the State to make "reasonably diligent inquiry" and to disclose non-privileged evidence as required by law, rules of procedure, or court opinions unless a protective order is entered.

10.7   Voluntary Disclosure by State

The Juvenile Code specifically provides that the State is not prohibited from making voluntary disclosure of evidence "in the interest of justice." G.S. 7B-2300(f). It is important, however, for counsel to file a broad motion for discovery even when the State voluntarily discloses evidence. The right to discovery under the statute requires that a motion be filed and an order for discovery be entered. *See supra* § 10.3A, Motion and Order Required. Although *Brady* does not necessarily require that a motion be filed to invoke the State's duty to disclose, counsel should file a written motion to highlight the information being sought and to strengthen the record in the event of appeal. If the prosecutor fails to produce discoverable information after receiving a specific request, the juvenile may have a stronger argument for sanctions.

10.8   Other Sources of Information

Juveniles also have access to a significant amount of information beyond the information available through discovery. Under G.S. 7B-2901(a), the juvenile and the juvenile's attorney are entitled to examine and obtain copies of written parts of the clerk's records for cases involving the abuse, neglect, or dependency of the juvenile under Subchapter I of the Juvenile Code. A motion or court order is not required to obtain the records.

G.S. 7B-2901(b) also gives the juvenile the right to examine DSS records of cases in which the juvenile is under placement by a court or has been placed under protective custody by DSS. These records include "family background information; reports of social, medical, psychiatric, or psychological information concerning a juvenile or the juvenile's family; interviews with the juvenile's family; or other information which the court finds should be protected from public inspection in the best interests of the juvenile." G.S. 7B-2901(b). There is no requirement that the juvenile file a motion or obtain a court order before examining the records. The Court of Appeals acknowledged, in *In re J.L.*, 199 N.C. App. 605, 609 (2009), that juveniles have a "right" under G.S. 7B-2901(b) to access such records.

The juvenile and the juvenile's attorney are also entitled to examine and obtain copies of records concerning the juvenile that are maintained by law enforcement and the Division of Adult Correction and Juvenile Justice. G.S. 7B-3001(b) and (c). No motion or court order are required to obtain the records. If the records are not turned over on request, however, counsel for the juvenile should file a motion for an order compelling production.

The juvenile's rights under G.S. 7B-2901 and 7B-3001 are not grounded in discovery principles, but rather effectuate the juvenile's right to access records that are shielded from public inspection. Counsel should be familiar with the provisions of these statutes and should seek the records available under them.

10.9 Public Records Request

Counsel may make a request to inspect and examine public records under Chapter 132 of the North Carolina General Statutes. For example, counsel may obtain operations manuals, policies, and standard operating procedures developed by police and sheriffs' departments. The right to access public records is governed by G.S. 132-6. The statute does not require a specific form for requesting access to public records. Instead, the custodian of public records must permit "any person" to inspect and examine public records "at reasonable times and under reasonable supervision." G.S. 132-6(a). G.S. 132-6.2 permits the custodian to charge fees for copies of public records. Such fees must only reflect the "actual cost" of making the copies, which is "limited to direct, chargeable costs related to the reproduction of a public record as determined by generally accepted accounting principles and does not include costs that would have been incurred by the public agency if a request to reproduce a public record had not been made." G.S. 132-6.2(b).

When the General Assembly enacted Chapter 132, it intended that, as a general rule, the public should have "liberal access to public records." *News & Observer Pub. Co. v. State*, 312 N.C. 276, 281 (1984). This policy is reflected in the definition of "public record," which includes "all documents, papers, letters, maps, books, photographs, films, sound recordings, magnetic or other tapes, electronic data-processing records, artifacts, or other documentary material, regardless of physical form or characteristics, made or received pursuant to law or ordinance in connection with the transaction of public business by any agency of North Carolina government or its subdivisions." G.S. 132-1.

For more information about public records requests, see DAVID M. LAWRENCE, PUBLIC RECORDS LAW FOR NORTH CAROLINA LOCAL GOVERNMENTS (UNC School of Government, 2d ed. 2009); and Frayda Bluestein, *Public Records in North Carolina* (UNC School of Government, 2012).

10.10 State's Statutory Right to Discovery

A. Names of Witnesses

The juvenile must provide, on motion and order, the names of all people to be called as witnesses. G.S. 7B-2301(a).

B. Right Based on Juvenile's Order for Discovery Following State's Motion and Order for Discovery

If a juvenile has obtained an order for discovery of *any* information under G.S. 7B-2300, the State has the right to discover the evidence or information listed below. G.S. 7B-2301(b), (c). The juvenile has no obligation to disclose evidence or information unless the State has filed a discovery motion and obtained an order compelling disclosure. Further, the categories apply only when the juvenile intends to make use of the evidence at trial, as described below.

Documents and tangible objects. On motion of the State, the court must order the juvenile to allow the State to inspect and copy books, papers, documents, photographs, motion pictures, mechanical or electronic recordings, and tangible objects *if* the materials are

- within the possession, custody, or control of the juvenile; *and*
- intended to be introduced as evidence by the juvenile.

G.S. 7B-2301(b).

Reports of examinations and tests. On motion of the State, the court must order the juvenile to allow the State to inspect and copy the results of certain tests and examinations. Results of physical or mental examinations, tests, measurements, or experiments made in connection with the case must be disclosed *if* the information is

- within the possession and control of the juvenile; *and*
- intended to be introduced as evidence or prepared by a witness whom the juvenile intends to call to testify about the result of the examination or test.

G.S. 7B-2301(c).

Physical evidence. On motion of the State, the court must order the juvenile to allow the State to inspect, examine, and test physical evidence that the juvenile intends to offer as evidence to the court. G.S. 7B-2301(c). The statute also permits the State to examine and test a sample of the physical evidence instead of the entire object. *Id.* Any examination or testing of the evidence by the State must be completed under "appropriate safeguards." *Id.* The juvenile must also permit the State to inspect and examine any tests or experiments made in connection with physical evidence that the juvenile intends to offer as evidence to the court. *Id.*

10.11 Protective Order

Either party is allowed to file a motion requesting an order that discovery be denied, restricted, or deferred. G.S. 7B-2302(a).

In the court's discretion, a party moving to restrict discovery may submit supporting affidavits or statements for in camera inspection. If the motion for relief is granted, the material inspected in camera by the court must be preserved for review by the Court of Appeals on appeal. G.S. 7B-2302(b).

Chapter 11
Motions to Suppress

11.1   Motions Practice in Juvenile Court

A. Goals

Advocacy through motions practice is essential to protection of a juvenile's constitutional and statutory rights. Filing motions can achieve several goals in a juvenile case. A pending motion may strengthen the juvenile's bargaining position with the State, while a successful motion may resolve the case, or some portions of it, in the juvenile's favor. Advocacy through motions practice will demonstrate to the court, the prosecutor, and the juvenile that counsel is dedicated to providing an effective and zealous defense. The court and the prosecutor may then be more likely to listen carefully and be persuaded by arguments of counsel.

Drafting a motion requires that counsel research the statutory, constitutional, or case law bases for the motion. A written motion and argument on the record and a memorandum of law submitted to the court, along with appropriate objections, protect the juvenile's rights and preserve issues in the event of an appeal.

B. Types of Motions

A variety of motions may be filed, including a motion requesting that a hearing be closed (*see supra* § 2.7, Right to an Open Hearing), that witnesses be sequestered (*see infra* § 12.5A, Sequestering Witnesses), for discovery (*see supra* § 10.3, Procedures for Obtaining Discovery), requesting an evaluation of capacity (*see supra* § 7.8, Obtaining an Expert Evaluation), requesting that an expert be appointed (*see supra* § 7.8A, Procedures to Obtain Expert Evaluation), and for dismissal of the petition (*see supra* § 6.3H, Defects in Petition: Timing of Motion).

Motions to suppress are particularly important in juvenile court because the State's case often rests on a statement or admission of a juvenile or on evidence obtained from a search of a juvenile. A successful suppression motion may result in the dismissal of the petition by the State or on motion of the juvenile. This chapter focuses on filing and arguing motions to suppress.

11.2   Filing Motions and Hearing Procedures

Before 2015, the Juvenile Code did not contain specific procedures for filing suppression motions in juvenile delinquency cases. However, suppression motions were routinely litigated in juvenile court. *See, e.g., In re V.C.R.*, 227 N.C. App. 80, 87 (2013) (reversing order denying the juvenile's motion to suppress). In 2015, the General Assembly amended several parts of the Juvenile Code. *See* 2015 N.C. Sess. Laws Ch. 58 (H 879). One of the amendments included a new statute—G.S. 7B-2408.5—that defined the procedures for suppression motions. Those procedures are described below.

A. Timing of Motions

G.S. 7B-2408.5 does not set any deadlines for filing suppression motions. Instead, the statute states that a suppression motion may be made either before or during the adjudicatory hearing. G.S. 7B-2408.5(a), (e). The language in G.S. 7B-2408.5 stands in contrast to G.S. 15A-975, the statute for suppression motions in adult court, which states that a defendant must file a suppression motion before trial unless certain limited exceptions apply.

If the motion to suppress would be dispositive if successful—that is, it would exclude evidence necessary for the State to prove the charged offense—the motion should be filed early in the case. If a motion to suppress is granted before the probable cause hearing, the State may be unable to establish probable cause.

There may be tactical reasons in some instances not to file a motion to suppress until the adjudicatory hearing begins. Counsel may decide to defer filing to avoid revealing to the State that certain evidence may not be admissible at adjudication. If the motion to suppress is granted at a later stage, the State may be unable to produce other sufficient evidence to prove the allegations in the petition.

B. Form and Contents of Motion

If counsel makes a suppression motion before the adjudicatory hearing, the motion must be in writing and a copy of the motion must be served on the State. G.S. 7B-2408.5(a). The motion must state the grounds for suppressing the evidence and must be accompanied by an affidavit containing facts supporting the motion. *Id.* Counsel may sign the affidavit based on information and belief rather than having the juvenile sign as long as counsel includes the source of the information and the basis for the belief in the affidavit. *Id.; see also State v. Chance*, 130 N.C. App. 107, 110–11 (1998) (observing that the adult statute governing suppression motions does not require the defendant to sign the affidavit in support of a suppression motion).

It is critical that counsel follow the requirements of G.S. 7B-2408.5(a). If the motion does not allege a legal basis for suppression or the affidavit does not support the ground alleged, the court may summarily deny the motion. G.S. 7B-2408.5(c). In adult cases, the failure to attach an affidavit to the motion waives the right to contest the evidence not only at trial, but also on appeal. *State v. Holloway*, 311 N.C. 573, 578 (1984). Although the reasoning in *Holloway* has not yet been extended to juvenile delinquency cases, counsel should ensure that the suppression motion complies with G.S. 7B-2408.5(a) to avoid waiver of the suppression issue.

If counsel makes a suppression motion during the adjudicatory hearing, the motion may be made "in writing or orally." G.S. 7B-2408.5(e). It is unclear whether a written suppression motion made during the adjudicatory hearing must include an affidavit. G.S. 7B-2408.5(e) states that a suppression motion made during the adjudicatory hearing "may be determined in the same manner as when made before the adjudicatory hearing." Although not specifically stated in the statute, if counsel files a written motion during the adjudicatory hearing, counsel should attach an affidavit to the motion.

The written motion should state both constitutional and statutory grounds for suppression. As part of the 2015 amendments to the Juvenile Code, the General Assembly added language making substantial violations of the G.S. Chapter 15A, the Criminal Procedure Act, a basis for suppression. *See infra* § 11.3C, Substantial Violations of Criminal Procedure Act.

Although not statutorily required, counsel should prepare a memorandum of law supporting the motion to suppress. A memorandum will place before the court the legal authority supporting the motion and will also supplement the record on appeal.

C. Renewal of Objection at Adjudicatory Hearing

If the juvenile files a suppression motion before the adjudicatory hearing and the court denies the motion, the juvenile must renew the motion during the adjudicatory hearing to preserve the motion for appeal. *State v. Grooms*, 353 N.C. 50, 66 (2000). The reason that suppression motions must be renewed is because courts consider pretrial rulings on suppression motions to be "preliminary." *State v. Waring*, 364 N.C. 443, 468 (2010). In practice, this means that the juvenile must object, based on the grounds included in the suppression motion as well as any other applicable grounds, when the State presents the evidence in court. *State v. Golphin*, 352 N.C. 364, 405 (2000).

If the juvenile preserves the suppression issue, but is adjudicated delinquent and appeals, the State bears the burden of proving on appeal that the error was harmless beyond a reasonable doubt. *State v. Robey*, 91 N.C. App. 198, 206 (1988). If the juvenile does not preserve the suppression issue, the issue will be subject to plain error review on appeal. *State v. Stokes*, 357 N.C. 220, 227 (2003). Under plain error review, the juvenile must show that the error had a "probable impact" on the trial court hearing. *State v. Lawrence*, 365 N.C. 506, 518 (2012). The difference between the two standards is critical and could affect the outcome of the appeal. *See, e.g., State v. Pullen*, 163 N.C. App. 696, 702 (2004) (stating that the court "might reach a different result" if the error were preserved and the State bore the burden of proving that the error was harmless beyond a reasonable doubt). Thus, it is crucial that counsel renew the motion to suppress at the adjudicatory hearing when the State presents the evidence that was at issue in the suppression motion.

By amendment to the North Carolina Rules of Evidence in 2003, the General Assembly tried to eliminate the requirement that counsel must renew an objection when evidence that was the subject of an unsuccessful motion to suppress is presented at the adjudication. N.C. R. Evid. 103(a)(2). The Court of Appeals initially enforced this rule.

See State v. Rose, 170 N.C. App. 284, 288 (2005) (defendant not required to renew objection when evidence is offered at trial after motion to suppress denied before trial); *In re S.W.*, 171 N.C. App. 335, 337 (2005) (to same effect). The Court of Appeals thereafter held, however, that the General Assembly impermissibly interfered with the North Carolina Supreme Court's exclusive authority to make rules of practice and procedure for appeals. *State v. Tutt*, 171 N.C. App. 518, 524 (2005). Counsel should therefore continue to object if evidence that has been the subject of a previous motion to suppress is offered at the adjudication.

Counsel should also object during the hearing if evidence that has been ordered suppressed is presented, whether by design or inadvertence. The evidence has been ruled inadmissible and should be excluded from consideration by the court. An objection should also be made during the hearing if evidence that is subject to suppression is introduced by the State without prior notice that it will be offered. If necessary, counsel should request a continuance to research and present legal authority supporting suppression.

D. Appeal of Denial of Motion to Suppress Following Admission

The juvenile's right to appeal the denial of a motion to suppress after admitting the allegations in the petition is subject to multiple rules imposed by statute and case law. Counsel should take great care to comply with the rules to preserve the juvenile's right to challenge the denial of a suppression motion on appeal.

First, the right to appeal an order denying a motion to suppress is limited by statute. According to G.S. 7B-2408.5(g), the juvenile has the right to appeal an order denying a motion to suppress "upon an appeal of a final order of the court in a juvenile matter." G.S. 7B-2408.5(g). A dispositional order is a final order. G.S. 7B-2602; *In re A.L.*, 166 N.C. App. 276, 277 (2004). In contrast, an adjudication order is not a final order. *In re M.L.T.H.*, 200 N.C. App. 476, 480 (2009). G.S. 7B-2602 permits a juvenile to appeal an adjudication order within 70 days if the court does not enter disposition within 60 days. In this instance, the juvenile may be able to challenge an order denying a suppression motion as part of an appeal of an adjudication order. Because the literal terms of G.S. 7B-2408.5(g) require a "final order," the safer practice is to have the judge enter a disposition order within 60 days.

Second, if the juvenile enters an admission instead of proceeding to an adjudication hearing, counsel should give notice of the juvenile's intent to appeal the suppression order before entering an admission. Under G.S. 15A-979(b), a defendant in adult court has the right to appeal an order denying a motion to suppress after pleading guilty. Courts have construed G.S. 15A-979(b) to mean that the defendant must give notice to the prosecutor and the court of his intent to appeal the suppression order before pleading guilty. *State v. Tew*, 326 N.C. 732, 735 (1990); *State v. Brown*, 142 N.C. App. 491, 492 (2001). Courts have not extended the requirement to juvenile delinquency cases and may never do so because, unlike in adult cases, there are no statutory limitations on the issues juveniles may raise on appeal following an admission. As a best practice, however, counsel should include a statement in the written transcript of admission reserving the right to appeal the order denying the motion to suppress.

Third, counsel must give proper notice of appeal. The juvenile's right to appeal is found in G.S. 7B-2602 and is discussed in more detail *infra* in § 16.3, Right to Appeal. According to G.S. 7B-2602, counsel must give notice of appeal in open court or in writing within 10 days after entry of a final order. In addition, if the juvenile enters an admission, counsel may not rely on the notice of the juvenile's intent to appeal the suppression order as a notice of appeal from a final order. "A Notice of Appeal is distinct from giving notice of intent to appeal." *State v. McBride*, 120 N.C. App. 623, 625 (1995). If the juvenile gives notice of intent to appeal the suppression order before entering an admission, but fails to give notice of appeal from a final order, the appeal will be subject to dismissal for lack of jurisdiction. *State v. Miller*, 205 N.C. App. 724, 725 (2010).

E. State's Right to Appeal Order Granting Motion to Suppress

G.S. 7B-2408.5 does not provide the State with the right to appeal an order granting a motion to suppress. Instead, the State's right to appeal a suppression order is in G.S. 7B-2604(b)(2). According to G.S. 7B-2604(b)(2), the State can only appeal from an order granting a motion to suppress if the order "terminates the prosecution of a petition." In *In re P.K.M.*, 219 N.C. App. 543, 545 (2012), the Court of Appeals dismissed the State's appeal from an order granting a motion to suppress because the trial court did not dismiss the case as part of its order on the motion to suppress. The Court of Appeals noted that an order granting a motion to suppress "does not, standing alone, dispose of a juvenile delinquency case" and suggested that a finding of insufficient evidence might be required to satisfy the requirement that the order terminate the prosecution of a petition. *Id.*

11.3 Bases for Motions to Suppress Statement or Admission of Juvenile

A. Constitutional Rights

A juvenile is protected by the constitutional right against self-incrimination guaranteed by the Fifth Amendment. *See In re Gault*, 387 U.S. 1 (1967); *Mincey v. Arizona*, 437 U.S. 385, 398–400 (1978) (involuntary or coerced confession not admissible); *see also supra* § 2.4A, Constitutional Right. After initiation of juvenile proceedings, the juvenile is afforded additional protection under the Sixth Amendment right to counsel, guaranteed to juveniles under *Gault*. *See Montejo v. Louisiana*, 556 U.S. 778 (2009) (a defendant has the right to counsel under the Sixth Amendment during police interrogation). If a juvenile has been questioned in violation of these rights, counsel should file a motion to suppress to prevent the court from admitting the statement into evidence. For a further discussion of these rights, see 1 NORTH CAROLINA DEFENDER MANUAL § 14.3, Illegal Confessions or Admissions (2d ed. 2013).

B. Statutory Rights under Juvenile Code

Juveniles in custody who are being questioned have statutory rights that include and go beyond the requirements of *Miranda* warnings. *See* G.S. 7B-2101; *see also supra* § 2.4B, Statutory Rights. These rights are afforded only if the juvenile is "in custody," a term that is not defined in the statutes but is the subject of case law. *See infra* § 11.4B, Definition of "In Custody."

In setting forth the information that the juvenile must receive before custodial interrogation, the statute tracks *Miranda* with the addition of the third provision below:

1. that the juvenile has a right to remain silent;
2. that any statement the juvenile makes can be and may be used against the juvenile;
3. that the juvenile has a right to have a parent, guardian, or custodian present during questioning; and
4. that the juvenile has a right to consult with an attorney and that one will be appointed for the juvenile if the juvenile is not represented and wants representation.

G.S. 7B-2101(a); *see infra* § 11.4E, Right to Have Parent, Custodian, or Guardian Present; § 11.4F, Right to Consult with and Have Attorney Appointed.

Questioning must cease "[i]f the juvenile indicates in any manner and at any stage . . . that the juvenile does not wish to be questioned further." G.S. 7B-2101(c). The court must find that the juvenile "knowingly, willingly, and understandingly waived the juvenile's rights" before the juvenile's in-custody statement can be admitted into evidence. G.S. 7B-2101(d); *see infra* § 11.4I, Knowing, Willing, and Understanding Waiver of Rights.

If a juvenile is under age 16, the presence of a parent, guardian, custodian, or attorney is required for an in-custody admission or confession to be admitted into evidence. G.S. 7B-2101(b). The parent, custodian, or guardian must also be advised of the juvenile's rights if an attorney is not present. *Id.* These requirements may not be waived by the juvenile or the parent, custodian, or guardian. *Id.*; *see infra* § 11.4E, Right to Have Parent, Custodian, or Guardian Present.

C. Substantial Violations of Criminal Procedure Act

As part of 2015 amendments to the Juvenile Code, the General Assembly added language stating that the "provisions of G.S. 15A-974 shall apply" to suppression motions in juvenile delinquency cases. G.S. 7B-2408.5(h). G.S. 15A-974 was enacted in 1973 and "broadened" the exclusionary rule to include evidence "obtained as a result of a substantial violation" of the Criminal Procedure Act—that is, Chapter 15A of the General Statutes. *State v. Williams*, 31 N.C. App. 237, 238-39 (1976) (citing G.S. 15A-974(2)). When a court determines whether a violation was substantial, it must consider "all the circumstances," including the importance of the interest that was violated, the extent of deviation from lawful conduct, the extent to which the violation was willful, and the extent to which exclusion of the evidence will deter future violations. G.S. 15A-974(2). A court may not suppress evidence for a statutory violation if the person who committed the violation "acted under the objectively reasonable, good faith belief that the actions were lawful." *Id.*

A number of North Carolina cases have addressed whether a statutory violation warranted suppression. For example, in *State v. Norris*, 77 N.C. App. 525, 529 (1985), *disapproved on other grounds by In re Stallings*, 318 N.C. 565 (1986), the Court of Appeals held that a one-on-one show-up, conducted without a court order before the juvenile was transferred to superior court, constituted a substantial violation and should have been suppressed. The Court held in *State v. McHone*, 158 N.C. App. 117, 122 (2003), that a "search warrant application supported only by a conclusory affidavit" constituted a substantial violation under G.S. 15A-974(2). In contrast, in *State v. Satterfield*, 300 N.C. 621, 626 (1980), the Court held that an officer's failure to remind the defendant of his right to counsel before taking fluid samples pursuant to a non-testimonial identification order did not warrant suppression under G.S. 15A-974(2). In *State v. Pearson*, 356 N.C. 22, 34 (2002), the court held that an officer's failure to return an inventory of evidence seized pursuant to a search warrant to the judge who issued the search warrant did not require suppression of the evidence pursuant to G.S. 15A-974(2). Additional cases involving statutory violations can be found by searching for cases citing G.S. 15A-974(2).

11.4 Case Law: Motions to Suppress In-Custody Statements of Juveniles

A. Scope of Discussion in this Manual

This section reviews cases involving in-custody statements by juveniles. There may be additional grounds for suppressing statements that do not require that the juvenile be in custody, such as involuntary statements under the Fifth Amendment and statements in violation of the Sixth Amendment right to counsel. *See* 1 NORTH CAROLINA DEFENDER MANUAL § 14.3, Illegal Confessions or Admissions (2d ed. 2013).

B. Definition of "In Custody"

Miranda and statutory warnings are required during questioning only when the juvenile is in custody. *See* G.S. 7B-2101. The court must first determine whether the juvenile was in custody in ruling on a motion to suppress. *In re Butts*, 157 N.C. App. 609, 612–13 (2003).

The standard for determining whether a person is in custody for *Miranda* purposes is, "based on the totality of the circumstances, whether there was a formal arrest or a restraint on freedom of movement of the degree associated with a formal arrest." *State v. Buchanan*, 353 N.C. 332, 339 (2001). This is an objective test of "whether a reasonable person in the position of the defendant would believe himself to be in custody or that he had been deprived of his freedom of action in some significant way," and is not based on the subjective intent of the interrogator or the perception of the person under questioning. *Butts*, 157 N.C. App. at 613, *quoting State v. Sanders*, 122 N.C. App. 691 (1996); *State v. Buchanan*, 353 N.C. 332 (2001). The juvenile's age is a factor in the custody analysis if the officer knew how old the juvenile was at the time of questioning or if the juvenile's age was "objectively apparent to a reasonable officer." *J.D.B. v. North Carolina*, 564 U.S. 261, 274 (2011); *see also* LaToya Powell, *Applying the Reasonable Child Standard to Juvenile Interrogations After J.D.B. v. North Carolina*, ADMINISTRATION OF JUSTICE BULLETIN No. 2016/01 (Feb. 2016).

The Court of Appeals has held that the failure of the trial court to determine whether the juvenile was in custody before admitting into evidence the juvenile's statement to law enforcement officers is error. *Butts*, 157 N.C. App. at 614. If the remaining evidence is not sufficient to support an adjudication of delinquency, the trial court must dismiss the case. *Id.* at 616; *see also In re J.L.B.M.*, 176 N.C. App. 613, 625 (2006) (directing trial court to grant juvenile's motion to dismiss on remand if the court found that the juvenile was in custody when he made statements to officers because the remaining evidence was insufficient to support an adjudication).

C. Application of Standard for Determining Whether In Custody

North Carolina appellate courts have applied the test for determining whether a juvenile was in custody in the following contexts. In cases in which the court did not consider the juvenile's age in determining custody, the opinions in those cases may need to be reassessed in light of the U.S. Supreme Court's decision in *J.D.B. v. North Carolina*, 564 U.S. 261 (2011).

School office. In *In re W.R.*, 363 N.C. 244 (2009), a principal and an assistant principal escorted the juvenile to a school office and questioned him. At some point, a school resource officer entered the office and joined the questioning. The officer also searched the juvenile for weapons. After approximately thirty minutes of questioning, the juvenile admitted that he had taken a knife to school the day before. When the case was heard for adjudication, the juvenile's attorney did not make a motion to suppress the juvenile's statement or object when the court admitted the statement into evidence. The North Carolina Supreme Court upheld the juvenile's adjudication, but noted that "no motion to suppress was made, no evidence was presented and no findings were made as to either the school resource officer's actual participation in the questioning of W.R. or the custodial or noncustodial nature of the interrogation." *Id.* at 248. Based on the "limited record" of the interrogation, the Court could not conclude that the juvenile was subject to custodial interrogation, which would have required *Miranda* warnings and the protections of G.S. 7B-2101. *Id.*

The Court of Appeals held in *In re K.D.L.*, 207 N.C. App. 453 (2010), that the juvenile was improperly subject to custodial interrogation without *Miranda* warnings or the warnings in G.S. 7B-2101. In *K.D.L.*, a teacher contacted a school resource officer after finding marijuana on a classroom floor. The teacher also suspected that the marijuana belonged to the juvenile. When the officer arrived, he patted the juvenile down and transported him in his patrol car to the principal's office. The juvenile was then questioned by the principal for several hours in the presence of the officer. The Court of Appeals held that it was objectively reasonable for the juvenile to believe he was under arrest because being frisked and transported in a patrol car was not one of the "usual restraints" generally imposed during school. *Id.* at 461.

Home. In *In re Hodge*, 153 N.C. App. 102 (2002), the Court of Appeals held that the juvenile was not in custody when he was questioned by a police officer in the living room of his home. The questioning occurred in the presence of the juvenile's mother and younger brother. No court proceedings had been initiated, and the officer informed the juvenile that he did not have to talk to her and that she was not going to arrest him. Under these circumstances, the Court held that the juvenile "was not subject to a restraint on his freedom of movement of the degree associated with a formal arrest." *Id.* at 109.

The Court of Appeals reached a similar conclusion in *In re D.A.C.*, 225 N.C. App. 547 (2013). There, two officers investigating gunshots asked the juvenile to step outside of his house and talk. The juvenile agreed and went to a point about ten feet outside of the house. The juvenile's parents remained inside the house. The officers then talked to the juvenile for approximately five minutes. One of the officers was in uniform; the other was in civilian clothes. The officers did not place the juvenile under arrest, put handcuffs on him, or search his person. Based on these circumstances, the Court of Appeals held that the juvenile's admission that he fired a gun in the direction of the neighbor's house "did not result from an impermissible custodial interrogation." *Id.* at 555. One of the factors that led to the Court's holding was that the juvenile "was questioned in an open area in his own yard with his parents nearby." *Id.* at 553.

Police station. In *State v. Smith*, 317 N.C. 100 (1986) (decided under former G.S. 7A-595, now G.S. 7B-2101), *overruled in part on other grounds*, *State v. Buchanan*, 353 N.C. 332 (2001), the North Carolina Supreme Court held that the juvenile was in custody when two officers went to the juvenile's home, waited while he dressed, transported him in a police car with doors that could not be opened from the inside, read him his juvenile rights, and took him to the police station where he was again read his rights.

Public housing development. In *In re N.J.*, 230 N.C. App. 140 (2013) (unpublished), two police officers encountered the juvenile while on foot patrol in a public housing complex. The juvenile was sitting on an electrical box with three other juveniles. The officers arrested one of the other juveniles after finding marijuana in his pants pocket. The officers then found thirteen individually wrapped bags of marijuana in a cap on the ground near the electrical box. When the officers asked who the marijuana belonged to, the juvenile said that it was his. The Court of Appeals held that circumstances of the case did not "objectively suggest that a reasonable fifteen-year-old juvenile would have believed he was under arrest" because he was never handcuffed, frisked, or searched. In addition, the discussion occurred in an open area during daylight hours and the officers asked the three juveniles who were not initially arrested only one question.

D. Definition of "Interrogation"

There is no requirement under the federal constitution that officers give *Miranda* warnings to a person in custody if there is no interrogation. *State v. Ladd*, 308 N.C. 272, 280 (1983). The term "interrogation" includes both "express questioning" and its "functional equivalent." *Rhode Island v. Innis*, 446 U.S. 291, 300–01 (1980). "That is to say, the term 'interrogation' under *Miranda* refers not only to express questioning, but also to any words or actions on the part of the police (other than those normally attendant to arrest and custody) that the police should know are reasonably likely to elicit an incriminating response." *Id.* at 301.

In *State v. Jackson*, 165 N.C. App. 763 (2004), the North Carolina Court of Appeals held that officers were not required to give the juvenile defendant *Miranda* warnings because they did not subject him to interrogation. When the officers were with the defendant after a court hearing, the defendant saw a cap that had previously been admitted into evidence at the hearing. According to one of the officers, the defendant "spontaneously" stated that he knew where the cap came from. The officer responded, "[S]o do I." *Id.* at 768. The defendant then made statements indicating that he participated in a robbery. The Court of Appeals held that the officer's response to the defendant did not amount to an interrogation because the officer would not have known that it was likely to elicit an incriminating response.

In contrast, in *In re L.I.*, 205 N.C. App. 155 (2010), the Court of Appeals reversed the trial court's order denying a motion to suppress statements the juvenile made to an officer because the officer asked questions that he should have known would elicit an incriminating response from the juvenile. The juvenile was in a car that was stopped by the officer. During the stop, the officer ordered the juvenile to get out of the car and then asked her for the marijuana that he "knew she had." *Id.* at 157. The juvenile denied having any marijuana, but turned away and reached into her pants. The officer then placed the juvenile under arrest when the juvenile would not allow him to search her pants. The officer also told the juvenile that she would face an additional charge if she took drugs to the jail. In response, the juvenile told the officer that she had drugs in her coat pocket. The Court of Appeals held that the officer's questions constituted an interrogation because the officer's "objective purpose" was to obtain an admission from the juvenile. *Id.* at 162.

The Court of Appeals also held in *In re K.D.L.*, 207 N.C. App. 453 (2010), that a school resource officer engaged in interrogation of a juvenile even though the officer did not ask the juvenile any questions. The officer was contacted after a teacher found marijuana on a classroom floor and suspected that it belonged to the juvenile. The officer frisked the juvenile and transported him to the principal's office. The officer then remained in the office while the principal questioned the juvenile for several hours. The Court of Appeals held that the officer's conduct "significantly increased the likelihood [the juvenile] would produce an incriminating response to the principal's questioning." According to the Court, the officer's "near-constant supervision" of the juvenile's interrogation would have caused a reasonable person to believe the principal was interrogating him "in concert" with the officer.

E. Right to Have Parent, Custodian, or Guardian Present

Scope of right. The right to have a parent, custodian, or guardian present during custodial interrogation applies to all juveniles, including those who are 16 or over and no longer under the jurisdiction of the juvenile court. G.S. 7B-2101(a)(3); *State v. Fincher*, 309 N.C. 1 (1983) (decided under former G.S. 7A-595(a)(3), now G.S. 7B-2101(a)(3)); *State v. Smith*, 317 N.C. 100 (1986), *overruled in part on other grounds, State v. Buchanan*, 353 N.C. 332 (2001). A juvenile is a person who is under the age of 18 and is not married, emancipated, or a member of the armed forces of the United States. G.S. 7B-1501(17).

Before 2015, G.S. 7B-2101(b) stated that only juveniles under the age of 14 could not waive the requirement that a parent, guardian, custodian, or attorney be present when the juvenile made a statement during custodial interrogation. In 2015, the General Assembly extended the protection of G.S. 7B-2101(b) to juveniles under the age of 16. *See* 2015 N.C. Sess. Laws Ch. 58 (H 879). If the juvenile is younger than 16 years old, in custody, and questioned by officers without the presence of a parent, custodian, guardian, or attorney, any statement the juvenile made to the officers is "inadmissible." *In re J.L.B.M.*, 176 N.C. App. 613, 624 (2006) (citing G.S. 7B-2101(b)). If the court admits a statement from a juvenile who was younger than 16 years old, it must affirmatively find that the juvenile made the statement while in the presence of a parent, guardian, or custodian. *In re Young*, 78 N.C. App. 440, 441 (1985).

Suppression of a statement by a juvenile who is 16 years old or older is not automatic when a parent, custodian, or guardian is not present. However, if officers obtain the statement in violation of G.S. 7B-2101—for example, without advising the juvenile of the right to their presence or obtaining a waiver—the statement "must be suppressed." *State v. Branham*, 153 N.C. App. 91, 99 (2002).

Meaning of "parent, custodian, or guardian." The term "parent" is not defined in G.S. 7B-1501 or 7B-2101. There are also no cases that define the term with respect to questioning under G.S. 7B-2101. In *State v. Stanley*, 205 N.C. App. 707, 710 (2010), a criminal appeal involving sex offender registration, the Court of Appeals surveyed various definitions of the term "parent" and determined that it meant "a biological or adoptive parent." If officers obtained a statement from a juvenile in the presence of someone other than a "biological or adoptive parent"—such as a stepparent—counsel should consider filing a motion to suppress on the ground that the statement was obtained in violation of G.S. 7B-2101. *See, e.g., In re M.L.T.H.*, 200 N.C. App. 476, 488 (2009) (holding that an officer gave the juvenile an "improper choice" when advising the juvenile that he could talk to the officer in the presence of the juvenile's brother, who was not a parent, guardian, or custodian).

The term "custodian" is defined under G.S. 7B-1501(6) as "[t]he person or agency that has been awarded legal custody of a juvenile by a court." Examples of custodians include individuals who are granted custody under Chapter 50 of the North Carolina General Statutes (Divorce and Alimony). For instance, a court might grant custody of a juvenile under Chapter 50 to a family member, neighbor, or teacher.

The term "guardian" is not defined in G.S. 7B-1501 or 7B-2101. In *State v. Jones*, 147 N.C. App. 527 (2001), the juvenile defendant moved to suppress a statement that he gave to an officer in the presence of his aunt on the ground that his aunt was not a guardian under G.S. 7B-2101. The Court of Appeals stated that a guardian was a person with legal authority over the juvenile through "court-appointed authority" or "any authority conferred by government upon an individual." The Court held that the juvenile's aunt constituted a guardian because "[b]oth DSS and the local school system . . . gave [her] authority over defendant." *Id.* at 540.

In contrast, the juvenile defendant in *State v. Oglesby*, 361 N.C. 550, 555 (2007), moved to suppress a statement that he gave to an officer because the officer would *not* permit his aunt to be present during questioning. The juvenile argued that his aunt was a guardian for purposes of G.S. 7B-2101. In denying the motion to suppress, the North Carolina Supreme Court narrowed the definition of guardian to mean a person who has established a relationship with the juvenile "by legal process." The Court held that the juvenile's aunt did not qualify as a guardian because evidence that she was a "mother figure" to the defendant did not establish the "*legal* authority" necessary for her to be treated as a guardian under G.S. 7B-2101. *Id.* at 556 (emphasis in original). Although the Court did not give examples of individuals who are granted legal authority to act as guardians, G.S. 7B-600 and 35A-1220, *et seq.*, provide procedures for the appointment of guardians. Based on *Oglesby*, it would appear that a person appointed to act as a guardian under G.S. 7B-600 or 35A-1220, *et seq.*, would qualify as a guardian for purposes of G.S. 7B-2101.

Jones and *Oglesby* demonstrate the different ways in which violations of G.S. 7B-2101 might occur. In *Jones*, the juvenile defendant argued that the presence of a person who was not a guardian violated his rights. In *Oglesby*, the juvenile defendant argued that the exclusion of a person who was a guardian violated his rights. Counsel should therefore carefully analyze the circumstances surrounding any statement the juvenile made during custodial interrogation to determine whether there are grounds for suppression under G.S. 7B-2101.

Invocation and waiver of right by juvenile under 16. A juvenile who is under the age of 16 need not invoke and may not waive the requirement that a parent, guardian, custodian, or attorney be present when a statement is made during a custodial interrogation. G.S. 7B-2101(b). The right applies automatically.

The juvenile's right under G.S. 7B-2101 to have a parent, guardian, or custodian present during questioning belongs to the juvenile. A parent, custodian, or guardian cannot waive the right on the juvenile's behalf. See G.S. 7B-2101(b); *In re Butts*, 157 N.C. App. 609,

614 (2003). In *Butts*, the juvenile, who was less than 14 years of age, was questioned at the police station and made a statement without a parent, custodian, guardian, or attorney present. The lower court admitted the juvenile's statement without determining whether he was in custody on the ground that custody was irrelevant because the juvenile's father waived the right to a parent's presence by voluntarily leaving the room. In reversing and ordering a new adjudicatory hearing, the Court held that a parent cannot waive the requirement of a parent's presence during a custodial interrogation of a juvenile under the age of 14 (now, 16). The juvenile's statement would therefore be inadmissible at adjudication if he was found to be in custody at the time it was given. Similarly, in a case under former G.S. 7A-595(b) (now G.S. 7B-2101(b)), the Court held that the lower court must affirmatively find that the 12-year-old juvenile's custodial statement was made in the presence of a parent, guardian, custodian, or attorney before admitting it into evidence. *In re Young*, 78 N.C. App. 440 (1985).

Invocation and waiver of right by juvenile 16 or over. For officers to question a juvenile who is 16 years old or older and in custody, they must obtain a waiver of the right to have a parent, custodian, or guardian present. For a discussion of the requirements for waiver, see *infra* § 11.4I, Knowing, Willing, and Understanding Waiver of Rights.

When a juvenile who is 16 years old or older invokes the right to have a parent, custodian, or guardian present, questioning must cease. *State v. Branham*, 153 N.C. App. 91, 99 (2002). In *State v. Smith*, 317 N.C. 100 (1986), the juvenile defendant asked that his mother be present during questioning after he was read his rights at the police station. Before his mother arrived, two officers resumed speaking to the juvenile, which resulted in the juvenile making a confession. Even though the juvenile stated that he wanted to make a statement without his mother present and signed a waiver form, the Court held that the officers violated his statutory rights by resuming questioning after he had invoked the right to have his mother present. In questioning a juvenile who is 16 years old or older, however, police officers are not required to inform the juvenile that his parents or attorney are actually present. *State v. Gibson*, 342 N.C. 142, 149 (1995).

A parent, custodian, or guardian may not waive the juvenile's right to the parent's presence after the juvenile has invoked the right. *State v. Branham*, 153 N.C. App. 91, 98 (2002). In *Branham*, the juvenile defendant requested that his mother be present as he was being questioned. Although she was in the police station, his mother did not want to be present. The Court of Appeals held that a parent may not waive the juvenile's right under G.S. 7B-2101(a)(3), and the juvenile defendant was entitled to a new trial at which his statement would be suppressed.

In some cases, it may not be clear whether the juvenile invoked the right to have a parent, custodian, or guardian present. In criminal cases, officers are not required to cease questioning unless the defendant "articulate[s] his desire to have counsel present sufficiently clearly that a reasonable police officer in the circumstances would understand the statement to be a request for an attorney." *Davis v. United States*, 512 U.S. 452, 459 (1994). In *State v. Saldierna*, 369 N.C. 401 (2016), the Supreme Court of North Carolina extended the reasoning of *Davis* to cases involving juveniles and held that officers have "no duty to ask clarifying questions or to cease questioning" without an "unambiguous, unequivocal invocation" of the juvenile's right under G.S. 7B-2101 to the presence of a parent, custodian, or guardian.

The Supreme Court in *Saldierna* reversed the Court of Appeals' decision, which held that "an ambiguous statement touching on a juvenile's right to have a parent present during an interrogation triggers a requirement for the interviewing officer to clarify the juvenile's meaning." *State v. Saldierna*, 242 N.C. App. 347, 359 (2015). The Court of Appeals based its holding on "concerns about the special vulnerability of juveniles subject to custodial interrogations." *Id.* The Court of Appeals relied on the U.S. Supreme Court's decision in *J.D.B. v. North Carolina*, 564 U.S. 261 (2011), which recognized that children often lack the judgment to avoid choices that could be detrimental to them and that children are more susceptible to outside pressures than adults. The U.S. Supreme Court raised similar concerns in previous opinions. *See, e.g., Thompson v. Oklahoma*, 487 U.S. 815, 835 (1988) (plurality opinion) ("Inexperience, less education, and less intelligence make the teenager less able to evaluate the consequences of his or her conduct while at the same time he or she is much more apt to be motivated by mere emotion or peer pressure than is an adult."); *Gallegos v. Colorado*, 370 U.S. 49, 54 (1962) (observing that juveniles are "not equal to the police in knowledge and understanding of the consequences of the questions and answers being recorded and . . . [are] unable to know how to protect [their] own interests or how to get the benefits of [their] constitutional rights"); *Haley v. Ohio*, 332 U.S. 596, 599-600 (1948) (plurality opinion) ("[W]e cannot believe that a lad of tender years is a match for the police in such a contest [as custodial interrogation]. . . . He needs someone on whom to lean lest the overpowering presence of the law, as he knows it, crush him.").

The Supreme Court in *Saldierna* did not discuss the impact of *J.D.B.* and other U.S. Supreme Court decisions recognizing the differences between adults and juveniles. These differences may be relevant to determining in particular cases whether a reasonable officer would have considered statements made by the juvenile to be a clear request to have a parent, guardian, or custodian present during questioning. The Supreme Court also did not address provisions giving juveniles greater protection than adults in the court system. *See* G.S. 7B-2101(c) (providing that if juvenile indicates "in any manner" and "at any stage of the questioning" that the juvenile does not wish to be questioned further, the officer must cease questioning); LaToya Powell, *A Juvenile's Request for a Parent During Custodial Interrogation Must Be Unambiguous*, ON THE CIVIL SIDE, UNC SCH. OF GOV'T BLOG (Mar. 8, 2017) (discussing impact of this statutory requirement). If there is some ambiguity in the juvenile's statements about having a parent present during questioning, counsel should consider arguing that concerns about providing greater protection to juveniles would have led a reasonable officer to believe the juvenile wanted a parent present while the officer spoke to the juvenile. *See, e.g., In re T.E.F.*, 359 N.C. 570, 575, (2005) (holding that the State has a "higher burden" to protect the rights of juveniles); *Lewis v. State*, 288 N.E.2d 138, 141 (Ind. 1972) ("The concept of establishing different standards for a juvenile is an accepted legal principle since minors generally hold a subordinate and protected status in our legal system").

Even where the juvenile has not clearly invoked the statutory right to have a parent, guardian, or custodian present, the juvenile's statements are inadmissible unless the juvenile knowingly, willingly, and understandingly waived that right, which is a separate question. In *Saldierna,* the Supreme Court remanded the case for a determination of whether there was a valid waiver. For a discussion of the requirements for waiver and the result on remand, see *infra* § 11.4I, Knowing, Willing, and Understanding Waiver of Rights.

F. Right to Consult with and Have Attorney Appointed

A juvenile has the right to consult with an attorney during questioning, and an attorney must be appointed if the juvenile so requests. G.S. 7B-2101(b). Although the statute provides for the appointment of counsel during questioning, in practice questioning ceases and an attorney is appointed only if a petition is filed. The U.S. Supreme Court held in *Davis v. United States*, 512 U.S. 452, 459 (1994) that officers are not required to stop an interrogation if the defendant in a criminal case makes an "ambiguous or equivocal reference to an attorney." Relying on *Davis*, the Supreme Court of North Carolina held in *State v. Saldierna*, 369 N.C. 401 (2016), that officers do not have a duty to clarify an ambiguous assertion of the juvenile's statutory right under G.S. 7B-2101 to the presence of a parent, custodian, or guardian. *See supra* "Invocation and waiver of right by juvenile 16 or over" in § 11.4E, Right to Have Parent, Custodian, or Guardian Present. However, the U.S. Supreme Court has recognized that different treatment is required of juveniles and adults with respect to constitutional rights under *Miranda* and in other contexts. *See id.* (discussing cases). Counsel should argue that these differences warrant clarifying questions when there is some ambiguity about whether the juvenile has invoked the constitutional right to an attorney.

G. Right to Remain Silent

A juvenile has the right to remain silent. *In re Gault*, 387 U.S. 1, 55 (1967). In criminal cases, a defendant must unambiguously state that he wishes to remain silent in order for an interrogation to end. *Berghuis v. Thompkins*, 560 U.S. 370, 382 (2010). The Supreme Court of North Carolina reached a similar conclusion in *State v. Saldierna*, 369 N.C. 401 (2016), with respect to the juvenile's statutory right to have a parent, custodian, or guardian present during questioning. *See supra* "Invocation and waiver of right by juvenile 16 or over" in § 11.4E, Right to Have Parent, Custodian, or Guardian Present. However, the U.S. Supreme Court has recognized that different treatment is required of juveniles and adults with respect to constitutional rights under *Miranda* and in other contexts. *See id.* (discussing cases). Counsel should argue that these differences warrant clarifying questions when there is some ambiguity about whether the juvenile has invoked the constitutional right to silence.

H. When Questioning Must Cease

Interrogation must cease if the juvenile invokes the right to remain silent, the right to have an attorney present, or the right to have a parent, guardian, custodian present. *State v. Branham*, 153 N.C. App. 91, 95 (2002); *see also supra* § 11.4E, Right to Have Parent, Custodian, or Guardian Present. Questioning may resume if the juvenile initiates further communication with officers. *Id.*

In *State v. Johnson*, 136 N.C. App. 683 (2000), the juvenile invoked his right to silence during a custodial interrogation in his mother's presence. His mother then interrupted and told him "we need to get this straightened out today and we'll talk with him anyway." *Id.* at 686. After the juvenile "nodded affirmatively" to the officer, the officer asked if he wanted to answer questions without a lawyer or parent present. *Id.* The juvenile answered "yes" and signed a waiver of rights form. The Court held that the juvenile's nod of his head re-initiated communication with the officer after he had invoked the right to remain silent and that his statement was therefore admissible.

I.   Knowing, Willing, and Understanding Waiver of Rights

Constitutional and statutory requirements. Constitutional and statutory rights may be waived by the juvenile, except for the requirement that a parent, guardian, custodian, or attorney be present during custodial interrogation of a juvenile under 16 years of age. G.S. 7B-2101(b). Before admitting into evidence a statement resulting from a custodial interrogation, the court must make a finding that a juvenile "knowingly, willingly, and understandingly waived" his or her rights. G.S. 7B-2101(d). The finding must be supported by record evidence. *State v. Brantley*, 129 N.C. App. 725, 729 (1998). The State bears the burden of proving by a preponderance of the evidence that the waiver of both constitutional and statutory rights was "knowing and intelligent." *State v. Flowers*, 128 N.C. App. 697, 701 (1998).

Test. In determining whether a waiver of rights was voluntary, the court must look at the "totality of the circumstances," including custody, mental capacity, physical environment, and manner of interrogation. *State v. Bunnell*, 340 N.C. 74, 80 (1995). The court must consider the "specific facts and circumstances of each case, including background, experience, and conduct of the accused." *State v. Johnson*, 136 N.C. App. 683, 693 (2000); *see infra* § 11.5B, Age as Factor in Legality of Search and Seizure. A lay witness, including the interrogating officer, may offer an opinion on the juvenile's understanding of his or her rights if based on personal observation. *See State v. Johnson*, 136 N.C. App. at 693 (opinion testimony of detectives regarding the juvenile's understanding of his waiver of rights was properly admitted because they were present when the juvenile was read his rights and when he signed the waiver form). When the interrogation involves a juvenile, the court must "carefully scrutinize" the circumstances to determine whether the juvenile "legitimately waived" his rights. *State v. Reid*, 335 N.C. 647, 663 (1994).

In *State v. Brantley*, 129 N.C. App. 725 (1998), the Court of Appeals held that the juvenile knowingly, voluntarily, and understandingly waived her rights before making a statement to officers where the officers informed the juvenile that she could have a parent or guardian present and the juvenile signed a waiver of rights form describing her *Miranda* rights. Similarly, the Court held in *State v. Williams*, 209 N.C. App. 441 (2011), that the juvenile knowingly and voluntarily waived his right to have his mother present during questioning. In *Williams*, the juvenile initially invoked his right to have his mother present during questioning on a murder charge. When officers later returned to the interrogation room, the juvenile said that the officers had "misunderstood" him and that he only wanted his mother present for questioning on a separate robbery charge. *Id.* at 443. He also said that he did not want his mother present when he talked to officers about the murder charge.

In contrast, on remand from the Supreme Court's decision in *State v. Saldierna*, discussed previously, the Court of Appeals held that the juvenile did not knowingly, willingly, and understandingly waive his rights before confessing to an interrogating officer. *State v. Saldierna*, ___ N.C. App. ___, 803 S.E.2d 33 (2017), *rev. granted*, ___ N.C. ___ (Nov. 1, 2017). The juvenile was 16 years old, had an 8th grade education, and had no prior experience with police officers. His primary language was Spanish. The juvenile was also interrogated in the presence of three officers and signed an English waiver form. Immediately after signing the form, the juvenile asked to call his mother. In ruling on the juvenile's waiver, the Court of Appeals explained, "[t]o be valid, a waiver should be voluntary, not just on its face, i.e., the paper it is written on, but *in fact*. It should be unequivocal and unassailable when the subject is a juvenile." *Id.* at 41 (emphasis in original). Based on the totality of the circumstances, the Court determined that the juvenile's waiver was invalid. *Id.* at 43.

The North Carolina Court of Appeals has held that an interrogating officer does not have a duty to explain constitutional or statutory rights to a juvenile in greater detail than is required by *Miranda* and the statute. *State v. Flowers*, 128 N.C. App. 697, 700 (1998) (decided under former G.S. 7A-595(a), now G.S. 7B-2101(a)), *cited by State v. Lee*, 148 N.C. App. 518, 521 (2002); *see also supra* "Invocation and waiver of right by juvenile 16 or over" in § 11.4E, Right to Have Parent, Custodian, or Guardian Present (discussing whether officer has obligation to clarify ambiguous invocation of this statutory right). However, the Supreme Court has more recently acknowledged that juveniles possess only an "incomplete ability to understand the world around them" and that the risk of false confessions is "all the more troubling . . . when the subject of custodial interrogation is a juvenile." *J.D.B. v. North Carolina*, 564 U.S. 261, 269, 273 (2011). In addition, there is now a growing body of research demonstrating that juveniles need more protections than adults. One study concluded that commonly-used juvenile *Miranda* warnings "are far beyond the abilities of the more than 115,000 preteen offenders charged annually with criminal offenses" Richard Rogers et al., *The Comprehensibility and Contents of Juvenile Miranda Warnings*, 14 PSYCHOL. PUB. POL'Y & L. 63 (2008). In another study, juveniles age 15 and younger were significantly more likely than older juveniles to make decisions that represented compliance with authority. Thomas Grisso et al., *Juveniles' Competence to Stand Trial: A Comparison of Adolescents' and Adults' Capacities as Trial Defendants*, 27 LAW & HUM. BEHAV. 333 (2003). If counsel is assigned to a case in which the interrogating officer did not explain *Miranda* warnings to the juvenile and there is a question of whether the juvenile understood his rights before waiving them, counsel should consider presenting these studies and arguing that the juvenile's waiver was not voluntary.

Express waiver not required. Although the court must make a finding that the juvenile knowingly waived his or her rights under the statute, the court is not required to base its finding on an express waiver by the juvenile of his or her rights. If there is not an express waiver, the State has a heavy burden to show a knowing and voluntary waiver. *State v. Flowers*, 128 N.C. App. 697, 701 (1998) (decided under former G.S. 7A-595(a), now G.S. 7B-2101(a)); *North Carolina v. Butler,* 441 U.S. 369, 375–76 (1979). In *Flowers*, the Court found that the juvenile made a legally sufficient waiver when he responded that he understood after being informed of his rights and then responded to questions. There can be no waiver if a juvenile has not been properly advised of the rights at issue. *State v. Fincher*, 309 N.C. 1, 11 (1983).

J. Recording of Statements

G.S. 15A-211 requires electronic recording of custodial interrogations of juveniles in criminal investigations conducted at any place of detention. The requirement is not limited to specific offenses. The statute does not define the term "juvenile" and may apply to any person under the age of 18. *See* G.S. 7B-101(14) (defining juvenile for purposes of Juvenile Code as person under age 18); *see also State v. Fincher*, 309 N.C. 1 (1983) (applying statutory juvenile warning requirements to defendants under age 18). If investigating officers violate the statute, the trial court must consider the officers' non-compliance in adjudicating any suppression motions based on the interrogation. G.S. 15A-211(f). The failure to comply with the statute is also admissible in support of any claims that the juvenile's statement was involuntary or unreliable. *Id*. For a further discussion of the legislation, see John Rubin, *2007 Legislation Affecting Criminal Law and Procedure*, ADMINISTRATION OF JUSTICE BULLETIN No. 2008/01, at 5–6 (UNC School of Government, Jan. 2008), and John Rubin, *2011 Legislation Affecting Criminal Law and Procedure* at 35, no. 63 (UNC School of Government, Dec. 12, 2011).

11.5 Suppression of Evidence Obtained through Illegal Search and Seizure

A. Scope of Discussion in this Manual

Much of the case law regarding search and seizure is derived from criminal proceedings. The discussion in this manual is limited to age as a relevant factor in determining whether a seizure has occurred within the meaning of the Fourth Amendment and a brief review of juvenile case law regarding search and seizure in the school setting.

The North Carolina Defender Manual contains a chapter devoted to the issues surrounding warrantless search and seizure cases. *See* 1 NORTH CAROLINA DEFENDER MANUAL Ch. 15, Stops and Warrantless Searches (2d ed. 2013).

B. Age as Factor in Legality of Search and Seizure

The North Carolina Court of Appeals held in a 2007 case that age is a relevant factor in determining whether a person has been seized within the meaning of the Fourth

Amendment. *In re I.R.T.*, 184 N.C. App. 579 (2007). In *I.R.T.*, the juvenile was 15 years old when he was questioned by two officers with gang unit emblems on their shirts and carrying visible guns, who had arrived in marked police cars. Under these circumstances, including the consideration of the age of the juvenile, the Court found that a reasonable person would not have felt free to leave and that the juvenile was therefore "seized" within the meaning of the Fourth Amendment. *Id.* at 585. The Court upheld the denial of the juvenile's motion to suppress the evidence resulting from a search, however, finding that based on the juvenile's conduct and other circumstances the officers had reasonable suspicion to seize the juvenile as well as probable cause to search the juvenile.

C. Case Law: Search and Seizure at School

Standard for school searches. In *New Jersey v. T.L.O.*, 469 U.S. 325, 341–42 (1985), the U.S. Supreme Court distinguished between a search of a student in school performed by a police officer and one conducted by a school official. Law enforcement officers must conform to the requirements of the Fourth Amendment. School officials, however, are held to a lower standard. To determine the legality of a search by a school official, the court must first determine whether the search was justified at its inception. Second, the court must determine whether the search was reasonably related to the circumstances that initially justified the search. In *In re Murray*, 136 N.C. App. 648, 652 (2000), the North Carolina Court of Appeals followed *T.L.O.* and held that the search of a student's book bag at school by a principal was reasonable under this standard.

In *In re D.D.*, 146 N.C. App. 309, 319 (2001), the Court of Appeals applied the standard from *T.L.O.* and upheld a search of a juvenile by police officers working "in conjunction with" school officials. The Court has since upheld other searches and seizures of juveniles by school resource officers under the *T.L.O.* standard. *See, e.g., In re J.F.M. & T.J.B.*, 168 N.C. App. 143 (2005) (upholding detention of a student by a school resource officer); *In re S.W.*, 171 N.C. App. 335 (2005) (affirming search of a student by an officer who worked "exclusively" as a school resource officer); *In re D.L.D.*, 203 N.C. App. 434, 439 (2010) (upholding search of a student at school by a sheriff's corporal assigned to the school and who had made "numerous arrests" there). The Court of Appeals has stated that the *T.L.O.* standard applies to officers who are "primarily responsible to the school district rather than the local police department." *In re J.F.M. & T.J.B.*, 168 N.C. App. at 147.

The Court has also recognized that a school search of a juvenile by "outside law enforcement officers" would be weighed against the standard of probable cause. *In re D.D.*, 146 N.C. App. at 318. Other courts have reached similar conclusions. *See, e.g., State v. Meneese*, 282 P.3d 83, 88 (Wash. 2012) (school resource officer with police duties, but no authority to discipline students, held to the standard of probable cause for search of juvenile's backpack); *Patman v. State*, 537 S.E.2d 118, 120 (Ga. App. 2000) (police officer working special duty at a high school required to have probable cause to search juvenile's jacket pocket), *overruled on other grounds by State v. Kazmierczak*, 771 S.E.2d 473, 479 (Ga. App. 2015).

Intrusive school searches. Although searches by school officials are not subject to probable cause, intrusive searches might not survive scrutiny under the lower standard outlined in *T.L.O.* In *Safford Unified Sch. Dist. No. 1 v. Redding*, 557 U.S. 364, 377 (2009), the U.S. Supreme Court held that a strip search of a 13-year-old student by an assistant principal was unreasonable where there was no indication of danger to students from the type and quantity of drugs that led to the search and where there was no reason to suspect that the student was carrying pills in her underwear. Based on *Redding*, the North Carolina Court of Appeals reversed a delinquency adjudication based on drugs found during a "bra-lift" that was conducted during a school-wide search because the search lacked "individualized grounds for suspecting" that the juvenile had drugs on her person. *In re T.A.S.*, 213 N.C. App. 273, 280-81 (2011). However, the North Carolina Supreme Court vacated the Court of Appeals opinion and remanded the case to district court for further findings. *In re T.A.S.*, 366 N.C. 269, 269 (2012).

11.6   Suppression of Illegal Identifications

A.   Constitutional Grounds

Due Process prohibits identification procedures that are impermissibly suggestive. For a discussion of applicable law and cases addressing whether identification procedures are impermissibly suggestive, see 1 NORTH CAROLINA DEFENDER MANUAL § 14.4, Illegal Identification Procedures (2d ed. 2013).

B.   Eyewitness Identification Reform Act

In 2007, the North Carolina General Assembly enacted the Eyewitness Identification Reform Act (hereinafter "the Act") in order to create uniform eyewitness identification procedures and reduce the risk of misidentification. *See* G.S. 15A-284.50 through G.S. 15A-284.53. The Act initially applied only to photo line-ups and live line-ups, not show-ups. *State v. Rawls*, 207 N.C. App. 415, 423 (2010). In 2015, the General Assembly amended the Act so that it would also apply to show-ups. *See* 2015 N.C. Sess. Laws Ch. 212 (H 566).

Although the Act does not specify that it is applicable to juvenile delinquency proceedings, the purpose of the Act is "to help solve crime, convict the guilty, and exonerate the innocent" by improving eyewitness identification procedures. G.S. 15A-284.51. As these ends are equally important in juvenile court, counsel should argue that any eyewitness identification of a juvenile by lineup must comply with the requirements of the Act.

The Act provides several requirements for photo line-ups. For instance, photo line-ups must be conducted by an independent administrator, who must show the photos to the witness sequentially, one at a time. G.S. 15A-284.52(b). The Act also provides requirements for show-ups. A show-up is only permitted "when a suspect matching the description of the perpetrator is located in close proximity in time and place to the crime, or there is reasonable belief that the perpetrator has changed his or her appearance in close time to the crime, and only if there are circumstances that require the immediate display of a suspect to an eyewitness." G.S. 15A-284.52(c1). Officers may not conduct a show-up with a photograph, but must use a live suspect. *Id.*

There are two remedies for non-compliance with the Act that could be argued in a juvenile case. First, failure to comply with any of the statutory requirements may be considered by the court in ruling on a motion to suppress an eyewitness identification. Second, failure to comply with any of the statutory requirements is admissible as evidence to support a claim of eyewitness misidentification if the evidence is otherwise admissible. G.S. 15A-284.52(d)(1), (2). If a juvenile line-up or show-up does not comply with statutory requirements, counsel should cite the Act in a written motion to suppress, in argument, and in questioning regarding eyewitness misidentification.

For a further discussion of the Eyewitness Identification Reform Act, *see* John Rubin, *2007 Legislation Affecting Criminal Law and Procedure,* ADMINISTRATION OF JUSTICE BULLETIN No. 2008/01, at 2–4 (Jan. 2008).

Chapter 12
Adjudicatory Hearings

12.1 Overview

The adjudicatory hearing is the hearing before a district court judge to determine whether a juvenile has committed a delinquent act. At the hearing, the juvenile can either enter an admission to the allegations in the petition or contest the allegations. If the juvenile contests the allegations, the State must prove the allegations beyond a reasonable doubt. Counsel for the juvenile may cross-examine the State's witnesses and may present testimony and other evidence. Procedures for adjudicatory hearings are set forth in Article 24 of the Juvenile Code, G.S. 7B-2400 through 7B-2414.

This chapter outlines the basic procedures for an adjudicatory hearing. Many aspects of the adjudicatory process are discussed in greater detail in other chapters, which are referenced throughout this chapter.

12.2 Preliminary Matters

A. Amendment of Petition

The petition may be amended with permission of the court if the amendment does not change the nature of the offense alleged. The juvenile must be granted time to prepare a defense to the amended petition. G.S. 7B-2400; *see supra* § 6.3D, Amendment of Petition.

B. Capacity to Proceed

The juvenile must have capacity to proceed before an adjudicatory hearing may commence. Several procedures for determining capacity in criminal court (G.S. 15A-1001, 15A-1002, and 15A-1003) apply to delinquency proceedings. G.S. 7B-2401; *see supra* Chapter 7, Capacity to Proceed.

C. Open or Closed Hearing

The adjudicatory hearing is generally open to the public. G.S. 7B-2402. It may be closed for good cause on motion of a party or the court, subject to the right of the juvenile to an open hearing. G.S. 7B-2402; *see supra* § 2.7, Right to an Open Hearing.

D. Motions before Adjudication

Motions concerning the adjudicatory proceedings, such as a motion to suppress, should generally be filed and set for hearing before the date of adjudication. *See supra* § 6.3H, Defects in Petition: Timing of Motion; § 11.2A, Timing of Motions. This will allow time for counsel to prepare based on the court's rulings on evidence and other matters. An oral motion can and should be made at the time of the adjudicatory hearing, however, where counsel has not been afforded the opportunity to file one in writing.

E. Continuances

Statutory grounds. A continuance may be granted by the court for good cause for as long as is reasonably required:

- to receive evidence, reports, or assessments requested by the court;
- to receive other information needed in the best interest of the juvenile;
- to allow a reasonable time for the parties to conduct expeditious discovery; or
- in "extraordinary circumstances" when necessary for the proper administration of justice or in the best interests of the juvenile.

G.S. 7B-2406; *see In re Lail*, 55 N.C. App. 238, 240 (1981) (grounds for continuance motion must be established and, if based on absence of a witness, an affidavit stating facts to be proved by the witness must be tendered).

Constitutional grounds. A continuance may also be based on the juvenile's right to effective assistance of counsel and right to confront one's accusers under the Sixth and Fourteenth Amendments to the United States Constitution and Article I, §§ 19, 23, and 24 of the North Carolina Constitution. *See* 1 NORTH CAROLINA DEFENDER MANUAL § 13.4A, Motion for Continuance (2d ed. 2013). Counsel should base a request for a continuance on both constitutional and statutory grounds.

Filing the motion. It is better practice to file a written motion for continuance stating the grounds for the continuance in advance of the hearing date if possible. The motion should be served on the prosecutor and discussed with the juvenile court counselor. At a minimum it is good practice to notify the prosecutor of a continuance request as early as possible and seek consent to the continuance or suggest that witnesses be placed on call so that they can come to court if the motion to continue is denied. An oral motion to continue may be necessary if discovery is delivered by the prosecutor on or just before the hearing date and counsel needs time to review the information with the juvenile.

If a continuance motion is denied, counsel should ensure that the motion for continuance and the reasons supporting it are on the record. Counsel could also request that the proceeding be bifurcated, with the State's evidence presented on one day and the juvenile's evidence presented at a subsequent session of court, so that a necessary defense witness can be called at a later date.

Limitations on continuances. Continuances of adjudicatory hearings may be limited based on the mandate of the Juvenile Code for the court to "proceed with all possible speed in making and implementing determinations." G.S. 7B-1500(4). Counsel should be prepared to provide a clear and compelling reason why a continuance is necessary.

Because continuances are limited by local rules in some districts, counsel should be familiar with local rules and policies restricting continuances. Local rules for each district are available on the Administrative Office of the Courts website.

F. Requirement of Separate Adjudicatory Hearing

Before 2015, the Court of Appeals held in *In re J.J., Jr.*, 216 N.C. App. 366, 369 (2011), that it was proper for the trial court to hold a probable cause hearing, transfer hearing, and adjudicatory hearing in "one proceeding." The Court reached a similar conclusion in *In re G.C.*, 230 N.C. App. 511, 522 (2013). In 2015, the General Assembly enacted a reform bill for the Juvenile Code. *See* 2015 N.C. Sess. Laws Ch. 58 (H 879). As part of the legislation, the adjudication hearing must now be a separate proceeding from probable cause or transfer hearings. G.S. 7B-2202(f)(2), 7B-2203(d). The legislation thus reverses the holdings of *In re J.J., Jr.* and *In re G.C.* and requires bifurcated hearings. In theory, the court could hold a separate adjudicatory proceeding on the same day as the earlier proceeding. Counsel should object if additional time is needed to prepare for the adjudicatory hearing or proceeding with the adjudicatory hearing would otherwise not be in the juvenile's interest.

G. Discovery

The State should provide counsel with all discovery before the adjudicatory hearing so that counsel can prepare to cross-examine witnesses and present a zealous defense against the allegations. *See supra* Chapter 10, Discovery. Counsel may need to contact the prosecutor if discovery is not delivered in a timely manner. If discovery is not provided sufficiently in advance for counsel to prepare, a motion to continue or for sanctions may be necessary. *See, e.g., In re A.M.*, 220 N.C. App. 136, 138 (2012) (trial court erred by depriving juvenile of any remedy, such as granting a motion in limine or continuing the case, for the State's failure to disclose the name of a witness during discovery).

H. Voluntary Dismissal by Prosecutor

For many years, there was some uncertainty among prosecutors about whether the State had the authority to dismiss juvenile delinquency petitions. As part of the 2015 reform of the Juvenile Code, the General Assembly made clear that prosecutors are permitted to voluntarily dismiss juvenile petitions with or without leave. G.S. 7B-2404(b). The statute allows the prosecutor to dismiss a petition with leave if the juvenile failed to appear in court; the prosecutor may refile the petition "if the juvenile is apprehended or apprehension is imminent." *Id.* The statute does not specify any other circumstances in which a prosecutor may dismiss a petition with leave.

I. Preparation for the Juvenile's Appearance

Counsel should advise the juvenile as to suitable courtroom attire and demeanor. If the juvenile is in detention, counsel should make arrangements with staff for the juvenile to wear appropriate clothing and to ensure that the juvenile will not be brought into court in handcuffs or shackles. *See supra* § 8.6B, Shackling.

12.3   Negotiating an Admission

A.   Juvenile Defender Performance Guidelines

Admissions and negotiations over admissions are discussed in Performance Guidelines
for Appointed Counsel in Juvenile Delinquency Proceedings at the Trial Level § 8 (2007)
adopted by the North Carolina Commission on Indigent Defense Services, and reprinted
infra in Chapter 18 of this manual.

B.   Negotiation with the Prosecutor

Counsel should contact the prosecutor in each case to discuss the possibility of
negotiating an admission. The prosecutor may be willing to accept an admission to a
misdemeanor rather than a felony or make some other concession that would benefit the
juvenile. In some districts, the prosecutor may be willing to continue adjudication with
the agreement that the petition will be dismissed if the juvenile abides by certain
conditions, or enter into a similar agreement that disposition will be continued. If the
prosecutor makes an admission offer, counsel must inform the juvenile of the offer even
if the offer does not seem favorable to the juvenile and is likely to be rejected. *See, e.g.,
State v. Simmons*, 65 N.C. App. 294, 299 (1983) (holding that a defense attorney in a
criminal case has a duty to advise the defendant if the State makes a plea offer).

C.   Discussion of Options with Juvenile

Counsel should discuss the allegations and evidence with the juvenile before the hearing,
advising the juvenile of the strengths and weaknesses of the case. The juvenile must be
informed of the right to contest the allegations and have the court adjudicate the matter
after hearing the evidence, and that these rights are waived by making an admission. The
juvenile should be informed that the petition must be dismissed if the court does not find
that the State has proven the allegations in the petition beyond a reasonable doubt.
Counsel should advise the juvenile regarding defense strategies and the consequences of
an adjudication based on the allegations.

Counsel should discuss the possible benefits and risks of a contested adjudicatory hearing
versus negotiating an admission. Considerations might include whether there is an
eyewitness, physical evidence, or an admissible confession or statement of a co-
respondent. The ability to expunge an adjudication of delinquency may also be an
important factor in making decisions about an admission because some records of
adjudication may not be expunged. G.S. 7B-3200(b); *see infra* Chapter 17, Expunction of
Juvenile Records. Additionally, certain juvenile adjudications may be used in subsequent
criminal proceedings. For example, prior adjudications may affect the juvenile in a
subsequent criminal case at the time bail is set, during plea negotiations, at trial for
impeachment purposes, and as an aggravating factor at sentencing. G.S. 7B-3000(e), (f);
see supra "Statutory exceptions for use in limited criminal court proceedings" in § 2.8A,
Juvenile Court Records. Counsel should advise the juvenile that an admission has the
same legal effect as an adjudication by the court. The juvenile must weigh the likelihood

of an adjudication for the offense alleged versus the potential for dismissal in considering a negotiated admission. Counsel should also advise the juvenile of the possible dispositional orders pursuant to an adjudication on the petition or a negotiated admission.

Counsel should advise the juvenile that he can appeal an admission and challenge errors in the court's acceptance of an admission. *See infra* § 16.3F, Appeal Involving an Admission by a Juvenile. However, counsel should also advise the juvenile that the State will have the opportunity to pursue any of the original charges again if the appeal is successful and the admission is vacated. *See In re D.A.F.*, 179 N.C. App. 832, 837 (2006) (holding that the juvenile's successful challenge to his admission "place[d] the parties as they were at the beginning of the proceedings"). In addition, counsel should advise the juvenile that any concessions by the State that were included in the admission agreement will no longer be enforceable if the admission is vacated. *See id.* (reinstating three charges that were dismissed as part of the juvenile's admission agreement with the State); *see also State v. Fox*, 34 N.C. App. 576, 579 (1977) ("Where a defendant elects not to stand by his portion of a plea agreement, the State is not bound by its agreement to forego the greater charge.").

There are special considerations in negotiations over an admission if the juvenile is not a citizen of the United States. Counsel should investigate negotiation of an admission that will not jeopardize the juvenile's opportunity to remain in the country or become a legal citizen. *See infra* § 12.7, Collateral Effects of Adjudication.

D. Decision of Juvenile

All admission offers must be conveyed to the juvenile by counsel in a confidential setting. Counsel should explain all considerations regarding an admission offer and may explain the offer to a parent with the juvenile's consent. It is the decision of the juvenile, however, whether to accept an admission offer or proceed to adjudication.

12.4 Conduct of the Hearing on an Admission

A. Entering an Admission

After preliminary matters are concluded the court must inquire of the juvenile whether the allegations in the petition are "admitted" or "denied." *In re Wilson*, 153 N.C. App. 196, 197 (2002), *citing* G.S. 7B-2407, 7B-2408 (proper inquiry by court is whether the juvenile "admits" or "denies" the allegations, and juvenile's counsel should respond in kind; use of terms "responsible" or "not responsible" is not correct).

Counsel should ensure that the hearing is on the record. This will allow appellate review of the procedures that resulted in the admission.

B. Admission by Juvenile

Court must personally address juvenile. Before an admission may be accepted, the judge must personally inform the juvenile of statutory rights and determine whether the juvenile understands the consequences of an admission. G.S. 7B-2407(a). Specifically, the judge must:

- inform the juvenile of the right to remain silent and that any statement the juvenile makes may be used against the juvenile;
- determine that the juvenile understands the nature of the charge;
- inform the juvenile of the right to deny the allegations;
- inform the juvenile that by making an admission the right to confront witnesses is waived;
- determine that the juvenile is satisfied with the juvenile's representation; and
- inform the juvenile of the most restrictive disposition on the charge.

G.S. 7B-2407(a)(1)–(6).

The language of G.S. 7B-2407(a) is mandatory, and the failure of the court to address any one of these statutory provisions with the juvenile constitutes reversible error. *In re T.E.F.*, 359 N.C. 570, 575-76 (2005). A signed transcript of admission will not cure an insufficient colloquy with the juvenile that omits the required inquiries. *In re A.W.*, 182 N.C. App. 159, 162 (2007). If the court imposes a disposition that exceeds the disposition described in the transcript of admission or the court's colloquy with the juvenile, the juvenile must be given an opportunity to withdraw the admission. *In re D.A.F.*, 179 N.C. App. 832, 837 (2006); *In re W.H.*, 166 N.C. App. 643, 647 (2004).

Discussions about admission. The court must determine that the admission is the result of an informed choice by the juvenile before accepting an admission. This determination must be based on inquiries by the court of the prosecutor, the juvenile's attorney, and the juvenile as to whether there were prior discussions regarding the terms of the admission and whether there was any improper pressure on the juvenile to admit. G.S. 7B-2407(b).

Factual basis for admission. An admission may be accepted by the court only if the judge determines that there is a factual basis for the admission. The court may base this decision on any of the following:

- a statement of the facts from the prosecutor;
- a written statement of the juvenile;
- sworn testimony, which may contain reliable hearsay; or
- a statement of facts by the juvenile's attorney.

G.S. 7B-2407(c).

The statute does not recognize other sources for a factual basis. In *In re D.C.*, 191 N.C. App. 246, 248 (2008), the Court of Appeals held that G.S. 7B-2407(c) "does not provide that a juvenile petition may serve as information for determining that there is a factual basis for admitting a juvenile's plea." Based on the limited number of sources described in G.S. 7B-2407(c) and the Court's strict interpretation of the statute in *In re D.C.*, it seems unlikely that a mere transcript of admission or stipulation to the existence of a factual basis, without supporting information from at least one of the above sources, would be sufficient to establish the factual basis for an admission.

If the prosecutor provides a statement of the facts, counsel should request an opportunity to supplement the statement with mitigating or conflicting information as appropriate. Counsel should ask to question witnesses if they might provide helpful information. Caution must be exercised by counsel in providing facts or asking additional questions, however, to avoid presenting or eliciting information that may be harmful to the juvenile.

Transcript of admission by juvenile. Counsel should always submit to the court a "Transcript of Admission by Juvenile," filled out by the juvenile, juvenile's counsel, and the prosecutor. *See* Form AOC-J-410 (Transcript of Admission by Juvenile) (Mar. 2012). This will confirm any negotiations and protect the record on appeal. Although judges in some districts do not require written transcripts of admissions for misdemeanors, counsel should insist that they be completed and filed.

The transcript form includes the information that the judge is required to address personally with the juvenile pursuant to G.S. 7B-2407. Completion and entry of the Transcript of Admission into evidence does not fulfill the court's statutory duties if the court does not, in fact, address the juvenile personally regarding the matters on the form. *In re A.W.*, 182 N.C. App. 159, 162 (2007).

Counsel should review the transcript of admission with the juvenile and assist the juvenile in completing the form. An admission should not be entered if the juvenile does not understand what is being admitted and the possible consequences thereof. A juvenile's inability to understand the information in the transcript may indicate the need for counsel to move for an evaluation of capacity to proceed. *See supra* § 7.5, Standard for Capacity to Proceed to Adjudication. Counsel should make a copy of the transcript to review with the juvenile as the judge is reciting the questions.

***Alford* Admission.** In *North Carolina v. Alford*, 400 U.S. 25 (1970), the U.S. Supreme Court held that a defendant may enter a guilty plea while maintaining innocence. The trial court may accept the plea as long as the defendant enters the plea knowingly, voluntarily, and intelligently. *State v. McClure*, 280 N.C. 288, 294 (1972). A conviction based on an *Alford* plea carries the consequences of a conviction based on a guilty plea. *State v. Alston*, 139 N.C. App. 787, 793 (2000).

In *In re C.L.*, 217 N.C. App. 109 (2011), the Court of Appeals upheld an *Alford* admission in a juvenile delinquency case. The juvenile did not challenge the validity of the *Alford* admission and argued instead that the trial court failed to ensure that he understood he would be treated as guilty based on his *Alford* admission. Applying a totality of circumstances test, the court found that the juvenile's admission was entered knowingly, voluntary, and intelligently. *Id.* at 116. The juvenile did not argue that the trial court failed to comply with the colloquy requirements in G.S. 7B-2407 for the taking of an admission; the Court of Appeals therefore declined to apply the "strict compliance" test articulated in *In re T.E.F.*, 359 N.C. 570 (2005), for the taking of admissions.

If the juvenile intends to enter an *Alford* admission as part of a negotiated arrangement, counsel should obtain the prosecutor's consent to avoid withdrawal of the arrangement if the prosecutor is dissatisfied with the juvenile's unwillingness to admit responsibility.

12.5 Conduct of Contested Adjudicatory Hearing

A. Sequestering Witnesses

Before the adjudicatory hearing begins, counsel should move to sequester witnesses who might be called to testify at the adjudicatory hearing if doing so would benefit the defense. It is usually helpful to the juvenile for the State's witnesses to be sequestered. This prevents subsequent witnesses from conforming their testimony to prior testimony and requires them to rely only on their own memory of events.

B. Attachment of Jeopardy

Jeopardy attaches when the court begins to hear evidence regarding the allegations in the petition. G.S. 7B-2414; *In re Phillips*, 128 N.C. App. 732, 734 (1998). If there is a procedural defect depriving the court of jurisdiction, however, jeopardy does not ordinarily attach. *See supra* § 6.3D, Amendment of Petition.

C. Rules of Evidence

The Juvenile Code provides that the rules of evidence in criminal cases are applicable to adjudicatory hearings. G.S. 7B-2408. Evidentiary rules are derived from the North Carolina Rules of Evidence, G.S. 8C-1; statutes governing criminal and delinquency cases; and case law. Pertinent rules include North Carolina Rules of Evidence 401 through 412, regarding relevance; Rules 701 through 706, regarding opinion testimony; and Rules 801 through 806, regarding hearsay. Pertinent statutory evidence provisions include G.S. 15A-1225.1, 15A-1225.2, and 15A-1225.3, which involve remote testimony of child witnesses, witnesses with developmental disabilities or mental retardation, and forensic analysts.

Several juvenile statutes concern admissibility of evidence at adjudication. G.S. 7B-2408 provides that no statement of a juvenile to a juvenile court counselor during the preliminary inquiry and evaluation process is admissible at adjudication. G.S. 7B-3201 provides that an adjudication of delinquency may be used to impeach the testimony of a juvenile respondent in a subsequent proceeding or of a juvenile witness in a delinquency proceeding, regardless of whether the juvenile's record has been expunged. *See also In re S.S.T.*, 165 N.C. App. 533, 534 (2004) (evidence of prior adjudications of delinquency properly admitted to impeach respondent under G.S. 7B-2408; Rule of Evidence 609(d), limiting use of juvenile adjudications for impeachment, does not apply to testimony by juvenile in juvenile delinquency proceeding). The Rules of Evidence give the court some discretion in deciding whether certain evidence regarding juvenile witnesses will be admitted. *See, e.g., In re Oliver*, 159 N.C. App. 451, 455 (2003) (court did not abuse discretion under Rule 608(b) by refusing to admit into evidence school disciplinary record of juvenile witness or by refusing to allow cross-examination concerning contents of record); *see also* N.C. R. EVID. 403 (court may exclude evidence if its probative value is substantially outweighed by unfair prejudice or other factors).

D. Burden of Proof

The State has the burden of proving the allegations in the petition and the identity of the juvenile as the perpetrator beyond a reasonable doubt. G.S. 7B-2409; *see supra* § 2.5, Right to Standard of Proof Beyond a Reasonable Doubt. Every element of the offense alleged in the petition must be proved by the State. *In re May*, 357 N.C. 423, 426 (2003). Although statutes and case law are clear on this point, it should be reiterated by counsel at the close of the evidence.

E. Record of the Proceedings

The adjudicatory hearing must be recorded by stenographic notes or by electronic or mechanical means. G.S. 7B-2410. Counsel should request a court reporter if there are concerns about the adequacy of a recording. Although an inaccurate transcript may be the basis for a new adjudication, the appellate court may find an incomplete transcript sufficient for appellate review. *In re D.W.*, 171 N.C. App. 496, 503–04 (2005) (although there was no record of the juvenile's testimony on direct examination, the transcript of the juvenile's cross-examination and his attorney's argument was an adequate alternative); *In re Lineberry*, 154 N.C. App. 246, 257 (2002) (tape recording of adjudicatory hearing was adequate under statute even though certain portions were inaudible and were not transcribed; transcript was not so inaccurate as to prevent meaningful review by appellate court).

F. Presentation of Evidence

State's evidence. If the juvenile denies the allegations in the petition, the State must proceed with presentation of evidence. Counsel should be alert for the need to object to inadmissible testimony and should state the grounds for the objection, such as hearsay or expert opinion without proper foundation. Failure to object is likely to constitute a waiver of the objection to admissibility. Unless the court allows a continuing or line objection to a particular line of testimony, an objection, with stated grounds, should be made each time the objectionable evidence is introduced.

The juvenile has the right to cross-examine the State's witnesses. G.S. 7B-2405(3). Counsel should prepare questions for cross-examination before the hearing, derived from discovery, investigation, and counsel's theory of defense. The direct testimony of the

State's witnesses may generate additional areas to pursue on cross-examination. In some instances it may be better not to cross-examine a witness, particularly if the direct testimony was not harmful to the juvenile's case or the answer is unknown and potentially harmful to the juvenile's case. Asking no questions also may underscore the lack of importance of the witness.

Counsel may contact a State's witness who is not represented by an attorney but generally cannot compel the witness to submit to an interview. *See* 1 NORTH CAROLINA DEFENDER MANUAL § 4.4C, Examinations and Interviews of Witnesses (2d ed. 2013). According to Rule 4.2 of the North Carolina Rules of Professional Conduct, counsel may not communicate with any witness who is represented by an attorney without the permission of the attorney.

The North Carolina State Bar has also adopted specific opinions on communication with child witnesses. North Carolina State Bar Ethics Opinion RPC 249 (1997) states that a lawyer may not communicate with a child who is represented by a guardian ad litem or an attorney advocate unless the lawyer obtains their consent. 2009 North Carolina State Bar Formal Ethics Opinion 7 (2012) states that neither a defense attorney nor prosecutor may interview an unrepresented child who is the alleged victim of physical or sexual abuse in a criminal case if the child is younger than the age of maturity as provided in G.S. 7B-2101(b). That statute addresses in-custody interrogations, but the State Bar adopted the age in that statute as the benchmark for interviews in this context. At the time of the State Bar's opinion, the age in G.S. 7B-2101(b) was 14, but the opinion states that the opinion would be modified if the General Assembly changed the age designation. The age of maturity under G.S. 7B-2101(b) was revised in 2015 and is currently 16. A lawyer may interview an unrepresented child under 16 in this kind of case with the consent of a non-accused parent or guardian or a court order allowing the lawyer to seek an interview with the child without such consent. If the child has a guardian ad litem or attorney advocate, the lawyer also must obtain that person's consent under the earlier State Bar opinion.

Important witnesses, such as investigating officers and eyewitnesses, often will need to be thoroughly cross-examined. Counsel must be careful, however, not to open the door through cross-examination to testimony that would otherwise be inadmissible.

Juvenile's evidence. Counsel should confer with the juvenile to decide whether evidence will be presented on behalf of the juvenile. If the State has presented a weak case, it may be good strategy to present no evidence and to renew the motion to dismiss. A motion that is not granted at the close of the State's evidence might be granted at the close of all evidence.

Counsel should interview all witnesses that will be called on behalf of the juvenile. A person who lacks credibility or who seems unsure of the facts may weaken the juvenile's case even if some of the testimony would be helpful. An expert witness must be qualified and tendered to the court as such in order for the expert's opinion to be admissible. *See* N.C. R. EVID. 702. Most experts who have testified in cases before are familiar with this process and will have documentation concerning education, research, publications, and work experience.

An important decision is whether the juvenile will testify. Counsel should explore with the juvenile those matters that could be raised during cross-examination, especially earlier contradictory statements of the juvenile, if any, and questions that might be posed to impeach the juvenile's credibility. A mock direct and cross-examination of the juvenile may be helpful. Although counsel should advise the juvenile on whether testifying will be beneficial, the decision whether to testify is ultimately the juvenile's.

G. Motion to Dismiss

The juvenile's right to appeal the denial of a motion to dismiss is subject to multiple rules imposed by the North Carolina Rules of Appellate Procedure and case law. Counsel should take great care to comply with the rules to preserve the juvenile's right to challenge the court's ruling on appeal should it deny the motion to dismiss.

First, counsel should always make a motion to dismiss at the close of the State's evidence and then at the close of all the evidence. The failure to do so waives any sufficiency arguments on appeal. *In re Rikard*, 161 N.C. App. 150, 155 (2003) (order of adjudication was affirmed on basis that juvenile failed to renew motion to dismiss at close of all evidence); *In re Hodge*, 153 N.C. App. 102, 107 (2002) (same); *In re Clapp*, 137 N.C. App. 14, 19 (2000) (juvenile was precluded from challenging the sufficiency of the evidence on appeal because he "failed to move for dismissal at the close of the evidence").

Second, as part of the motion, counsel should always assert that the evidence is insufficient to support each element of each offense. The failure to challenge each element could harm the juvenile's chance of relief on appeal. If counsel challenges a specific element in district court and loses and the appellate attorney challenges a different element on appeal, the Court of Appeals might dismiss the sufficiency argument. *See, e.g., State v. Euceda-Valle*, 182 N.C. App. 268, 271 (2007) (rejecting sufficiency argument because the defendant presented "a different argument on appeal than that which he argued to the trial court"). If there are specific weaknesses in the State's evidence, counsel should identify those weaknesses for the court after asserting that the evidence is insufficient for each element.

Third, counsel should always assert as part of the motion to dismiss that there is a variance between the crime alleged in the petition and any crime that might be supported by the evidence. If counsel does not argue as part of the motion to dismiss that there is a variance, any argument involving a variance that the juvenile raises on appeal will be waived. *State v. Pickens*, 346 N.C. 628, 645 (1997); *State v. Mason*, 222 N.C. App. 223, 226 (2012). Thus, counsel should first say that he or she is moving to dismiss for insufficient evidence of each element of each offense. Counsel should then argue for dismissal on the basis of a variance between the offense or theory alleged in the petition and the evidence presented at the adjudicatory hearing. If the variance argument is successful, the trial court must dismiss the offense alleged in the petition for insufficient evidence. The trial court may not adjudicate the juvenile delinquent of an offense not alleged in the petition. *See In re Griffin*, 162 N.C. App. 487, 494 (2004) (vacating adjudication for first-degree sexual offense where the theory alleged in the petition was based on the use of force, but the evidence presented at the adjudicatory hearing involved a separate theory of guilt based on the relative ages of the juvenile and the victim).

Fourth, counsel should always constitutionalize the motion to dismiss for insufficient evidence by asserting that the denial of the motion would violate the Fourteenth Amendment to the United States Constitution and Article I, § 19 of the North Carolina Constitution. Counsel should constitutionalize the motion to dismiss for fatal variance by asserting that adjudicating the juvenile on a theory not supported by the petition would violate the Fourteenth Amendment of the United States Constitution and Article I, §§ 19, 12, and 24 of the North Carolina Constitution.

When the trial court rules on a motion to dismiss a petition in a juvenile delinquency case, the juvenile "is entitled to the application of the same rules in weighing the evidence against him on a motion for nonsuit or to dismiss as if he were an adult criminal defendant." *In re Vinson*, 298 N.C. 640, 656 (1979). The court must determine whether the State presented "substantial evidence of each of the material elements of the offense alleged." *In re Eller*, 331 N.C. 714, 717 (1992). When the evidence raises no more than a suspicion that the juvenile committed the offense, the court must grant the motion to dismiss. *In re R.N.*, 206 N.C. App. 537, 540 (2010). "This is true even though the suspicion so aroused by the evidence is strong." *Vinson*, 298 N.C. at 657. The court must consider the evidence in the light most favorable to the State and give the State any reasonable inference that can be drawn therefrom. *In re A.W.*, 209 N.C. App. 596, 599 (2011). The court must also consider evidence offered by the juvenile that explains or clarifies the State's evidence, as well as exculpatory evidence presented by the State. *State v. Bates*, 309 N.C. 528, 535 (1983); *State v. Bruton*, 264 N.C. 488, 499 (1965).

12.6 Order of Adjudication

If the court does not find that the allegations in the petition have been proved beyond a reasonable doubt, it must dismiss the petition with prejudice. G.S. 7B-2411. The juvenile must be released if in custody. *Id.*

If the court finds that the allegations have been proved beyond a reasonable doubt, it must state this in a written adjudication order. G.S. 7B-2409, 7B-2411. If the court fails to apply the reasonable doubt standard or it is unclear which standard the court applied, the adjudication order is subject to reversal. *See In re C.B.*, 187 N.C. App. 803, 807 (2007) (reversing adjudication order that applied both the reasonable doubt and clear, cogent, and convincing standards to the evidence); *In re Eades*, 143 N.C. App. 712, 714 (2001) (remanding adjudication because the trial court failed to state that the allegations in the petition were proven beyond a reasonable doubt).

Before 2009, courts were not required to issue written adjudication orders. *In re Rikard*, 161 N.C. App. 150, 154 (2003). Based on 2009 amendments, adjudication orders must now be in writing. G.S. 7B-2411. The written order must include the offense date, misdemeanor or felony classification of the offense, and the date of adjudication. In *In re J.V.J.*, 209 N.C. App. 737, 740–41 (2011), the Court of Appeals reversed an adjudication order in which although the trial court found beyond a reasonable doubt that the juvenile was "responsible," the order did not address the allegations and stated only "through a fragmentary collection of words and numbers" that the offense described in the petition occurred. In contrast, in *In re K.C.*, 226 N.C. App. 452, 461 (2013), the Court upheld an adjudication order because the order "provide[d] the date of the offense, the fact that the assault is a class 2 misdemeanor, the date of the adjudication, and clearly state[d] that the court considered the evidence and adjudicated [the juvenile] delinquent as to the petition's allegation of simple assault beyond a reasonable doubt."

Counsel should review the written order to ensure that it is consistent with the oral order announced in open court and, if inconsistencies exist, move that the trial court make appropriate modifications.

12.7 Collateral Effects of Adjudication

An adjudication of delinquency is not a conviction of a criminal offense. A juvenile who has been found to be delinquent does not forfeit any citizenship rights. G.S. 7B-2412. There may be adverse consequences, however, for a noncitizen.

Because it is not considered a conviction, an adjudication of delinquency generally does not have the adverse immigration consequences that result from convictions. However, certain adverse immigration consequences do not require a conviction; mere bad acts can trigger a penalty. Examples include being a drug addict or abuser, engaging in prostitution, using false documents, smuggling aliens, or drug trafficking. *See* IMMIGRATION CONSEQUENCES OF A CRIMINAL CONVICTION IN NORTH CAROLINA § 4.2F, Juvenile Delinquency Adjudication (Sept. 2017). A juvenile adjudication involving offenses of this nature may be grounds for deportation or bar admission to the country as a legal immigrant. Adjudications involving these offenses can also be used to deny an application for Special Immigrant Juvenile Status, which helps certain undocumented children in the state juvenile/foster care system obtain lawful immigration status. *See id.* A delinquency adjudication may be considered an adverse factor if the juvenile applies for a discretionary benefit under the immigration laws, such as citizenship or a green card. *See id.* Counsel should contact an immigration lawyer for additional information when representing a juvenile who is not a citizen.

An adjudication may be used to impeach a juvenile witness in a juvenile delinquency proceeding and in some instances in subsequent criminal proceedings. *See supra* § 12.5C, Rules of Evidence; "Statutory exceptions for use in limited criminal court proceedings" in § 2.8A, Juvenile Court Records. An adjudication for a Class A, B1, B2, C, D, or E felony can be used to impose an aggravated sentence for a conviction in adult court or to impose a death sentence in a capital case if the felony involved the use or threat of violence. G.S. 15A-1340.16(d)(18a), 15A-2000(e)(3).

Adjudication of an offense that would be a felony if committed by an adult bars participation in high school sports for as long as the juvenile is in school. This is by rule of the North Carolina High School Athletic Association, which governs high school sports. The policy is available on the Association's website. Counsel should inform the juvenile of this consequence if the juvenile is admitting a felony offense or might be adjudicated for such an offense.

The court also might require registration as a sex offender for certain offenses, discussed *infra* in § 13.9, Registration of Juvenile Adjudicated for Certain Sex Crimes.

12.8   Expunction of Juvenile Record

Some records of delinquency may be expunged under prescribed statutory conditions. G.S. 7B-3200 through 7B-3202; *see infra* Chapter 17, Expunction of Juvenile Records; *see also* "Expunction of Delinquency Matters" in John Rubin, Relief from a Criminal Conviction: A Digital Guide to Expunctions, Certificates of Relief, and Other Procedures in North Carolina (UNC School of Government 2016). This may be an important consideration if the juvenile is offered the opportunity to admit to an allegation that would be subject to expunction.

If the juvenile is adjudicated delinquent for an offense that is subject to expunction, counsel should advise the juvenile and the parent, with the juvenile's consent, of the expunction process. Anyone wishing to pursue expunction should be advised to contact the Clerk of Superior Court's office for appropriate paperwork if and when the criteria for expunction are met.

Chapter 13
Dispositional Hearings

13.1　Overview

Following an adjudication of delinquency, the court proceeds to a dispositional hearing for entry of an order of disposition within the statutory alternatives. The court must determine the proper disposition level based on both the seriousness of the offense adjudicated and the juvenile's history of delinquency. Once the court determines the disposition level, it must order a disposition that meets the needs of the juvenile and provides for protection of the public. Statutory alternatives range from dismissal of the case to commitment to the Division of Adult Correction and Juvenile Justice. Counsel should advise the juvenile of possible dispositions within the available dispositional alternatives but must advocate for the disposition desired by the juvenile.

This chapter will review dispositional hearing procedures and statutory provisions for determining the classification of the offense and the juvenile's delinquency history level. Alternatives for each dispositional level and the court's discretion within the statutory mandates are discussed.

13.2　Terminology Used in this Chapter

Delinquency history level determines the permissible dispositional alternatives based on points assigned for the juvenile's prior adjudications and the classification of the current adjudicated offense. *See infra* § 13.7, Delinquency History Levels and Offense Classification.

Division is the Division of Adult Correction and Juvenile Justice of the Department of Public Safety. G.S. 7B-1501(10a).

Disposition is the order entered by the court following an adjudication of delinquency. A dispositional hearing is held, which may be informal, for the court to consider the predisposition report, along with evidence from the State and the juvenile. The court must order a disposition within the statutory guidelines based on both the seriousness of the offense adjudicated and the juvenile's history of delinquency.

Predisposition report is prepared by a juvenile court counselor and contains information regarding the juvenile and recommendations for disposition. The predisposition report must contain a risk and needs assessment and is submitted at the dispositional hearing. G.S. 7B-2413; *see infra* § 13.4, Predisposition Investigation and Report.

A risk and needs assessment is attached to the predisposition report submitted by the juvenile court counselor at the dispositional hearing. It must contain information regarding the juvenile's social, medical, psychiatric, psychological, and educational history, as well as any factors indicating the probability of the juvenile committing further delinquent acts. G.S. 7B-2413; *see infra* § 13.4B, Contents of Report; § 13.4C, Risk Factors.

13.3 Preliminary Matters

A. Continuance of Dispositional Hearing

After adjudication the court may continue the dispositional hearing for preparation of the predisposition report and risk and needs assessment or at the request of the juvenile. G.S. 7B-2413, 7B-2501(b); *see also In re Vinson*, 298 N.C. 640, 661–62 (1979) (stating that dispositional hearing must be continued at juvenile's request under recently enacted G.S. 7A-639 (now G.S. 7B-2413), G.S. 7A-640 (now G.S. 7B-2501(a),(b)), and G.S. 7A-632 (now G.S. 7B-2406); case decided under earlier, different version of Code and remanded on other grounds). The statute providing for continuances under the hearing procedures statute, G.S. 7B-2406, has been held to apply to dispositional hearings, giving the court discretion to continue a dispositional hearing "for good cause." *In re R.D.R.*, 175 N.C. App. 397, 401 (2006) (court had discretion to continue disposition on its own motion for one week, until adjudicatory date for another petition involving juvenile). This statute states that the continuance is only "for as long as is reasonably required to receive" evidence or other information. G.S. 7B-2406.

If the juvenile is opposed to a continuance of disposition, counsel should cite the statute setting forth that one of the purposes of the subchapter on delinquent juveniles is to provide "swift, effective dispositions." G.S. 7B-1500(2)a. Additionally, G.S. 7B-2413 provides that the court "shall proceed to the dispositional hearing upon receipt of the predisposition report," indicating that the dispositional hearing should not be continued in the absence of a sufficient reason if the report has been prepared.

If the court continues the dispositional hearing for more than sixty days after adjudication and the juvenile appeals the adjudication order (permissible under G.S. 7B-2602), the trial court is divested of jurisdiction over the case and may not conduct a dispositional hearing while the appeal is pending. *In re J.F.*, 237 N.C. App. 218, 228 (2014).

B. Secure Custody Pending Dispositional Hearing

The court may order the juvenile into secure custody after an adjudication of delinquency pending the dispositional hearing. G.S. 7B-1903(c). This will not be an issue if disposition immediately follows adjudication. There may be reasons for a continuance, however, such as the need for preparation of a predisposition report or the juvenile's need for time to subpoena witnesses or documents.

If the court indicates that it is considering secure custody pending disposition, counsel should consider arguing that secure custody is not warranted. The criteria for secured custody in G.S. 7B-1903(b)(1)–(6) may apply at this stage of the proceedings and at least provides guidance on deciding whether secure custody is warranted. For example, if the juvenile was adjudicated for a misdemeanor that did not involve dangerous conduct and the juvenile did not miss any court dates, counsel should assert that there are insufficient grounds to place the juvenile in secure custody.

If the court orders the juvenile to be placed in secure custody, it must issue a written order with "appropriate findings of fact." G.S. 7B-1903(c). The court must also hold review hearings every 10 calendar days. *Id.* The juvenile may waive review hearings for up to 30 calendar days. *Id.*

For a further discussion of secure custody after adjudication, see "Criteria for secure custody" in § 8.6G, Secure Custody Following Adjudication of Delinquency.

13.4   Predisposition Investigation and Report

A. Consent for Preparation of the Report

The juvenile court counselor must obtain consent of the juvenile, the juvenile's parent, guardian, or custodian, or the juvenile's attorney to prepare the predisposition report and risk and needs assessment (also called the disposition report) before adjudication. G.S. 7B-2413. Without consent, the predisposition report cannot be prepared until after an adjudication, and the dispositional hearing will be continued unless the court makes a written finding that a report is not needed for disposition to proceed. *Id.* This consent is typically granted by the juvenile or a parent, guardian, or custodian at the intake meeting with the court counselor. *See infra* Appendix 13-1: Authorization to Prepare Pre-Disposition Report. If the juvenile or the juvenile's parents consent to preparation of the pre-disposition report before adjudication, counsel should advise the juvenile and the juvenile's parents that they should not discuss the allegations in the petition with the court counselor.

In most cases it will be beneficial to the juvenile for the report to be written before adjudication. If the petition is dismissed at adjudication, the report is of no consequence. If the juvenile is found to be delinquent, having the prepared report may prevent the need for a continuance. This is particularly important if the juvenile is being held in secure custody. It will also give counsel more time to review the report, affording the opportunity to bring factual mistakes to the attention of the court counselor, to provide positive information to the court counselor that was omitted, and to subpoena witnesses regarding the information in the report.

B. Contents of Report

A predisposition report prepared by the juvenile court counselor must be submitted before the dispositional hearing. A risk and needs assessment, which is a comprehensive evaluation of the juvenile, must be part of the predisposition report. The risk and needs assessment must contain information regarding the juvenile's social, medical, psychiatric, psychological, and educational history. G.S. 7B-2413.

C. Risk Factors

G.S. 7B-2413 require that the report include any factors indicating the probability that the juvenile will commit further offenses. Counsel should review the court counselor's file and be prepared to cross-examine the juvenile court counselor and subpoena necessary witnesses about any asserted factors. Through cross-examination and direct testimony from the juvenile's witnesses, mistakes in the report may be corrected and positive information elicited.

Because the section of the report on risk factors is more subjective, there may be more reason to cross-examine the juvenile court counselor about its contents, especially if the report concludes that there is a high risk of the juvenile committing further delinquent acts or otherwise contains information that could be harmful to the juvenile. Cross-examination should explore whether the risk factors are based on incorrect information or faulty assumptions. Counsel should be careful in questioning, however, because it might allow the juvenile court counselor to discuss the risk factors in more detail to the detriment of the juvenile's case. An alternative is to argue that the factors listed do not put the juvenile at risk for re-offending or that the juvenile court counselor has made unwarranted or contradictory assumptions.

D. Right to Review before Dispositional Hearing

The juvenile, as well as counsel, has the right to review the predisposition report with the attached risk and needs assessment before the dispositional hearing. G.S. 7B-2413. However, the trial court may withhold the report if it determines that disclosure of the report would "seriously harm the treatment or rehabilitation of the juvenile or would violate a promise of confidentiality." *Id.*

In many districts the report is presented to counsel at the same time the report is presented to the court, affording counsel little time to review the report and consult with the juvenile. Counsel should consider pressing for delivery of the report before the hearing or requesting additional time to review the report.

Some juveniles will want to read the report, although others may be satisfied if counsel explains it to them. If the juvenile wants to read the report, counsel should review it with the juvenile to assist in interpretation.

Although the statute concerning the predisposition report does not specify a parent, guardian, or custodian as a person entitled to review the report, these people may have the right to do so pursuant to their statutory right to review files concerning the juvenile. *See* G.S. 7B-3001. Because the statutory right is not clear, counsel should direct the parent, guardian, or custodian to address a request for the predisposition report to the court.

E. Right to Present Rebuttal Evidence to Predisposition Report

The juvenile and the juvenile's parent, guardian, or custodian are entitled to present evidence to rebut the information in the predisposition report. G.S. 7B-2413. Both the juvenile and the juvenile's parent, guardian, or custodian are generally entitled to present evidence at disposition and to present a proposed dispositional plan. G.S. 7B-2501; *see supra* "Disposition" in § 3.5E, Parent, Guardian, or Custodian. Counsel should present rebuttal evidence as well as positive information regarding the juvenile.

13.5 Dispositional Hearing

A. Conduct of the Hearing

Hearing may be informal. The dispositional hearing may be informal, with the rules of evidence relaxed. G.S. 7B-2501(a). Counsel still must be vigilant in taking necessary steps to protect the juvenile's interests. An objection should be made to any parts of the predisposition report that are not admissible under the hearsay rules discussed below. The juvenile court counselor can be cross-examined as to the sources of information. If necessary, counsel should subpoena and cross-examine the people who are the sources of information in the report.

There is no statutory prohibition on the presentation of evidence by the juvenile. Counsel should call witnesses if testimony would be more effective than a report. Reports that are helpful to the juvenile should be offered into evidence, however, to counter negative information contained in the dispositional report.

Dispositional guidelines. G.S. 7B-2501(c) mandates that the court consider both the protection of the public and the needs and best interests of the juvenile in developing a dispositional order. Counsel should argue that the court should tailor the dispositional order to meet the juvenile's needs in advocating for the disposition sought by the juvenile.

Pursuant to G.S. 7B-2501(c)(1)–(5), the following factors are to be considered by the court:

- the seriousness of the offense,
- the need to hold the juvenile accountable,
- the importance of protecting the public safety,
- the degree of culpability indicated by the circumstances of the particular case, and
- the rehabilitative and treatment needs of the juvenile indicated by a risk and needs assessment.

Evidence. "Any evidence" is admissible, including hearsay, that the court finds to be "relevant, reliable, and necessary to determine the needs of the juvenile and the most appropriate disposition." G.S. 7B-2501(a). Written reports concerning the needs of the juvenile are admissible. *Id.*

Counsel should continue to object to evidence that does not meet the statutory standard of relevance, reliability, and necessity. For example, statements based on double hearsay ("The mother/neighbor/co-respondent stated that the teacher/doctor/counselor said . . .") or evaluations that are no longer current may be objectionable. Inappropriate recommendations of the court counselor, such as for substance abuse treatment when there is no evidence of substance abuse, should be objected to and argued against. A motion for a continuance to subpoena a witness for cross-examination may be made if unreliable hearsay information is admitted over counsel's objection.

Right of juvenile and parent to present evidence. The juvenile and the juvenile's parent, guardian, or custodian have the right to present evidence and make argument to the court concerning the appropriate disposition. G.S. 7B-2501(b). Counsel should talk with the parent concerning the parent's position on disposition and explain the possible consequences of the parent making negative statements regarding the juvenile at disposition. *See supra* "Disposition" in § 3.5E, Parent, Guardian, or Custodian.

Defense dispositional plan. Counsel should prepare a dispositional plan and, where appropriate, a dispositional memorandum. Topics that may be included are:

- favorable information, including mitigating factors and relative culpability concerning the offense, and information regarding the juvenile's personal background, educational history, employment record and opportunities, and financial status;
- factors supporting a disposition other than confinement, such as the potential for rehabilitation or the nonviolent nature of the crime;
- the availability of treatment programs, treatment facilities, and community service work opportunities;
- challenges to incorrect or incomplete information or inappropriate references and characterizations in the State's evidence; and
- if appropriate, a counterproposal to confinement.

See N.C. Commission on Indigent Defense Services, Performance Guidelines for Appointed Counsel in Juvenile Delinquency Proceedings at the Trial Level § 10.5 (2007) reprinted *infra* in Chapter 18 of this manual.

Dismissal. The court may dismiss the case after an adjudication of delinquency, although the statute provides no guidelines for doing so. G.S. 7B-2501(d). Dismissal of the case might be appropriate, for example, for a first offense that is relatively minor, when the juvenile's parents have taken adequate steps to address underlying problems, or when the experience of being in juvenile court has had a positive effect on the juvenile's behavior.

Continuance of disposition. A continuance of up to six months may be ordered specifically to allow the juvenile's family to address the juvenile's needs. G.S. 7B-2501(d). The needs of the juvenile may be met by providing more adequate home supervision, through placement in a private or specialized school or agency, or through some other plan approved by the court. G.S. 7B-2501(d). Even if the case involves a serious offense, the court might grant a continuance of disposition under this statute if counsel presents a comprehensive plan. If the plan has been successful when the case is rescheduled, the court may dismiss the case or impose a more lenient disposition than it might have originally entered.

Counsel should move for a continuance of disposition when appropriate and consider filing a written motion and supporting memorandum of law. Documentation outlining the family's efforts to explore community resources and the resulting proposed dispositional plan may persuade the court to continue the dispositional hearing.

B. Court-Ordered Evaluation and Treatment

Evaluation. To assist in developing an appropriate disposition, the court may order that the juvenile be examined by a physician, psychiatrist, psychologist, or other qualified expert. G.S. 7B-2502(a).

The court must allow the parent to arrange for the ordered evaluation as the first option. G.S. 7B-2502(b). If the parent accepts this responsibility, counsel should seek to work with the parent in selecting the most appropriate expert to perform the evaluation. Counsel may suggest someone who has worked with juveniles and who has performed thorough and effective juvenile court evaluations in other cases.

If the parent refuses or is unable to make the arrangements, the court may enter an order specifying who will perform the evaluation. G.S. 7B-2502(b). Counsel might suggest that the court appoint an expert with whom the juvenile has an existing relationship or an expert who has worked with juveniles and has done other juvenile court evaluations. After the court has ordered a particular expert to perform an evaluation, counsel should contact the expert to provide background material or other information that might be helpful to the juvenile's position.

The Juvenile Code suggests that the evaluation might be done on an inpatient basis, as it directs the court to consider whether it is in the juvenile's interest to remain in the county of residence "[i]n placing a juvenile in out-of-home care under this section." G.S. 7B-2502(a). Typically, the juvenile will prefer to be evaluated on an outpatient basis.

Counsel should obtain a copy of any report resulting from the examination before further proceedings occur. The expert may be contacted to provide clarifying information to supplement the report. If necessary, counsel should subpoena the expert for cross-examination about the evaluation.

Hearing. A hearing must be held after completion of the examination to determine whether the juvenile is in need of medical, surgical, psychiatric, psychological, or other evaluation or treatment. G.S. 7B-2502(b). Generally, the court will review any written report regarding the evaluation or receive testimony from the evaluator regarding the report and recommendations. Counsel should cross-examine any witnesses and present evidence favorable to the juvenile's position. The juvenile might have an ongoing relationship with a counselor, therapist, teacher, or other person who could present testimony helpful to the court and to the juvenile's position. In some cases, the juvenile's parent might be called on the juvenile's behalf. There is a danger, however, in presenting testimony from a parent who downplays the juvenile's problems and does not understand the need for or intend to pursue an appropriate plan.

The county manager of the county of the juvenile's residence, or other designated person, must be given notice of the hearing and be allowed to be heard. This is required because the county may be required to pay for the cost of the juvenile's evaluation and treatment, discussed next. G.S. 7B-2502(b).

Cost of treatment. If the court decides to order treatment, it must also determine who will be responsible for the cost. The statute presumes that the parent who arranges for evaluation and treatment will pay for the cost. If the court determines that the parent is unable to pay, however, the court must order the county of the juvenile's residence to pay for evaluation and treatment. In that case, the county department of social services is required to recommend the facility that will evaluate and treat the juvenile. G.S. 7B-2502(b).

C. Court-Ordered Drug Testing

If a juvenile is adjudicated delinquent for an offense that involves the possession, use, sale, or delivery of alcohol or a controlled substance, the court *must* order that the juvenile be tested for use of a controlled substance or alcohol within 30 days of the adjudication. In other cases, the court *may* order that the juvenile be tested for use of a controlled substance or alcohol. Counsel should object if no evidence of drug use has been presented. If ordered, the results of these initial tests, as opposed to regular testing ordered as part of disposition, may be used for evaluation and treatment purposes only. G.S. 7B-2502(a).

A juvenile court counselor may require the juvenile to submit to drug testing if the court makes this a condition of probation. G.S. 7B-2510(a)(7)c., 7B-2510(b)(2); *see In re Schrimpsher*, 143 N.C. App. 461, 466–67 (2001) (court did not have authority to order as a condition of probation that the juvenile submit to urinalysis, blood, or breathalyzer testing on request of any law enforcement officer; juvenile conceded that court had authority to order juvenile to submit to testing on request of court counselor).

D. Evaluation and Treatment of Mentally Ill or Developmentally Disabled Juvenile

Referral to area program. The court must refer a juvenile to the area mental health, developmental disabilities, and substance abuse services director (hereinafter the director) for "appropriate action" if it believes or if there is evidence presented that the juvenile is mentally ill or developmentally disabled. G.S. 7B-2502(c). The director must obtain an interdisciplinary evaluation and arrange for services to meet the juvenile's needs. *Id.* These services could include a specialized school, therapy, counseling, a personal aide, or residential treatment.

Inpatient treatment. A juvenile may be admitted to a mental health facility or mental retardation center with the consent of the parent, guardian, or custodian (hereinafter the parent) if the area program evaluation determines that this is the best service for the juvenile. G.S. 7B-2502(c). If the parent refuses to consent after admission is recommended by the director, the court may provide the consent and signature required for admission. *Id.* This commitment is called a voluntary admission although from the juvenile's standpoint it is involuntary.

If the juvenile is refused admission by a regional mental hospital or is discharged before treatment is complete, the hospital must report this to the court. G.S. 7B-2502(c). There must be a written report outlining the reasons for denial of admission or discharge and the juvenile's diagnosis, symptoms of mental illness, indications of need for treatment, and a referral to another facility that could provide appropriate treatment for the juvenile. *Id.*

Voluntary admission of a juvenile to an inpatient facility must conform to the procedures in G.S. Chapter 122C. *See* NORTH CAROLINA CIVIL COMMITMENT MANUAL Ch. 6, Voluntary Admission of Minors (2d ed. 2011). A district court judge must review the voluntary admission in a separate proceeding in which the juvenile is represented by counsel. *See* G.S. 122C-221 through 122C-224.7. Special counsel generally represents juveniles at State hospitals, and counsel is usually appointed for juveniles at other facilities. A juvenile *must* be discharged by the "responsible professional" at any time it is determined that the juvenile is no longer mentally ill or is no longer in need of treatment at the facility. The juvenile must meet *and* continue to meet the criteria for voluntary admission for inpatient treatment—that is, being mentally ill or a substance abuser and in need of treatment at the facility. G.S. 122C-224.7.

At the hearing to review the voluntary admission, the court may concur with the admission and authorize continued treatment for up to 90 days at the initial hearing, continue the admission for an additional 15 days for additional diagnosis and evaluation, or discharge the juvenile. G.S. 122C-224.3(g).

13.6   Dispositional Alternatives

A. Purpose of Disposition

The philosophy underlying dispositional alternatives available under the Juvenile Code was changed by the repeal of former G.S. 7A-646, which required that the court impose the least restrictive dispositional alternative and order commitment to the Division of Youth Services only after other alternatives were found to be inappropriate or were proven to be unsuccessful. Under the current statute, G.S. 7B-2501, the court must balance the needs of the juvenile with the need for public safety within the permissible dispositional alternatives. It remains the role of counsel to advocate on behalf of the juvenile for the least restrictive and least punitive disposition desired by the juvenile.

B. Statutory Categories

The court must choose dispositional alternatives within the appropriate dispositional level, which is determined by the juvenile delinquency history level and the offense classification. *See infra* § 13.7, Delinquency History Levels and Offense Classification. There are 24 dispositional alternatives. G.S. 7B-2506(1) through (24). Some Level 1 and Level 2 alternatives are identical except that a more severe disposition is allowed under Level 2. For example, alternative (4) provides for restitution up to $500, and alternative (22) provides for restitution over $500. Likewise, alternative (6) allows up to 100 hours of community service, and alternative (23) allows up to 200 hours; alternative (12) provides for a limit of five 24-hour periods of intermittent detention, and alternative (20) provides for up to fourteen 24-hour periods.

Each alternative is described briefly below, along with case law applicable to that alternative. Within the dispositional limits for each class of offense and delinquency history level under G.S. 7B-2508, the court may:

1. If a juvenile needs more adequate care or supervision, or is in need of placement:

    a. require supervision in the home by a designated person or agency, subject to court-ordered conditions;
    b. make a change in the juvenile's custody; or
    c. place the juvenile in the custody of the department of social services.

2. Excuse the juvenile from compulsory school attendance if the court finds that a suitable alternative plan can be arranged.

3. Order the juvenile to cooperate with a community-based program, an intensive substance abuse program, or a residential or nonresidential program, not to exceed 12 months.

    - *In re M.A.B.*, 170 N.C. App. 192, 194 (2005) (court did not improperly delegate its authority under G.S. 7B-2506(3) by ordering juvenile to cooperate with placement in a residential or nonresidential treatment program as directed by juvenile court counselor or mental health agency, as court ordered participation in program but allowed another person or agency to determine specifics)

- *In re S.R.S.*, 180 N.C. App. 151, 159 (2006) (citing *Hartsock*, below, the Court of Appeals held that the trial court improperly delegated authority to juvenile court counselor to decide on type and provider of counseling)

- *In re Hartsock*, 158 N.C. App. 287, 292 (2003) (court could not delegate its authority under G.S. 7B-2506(14) to juvenile court counselor or counselor from treatment program to place juvenile in residential treatment)

4. Require restitution up to $500 payable within 12 months.

- *In re D.A.Q.*, 214 N.C. App. 535, 538 (2011) (court erred by failing to find that restitution was in the juvenile's best interest before ordering the juvenile to pay restitution)

- *In re Z.A.K.*, 189 N.C. App. 354, 362 (2008) (court improperly ordered restitution without finding that restitution was in the juvenile's best interest)

- *In re M.A.B.*, 170 N.C. App. 192, 194 (2005) (court did not improperly delegate authority by ordering juvenile to pay up to $500 restitution payable within 12 months with amount to be determined on submission of medical bills to court)

- *In re McDonald*, 133 N.C. App. 433, 436 (1999) (court erred in ordering juvenile to pay $200 restitution as it failed to make findings of fact regarding amount of damage suffered by victim and only evidence presented were pictures of damaged property)

5. Impose a fine.

6. Order up to 100 hours of supervised community service to be done within 12 months.

7. Order participation in the victim-offender reconciliation program.

8. Place the juvenile on probation under supervision of the juvenile court counselor. *See infra* § 13.6C, Probation.

9. Prohibit the juvenile from obtaining a driver's license for as long as the juvenile is under the court's jurisdiction.

10. Impose a curfew.

11. Order the juvenile not to associate with specified persons or be in specified places.

12. Impose intermittent detention, limited to five 24-hour periods.

- *In re Hartsock*, 158 N.C. App. 287, 292 (2003) (order for intermittent confinement of no effect as court failed to specify when confinement would occur; delegation of authority would have been contrary to express language of statute)

13. Order placement in a wilderness program.

14. Order placement in a residential treatment facility, an intensive nonresidential treatment program, an intensive substance abuse program, or a group home other than a multi-purpose group home operated by a State agency.

   - *In re Hartsock*, 158 N.C. App. 287, 292 (2003) (court could not delegate its authority under G.S. 7B-2506(14) to juvenile court counselor or counselor from treatment program to place juvenile in residential treatment)

   - *In re M.A.B.*, 170 N.C. App. 192, 194 (2005) (court did not improperly delegate its authority under G.S. 7B-2506(3) by ordering juvenile to cooperate with placement in residential or nonresidential treatment program as directed by juvenile court counselor or mental health agency, as court ordered participation in program but left specifics to another person or agency)

   - *In re S.R.S.*, 180 N.C. App. 151, 159 (2006) (citing *Hartsock*, above, the Court of Appeals held that the trial court improperly delegated authority to juvenile court counselor to decide whether there would be out-of-home placement)

15. Place the juvenile on intensive probation under the supervision of a juvenile court counselor. *See infra* § 13.6C, Probation.

16. Order the juvenile to cooperate with a supervised day program under specified terms and conditions.

17. Order the juvenile to participate in a regimented training program. (There are no programs of this type, also called "boot camps," in North Carolina as of the writing of this manual.)

18. Order house arrest.

19. Suspend imposition of a more severe, permissible disposition on the juvenile's agreement to court-imposed conditions.

20. Order confinement in detention for up to fourteen 24-hour periods, not to be imposed consecutively with any intermittent detention under (12) above.

   - *In re Hartsock*, 158 N.C. App. 287, 292 (2003) (order for intermittent confinement of no effect as court failed to specify when confinement would occur; delegation of authority would have been contrary to express language of statute)

21. Order residential placement in a multi-purpose group home operated by a State agency.

22. Order restitution of more than $500 payable within 12 months.

  - *In re Schrimpsher*, 143 N.C. App. 461, 465–66 (2001) (court must make findings of fact to determine whether others were jointly and severally liable for damages, total amount of damages, and amount of damages attributable to juvenile)

23. Order up to 200 hours supervised community service.

24. Commit the juvenile to the Division for placement in a youth development center, also known as "training school," for a period of not less than six months.

  - *In re T.B.*, 178 N.C. App. 542, 546 (2006) (commitment to Department of Youth Services may be ordered only for juvenile who is eligible to receive Level 3 disposition)

  - *In re D.A.F.*, 179 N.C. App. 832, 835 (2006) (trial court did not abuse its discretion in ordering the juvenile to be committed to a youth detention center because it was a "reasoned decision" based on factors regarding juvenile's needs and risk to public safety)

C. Probation

The court may place the juvenile either on probation or intensive probation. G.S. 7B-2506(8), (15). During the probationary period, the juvenile is under the supervision of a juvenile court counselor and may be subject to conditions ordered by the court. The juvenile may be brought back into court on a motion alleging violation of the conditions of probation, possibly subjecting the juvenile to further dispositional orders of the court. G.S. 7B-2510(e). If the court indicates at disposition that it is considering probation, counsel should consider arguing against probation or seeking to limit the conditions imposed by the court. *See infra* § 14.3, When Probation May Be Ordered.

The conditions of probation are often one or more of the other dispositional alternatives listed in G.S. 7B-2506. *See infra* Chapter 14, Probation.

13.7 Delinquency History Levels and Offense Classification

A. Statutory Classifications

The classification structure for juvenile offenses and delinquency history levels requires that the court impose a dispositional alternative within one of three levels determined by the statutory classification of the offense (violent, serious, or minor) and the juvenile's delinquency history level, determined by points assigned for each adjudicated offense.

G.S. 7B-2506 through 7B-2508. Counsel must be familiar with the statutory scheme to be prepared to argue for the least restrictive disposition within the juvenile's delinquency level and to advise the court if an impermissible disposition is considered.

The Administrative Office of the Courts has created a delinquency history worksheet, which includes a section for prior adjudications and a table to calculate the number of delinquency history points. *See* AOC-J-469 (Delinquency History Level Worksheet) (Oct. 2016). The Office of the Juvenile Defender has also created a quick reference guide that summarizes many of the statutes that govern the process for determining the dispositional level and a chart describing dispositional alternatives available for each dispositional level. *See infra* Appendix 13-2: Quick Reference Guide for Dispositional Hearings, and Appendix 13-3: Juvenile Disposition Options.

B.　Determining the Classification of the Offense

The dispositional alternatives that the trial court may impose are determined in part by the classification of the offense for which the juvenile is adjudicated delinquent. Offenses are divided into the following three categories under G.S. 7B-2508(a):

Offense Category	Offense Class
Violent	Class A through E felony
Serious	Class F through I felony or Class A1 misdemeanor
Minor	Class 1, 2, or 3 misdemeanor

C.　Determining Delinquency History Levels

Generally. The dispositional alternatives available to the trial court are also determined by the total points assigned to the juvenile's prior adjudications and the juvenile's probation status, if any. G.S. 7B-2507(a). Counsel should review the court file and use the delinquency history worksheet to determine the juvenile's delinquency history level prior to the dispositional hearing. *See* AOC-J-469 (Delinquency History Level Worksheet) (Oct. 2016). The delinquency history provided to the court by the prosecutor or court counselor may be inaccurate and could result in an improper disposition if counsel does not object. The provisions for assigning points and determining the delinquency history level based on those points are set forth in G.S. 7B-2507(b) and (c), respectively.

Points. Points are assigned for each prior adjudication as follows:

Offense Class	Points
Class A through E felony	4 points
Class F through I felony or Class A1 misdemeanor	2 points
Class 1, 2, or 3 misdemeanor	1 point
On probation at time of offense	2 points

Delinquency history levels by points. Delinquency history levels as determined by points are as follows:

Delinquency History Level	Points
Low	No more than 1 point
Medium	2 or 3 points
High	4 or more points

Reviewing the juvenile's history of prior adjudications. Counsel should carefully review the juvenile's prior adjudications before the dispositional hearing. A juvenile who is adjudicated delinquent for more than one offense in a single session of court is assigned points based only on the offense having the highest points. G.S. 7B-2507(d). Based on this provision, it is generally advantageous for a juvenile to have multiple petitions that are filed within a short period of time adjudicated in the same session of court. If the petitions are adjudicated in separate court sessions, the juvenile may receive a higher point total at a later dispositional hearing on a new petition.

Although the court may assign points for adjudications that arose in different sessions of court, there is one limitation on the court's authority to assign points in those circumstances. As part of the 2015 Juvenile Code reform bill, the General Assembly defined a prior adjudication as "an adjudication of an offense that occurs before the adjudication of the offense before the court." G.S. 7B-2507(a); 2015 N.C. Sess. Laws Ch. 58 (H879). The legislation reversed the holding of *In re P.Q.M.*, 232 N.C. App. 419, 434 (2014), which held that it was proper for the trial court to assess delinquency history level points for an adjudication that arose after the adjudication that was the subject of the dispositional order.

Additionally, the juvenile's delinquency history level is determined by the classification of the prior offense at the time the current offense was committed. G.S. 7B-2507(c). In other words, the court must classify the prior adjudication based on the classification of the crime on the offense date for the current offense. Counsel should ensure that the court assigns the proper classification for any prior adjudications for crimes that have been assigned a lower classification since the juvenile was adjudicated.

Proof of prior adjudications. The State bears the burden of proof by the preponderance of the evidence to show that the prior adjudication exists and that the juvenile is the person who committed the offense. Prior adjudications must be proved by stipulation of the parties, an original or copy of the court record of the prior adjudication, a copy of the record maintained by the Division of Criminal Information or by the Division of Juvenile Justice, or by any other method found by the court to be reliable. G.S. 7B-2507(f).

The prosecutor must make "all feasible efforts" to obtain and present to the court the full record of the juvenile. It must be provided to the juvenile on request. G.S. 7B-2507(f). Counsel should submit a request for the Division of Juvenile Justice record directly to the chief court counselor as well as make a timely request to the prosecutor for the record that will be submitted in court. A sample form for requesting the release of the Division's files for the juvenile is available on the Office of the Juvenile Defender website.

The delinquency history worksheet contains a section in which counsel can affirmatively stipulate in writing to prior adjudications. *See* AOC-J-469 (Delinquency History Level Worksheet) (Oct. 2016). However, counsel can also stipulate orally at the dispositional hearing or by failing to object to reports that describe prior adjudications. *See In re D.R.H.*, 194 N.C. App. 166, 172 (2008) (juvenile's attorney stipulated to prior adjudications by failing to contest or inquire into prior adjudications that were listed in a report prepared by the court counselor for the juvenile's disposition hearing).

Even if counsel stipulates to prior adjudications, the stipulation is not binding if the court miscalculates the juvenile's delinquency history level. *See State v. Fraley*, 182 N.C. App. 683, 691 (2007) (remanding for resentencing despite the defendant's stipulation to prior convictions because the convictions did not support the prior record level chosen by the trial court).

Classification of prior adjudications from other jurisdictions. An adjudication of a felony in a jurisdiction outside of North Carolina is generally classified as a Class I felony. An adjudication of a misdemeanor is generally classified as a Class 3 misdemeanor. G.S. 7B-2507(e).

The juvenile may have a felony from another jurisdiction treated as a misdemeanor on proof by a preponderance of the evidence that the offense in the other jurisdiction is "substantially similar" to a misdemeanor offense in North Carolina. G.S. 7B-2507(e).

If the State proves by a preponderance of the evidence that an offense classified as a misdemeanor in another jurisdiction is "substantially similar" to an offense that is classified as a Class I felony or higher in North Carolina, the offense is treated as that specific class of felony for the purpose of assigning points. For example, if the State establishes that the offense from another jurisdiction is substantially similar to a common law robbery in North Carolina, the offense would be treated as a Class G felony. If the State proves by a preponderance of the evidence that an offense classified in another jurisdiction as a misdemeanor is "substantially similar" to an offense classified as a Class A1 misdemeanor in North Carolina, the offense is treated as a Class A1 misdemeanor for the purpose of assigning points.

Assessing points for committing the offense while on probation. The trial court may assess two delinquency history points under G.S. 7B-2507(b)(4) if the juvenile committed the offense while on probation. Counsel should therefore review the juvenile's probationary status before the dispositional hearing.

In *In re A.F.*, 231 N.C. App. 348 (2013), the juvenile's attorney stipulated that the juvenile was on probation on the offense date for the case. The trial court originally placed the juvenile on probation during an earlier dispositional hearing. However, the court never extended the probationary period, which expired before the offense date for the adjudication that was the subject of the appeal. As a result, both the stipulation and the court's assessment of two points under G.S. 7B-2507(b)(4) were improper. *Id.* at 356.

13.8 Dispositional Limits for Each Class of Offense and History Level

G.S. 7B-2508 outlines three dispositional levels for delinquency cases. The following chart from G.S. 7B-2508(f) prescribes the dispositional levels that are available to the trial court based on the offense classification and delinquency history level.

DISPOSITION CHART			
OFFENSE	DELINQUENCY HISTORY		
	Low	Medium	High
Violent	Level 2 or 3	Level 3	Level 3
Serious	Level 1 or 2	Level 2	Level 2 or 3
Minor	Level 1	Level 1 or 2	Level 2

The chart is also available in section I of the delinquency history worksheet. *See* AOC-J-469 (Delinquency History Level Worksheet) (Oct. 2016).

The three dispositional levels described in G.S. 7B-2508, as well as the dispositional alternatives available for each level, are described below.

Level 1 (Community Disposition)

- Dispositional alternatives (1)–(13) and (16) under G.S. 7B-2506 are available to the court. G.S. 7B-2508(c).

- In choosing among the alternatives, the court must consider the juvenile's needs as outlined in the risk and needs assessment section of the predisposition report, the appropriate community resources available to meet those needs, and the protection of the public. G.S. 7B-2508(c).

Level 2 (Intermediate Disposition)

- Dispositional alternatives (1)–(23) under G.S. 7B-2506 are available to the court with the proviso that at least one disposition listed in (13)–(23) must be ordered. The court may order a Level 3 disposition if the juvenile has received a Level 3 disposition in a prior proceeding. G.S. 7B-2508(d).

- The standard for determination of the appropriate disposition is the same as for a Level 1 disposition. G.S. 7B-2508(d).

- The court may impose a Level 2 disposition even if the juvenile is subject to a Level 3 disposition if the court makes written findings that substantiate extraordinary needs of the juvenile. G.S. 7B-2508(e).

Level 3 (Commitment)

- Only alternative (24), commitment to the Division of Juvenile Justice of the Department of Public Safety, is allowed as a disposition under Level 3. G.S. 7B-2508(e); *see also infra* Chapter 15, Commitment to the Division of Adult Correction and Juvenile Justice.

- The court may order a Level 3 disposition if the juvenile has four or more separate adjudications of delinquency. G.S. 7B-2508(g). The prior adjudications must be non-overlapping, that is, the juvenile must have committed each successive offense after being adjudicated of the preceding offense. *Id.*

- If the juvenile is subject to a Level 2 disposition based on the offense classification and the delinquency history level, the court may order a Level 3 disposition if the juvenile has previously received a Level 3 disposition in a prior juvenile case. G.S. 7B-2508(d).

- If the juvenile is subject to a Level 2 disposition based on the offense classification and the delinquency history level, the court may order a Level 3 disposition if the court, after notice and a hearing, finds by the greater weight of the evidence that the juvenile has violated the conditions of probation. G.S. 7B-2510(e).

See supra § 13.6B, Statutory Categories; s*ee also* Janet Mason, Determining Dispositional Options for Delinquent Juveniles, 2007 New Juvenile Defender Program (UNC School of Government).

Consolidation of offenses. If a juvenile is adjudicated delinquent for more than one offense during a single session of court, the court must consolidate the offenses for disposition and impose a single disposition for the consolidated offenses based on the class of offense and delinquency history level for the most serious offense. G.S. 7B-2508(h).

The term "session" is not defined in the Juvenile Code. The Court of Appeals has indicated that "session" refers to a week-long period in juvenile court. *In re D.R.H.*, 194 N.C. App. 166, 169 (2008). If the juvenile is adjudicated for multiple offenses during separate sessions of court but a single disposition hearing is held for all of the offenses, the court may still consolidate the offenses for disposition.

The statute does not address the situation in which the juvenile is adjudicated delinquent while subject to the terms of a prior dispositional order. In *In re Thompson*, 74 N.C. App. 329, 330 (1985), the Court of Appeals held that a trial court could set a dispositional order to run consecutive to an existing dispositional order. Although *Thompson* has not been overruled, its precedential value is limited under the current version of the Juvenile Code. Under G.S. 7B-2513, most Level 3 commitments involve an indefinite maximum term. Further, the decision to extend the juvenile's commitment is determined by the Division. G.S. 7B-2515. Consequently, if a trial judge wanted to impose a consecutive Level 3 dispositional order, there would likely be no fixed date by which the judge could set the new disposition to begin. Additionally, while there is no specific procedure in the Juvenile Code that addresses this situation, counsel should argue that the trial court should consolidate the new Level 3 disposition into the prior disposition and permit the Division to determine when the juvenile should be released.

If the juvenile is adjudicated for an offense while serving an existing term of probation, counsel should argue against the imposition of an additional term of probation for the new adjudication. Counsel should assert that subjecting the juvenile to two concurrent periods of probation would be confusing, especially if the orders contain different conditions. Counsel should therefore advocate for modification of the existing period of probation based on the new adjudication.

Court's discretion. The court has wide discretion in ordering a disposition within this statutory scheme. For example, it can order dismissal or a continuance of disposition in any case. G.S. 7B-2501(d); *see supra* "Dismissal" and "Continuance of disposition" in § 13.5A, Conduct of the Hearing. Level 1 dispositional alternatives may be ordered in every case. Level 2 dispositional alternatives are permissible for Level 3 cases on the court's finding of extraordinary needs of the juvenile. G.S. 7B-2508(e). For Level 2 cases, the court must order at least one intermediate dispositional alternative in G.S. 7B-2506(13)–(23). G.S. 7B-2508(d).

In some cases, the court also has discretion to determine the disposition level. *See In re Robinson*, 151 N.C. App. 733, 738 (2002) (court had discretion to impose either Level 2 or Level 3 disposition as juvenile committed offense classified as "violent" and had "low" delinquency history level; no abuse of discretion in ordering a Level 3 disposition because court based its order on juvenile's high risk of reoffending and needs of juvenile); *In re N.B.*, 167 N.C. App. 305, 311 (2004) (court had discretion to impose either Level 2 or Level 3 disposition because juvenile committed offense classified as "violent" and had "low" delinquency history level; no abuse of discretion in ordering Level 3 disposition based on juvenile's continued excessive absences from school).

Counsel should emphasize this statutory discretion to the court in arguing for an appropriate disposition at the lowest dispositional level. This is particularly important because after a juvenile is placed on Level 2, even for a low-level felony or Class A1 misdemeanor, the court may order commitment to a youth development center upon adjudication of a probation violation. G.S. 7B-2510(e); *see also infra* § 14.8E, Alternatives on Finding of a Violation.

13.9   Registration of Juvenile Adjudicated for Certain Sex Crimes

Registration requirements. A juvenile convicted as an adult of an offense requiring sex offender registration or monitoring is subject to the requirements, restrictions, and procedures applicable to adults, which are numerous. *See* G.S. 14-208.32 (so stating). If adjudicated in juvenile court, the restrictions are fewer and the offenses triggering them narrower.

A juvenile who is at least 11 years old may be ordered to register with the county sheriff for a sex crime if the court finds the juvenile to be a danger to the community and the juvenile is adjudicated delinquent for a violation of one of the following criminal statutes: G.S. 14-27.21 (first-degree forcible rape), G.S. 14-27.22 (second degree forcible rape), G.S. 14-27.24 (first-degree statutory rape), G.S. 14-27.26 (first-degree forcible sexual offense), G.S. 14-27.27 (second-degree forcible sexual offense), or G.S. 14-27.29 (first-degree statutory sexual offense). G.S. 7B-2509. The registration statute also refers to G.S. 14-27.6, but that statute has been repealed. Also included are an attempt, conspiracy, or solicitation of another to commit any of the offenses, or aiding or abetting any of the offenses. G.S. 14-208.26(a1). The court must specifically find that the juvenile is a danger to the community before ordering the juvenile to register.

If the court orders the juvenile to register, it must conduct the notification procedures specified in G.S. 14-208.8. The court must inform the juvenile of the requirement to register and obtain a statement signed by the juvenile stating that the juvenile was informed of the registration requirement. The court must also obtain biographical information from the juvenile, any aliases the juvenile might have, a statement indicating whether the juvenile is a student, and any online identifier the juvenile uses. G.S. 14-208.8(a)(2). The chief court counselor, not the juvenile, is responsible for filing the registration information with the sheriff. G.S. 14-208.26(b).

The Department of Public Safety must include the registration information in the Criminal Information Network. G.S. 14-208.31. That statute provides that the Department must maintain the registration information permanently. The information does not appear to be subject to expunction because all of the triggering offenses are Class C felonies or higher and therefore not subject to expunction under the applicable statutes. *See infra* Chapter 17, Expunction of Juvenile Records.

The information must also be maintained separately by the sheriff. It may be released only to law enforcement agencies and local boards of education. G.S. 14-208.29(b). The information is not a public record and not open to public inspection. G.S. 14-208.29(a). The statute also states that the information must not be included in the county or statewide registries of adults convicted of sex crimes or be made available to the public through the internet. *Id.*; *see also* G.S. 14-208.31 (stating that information maintained by Department of Public Safety is confidential).

Every year on the anniversary of the juvenile's initial registration and six months after that date, the sheriff must mail a verification form to the juvenile court counselor assigned to the juvenile. G.S. 14-208.28. The form must be signed by the court counselor and the juvenile and must indicate whether the juvenile still resides at the address last reported to the sheriff. If the juvenile has a new address, the court counselor must include the new address on the form. The court counselor must also return the form to the sheriff within three business days of receiving the form.

If the juvenile is ordered to register, the registration requirement automatically terminates on the juvenile's eighteenth birthday or when the jurisdiction of the juvenile court ends, whichever first occurs. G.S. 14-208.30.

Other requirements based on sex crimes. Adults convicted of sex crimes are subject to an array of regulations and restrictions, such as satellite-based monitoring and limitations on areas where they can reside and premises where they can go. It is clear that some of these provisions do not apply to juveniles. For example, juveniles are not subject to satellite-based monitoring. The satellite-based monitoring program is generally limited to individuals who are "convicted of a reportable conviction." G.S. 14-208.40(a). An adjudication is not a conviction, G.S. 7B-2412, and thus does not subject the juvenile to satellite-based monitoring. Likewise, the sexually violent predator registration program, which provides for lifetime registration, requires a conviction for a crime classified as a sexually violent offense. G.S. 14-208.20. Therefore, that program, too, does not apply to a juvenile adjudicated of a sex crime in juvenile court.

It is less clear whether other provisions applicable to adults, such as residential and premises restrictions or the crime of failure to register, apply to juveniles adjudicated of sex crimes. On the one hand, these provisions state that they apply to "registrants" or individuals "required to register under this Article"—that is, Article 27A of G.S. Chapter 14. *See, e.g.*, G.S. 14-208.11 (penalties for the failure to register), 14-208.16 (residential restrictions), and 14-208.18 (premises restrictions). The juvenile registry is one of four parts in Article 27A, which includes the residential and premises restrictions and the crime of failure to register.

On the other hand, the term "statewide registry" is defined under G.S. 14-208.6(8) as the adult registry described in G.S. 14-208.14 and does not include the juvenile registry. Thus, the general references to "registrants" in the various restrictions noted above do not necessarily apply to juvenile registrants. To the contrary, G.S. 14-208.26(a) states that a juvenile required to register on the juvenile registry is only required to register and maintain that registration as provided by "this Part"—that is, Part 4 of Article 27A— which does not contain any residential or premises restrictions or penalties for the failure to register or maintain registration. Those provisions are contained in Parts 2 and 3 of Article 27A. G.S. 14-208.32 states that the requirements of Parts 2 and 3 apply only to juveniles convicted as adults, suggesting that the residential, premises, and other restrictions in Parts 2 and 3 do not apply to juveniles on the juvenile registry.

Beyond a close reading of the relevant statutes, some of the restrictions applicable to adults are a poor fit for those on the juvenile registry. For example, some of the adult failure to register provisions in G.S. 14-208.11 center on the adult's failure to report to the sheriff or return verification forms. However, the juvenile court counselor, not the juvenile registrant, is required to complete those responsibilities. G.S. 14-208.26(b), 14-208.28. As a practical matter, the residential and premises restrictions are also difficult to apply to juveniles. If applicable, those restrictions could bar a juvenile from living at home with parents or from being present at any place intended for the use, care, or supervision of minors. It seems unlikely that the General Assembly intended this result.

Although there is no case law addressing whether residential and premises restrictions or the crime of failure to register apply to juveniles, counsel should argue that those provisions do not apply if the State intends charge a violation against a juvenile.

Impact of potential federal requirements. In 2006, Congress enacted the Adam Walsh Child Protection and Safety Act, which set federal sex offender registration requirements. The legislation provided financial incentives for states to create comparable registration requirements for convictions and adjudications for sex crimes. *In re McClain*, 226 N.C. App. 465, 468 (2013). North Carolina, like many other states, did not adopt the more stringent federal requirements for juveniles. *See* Jamie Markham, *The SORNA-Compliance Dog That Didn't Bark*, N.C. CRIM. L., UNC SCH. OF GOV'T BLOG (June 23, 2011). Nevertheless, counsel must advise juvenile clients adjudicated of sex crimes about the possible need for registration if they move to a state that has adopted the federal standards or if North Carolina adopts a fully compliant registration regime in the future. The law in other states is beyond the scope of this manual. For more information, consult the federal Office of Sex Offender Sentencing, Monitoring, Apprehending, Registering, and Tracking website.

13.10 Dispositional Order

A dispositional order must be in writing and must contain appropriate findings of fact and conclusions of law. G.S. 7B-2512(a). The findings must demonstrate that the court considered the factors under G.S. 7B-2501(c), discussed *supra* in "Dispositional guidelines" in § 13.5A, Conduct of the Hearing. *In re K.C.*, 226 N.C. App. 452, 462 (2013). If the court fails to make written findings on those factors, the dispositional order is subject to reversal. *In re V.M.*, 211 N.C. 389, 390–91 (2011).

At a minimum, the dispositional order must indicate that the court considered all of the factors in G.S. 7B-2501(c). Some cases indicate that the court must make findings on all of the factors and that reversal is required if the court makes findings on some but not all of the statutory factors. *See, e.g., In re K.C.*, 226 N.C. App. at 462–63. In *In re D.E.P.*, 796 S.E.2d 509 (2017), however, the Court of Appeals held that prior decisions did not impose such a requirement. Reviewing earlier decisions, the court asserted that it was not overruling decisions of other panels because there was "no support for a conclusion that in every case the 'appropriate' findings of fact must make reference to all of the factors listed in [G.S.] 7B-2501(c) . . . ." The court in *In re D.E.P.* concluded that a trial court's findings of fact are sufficient if they demonstrate consideration of all of the statutory factors.

In unpublished opinions, the Court of Appeals has also held that a court may satisfy its fact-finding duty under G.S. 7B-2512 by incorporating reports and assessments into the dispositional order. *In re T.L.M.*, 787 S.E.2d 464 (2016) (unpublished); *In re D.O.B.*, 213 N.C. App. 422 (2011) (unpublished). Incorporation may not always be adequate, however. Cases have recognized that the trial court "should not broadly incorporate . . . written reports from outside sources as its findings of fact," *In re J.S.*, 165 N.C. App. 509, 511 (2004), or use reports "as a substitute for its own independent review." *In re M.R.D.C.*, 166 N.C. App. 693, 698 (2004). In *In re V.M.*, 211 N.C. App. 389, 392 (2011), the trial court checked boxes on the dispositional order stating that the juvenile was adjudicated for a violent or serious offense and that he had violated the terms of probation. The court also incorporated reports and assessments into the order. The Court of Appeals reversed the dispositional order because the order contained insufficient findings of fact.

The court must state with particularity, both orally and in the written order, the precise dispositional terms, including the kind and duration, as well as the person who is responsible for implementation of the disposition and the person or agency granted custody if there is an order changing custody. G.S. 7B-2512(a). In addition, the court must provide information about the possibility of expunction of juvenile records either orally or in writing. G.S. 7B-2512(b). For information on expunging juvenile court records, *see infra* Chapter 17, Expunction of Juvenile Records.

13.11 Modification of Dispositional Order

A. Jurisdiction

The court has jurisdiction pursuant to G.S. 7B-2600(c) to modify a dispositional order during the following periods:

- during the minority of the juvenile;
- until the juvenile reaches the age of 19 years if the juvenile has been committed to the Division for the offenses specified;
- until the juvenile reaches the age of 21 years if the juvenile has been committed to the Division for first-degree murder, first-degree forcible rape, or first-degree forcible sexual offense; or
- until terminated by order of the court (but not later than the above time periods).

B. Procedures for Modifying a Dispositional Order

After the court orders a disposition, it can enter an order modifying the disposition on motion of the juvenile or the State. A sample motion to modify a dispositional order is available on the Juvenile Defender website.

There are three circumstances in which the court can modify the disposition. First, the court may hold a hearing on the modification of a dispositional order on the filing of a motion or petition under G.S. 7B-2600(a). Since the statute does not specify that the motion or petition must be filed by the juvenile, the State may also file a motion or petition. At the hearing on the dispositional order, the court must determine whether the dispositional order is in the best interests of the juvenile and may modify or vacate the order based on "changes in circumstances" or the "needs of the juvenile." G.S. 7B-2600(a). In *In re D.G.*, 191 N.C. App. 752, 756 (2008), the Court of Appeals upheld an order striking residential sex offender treatment from a dispositional order because the court counselor determined that the juvenile was not eligible for the treatment. The Court held that the modification was proper under G.S. 7B-2600(a) because the court counselor's determination the juvenile was not eligible for the treatment program qualified as a change in circumstances under G.S. 7B-2600(a).

Second, the court may reduce the nature or duration of the disposition under G.S. 7B-2600(b) if the dispositional order was imposed in an illegal manner or is unduly severe with respect to the seriousness of the offense, the culpability of the juvenile, or the dispositions given to juveniles adjudicated delinquent for similar offenses. In *In re A.F.*, 231 N.C. App. 348 (2013), the Court of Appeals reversed the denial of a motion to modify filed under G.S. 7B-2600(b). According to the Court of Appeals, the trial court improperly assessed two delinquency history points under G.S. 7B-2507 for committing the offense while on probation because the juvenile was not on probation on the offense date for the case. Based on the improper assessment of the two points, the Court of Appeals concluded that the trial court did not have the authority to impose a Level 3 disposition in its original dispositional order and that the trial court erred by denying the motion to modify the order.

Third, the court may order an alternative disposition under G.S. 7B-2601 if the Division of Juvenile Justice determines that the juvenile is not suitable for its program. If the court orders an alternative disposition under G.S. 7B-2601, the alternative disposition must be consistent with G.S. 7B-2508.

C. Appeal of Denial of Motion to Modify Disposition

Although the Court of Appeals discussed motions filed under G.S. 7B-2600 in *In re D.G.*, 191 N.C. App. 752, 756 (2008), and *In re A.F.*, 231 N.C. App. 348 (2013), it did not discuss whether a juvenile has the right to appeal the denial of a motion to modify a dispositional order. In both cases, the right to appeal was not in dispute because the juveniles appealed both the dispositional orders and the orders denying their motions to modify disposition. There are no other cases that discuss the right to appeal the denial of a motion to modify a dispositional order. The juvenile may have the right to appeal such an order under G.S. 7B-2602. According to subsection (3) of the statute, a juvenile may appeal from "[a]ny order of disposition . . . ." An order denying a motion to modify disposition arguably falls under subsection (3). For a further discussion of the juvenile's right to appeal, see *infra* Chapter 16, Appeals.

N★C
DPS
DEPARTMENT OF PUBLIC SAFETY
PREVENT · PROTECT · PREPARE

JUVENILE JUSTICE
Consent for Preparation of a Pre-Disposition Report

Juvenile's Full Name: *[Juvenile Name]*   Juvenile's DOB: *[Juvenile Date of Birth]*

If the above listed complaint(s) is/are approved for filing as a petition with the court, this consent allows a pre-disposition report to be prepared prior to adjudication. An adjudicatory hearing is a court hearing to decide if the facts of the petition are true. A pre-disposition report will contain information about your child and recommendations to the court for an appropriate plan to meet the needs of your child and to protect the public. The pre-disposition report includes Juvenile Family Data Sheet/social history information (e.g. family history, medical, psychiatric, psychological, and educational information), a Risk and Needs Assessment/Summary, and Service Plan.

I understand the pre-disposition report may be reviewed by my child's attorney. The report may be shared with the District Attorney and the presiding judge only if the petition(s) is/are found to be true. All juvenile information shall remain confidential.

I understand that I am not required to sign this consent form, and that services will not be adversely affected if I choose not to sign.

I understand that I have the right to revoke this authorization at any time by signing the *Action to Revoke* section at the bottom of this form, except for information that has already been released. Unless revoked sooner, this authorization expires at the completion of JJ involvement or the termination of court jurisdiction.

Juvenile: _____

Parent, Guardian, or Custodian: _____

Parent, Guardian, or Custodian: _____

Witness: _____

Attorney (Optional): _____

Date: _____

ACTION TO REVOKE

I _____, on this day _____, attest that I revoke this authorization.

_____   _____
Signature   *Date*

Form CS 011a Consent for Preparation of a Pre-Disposition Report
Form structure last revised May 2016
NC Department of Public Safety, Juvenile Justice

Page 26 or 1

Appendix 13-2: Quick Reference Guide for Dispositional Hearings

Offense Classification
[G.S. 7B-2508(a)(1), (2), (3)]
- **Violent:** Adjudication of a Class A through E felony
- **Serious:** Adjudication of a Class F through I felony or a Class A1 misdemeanor
- **Minor:** Adjudication of a Class 1, 2, or 3 misdemeanor

Delinquency History Points
[G.S. 7B-2507(b)(1), (2), (3), (4)]
- Each prior adjudication of a Class A through E felony = 4 points
- Each prior adjudication of a Class F through I felony or Class A1 misdemeanor = 2 points
- Each prior adjudication of a Class 1, 2, or 3 misdemeanor = 1 point
- If the juvenile was on probation at the time of offense = 2 points

Multiple Prior Adjudications
[G.S. 7B-2507(d)]
- For purposes of determining the delinquent history level, if a juvenile is adjudicated delinquent for more than one offense in a single session of district court, only the adjudication for the offense with the highest point total is used.

Special Dispositional Circumstances
- If the disposition chart prescribes a Level 2 disposition, the court may impose a Level 3 disposition if the juvenile was previously committed to a youth development center in a prior juvenile action. [G.S. 7B-2508(d)]
- The court may impose a Level 2 disposition rather than a Level 3 disposition if the court submits written findings that substantiate extraordinary needs of the juvenile. [G.S. 7B-2508(e)]
- A juvenile who has been adjudicated for a minor offense may be committed to a Level 3 disposition if the juvenile has been adjudicated of four or more prior offenses. For purposes of determining the number of prior offenses, each successive offense is one that was committed after adjudication of the preceding offense. [G.S. 7B-2508(g)]

Violation of Probation
- The court shall not order a Level 3 disposition for violation of the conditions of probation by a juvenile adjudicated delinquent for a minor offense. [G.S. 7B-2510(f)]
- If the court finds that the juvenile has violated the conditions of probation, the court may continue the original conditions of probation, modify the conditions of probation, or order a new disposition at the next higher level on the disposition chart (except that the court may not impose a Level 3 disposition for a juvenile adjudicated delinquent for a minor offense). Part of the new disposition may include an order of confinement in a secure juvenile detention facility for up to twice the term authorized by G.S. 7B-2508. [G.S. 7B-2510(e)]

Appendix 13-3: Juvenile Disposition Options

LEVEL 1: COMMUNITY	LEVEL 2: INTERMEDIATE*	LEVEL 3: COMMITMENT**
1. custody of juvenile to home/custodian/DSS	Any Level 1 disposition may be imposed but <u>at least one</u> of the following must be imposed:	1. training school not less than 6 months
2. alternative schooling	1. wilderness program	** Court may impose a Level 2 disposition if it submits written findings of extraordinary needs of the juvenile
3. community based/substance abuse/residential or nonresidential treatment up to 12 months	2. placement in resident treatment/intensive nonresidential treatment/intensive substance abuse or non-State group home	
4. restitution up to $500	3. intensive probation	
5. fine	4. supervised day program	
6. community service up to 100 hours	5. regimented training program	
7. victim-offender reconciliation program	6. house arrest	
8. probation	7. suspend disposition with conditions	
9. driver's license not issued	8. detention up to 14 24-hour periods	
10. curfew	9. residential placement in a State multipurpose group home	
11. not associate with persons/places	10. restitution more than $500	
12. intermittent detention up to 5 24-hour periods	11. community service up to 200 hours	
13. wilderness program	* Court may impose a Level 3 disposition if the juvenile has previously received a Level 3 disposition in a prior juvenile action	

Chapter 14
Probation

14.1   Overview

Probation is a dispositional alternative that may be ordered by the court pursuant to either a Level 1 or Level 2 disposition. A juvenile who is on probation is placed under the supervision of a juvenile court counselor and may be subject to a number of statutory conditions.

Violation of a condition of probation may subject a juvenile to extension of probation, modification of the conditions of probation, or in some cases entry of disposition at the next higher level. A juvenile who is moved from a Level 2 to Level 3 disposition as a result of a probation violation will usually receive a commitment to the Division of Adult Correction and Juvenile Justice for confinement in a locked facility.

14.2   Terminology Used in this Chapter

Division is the Division of Adult Correction and Juvenile Justice.

Intensive probation is a dispositional alternative under G.S. 7B-2506(15), although the term is not defined by either statute or policy. Under Division policy, intensive probation is treated as a form of intensive supervision.

Intensive supervision is court-ordered supervision by a juvenile court counselor. G.S. 7B-2510(b)(5). The intensive supervision counselor maintains a small caseload and makes frequent contacts with the juvenile, the juvenile's parent, guardian, or custodian, and others involved with the juvenile. *See infra* "Intensive Supervision" in § 14.4C, As Directed by Chief Court Counselor: Level 2.

Motion for review hearing is a hearing pursuant to G.S. 7B-2510(d) to review the progress of a juvenile on probation at any time during probation or at the end of probation. Although a motion for review may contain an allegation of a violation of probation, a review hearing should not be a probation violation hearing unless proper notice has been given. *See infra* § 14.8A, Motion and Notice Required.

Probation is a dispositional alternative in which the juvenile is ordered to comply with specified conditions under the supervision of a juvenile court counselor. A juvenile may be returned to court for violation of those conditions during the probationary period. G.S. 7B-1501(22).

Probation violation hearing is a hearing to review a juvenile's probation on motion and notice pursuant to G.S. 7B-2510(d), alleging a specific violation of probation. *See infra* § 14.8, Violation of Probation.

14.3   When Probation May Be Ordered

A. Generally

Probation is a dispositional alternative after an adjudication of delinquency if the juvenile is eligible for a Level 1 or Level 2 disposition. *See supra* § 13.8, Dispositional Limits for Each Class of Offense and History Level. Under Level 1 (community disposition), regular probation may be ordered. G.S. 7B-2506(8), 7B-2508(c). Under Level 2 (intermediate disposition), the juvenile may be placed on either regular or intensive probation. G.S. 7B-2506(8), (15); 7B-2508(d).

B. Advocacy at Dispositional Hearing when Probation Is Ordered

Although probation is not a required dispositional alternative, it is routinely ordered. Counsel should work to create a dispositional plan that meets the juvenile's expressed interests and limits exposure to further sanctions. Counsel should argue against an order of probation when not warranted by the evidence to avoid exposing the juvenile to a possible allegation of violation of probation in the future, which could lead to commitment to a youth development center on revocation of probation in a case with a Level 2 disposition.

G.S. 7B-2510(a) authorizes courts to impose conditions of probation that are "related to the needs of the juvenile" and that are "reasonably necessary to ensure that the juvenile will lead a law-abiding life . . . ." *See also infra* § 14.5, Conditions of Probation: Case Law. If the juvenile does not have a significant record in juvenile court and the predisposition report and risk and needs assessment indicate that the juvenile has a supportive family, counsel should argue that probation would not address the juvenile's needs and is not necessary to ensure that the juvenile leads a law-abiding life.

If the court orders probation, counsel should seek to limit the conditions imposed as part of probation. Any conditions must be related to the adjudicated offense and the needs of the juvenile. *See* G.S. 7B-2501(c) (requiring court to select disposition that protects the public but also meets the needs and best interests of the juvenile). Also, if the court imposes multiple conditions, there is a risk that the juvenile will not understand all of the conditions and will be more likely to violate them. "Research shows that young adolescents have lower cognitive capacities, particularly in stressful situations, than adults." Theresa Hughes, *A Paradigm of Youth Client Satisfaction: Heightening Professional Responsibility for Children's Advocates*, 40 COLUM. J.L. & SOC. PROBS. 551, 566 (2007). A "long recitation of rules" may also be difficult to understand by a person with impaired language skills, regardless of whether it is oral or in writing. Michele LaVigne & Gregory J. Van Rybroek, *Breakdown in the Language Zone: The Prevalence of Language Impairments Among Juvenile and Adult Offenders and Why It Matters*, 15 U.C. DAVIS J. JUV. L. & POL'Y 37, 80 (2011). Additionally, some of the conditions that the court can impose, such as remaining on "good behavior," are vague. Others, such as making "specified financial restitution," involve legal terminology. If the court imposes multiple conditions, there is a risk that the juvenile will not understand all of the conditions and will be more likely to be found in violation of the conditions of probation.

The risk is greater as the number of conditions increases. A court may impose 14 conditions of probation, plus community service, substance abuse monitoring, life skills or educational skills programs, electronic monitoring, and intensive supervision. G.S. 7B-2510. These conditions are in addition to the 14 dispositional alternatives that a court may impose for a Level 1 Disposition and the 23 dispositional alternatives that a court may impose for a Level 2 Disposition. G.S. 7B-2508(c), (d). Additionally, the forms that courts use to impose dispositional alternatives and conditions of probation reflect the language used in the statutes and do not provide simplified language that can be understood by juveniles. *See e.g.,* AOC-J-464 (Supplemental Order for Conditions of Probation) (Dec. 2015). The court should explain each condition of probation to the juvenile in developmentally appropriate language during the dispositional hearing. Counsel should also carefully explain the conditions to the juvenile after the hearing and ensure that the juvenile understands each condition.

14.4 Conditions of Probation

This section describes statutorily authorized conditions of probation. Limitations on certain conditions of probation are discussed *infra* in § 14.5, Conditions of Probation: Case Law.

A. Generally

A juvenile court counselor has the authority to visit a juvenile's residence if the juvenile is on probation. G.S. 7B-2510(a). In addition, the court may order a juvenile to comply with regular conditions of probation that are "related to the needs of the juvenile and that are reasonably necessary to ensure that the juvenile will lead a law-abiding life . . . ." G.S. 7B-2510(a). The statute lists 14 regular conditions that are specifically authorized. The court may order that a juvenile:

- remain on good behavior;
- not violate any laws;
- not violate any reasonable and lawful rules of a parent, guardian, or custodian;
- attend school regularly;
- maintain passing grades in up to four courses and cooperate with planning for such;
- not associate with specified people or be in specified places;
- refrain from use or possession of any controlled substance, refrain from use or possession of any alcoholic beverage, and submit to random drug testing;
- abide by a prescribed curfew;
- submit to a warrantless search at reasonable times;
- possess no firearm, explosive device, or other deadly weapon;
- report to a juvenile court counselor as required by the counselor;
- make specified financial restitution;

- be employed regularly if not attending school; and
- satisfy any other conditions determined appropriate by the court.

B. As Directed by Chief Court Counselor: Generally

The juvenile may also be ordered to comply with other conditions "if directed to comply by the chief court counselor." G.S. 7B-2510(b). Under G.S. 7B-2510(b)(1)–(3), the juvenile may be required by the chief juvenile court counselor to:

- perform up to 20 hours of community service,
- submit to substance abuse monitoring and treatment, and
- participate in a life skills or educational skills program administered by the Division.

C. As Directed by Chief Court Counselor: Level 2

Under G.S. 7B-2510(b)(4)–(5), a juvenile who is eligible for a Level 2 disposition may be ordered to comply with the following conditions at the direction of the chief court counselor:

- cooperate with electronic monitoring, and
- cooperate with intensive supervision.

Electronic monitoring. Electronic monitoring is a form of supervision over a juvenile that involves checking the juvenile's location through an electronic monitoring device that is fastened to the juvenile's body. *See* Number CS 13.1, "Electronic Monitoring Requirements and Procedures (R&P) Document," Department of Juvenile Justice and Delinquency Prevention (Oct. 3, 2013). Electronic monitoring is not the same as a dispositional order for house arrest under G.S. 7B-2506(18). If the court orders electronic monitoring as part of probation, the juvenile court counselor must oversee the installation of electronic monitoring equipment in the juvenile's residence. The juvenile court counselor must then establish exclusion and inclusion zones for the juvenile. Exclusion zones are geographic areas that the juvenile is prohibited from entering, such as a victim's home or a particular neighborhood. Inclusion zones are geographic areas where the juvenile is required to be during specific time periods, such as a school or business where the juvenile works. The juvenile court counselor must monitor notifications from the electronic monitoring equipment and respond when there are alerts involving tampering with the electronic monitoring device or violations of exclusion or inclusion zones by the juvenile.

Intensive supervision. The requirements for intensive supervision are outlined by Division policy, but are not defined by statute. *See* Number CS 3.1, "Supervision," Department of Juvenile Justice and Delinquency Prevention (Oct. 17, 2006). Under Division policy, a juvenile court counselor may supervise a maximum of 12 juveniles on intensive supervision. The counselor must contact the juvenile and the juvenile's parent, guardian, or custodian immediately after the juvenile is assigned to intensive supervision. Face-to-face contact must be made by the counselor with the juvenile at least three times every seven days, with at least one contact to be on the weekend or outside of regular school hours. In addition, contact with the parent must be made in person at least once every seven days, with a visit to the juvenile's residence at least every seven days. Finally, the counselor is required to make one contact per week with someone at the juvenile's school, the juvenile's work, or others involved significantly with the juvenile.

Contacts may gradually become less frequent with the approval of the chief court counselor. At a minimum, the counselor must have contact with the juvenile at least once every seven days, with the parent, guardian, or custodian every 14 days, and with school personnel and others at least once every 21 calendar days. Counsel will generally have to ask the juvenile court counselor or review the juvenile court counselor's file to learn if less frequent contacts have been approved.

14.5 Conditions of Probation: Case Law

North Carolina appellate courts have considered the propriety of some of the regular conditions of probation, including the provision under G.S. 7B-2510(a)(14) permitting courts to impose "other conditions determined appropriate by the court." This section contains a brief review of some of these cases as well as pertinent statutory limitations.

Although courts in some districts routinely order certain regular conditions of probation, G.S. 7B-2510(a) states that courts can only impose regular conditions that are "related to the needs of the juvenile" and that are "reasonably necessary to ensure that the juvenile will lead a law-abiding life." In adult criminal cases, courts are permitted to impose non-statutory special conditions of probation that are "reasonably related" to the defendant's rehabilitation. G.S. 15A-1343(b1)(10). This language "operates as a check on the discretion of trial judges." *State v. Lambert*, 146 N.C. App. 360, 367 (2001). Likewise, where appropriate, counsel should argue that the statutory language in G.S. 7B-2510(a) limits the discretion of judges to impose certain regular conditions of probation in juvenile cases.

A. Restitution

The court may require the juvenile to pay restitution as a condition of probation, G.S. 7B-2510(a)(12). However, the following limitations apply to any order of restitution:

1. If the court imposes a Level 1 disposition, it may not order more than $500.00 of restitution. G.S. 7B-2506(4), 7B-2508(c). The court may order more than $500.00 if the court imposes a Level 2 disposition. G.S. 7B-2506(22), 7B-2508(d).
2. The court may not order restitution without finding that payment of restitution is in the juvenile's best interest. *In re Z.A.K.*, 189 N.C. App. 354, 362 (2008).
3. The court may not order restitution if the juvenile is unable to pay the restitution amount. G.S. 7B-2506(4). The burden is on the juvenile to establish an inability to pay. *Id.*; *see also In re Schrimpsher*, 143 N.C. App. 461, 464 (2001) (holding that

imposition of restitution was proper where the juvenile, when given an opportunity to be heard, presented no evidence that he lacked the means to pay restitution).

4. Unless the juvenile stipulates to the amount of restitution, an order of restitution must be supported by findings of fact, which in turn must be supported by some evidence in the record. *In re McDonald*, 133 N.C. App. 433, 436 (1999).

5. The period within which the court may require the juvenile to pay restitution may not exceed 12 months. G.S. 7B-2506(4); *In re Heil*, 145 N.C. App. 24, 31–33 (2001).

The court may hold multiple individuals jointly and severally liable for payment of restitution. G.S. 7B-2506(4), (22). However, restitution will not be upheld even if the record indicates that the others participated in the crime if the court fails to make any findings from which the appellate court can determine that the others "acted jointly in causing harm." *In re Schrimpsher*, 143 N.C. App. 461, 465–66 (2001).

B. Submission to Urinalysis, Blood, or Breathalyzer Testing

The trial court may require the juvenile to submit to random drug testing as a condition of probation. G.S. 7B-2510(a)(7)c. However, as with other probation conditions, any testing must be "related to the needs of the juvenile" and "reasonably necessary to ensure that the juvenile will lead a law-abiding life." G.S. 7B-2510(a). Counsel should carefully review the predisposition report and risk and needs assessment. If the predisposition report and risk and needs assessment indicate that the juvenile has not used alcohol or drugs, and the juvenile has not been adjudicated of an offense involving alcohol or drugs, counsel should argue that testing is not warranted. If the court imposes drug testing, it may not require the juvenile to submit to testing requested by "any law enforcement." *In re Schrimpsher*, 143 N.C. App. 461, 466–67 (2001). Any testing must instead be requested by the juvenile court counselor. *Id.*

The trial court also may impose substance abuse monitoring and treatment as a condition of probation under G.S. 7B-2510(b)(2). However, monitoring and treatment under this provision may only occur if it is directed by the chief court counselor. G.S. 7B-2510(b).

If it is unclear whether the court has ordered random drug testing under G.S. 7B-2510(a)(7)c. or substance abuse monitoring and treatment under G.S. 7B-2510(b)(2), counsel should ask the court to clarify which condition it intended to impose and the basis for doing so.

C. Other Conditions

Requiring others to consent to warrantless searches. Pursuant to G.S. 7B-2510(a)(6), the court may order that the juvenile "not associate with specified persons or be in specified places." That authority does not extend, however, to ordering that those with whom the juvenile resides or rides consent to warrantless searches. *In re Schrimpsher*, 143 N.C. App. 461, 468–69 (2001). The Court found that it was "unfair and unreasonable" to require those not under the court's jurisdiction to consent to warrantless searches. Additionally, such a requirement would give people other than the juvenile control over the success or failure of the probation.

Wearing sign. The court may not order a juvenile to wear a sign in public that identifies the juvenile as delinquent. *In re MEB*, 153 N.C. App. 278, 282 (2002). In *MEB*, the juvenile was ordered to wear a large sign in public stating "I am a juvenile criminal." This requirement was held to violate the juvenile's right to confidentiality pursuant to G.S. 7B-3001(b), and to subject the juvenile to a choice between public ridicule and de facto house arrest in violation of the Juvenile Code and public policy.

Wearing necklace with victim's picture and visiting gravesite on anniversaries of victim's birth and death. The court distinguished the condition in *MEB* from requirements that a juvenile wear a necklace containing the victim's picture and place flowers on the victim's grave on the anniversaries of the victim's birth and death. *In re J.B.*, 172 N.C. App. 747, 751–53 (2005). In *J.B.*, which involved the offense of involuntary manslaughter, the Court found that the special conditions of probation, unlike those in *MEB*, did not expose the juvenile's record of delinquency to the public and did not amount to de facto house arrest. The juvenile could wear the victim's picture enclosed in a locket, which could be worn under clothing; visiting the gravesite was not addressed. The Court found that there was no requirement that the lower court solicit or consider a therapist's opinion regarding the potential for either benefit or damage to the juvenile from these conditions.

Restricting participation in activities. A prohibition on watching television for one year has been upheld as a condition of probation. *In re McDonald*, 133 N.C. App. 433, 435 (1999). In *McDonald*, the juvenile stated in court that she spray-painted the words "Charles Manson Rules" on someone else's property because she had recently watched a television documentary about him. Because the condition was related to the juvenile's misconduct, the injury to property, and her need to be free of negative influences, the Court found that the special condition was proper.

A restriction on participating in school activities, such as football or dances, was held to be proper where the court had evidence that the juvenile had difficulty engaging in age-appropriate behavior during complex social interactions. *In re J.B.*, 172 N.C. App. 747, 753 (2005). The Court noted that the juvenile could continue to interact with his peers in more structured settings, such as during regular school hours and at church, and was restricted only from those activities that posed the greatest danger for inappropriate or delinquent conduct.

Requiring admission of sex offense. The decision of the U.S. Supreme Court in *Minnesota v. Murphy*, 465 U.S. 420 (1984), that the constitutional right against self-incrimination prohibits making a waiver of the right a condition of probation, has been held applicable to juvenile cases. *In re T.R.B.*, 157 N.C. App. 609, 620 (2003). In *T.R.B.*, the Court of Appeals held that under *Murphy* a condition of probation ordering that the juvenile complete a sex offender evaluation and treatment program, which required attendance at all meetings and admission of responsibility for the offense, was impermissible. The Court noted that there may be an exception if the juvenile is granted immunity from use of the statements in subsequent prosecutions. *Id.* at 621–22 (*quoting Murphy*, 465 U.S. at 435 n.7).

14.6 Intensive Probation

Although the court may order intensive probation as a disposition pursuant to G.S. 7B-2506(15), the term is not defined by statute. The policies of the Division do not address the requirements for intensive probation, but appear to categorize it under court-ordered supervision as the same as intensive supervision. *See supra* "Intensive supervision" in § 14.4C, As Directed by Chief Court Counselor: Level 2; *see also* Number CS 3.1, "Supervision," Department of Juvenile Justice and Delinquency Prevention (Oct. 17, 2006).

14.7 Term of Probation

A. Generally

A term of probation is limited to one year but may be extended by the court. If the court orders probation or extends probation, counsel should ask the court to specify a date certain for the end of probation or a time for a review hearing before the period of probation expires to ensure that there is no confusion about when the juvenile's probation ends.

B. Extending Probation

There are two ways that a court can extend probation, discussed below.

To protect community or safeguard juvenile. The court may extend probation under G.S. 7B-2510(c) if the extension is "necessary to protect the community or to safeguard the welfare of the juvenile." The juvenile must be provided notice and a hearing before probation is extended. Although G.S. 7B-2510(c) does not specify the type of notice that is required, G.S. 7B-1807 states that the clerk must give the juvenile five days written notice of the date and time of hearings unless the juvenile is notified in open court. The hearing under G.S. 7B-2510(c) should occur before probation expires. However, the court has discretion to extend probation after probation expires if the hearing occurs "at the next regularly scheduled court date or if the juvenile fails to appear in court."

If the court extends probation, it must make findings to support the conclusion that the extension is necessary to protect the community or to safeguard the welfare of the juvenile. *See In re D.L.H.*, 198 N.C. App. 286, 296 (2009) (upholding extension order where the trial court made multiple findings indicating that the juvenile was absent from school and the juvenile's mother was not willing to have the juvenile placed in her home), *overruled on other grounds*, 364 N.C. 214 (2010).

Appellate courts have not interpreted this part of subsection (c). Some trial courts may interpret this language to mean that they can extend probation multiple times for up to a year. Regardless of how the language is interpreted, counsel should oppose any efforts to extend the juvenile's probation beyond a year.

For probation violations. The court may extend probation under G.S. 7B-2510(d) and (e) if it finds by the greater weight of the evidence that the juvenile has violated the conditions of probation. The juvenile must be given notice and a hearing before the court extends the juvenile's probation. G.S. 7B-2510(d). A stipulation by the juvenile at a later hearing that probation had previously been extended is not a substitute for the notice and hearing requirements of G.S. 7B-2510(d). *In re A.F.*, 231 N.C. App. 348, 356 (2013). Additionally, G.S. 7B-2510(d) provides that "the conditions or duration of probation may be modified *only as provided in this subchapter* . . . ." (emphasis added). Under G.S. 7B-2510(c), probation may not be extended beyond a year. Based on the language in subsection (c), counsel should argue that an extension under subsections (d) and (e) should not exceed a year.

The court has limited authority to extend probation under G.S. 7B-2510(d) and (e) after the original term of probation expires. In *In re T.J.*, 146 N.C. App. 605 (2001), the juvenile court counselor filed a motion for review before the expiration of the probationary term. The court then held a hearing two weeks after the probationary period was set to end and extended the juvenile's probation for six months. Citing G.S. 7B-2510(d), which provides that the court may review the juvenile's progress "at any time during the period of probation or at the end of probation," the Court held that the court had limited discretion to modify probation within a reasonable time after its expiration. *Id.* at 607.

If the court counselor files a motion for review *after* the probationary term has ended, counsel should move to dismiss the motion on the ground that probation has expired. Counsel should distinguish *T.J.*, where the motion was filed during the probationary period, and assert that the court's jurisdiction to extend probation expired when the period of probation ended. *See, e.g., State v. Moore*, 148 N.C. App. 568, 570 (2002) (trial court did not have jurisdiction to modify the defendant's probation where the State failed to establish that the violation report was filed before the probationary period expired).

Practice note: Counsel should object if the State seeks to extend probation for a reason not provided in the notice for the hearing. For example, the juvenile court counselor might file a motion for review alleging that the juvenile violated the conditions of probation, but then argue at the hearing on the motion that probation should be extended to safeguard the welfare of the juvenile. Counsel should oppose the extension and argue that extending probation for a reason that was not included in the motion for review would violate the juvenile's rights to notice and due process.

14.8   Violation of Probation

A.   Motion and Notice Required

The progress of the juvenile on probation may be reviewed on motion of the juvenile
court counselor, the juvenile, or the court. Conditions or the duration of probation may be
modified only after notice and a hearing. G.S. 7B-2510(d). The juvenile and the
juvenile's parent, guardian, or custodian are entitled to five days written notice before a
hearing on an alleged violation of probation. G.S. 7B-1807. If the clerk gives less than
five days notice of the violation hearing and counsel has not had sufficient time to
prepare, counsel should ask for a continuance.

Counsel should also oppose any motion for review filed by the prosecutor. A sample
motion to dismiss for lack of standing is available on the Office of the Juvenile Defender
website. According to G.S. 7B-2510(d), the only individuals who are permitted to file a
motion for review are the juvenile court counselor, the juvenile, and the court, not the
prosecutor. Based on G.S. 7B-2510(d), counsel should argue that any violations
described in the prosecutor's motion for review that are not included in a motion for
review filed by the juvenile court counselor cannot form the basis of a finding that the
juvenile violated the conditions of probation.

Counsel should also object on notice and due process grounds to any other violations that
were not included in the motion for review filed by the juvenile court counselor.
Juveniles have the right to notice before a hearing on an alleged probation violation. G.S.
7B-2510(e). In criminal court, it is improper for a court to revoke probation based on
conduct not alleged in the violation report. *State v. Cunningham*, 63 N.C. App. 470, 475
(1983); *cf. State v. Hubbard*, 198 N.C. App. 154 (2009) (trial court properly revoked
probation based on a condition not described in the violation report because the report
contained facts that supported the violation found by the court). Counsel should argue
that the same principles apply to juvenile cases and that finding a violation that was not
alleged would violate the juvenile's rights to notice and due process.

B.   Secure Custody Pending Hearing

Where the juvenile is alleged to have violated probation, the court may order secure
custody pending the probation violation hearing if the juvenile is alleged to have
damaged property or injured persons. G.S. 7B-1903(d).

C.   Preparation for Hearing

Preparation for a hearing on a motion alleging a violation of probation is generally the
same as for a hearing on a petition. Counsel should meet with the juvenile and prepare
the juvenile to testify when helpful to the case, talk with the juvenile court counselor and
review the counselor's records, and make other contacts as required to investigate and
respond to the alleged violation. Witnesses and records should be subpoenaed as

necessary. If appropriate, counsel should explore negotiating an agreement with the juvenile court counselor or prosecutor.

Counsel should check the following items during hearing preparation to determine whether:

- the motion alleging violation of probation was filed within the probationary period;
- the juvenile was given adequate written notice of the alleged violation and hearing;
- the juvenile court counselor has correctly calculated the period of probation;
- the original order of probation was for a period of probation within the statutory provisions of G.S. 7B-2510(c); and
- the condition of probation that is alleged to have been violated was set forth in the dispositional order and was a condition of probation allowed under G.S. 7B-2510(a).

D. Burden of Proof

To establish that the juvenile violated the terms of probation, the State must prove the violation "by the greater weight of the evidence." G.S. 7B-2510(e). If the State establishes a violation, the trial court may not revoke probation unless the violation was willful or without a lawful excuse. The juvenile has the burden of showing one of these grounds. *In re Z.T.W.*, 238 N.C. App. 365, 369–70 (2014). Evidence showing inability to comply satisfies this burden. *Id.* If the juvenile presents evidence of an inability to comply with the terms of probation, the court must consider and evaluate the evidence before ruling on the violation. *Id.*

The rules of evidence do not apply at probation violation hearings because they are considered "dispositional." *In re D.J.M.*, 181 N.C. App. 126, 131 (2007); *see also* G.S. 7B-2501. The court therefore may rely on hearsay to find that the juvenile violated the terms of probation. *In re Z.T.W.*, 238 N.C. App. at 368–69. Counsel should still object to evidence that is not relevant or reliable, including hearsay, and argue that such evidence is insufficient to support a finding that the juvenile violated the terms of probation.

Practice note: Counsel should argue against an allegation that the juvenile has violated probation by virtue of having been alleged to be delinquent or charged with a new offense. Under G.S. 7B-2510(a)(2), the court may order the juvenile not to violate any laws. The juvenile is not in violation, however, by merely being accused of violating a law. The State must produce sufficient evidence to meet its burden of proof of the acts allegedly committed by the juvenile. *See State v. Seagraves*, 266 N.C. 112, 113 (1965) (per curiam) (holding that the "burden of proof is on the State to show that the defendant has violated one of the conditions of his probation").

E. Alternatives on Finding of a Violation

If the court finds that the juvenile violated conditions of probation, it may keep in place the original conditions, modify the conditions or, with one exception, order a new disposition at the next higher level from the original disposition. G.S. 7B-2510(e). The exception is that the court may not order a Level 3 disposition for a violation of probation if the original adjudication was for an offense classified as minor under G.S. 7B-2508. G.S. 7B-2510(f). Counsel should ask the court to enter a new disposition immediately rather than hold the juvenile in detention and continue the matter.

If the court orders a new disposition, it may order a period of confinement in a secure juvenile detention facility for up to twice the term authorized by G.S. 7B-2508, which sets forth dispositional limits for each class of offense and delinquency history level. G.S. 7B-2510(e). If the court orders detention, counsel should request that the juvenile be given credit for any time already served. Although the court is not required to give the juvenile credit for time served, *In re D.L.H.*, 364 N.C. 214, 216 (2010), counsel should advise the court that there is no prohibition against giving the juvenile credit. If the probation violation hearing was delayed and the juvenile spent a significant amount of time in detention, counsel should argue that many of the purposes of dispositions under G.S. 7B-2500, such as promoting public safety and emphasizing accountability, have already been met. *See supra* "Credit for time served" in § 8.6F, Secure Custody Hearing.

F.   Use of Previously-Adjudicated Violations at Subsequent Proceedings

Subsequent adjudication proceedings. A finding by the court of a violation of probation for a certain act does not bar the filing of a petition and an adjudication of delinquency based on the same act. In *In re O'Neal*, 160 N.C. App. 409 (2003), the trial court found that the juvenile willfully violated the conditions of probation by becoming "physically aggressive" with another juvenile. The State later filed a petition for misdemeanor assault based on the same conduct and the juvenile was adjudicated delinquent for the offense. The Court of Appeals rejected the juvenile's argument that the adjudication for the assault charge after the probation determination violated the protection against double jeopardy. The Court held that double jeopardy protections do not apply to probation revocation proceedings.

Subsequent probation hearings. A separate question is whether the court may modify probation or enter a new disposition for conduct that was the subject of a previous probation hearing. If the juvenile court counselor files a motion for review alleging a violation that was adjudicated at a prior probation violation hearing, counsel should move to dismiss on res judicata and collateral estoppel grounds.

Under the doctrine of res judicata, "a final judgment on the merits in one action precludes a second suit based on the same cause of action between the same parties." *Whitacre P'ship v. BioSignia, Inc.*, 358 N.C. 1, 15 (2004). Under the doctrine of collateral estoppel, the determination of an issue in a prior proceeding "precludes the relitigation of that issue in a later action, provided the party against whom the estoppel is asserted enjoyed a full and fair opportunity to litigate that issue in the earlier proceeding." *Id.* Counsel must assert res judicata and collateral estoppel at the hearing on the alleged violation; otherwise, the claims are waived. *State v. McKenzie*, 292 N.C. 170, 177 (1977).

Appellate courts elsewhere have reversed probation revocation orders in adult cases based on res judicata and collateral estoppel grounds. *See People v. Quarterman*, 136 Cal. Rptr. 3d 419 (Cal. Ct. App. 2012); *Shumate v. State*, 718 N.E.2d 1133 (Ind. Ct. App. 1999); *Knox v. Pennsylvania Bd. of Probation and Parole*, 588 A.2d 79, 82 (Pa. Commw. Ct. 1991).

In *State v. Powell*, ___ N.C. App. ___, 793 S.E.2d 282 (2016) (unpublished), the North Carolina Court of Appeals refused to recognize that collateral estopped barred revocation at a later probation hearing based on a violation decided at an earlier hearing. In *Powell*, the defendant violated a condition of his probation by possessing a firearm in March 2015. The probation officer filed a violation report and, after a hearing, the trial court extended the defendant's probation based on the violation. In August 2015, the probation officer filed another violation report based on the March 2015 possession of a firearm and on absconding, but the State presented no evidence on absconding. The trial court revoked the defendant's probation based on the March 2015 possession of a firearm alone. The Court of Appeals held that collateral estoppel did not apply because the State was not contesting the finding from the prior probation hearing that the defendant possessed a firearm. Rather, the State was relying on it. The Court of Appeals did not consider whether the trial court's earlier judgment to extend probation barred the State from relitigating that judgment and requesting revocation. Counsel should continue to argue that both the judgment as well as findings from a prior probation hearing should be given res judicata and collateral estoppel effect.

The *O'Neal* decision, discussed at the beginning of this subsection G., is distinguishable from a case in which the State seeks to revoke a juvenile's probation based on a violation decided at previous probation hearing. *O'Neal* held only that double jeopardy principles do not apply to probation violation hearings and do not bar a subsequent adjudication of delinquency for the same act. The argument here is based on the separate doctrines of res judicata and collateral estoppel. *But see State v. Powell*, ___ N.C. App. ___, 793 S.E.2d 282 (2016) (unpublished) (stating without analysis that the defendant's collateral estoppel argument was in essence a double jeopardy argument despite their differences).

14.9   Termination of Probation

The court may enter a written order terminating probation on finding that there is no further need for supervision, either at the end of the probationary term originally ordered or at any time during probation. G.S. 7B-2511. At the election of the court, an order may be entered in chambers based on a report of the juvenile court counselor or may be entered after notice and a hearing with the juvenile's attendance. *Id.* Termination of probation does not terminate the court's jurisdiction unless ordered by the court, or when statutory conditions ending jurisdiction are met. G.S. 7B-1601(b); *see supra* § 3.3, Jurisdiction. Counsel should therefore request that the court terminate jurisdiction as well as probation, which may be done by checking a box on the order terminating probation. *See* Form AOC-J-465 (Order to Terminate Supervision (Undisciplined/Delinquent)) (Apr. 2000).

Chapter 15
Commitment to the Division of Adult Correction and Juvenile Justice

Appendix 15-1: Youth Development Centers in North Carolina   15-12

15.1 Overview

Commitment to the North Carolina Department of Public Safety, Division of Adult Correction and Juvenile Justice (DACJJ) is the most severe disposition under the Juvenile Code. Juveniles who are committed are confined in a youth development center, a locked facility operated by the State. The term of commitment is almost always indefinite with a six-month minimum. A juvenile who is committed must be released on post-release supervision, which is subject to revocation for violation of the terms of release.

15.2 Terminology Used in this Chapter

Division is the Division of Adult Correction and Juvenile Justice. G.S. 7B-1501(10a). The Division is charged with far-reaching duties, which include responsibility for State juvenile facilities and youth development centers and establishment of community-based treatment and prevention services. *See* G.S. 143B-806.

Detention facility is a facility approved to provide secure, or locked, confinement and care for juveniles. G.S. 7B-1501(9).

Holdover facility is a place in a jail that has been approved by the Department of Health and Human Services as meeting the State standards for detention as required under G.S. 153A-221 (Law Enforcement and Confinement Facilities: Minimum Standards). A holdover facility must provide close supervision of the juvenile, and the juvenile must not be able to talk with, see, or be seen by the adult population of the jail. G.S. 7B-1501(11).

Post-release supervision is supervision of a juvenile in the community after release from commitment to the Division. G.S. 7B-1501(21); *see infra* § 15.8, Post-Release Supervision.

Youth development center is a secure residential facility authorized to provide long-term treatment, education, and rehabilitative services for juveniles committed to the Division after an adjudication of delinquency. G.S. 7B-1501(29).

15.3 Juveniles Subject to Commitment

Commitment to the Division is a dispositional alternative only for a juvenile who is at least 10 years old and who has been adjudicated delinquent and for whom the dispositional chart in G.S. 7B-2508(f) prescribes a Level 3 disposition. G.S. 7B-2506(24), 7B-2513(a). An order of commitment may not be imposed for a juvenile who has been found to be undisciplined, or for one who has been adjudicated to be abused, neglected, or dependent. *See* G.S. 7B-2503 (Dispositional alternatives for undisciplined juveniles); G.S. 7B-903 (Dispositional alternatives for abused, neglected, or dependent juvenile).

A juvenile must be committed if the statutory dispositional chart prescribes a Level 3 disposition unless the court makes written findings that the juvenile has "extraordinary needs" that justify a Level 2 disposition. G.S. 7B-2508(e); *see supra* Appendix 13-3: Juvenile Disposition Options. Commitment may also be ordered for a juvenile who is eligible for a Level 2 disposition if a Level 3 disposition has been ordered in a prior juvenile proceeding, or for a juvenile who has been adjudicated of four or more prior non-overlapping offenses in which the juvenile committed each successive offense after being adjudicated of the preceding offense. G.S. 7B-2508(d), (g). A juvenile may also be subject to commitment upon a finding of a violation of probation if the juvenile is currently on a Level 2 disposition. G.S. 7B-2510(e), (f).

It is within the court's discretion to choose between two appropriate dispositional levels. *In re Robinson*, 151 N.C. App. 733 (2002) (court did not abuse discretion in committing juvenile under Level 3 where he was adjudicated delinquent for two "violent" and one "serious" offense and had a "low" delinquency history level; court considered risk and needs assessment, severity of case, lack of progress to date, and community alternatives in determining that commitment was in juvenile's best interest). Counsel should be prepared to argue for the lower dispositional level based on factors relating to the offense and the juvenile's needs.

The court does not have discretion to order a disposition at a level higher than that authorized by statute. In *In re T.B.*, 178 N.C. App. 542 (2006), the court found that the juvenile had violated the conditions of his probation. Because the juvenile's original disposition had been at Level 1, the court had discretion to order either a Level 1 or a Level 2 disposition for the probation violation. It did not have statutory authority, however, to order a Level 3 disposition. An order of commitment was therefore impermissible.

15.4 Holdover Facility Pending Placement

A juvenile committed to the Division following adjudication for an offense that would be a Class A, B1, B2, C, D, or E felony if committed by an adult may be held for up to 72 hours in a holdover facility pending placement in a youth development center. The court must make a determination, based on information provided by the juvenile court counselor, that there is no acceptable alternative placement and that the protection of the public requires that the juvenile be housed in a holdover facility. G.S. 7B-2513(h).

15.5 Role of Attorney Following Commitment

No statutory role is defined for the juvenile's attorney following an order of commitment unless the matter comes back before the court for further proceedings, such as a hearing on a motion alleging violation of the terms of post-release supervision. *See infra* § 15.9, Revocation of Post-Release Supervision. There is also no provision for payment of attorney's fees by the Office of Indigent Defense Services for follow-up or other involvement after commitment in the absence of a subsequent court proceeding requiring representation of the juvenile. A juvenile could benefit from representation by counsel regarding many issues arising from commitment, including placement, post-release planning, and extension of commitment. Local practice varies in the degree of involvement by counsel following commitment, from formal release of the attorney to the attorney maintaining some contact and providing advice to the juvenile on a pro bono basis. The issue is being reviewed by the Office of the Juvenile Defender and the Office of Indigent Defense Services.

15.6 Term of Commitment

A. Indefinite Term of at Least Six Months

Minimum term. Commitment is for an indefinite term of at least six months. G.S. 7B-2513(a); *see In re Allison*, 143 N.C. App. 586, 596 (2001) (statute does not violate the Equal Protection Clause by authorizing a longer period of confinement for a juvenile than could be imposed on an adult committing the same offense because a rational basis exists for disparate treatment of adults and children based on juvenile's need for supervision and control).

Maximum term. An indefinite commitment must end by the following birthdays of the juvenile pursuant to G.S. 7B-2513(a)(1)–(3):

- 21st birthday if the juvenile is committed for an offense that would be first-degree murder pursuant to G.S. 14-17, first-degree forcible rape pursuant to G.S. 14-27.21, first-degree statutory rape pursuant to G.S. 14-27.24, first-degree forcible sexual offense pursuant to G.S. 14-27.26, or first-degree statutory sexual offense pursuant to G.S. 14-27.29 if committed by an adult;
- 19th birthday if the juvenile is committed for an offense that would be a Class B1, B2, C, D, or E felony if committed by an adult, other than those listed immediately above;
- 18th birthday if the juvenile is committed for an offense other than those listed above.

Additionally, if the juvenile is adjudicated for a felony, the juvenile may not be committed to a term that exceeds the maximum term of imprisonment in the aggravated range for the felony that an adult with a prior record level VI could receive. G.S. 7B-2513; *In re C.J.J.*, 241 N.C. App. 655 (2015) (unpublished). If the juvenile is adjudicated for a misdemeanor, the juvenile may not be committed to a term that exceeds the maximum term of imprisonment for the misdemeanor than an adult with a prior conviction level III could receive. G.S. 7B-2513. As an exception, the juvenile's commitment may be extended beyond these limits under G.S. 7B-2515 if the Division determines that the juvenile's commitment should be extended to continue care or treatment under its statutory plan. G.S. 7B-2513(a); *see infra* § 15.7B, Assessment by the Division and Plan of Care.

For misdemeanor offenses, six months is both the minimum and maximum term of commitment because the maximum sentence an adult could receive for these offenses is less than six months. A commitment for a Class H or I felony could be similarly limited. An adult could receive up to 24 months for a Class I felony and up to 39 months for a Class H felony. The maximum term of a juvenile's commitment for these offenses might therefore expire before the juvenile's 18th birthday. The Division may extend commitment beyond the maximum adult sentence in some circumstances. *See infra* 15.6D, Extension of Commitment.

B. Definite Term

A juvenile who is at least 14 years old, who has been previously adjudicated delinquent for two or more felony offenses and who has previously been committed, may be committed to a definite term of not less than six months and not more than two years. G.S. 7B-2513(b).

C. Credit for Time in Detention Before Disposition

In *In re D.L.H.*, 364 N.C. 214, 216 (2010), the Supreme Court of North Carolina held that trial courts are not required to give credit for time served in secure custody before disposition. The opinion overruled prior decisions on the question by the court of appeals, such as *In re R.T.L.*, 183 N.C. App. 299 (2007) (unpublished), and *In re Allison*, 143 N.C. App. 586 (2001). Although trial courts are not required to give juveniles credit for time spent in secure custody, courts are not prohibited from taking the time into account when considering the most appropriate disposition for the juvenile. Courts have considerable leeway at the dispositional hearing. *See In re Doe*, 329 N.C. 743, 749 (1991) ("Flexibility in determining dispositions was one of the aims of the General Assembly in drafting the Juvenile Code."). According to G.S. 7B-2500, a dispositional order should promote public safety, emphasize accountability and responsibility, and provide the appropriate consequences, treatment, training, and rehabilitation to assist the juvenile in becoming a responsible and productive member of the community. If the juvenile spent a significant amount of time in secure custody or received services before the dispositional hearing, counsel should argue that many of the purposes of disposition have already been met.

D. Extension of Commitment

The Division may extend commitment beyond the maximum adult sentence or beyond the juvenile's 18th birthday if it determines that extension will promote protection of the public and will be likely to lead to further rehabilitation. G.S. 7B-2515(a). It must also determine that the statutorily-mandated plan of care needs to be continued for an additional period of time. G.S. 7B-2513(a). The juvenile has the right to contest the proposed extension at a review hearing.

The Division may determine that a juvenile's commitment should be extended if it decides that the juvenile needs additional treatment or rehabilitation. If the Division determines that commitment should be extended beyond the maximum adult sentence or past the juvenile's 18th birthday, it must notify the juvenile and the juvenile's parent, guardian, or custodian in writing at least 30 days in advance of those dates. G.S. 7B-2515(a); *In re J.L.H.*, 230 N.C. App. 214, 222 (2013) (holding that oral notice that the juvenile's commitment would be extended did not satisfy G.S. 7B-2515).

A court review of the Division's decision to extend commitment may be requested by the juvenile and the juvenile's parent, guardian, or custodian. G.S. 7B-2515(c). If a review is requested, the court must hold a hearing. The statute does not provide procedures for this hearing or specify that the juvenile must be represented at the hearing. However, a juvenile has the right to counsel in "all proceedings" pursuant to G.S. 7B-2000 and therefore should be entitled to representation. Additionally, a juvenile should be afforded counsel because an extension of commitment is a restraint on the juvenile's liberty that was not imposed by the original disposition.

15.7 Placement by Division

A. Youth Development Centers

A juvenile may be placed in a particular youth development center in the discretion of the Division. Placement is to be made based on best serving the juvenile's needs and may be in a Division institution or one licensed by the Division. G.S. 7B-2513(e).

There are currently four youth development centers operated by the Division: Chatham Youth Development Center in Siler City; Lenoir Youth Development Center located near Kinston; Edgecombe Youth Development Center in Rocky Mount; and Stonewall Jackson Youth Development Center in Concord. Chatham Youth Development Center is the only facility that serves females. For more information on the facilities, see *infra* Appendix 15-1: Youth Development Centers in North Carolina.

B. Assessment by the Division and Plan of Care

Upon commitment to a youth development center, a juvenile undergoes a screening and assessment of developmental, educational, medical, neurocognitive, mental health, psychosocial, and relationship strengths and needs. Results from these assessments, in combination with other current and historical data, are used by staff, parents or other caregivers, community providers, and stakeholders to develop a service plan for the juvenile involving treatment and educational, medical, and mental health services. These assessments also provide a framework for post-release supervision services. For more information on these assessments, see the Division's webpage on youth development centers.

This plan for care and treatment of the juvenile must be prepared by the Division within 30 days of assuming physical custody of the juvenile. G.S. 7B-2513(f). The chief court counselor is charged with providing the Division with all required records of the juvenile. The records are to be sent with the juvenile when the juvenile is transported to the youth development center, or if not obtainable at the time of admission, within 15 days of admission. G.S. 7B-2513(d).

Any confidential records that are provided to the Division pursuant to this section must remain confidential. The statute provides that these records may only be "used in a manner consistent with the best interests of the juvenile." G.S. 7B-2513(d).

Each juvenile committed to the Division for placement in a youth development center must be tested for controlled substances and alcohol. These initial test results must be incorporated into the plan of care but may be used for evaluation and treatment purposes only. G.S. 7B-2513(i). Subsequent testing may presumably be used to monitor compliance with rules and restrictions and could be used for other purposes.

The Division must evaluate the juvenile's progress at least once every six months as long as the juvenile remains in placement with the Division. G.S. 7B-2514(a).

C. Provision of Commitment Services in Non-YDC Facility

The Division may provide services in a placement that is not a youth development center or detention facility, sometimes referred to as a "community commitment," after assessing the needs of the juvenile. Before doing so, it must file a motion with the committing court outlining services to be provided and give notice of the motion to the prosecutor, the juvenile, and the juvenile's attorney. The court may enter an order approving the placement without a hearing unless the juvenile or the juvenile's attorney requests a hearing. If the court determines that it will hold a hearing, it must notify the Division of the hearing, and the Division must place the juvenile in a youth development center or detention facility pending the hearing. G.S. 7B-2513(e).

Counsel should be prepared to argue for a community commitment if that is an acceptable alternative for the juvenile. Examples of community placements are Eckerd Wilderness Camp, which is a structured outdoor living program, and psychiatric residential treatment facilities, or PRTFs, which are non-hospital facilities that provide psychiatric treatment, such as a secure group home with a trained staff.

D. No Effect on Jurisdiction of Court or Legal Custody

Commitment to the Division for placement does not terminate the court's jurisdiction over the juvenile and the juvenile's parent, guardian, or custodian. It also has no effect on legal custody, which remains with the parent or other person or agency previously having custody, although physical custody is placed with the Division. G.S. 7B-2513(g).

15.8 Post-Release Supervision

A. Post-Release Planning Process

The Division is required to begin formulating a post-release plan upon determining that the juvenile is ready for release from commitment. Written notice of the post-release supervision planning process must be given to the committing court. G.S. 7B-2514(a)(1).

A post-release planning conference is required by statute and must include the juvenile, the juvenile's parent, guardian, or custodian, juvenile court counselors who have supervised the juvenile on probation or who will supervise the juvenile after release, and the staff of the facility recommending release. G.S. 7B-2514(a).

There is no provision for notifying or involving the juvenile's attorney in this process.

B. Post-Release Plan Requirements

Each post-release plan must be in writing and must provide for at least 90 days, but not more than one year, of post-release supervision. The plan must address both the needs of the juvenile and the protection of the public. G.S. 7B-2514(b). A juvenile court counselor must supervise the juvenile during post-release supervision. G.S. 7B-2514(g).

C. Date of Release

Pursuant to G.S. 7B-2514(c), the Division is required to release the juvenile under a plan of post-release supervision at least 90 days prior to one of the following:

- completion of a definite term of commitment, which includes credit for time spent on post-release supervision under G.S. 7B-2514(f);
- the juvenile's 21st birthday if the juvenile was committed for an offense that would be first-degree murder, first-degree forcible rape, or first-degree forcible sexual offense if committed by an adult;
- the juvenile's 19th birthday if the juvenile was committed for an offense that would be a Class B1, B2, C, D, or E felony if committed by an adult, other than an offense set forth in G.S. 7B-1602(a) (first-degree murder, first-degree forcible rape, or first-degree forcible sexual offense if committed by an adult); or
- the juvenile's 18th birthday if the juvenile was committed for an offense other than an offense that would be a Class A, B1, B2, C, D, or E felony if committed by an adult.

The release date is subject to the proviso that a juvenile under an indefinite commitment may be released to post-release supervision only after a commitment period of at least six months. G.S. 7B-2514(e). The Division may only extend commitment beyond the maximum adult sentence or beyond the juvenile's 18th birthday in limited circumstances. *See supra* § 15.6D, Extension of Commitment.

D. Notification of Victim and Others of Release

If a juvenile is committed to the Division for an offense that would have been a Class A or B1 felony if committed by an adult, the chief court counselor must notify the victim and members of the victim's immediate family that they may request in writing to be notified in advance of the juvenile's scheduled release date. G.S. 7B-2513(j). If a request for notification is received, the Division must notify the person filing the request at least 45 days in advance of the scheduled release. The notice must include the juvenile's name, offense, date of commitment, and the date of the proposed release. G.S. 7B-2514(d). There is no statutory provision for filing an objection to the release.

People who must be notified at least 45 days before release to post-release supervision of a juvenile who was committed for an offense that would be a Class A or B1 felony if committed by an adult are: the juvenile, the juvenile's parent, guardian, or custodian, the district attorney where the juvenile was adjudicated, and the head of the law enforcement agency that took the juvenile into custody. These persons are not required to request notification of release. The notice must contain the information provided in the notice to the victim and must also be sent to the clerk of court for placement in the juvenile court file. G.S. 7B-2514(d).

E. Termination of Post-Release Supervision

The maximum period of post-release supervision is one year. G.S. 7B-2514(b). Termination of post-release supervision is by order of the court. G.S. 7B-2514(g).

15.9 Revocation of Post-Release Supervision

A. Motion and Notice

The juvenile, the juvenile court counselor providing post-release supervision, or the court on its own motion, may request a review hearing concerning the juvenile's progress on post-release supervision. Written notice of the allegations must be provided to the juvenile within a reasonable time. The notice must specify that the purpose of the hearing is to determine whether the juvenile has violated the terms of post-release supervision and whether revocation is warranted. G.S. 7B-2516(a).

B. Hearing on Motion

A hearing must be held to determine whether the allegation that the juvenile has violated the terms of post-release supervision is true. The statute provides that the juvenile shall be represented by an attorney at the hearing and has the right to confront and cross-examine witnesses. Additionally, the juvenile is allowed to admit, deny, or explain the violation alleged and to present proof, including affidavits and other evidence. A record of the proceeding must be made and maintained in the juvenile's record. G.S. 7B-2516(a).

Preparation for a hearing on allegations of violation of the terms of post-release supervision involves elements of preparation for both adjudicatory and dispositional hearings. Counsel should meet with the juvenile and contact necessary witnesses regarding the alleged violation. Witnesses should be subpoenaed or affidavits obtained supporting the juvenile's position on the allegations. Records should be reviewed, particularly those of the supervising juvenile court counselor. If a violation is found, counsel should be prepared to offer alternatives to revocation of post-release supervision.

The standard of proof is by the greater weight of the evidence. If violation of the terms of post-release supervision is found, the court may, but is not required to, revoke the post-release supervision. The court may also impose any other disposition provided by statute. G.S. 7B-2516(b).

C. Disposition on Revocation

The juvenile must be placed in a youth development center for an indefinite term of at least 90 days if post-release supervision is revoked. G.S. 7B-2516(c). The statute contains outer age limits on commitment after revocation. The juvenile may not remain committed past the juvenile's:

- 21st birthday if the juvenile is committed for an offense that would be first-degree murder pursuant to G.S. 14-17, first-degree forcible rape pursuant to G.S. 14-27.21, first-degree statutory rape pursuant to G.S. 14-27.24, first-degree forcible sexual offense pursuant to G.S. 14-27.26, and first-degree statutory sexual offense pursuant to G.S. 14-27.29 if committed by an adult;
- 19th birthday if the juvenile is committed for an offense that would be a Class B1, B2, C, D, or E felony if committed by an adult, other than those listed immediately above; and
- 18th birthday if the juvenile is committed for an offense other than those listed above.

It is unsettled whether the term of commitment is subject to the same limitations on the maximum set forth for the original commitment in G.S. 7B-2513(a)—basically, the maximum that an adult could receive for that class of offense. *See supra* "Maximum term" in § 15.6A, Indefinite Term of at Least Six Months. G.S. 7B-2516(c) does not restate these maximums, which supports the view that they do not apply. *See* LaToya Powell, *Extended YDC Commitments and the 30-Day Notice Requirement*, ON THE CIVIL SIDE, UNC SCH. OF GOV'T BLOG (July 12, 2017). However, the General Assembly may not have intended to authorize a greater term of commitment than initially permitted based solely on a violation of post-release supervision. G.S. 7B-2513(a) contains a single exception to these maximums—a determination by the Division pursuant to G.S. 7B-2515 that a greater period of commitment is needed for care or treatment. G.S. 7B-2513(a) does not contain an exception to the maximums based on revocation of post-release supervision under G.S. 7B-2516. Whether or not the maximums apply, counsel should consider requesting a hearing at an appropriate time to review the juvenile's commitment.

15.10 Transfer Authority of Governor from Jail or Prison to Division

The governor has the authority to order a person who is less than 18 years of age who is being held in a jail or penal facility of the State to be transferred to a residential facility operated by the Division. This must be done in consultation with the Division regarding the appropriateness of the transfer in terms of available space, staff, and suitability of programs for the juvenile. G.S. 7B-2517.

Although this provision does not apply to a juvenile delinquency case, it may be applicable to a case transferred from juvenile court to superior court. A juvenile who is transferred to superior court and convicted may request that the governor order a transfer from the jail or prison to a youth development center for confinement. There are no guidelines set forth in the statute, but special needs, immaturity, suitability of Division programs, and danger from the prison population are examples of issues that the attorney should consider when making an application to the governor requesting transfer. Under G.S. 7B-2517, the Division has discretion to release the juvenile after transfer based on the needs of the juvenile and the best interests of the State.

Appendix 15-1: Youth Development Centers in North Carolina

CHATHAM
CENTRAL CAROLINA BUSINESS PARK
560 PROGRESS BLVD.
SILER CITY, NC 27344
Director: Charles Dingle
Telephone: 919.742.6220
Attorney Visiting Hours: Flexible, call first
Regular Visiting Hours: Wednesday (1:00-5:00 p.m., 5:30-8:00 p.m.)
Sunday (9:00 a.m-12:00 p.m., 12:30-3:30 p.m.)
Available to Visit: Social workers and relatives approved by the juvenile court counselor

LENOIR
3055 DOBBS FARM ROAD
KINSTON, NC 28504
Director: Tangi Jordan
Telephone: 252.208.4920
Attorney Visiting Hours: Any time
Regular Visiting Hours: Wednesday (5:00-7:00 p.m.); Sunday (8:00 a.m-3:45 p.m.)
Available to Visit: Parents and relatives over 16 years old and approved by the juvenile court
counselor and social worker

EDGECOMBE
78 POSITIVE WAY
ROCKY MOUNT, NC 27801
Director: Crystal Wynn-Lewis
Telephone: 252.544.5730
Attorney Visiting Hours: Monday-Friday (8:30 a.m.-5:00 p.m.)
Saturday and Sunday (by appointment)
Regular Visiting Hours: Sunday (9:00-10:30 a.m.)
Monday-Friday by appointment (9:00 a.m.-5:00 p.m.)
Available to Visit: Immediate family including parents, siblings, and grandparents (ID required);
other relatives approved by the juvenile's social worker

STONEWALL JACKSON
850 HOLSHOUSER ROAD
CONCORD, NC 28027
Director: Peter Brown
Telephone: 704.652.4300
Attorney Visiting Hours: Flexible, schedule through the juvenile's social worker
Regular Visiting Hours: Wednesday (8:30-11:30 a.m., 12:30-3:30 p.m.), Sunday (9:00-10:30 a.m.,
11:30-1:00 p.m., 1:30-3:00 p.m.)
Available to Visit: Parents, grandparents, guardians, and relatives approved by the juvenile court
counselor and the director

Chapter 16
Appeals

16.1 Overview

Appeals in juvenile delinquency cases are heard in the North Carolina Court of Appeals. G.S. 7B-2602. Some juvenile delinquency appeals are then heard in the Supreme Court of North Carolina. Discussion of appeals in this manual involves the rights of the parties and participants to juvenile delinquency appeals and the orders that may be appealed in those cases.

It is the responsibility of appointed counsel in district court to protect the record for appeal by presenting evidence favorable to the juvenile, making an offer of proof if the court finds evidence for the juvenile inadmissible, cross-examining the State's witnesses, and making appropriate objections and motions. *See* Staples Hughes, *Preserving Error for Appeal: A Checklist* (2012); 2 NORTH CAROLINA DEFENDER MANUAL Appendix B: Preserving the Record (2d ed. 2013). The appointed attorney must advise the juvenile of the right to appeal and must file a timely notice of appeal if the juvenile decides to appeal. *See infra* § 16.2, Notice of Appeal. Counsel should communicate with the appellate attorney to ensure that all necessary information is transmitted for representation of the juvenile on appeal.

16.2 Notice of Appeal

Notice of appeal must be given in open court at the time of the hearing or in writing within 10 days after entry of a final order. G.S. 7B-2602. Giving oral notice of appeal is preferable as it avoids many of the complications that arise when filing a written notice of appeal. If no disposition is made within 60 days after entry of the order, written notice of appeal of the adjudication may be given within 70 days after entry of the adjudicatory order. *Id.* Counsel should maintain a calendaring system to ensure that appeals are filed within the strict statutory time limits.

If counsel files a written notice of appeal, counsel must ensure that the notice of appeal is in proper form. Although notice of appeal in juvenile delinquency cases is governed by G.S. 7B-2602, the Court of Appeals has applied Rule 3 of the N.C. Rules of Appellate Procedure to the contents of written notices of appeal filed in delinquency cases. *See, e.g., In re A.V.*, 188 N.C. App. 317, 321 (2008) (declining to review dispositional order because the order was not included in the written notice of appeal as required by Rule 3). According to Rule 3(d), a written notice of appeal must specify the party appealing, designate the judgment from which the appeal is taken, and designate the court to which the appeal is taken. The notice of appeal must also be signed by counsel and contain proof of service on the State. A sample notice of appeal is available on the Juvenile Defender website. Counsel should be sure to comply with the requirements of Rule 3 when entering written notice of appeal as a violation of the rule could provide grounds for dismissal of the appeal. *See, e.g., Ribble v. Ribble*, 180 N.C. App. 341, 343 (2006) (dismissing appeal under Rule 3 where the written notice of appeal lacked a certificate of service).

When entering notice of appeal, counsel should be sure to give notice of appeal from an order that can be appealed. If the order cannot be appealed, the appeal will be dismissed. *See In re A.L.*, 166 N.C. App. 276, 277–78 (2004) (dismissing appeal because the juvenile gave notice of appeal from adjudication order, which was not appealable). Appealable orders are discussed *infra* in § 16.3, Right to Appeal.

16.3   Right to Appeal

A. Who Can Appeal

The juvenile, the juvenile's parent, guardian, or custodian and, in limited circumstances, the State and county, may appeal. G.S. 7B-2604. This statute imposes no limitation on appeals by the juvenile or the juvenile's parent, guardian, or custodian.

Counsel should advise the juvenile of the right to appeal, as well as discuss the strengths and weaknesses of an appeal. *See generally Becton v. Barnett*, 920 F.2d 1190, 1194 (4th Cir. 1990) (trial attorney's failure to give notice of appeal prevented the defendant from demonstrating that "his conviction was unlawful through the appellate process"). A juvenile who has been committed or is otherwise detained should also be advised of the right to release pending appeal. *See infra* § 16.5, Disposition Pending Appeal. The juvenile makes the decision whether to appeal.

Pursuant to G.S. 7B-2604(b)(1) and (2), appeal by the State is limited to appeal of an order:

- finding a State statute unconstitutional; or
- terminating the prosecution of a petition by upholding the defense of double jeopardy, by holding that a cause of action is not stated under a statute, or by granting a motion to suppress.

Appeal by a county is limited to an order requiring the county to pay for medical, surgical, psychiatric, psychological, or other evaluation or treatment pursuant to G.S. 7B-2502 (Evaluation and treatment of undisciplined and delinquent juveniles) or pursuant to G.S. 7B-2702 (Medical, surgical, psychiatric, psychological evaluation or treatment of juvenile or parent). G.S. 7B-2604(c); *see also supra* § 13.5B, Court-Ordered Evaluation and Treatment.

B. Appeal of Final Order

Final order. Any "final order" may be appealed to the North Carolina Court of Appeals. G.S. 7B-2602. Under G.S. 7B-2602(1)–(4), a final order is defined to include the following:

- any order finding absence of jurisdiction;
- any order that in effect determines the action and prevents a judgment from which appeal might be taken;
- any order of disposition after an adjudication that a juvenile is delinquent; and
- any order modifying custodial rights.

Appeal from dispositional order. Even where counsel intends to appeal only the adjudication, the appeal under G.S. 7B-2602(3) must be from the *dispositional order* following the adjudication. For instance, the Court of Appeals dismissed the juvenile's appeal in *In re A.L.*, 166 N.C. App. 276, 277–78 (2004) because the juvenile's written notice of appeal referred only to the "adjudication of delinquency," which was not an appealable order under G.S. 7B-2602. In *In re D.K.L.*, 201 N.C. App. 443, 444 (2009), the juvenile's attorney stated at the beginning of the dispositional hearing that he "intended to appeal from the adjudication of delinquency." Although the court did not issue a dispositional order during the hearing, the juvenile's attorney gave oral notice of appeal when the hearing ended. The Court of Appeals later dismissed the juvenile's appeal because the oral notice of appeal given during the dispositional hearing was premature. *Id.* at 445.

Appeal of adjudication if no dispositional order entered. An adjudicatory order is not a final order under G.S. 7B-2602. However, the statute permits a juvenile to appeal an adjudicatory order by written notice of appeal within 70 days of adjudication if no disposition is made within 60 days after entry of the adjudicatory order. *Id.*; *In re D.F.-M.*, 176 N.C. App. 189 (2006) (unpublished) (appeal of adjudication not premature where notice of appeal was filed 65 days after entry of order of adjudication and court terminated jurisdiction over juvenile without order of disposition); *compare In re Taylor*, 57 N.C. App. 213 (1982) (appeal of adjudication dismissed as premature where notice of appeal was filed eight days after adjudication and no disposition was made); *In re T.E.B.*, 241 N.C. App. 175 (2015) (unpublished) (dismissing the juvenile's appeal because the juvenile "did not wait until after the 60-day period had expired before appealing"). If the court does not enter disposition within 60 days of the adjudicatory order and the juvenile wants to appeal the adjudicatory order, counsel should be sure to give notice of appeal during the 10-day window between the 60th and 70th day after the adjudicatory order is entered. Failure to do so may subject the appeal to dismissal.

If the juvenile properly appeals an adjudication order under G.S. 7B-2602 when there has been no disposition within 60 days, the trial court is divested of jurisdiction and may not conduct a dispositional hearing while the appeal is pending. *In re J.F.*, 237 N.C. App. 218, 228 (2014); *In re Rikard*, 161 N.C. App. 150, 153–54 (2003). If the juvenile does not appeal the adjudicatory order during the 10-day window, the juvenile may still appeal if the court enters disposition at a later date. *In re M.W.*, 204 N.C. App. 210 (2010) (unpublished).

Appeal from other final orders. There are no opinions in any juvenile delinquency appeals that involve orders finding an absence of jurisdiction, orders determining the action and preventing a judgment from which appeal might be taken, or orders modifying custodial rights, which are appealable under G.S. 7B-2602. Instead, the vast majority of juvenile delinquency appeals are from dispositional orders. These provisions in G.S. 7B-2602 authorize appeal, although they appear to be a vestige of when juvenile delinquency and juvenile abuse, neglect, and dependency cases were combined in a single code.

C. Appeal of Finding of Probable Cause

A finding of probable cause is not a final order for the purpose of an appeal. *In re K.R.B.*, 134 N.C. App. 328, 331 (1999) (finding of probable cause is not a final order that is immediately appealable; proper time for appeal is following entry of dispositional order); *see supra* § 9.7, Appeal of Finding of Probable Cause.

D. Appeal of Order Transferring Jurisdiction

An order transferring jurisdiction to superior court may be immediately appealed to superior court. G.S. 7B-2603(a). The order must be appealed to superior court to preserve the issue for review by the Court of Appeals. *State v. Wilson*, 151 N.C. App. 219, 222 (2002); *see supra* § 9.10, Appeal of Order of Transfer.

E. Appeal of Order Finding Capacity to Proceed

An order finding a juvenile capable of proceeding is not a final order that may be immediately appealed pursuant to G.S. 7B-2602. Counsel should make an objection on the record to the finding of capacity to proceed and should renew the objection at the outset of the adjudicatory hearing to preserve the issue for appeal. *In re Pope*, 151 N.C. App. 117, 119 (2002) (failure of juvenile to object to court's finding of capacity to proceed or at adjudicatory hearing waived issue on appeal); *see supra* § 7.11D, Objection to Finding of Capacity. *But see* 1 NORTH CAROLINA DEFENDER MANUAL § 2.7E, Objection to Finding of Capacity (2d ed. 2013) (suggesting that failure to object may not waive issue).

F. Appeal Involving an Admission by a Juvenile

In adult criminal appeals, the defendant has a limited right to appeal from a judgment entered on a guilty plea. *See* G.S. 15A-1444; *State v. Royster*, 239 N.C. App. 196, 200 (2015) (dismissing the defendant's appeal because the only argument he presented did not involve any of the issues under G.S. 15A-1444 that can be raised in an appeal from a guilty plea). In contrast, G.S. 7B-2602 does not impose limitations on juvenile delinquency appeals involving admissions. Thus, if the juvenile properly appeals under G.S. 7B-2602, there are no statutory limitations on issues that juveniles can raise in the appeal after entering an admission.

G. Appeal Involving the Denial of a Motion to Suppress

G.S. 7B-2408.5(g) allows the juvenile to appeal the denial of a motion to suppress "upon an appeal of a final order of the court in a juvenile matter." G.S. 7B-2408.5(g). Thus, the juvenile may not appeal from the order denying the motion to suppress but can challenge the order as part of an appeal from a final order. *See supra* § 16.3B, Appeal of Final Order. Additionally, the term "final order" under G.S. 7B-2602 includes a dispositional order, but not an adjudication order. *In re M.L.T.H.*, 200 N.C. App. 476, 480 (2009). A juvenile may appeal an adjudication order within 70 days if no dispositional order is entered within 60 days. G.S. 7B-2602. Although the juvenile may be able to challenge an order denying a suppression motion in an appeal from an adjudication order within the 10-day window if the court does not immediately order a disposition, the safer practice is to ask the court enter disposition within 60 days or enter notice of appeal when the court finally issues a dispositional order.

Although the juvenile may not appeal from an order denying a motion to suppress, counsel should give notice of the juvenile's *intent to appeal* if the juvenile plans to enter an admission. In adult cases, a defendant who pleads guilty has the right to appeal an order denying a motion to suppress. G.S. 15A-979(b). However, courts have interpreted the statute to mean that the defendant must give notice to the prosecutor and the court of his intent to appeal the order denying the motion to suppress before pleading guilty. *State v. Tew*, 326 N.C. 732, 735 (1990); *State v. Brown*, 142 N.C. App. 491, 492 (2001). Courts have not imposed a similar requirement in juvenile delinquency appeals and may never do so because, unlike in adult cases, juveniles are not limited in the issues they may raise following an admission. As a best practice, however, counsel should include a statement in the written transcript of admission reserving the right to appeal the order denying the motion to suppress.

H. Appeals by the State

G.S. 7B-2604 addresses the State's right to appeal in a juvenile delinquency case. The State's right is limited. Under G.S. 7B-2604(b)(2), the State may appeal an order granting a motion to suppress, but only if the order "terminates the prosecution of the petition." In *In re P.K.M.*, 219 N.C. App. 543, 545 (2012), the Court of Appeals dismissed the State's appeal from an order granting a motion to suppress. The Court reasoned that an order granting a motion to suppress "does not, standing alone, dispose of a juvenile delinquency case" and suggested that a finding of insufficient evidence might be necessary to satisfy the requirement that the order terminate the prosecution of a petition. *Id.* The Court also observed that the certification required under G.S. 15A-979(c) in State's appeals in adult criminal cases does not apply to State's appeals in juvenile delinquency cases. In adult cases, if the State wants to take an immediate appeal of an order granting a suppression motion, the prosecutor must certify that the appeal is not taken for the purpose of delay and that the evidence is essential to the case.

If the State appeals an order granting a motion to suppress, counsel should ensure that the trial court enters an order of appellate entries appointing the Appellate Defender to represent the juvenile in the appeal. *See generally infra* § 16.4, Transmitting the Appeal to the Appellate Defender.

I. Writ of Certiorari

Counsel may petition by writ of certiorari for review of a judgment or order from a trial court when the right to appeal has been lost by failure to file timely notice of appeal or when no right of appeal from an interlocutory order exists. N.C. Rules of Appellate Procedure, Rule 21(a)(1). Appellate counsel may file a petition for writ of certiorari to address a defect in a notice of appeal. There are few circumstances in which it would be appropriate for trial counsel to file a petition for writ of certiorari from an interlocutory order, and there is a significant likelihood that the appellate courts would deny the petition. Counsel should contact the North Carolina Office of the Appellate Defender when considering whether to seek review by writ of certiorari.

J. Supreme Court Jurisdiction

If there is a dissent in the Court of Appeals, appeal lies of right to the Supreme Court of North Carolina. G.S. 7A-30. If the opinion in the Court of Appeals is unanimous, a party may file a petition for discretionary review in the Supreme Court of North Carolina. G.S. 7A-31. The Supreme Court is under no obligation to hear the case and may deny the petition. If the Court grants the petition, the parties must file new briefs in the Supreme Court and present oral arguments.

16.4 Transmitting the Appeal to the Appellate Defender

Once the trial court enters disposition and counsel has filed notice of appeal, counsel should take steps to ensure that the appeal proceeds in a timely manner. Although some juveniles might be represented by retained counsel on appeal, most are represented by the Office of the Appellate Defender or an attorney assigned by the Office of the Appellate Defender. If the juvenile will not be represented by a retained attorney on appeal, counsel should make sure that the trial court enters an order of appellate entries appointing the Office of the Appellate Defender to the case. Counsel should make sure that the clerk sends a copy of the signed order of appellate entries to the Office of the Appellate Defender.

A. The Appellate Entries

An order of appellate entries is a court order that appoints the Appellate Defender to an appeal. In adult criminal appeals, the court will not appoint the Appellate Defender unless the court finds that the defendant is indigent. Juveniles in delinquency cases are presumed to be indigent. G.S. 7B-2000(b). Thus, no finding of indigency is required. Counsel should still review the appellate entries to ensure that the box identifying the Appellate Defender as the juvenile's initial appellate counsel is checked. If the box is not checked, the Appellate Defender must return the form to the clerk to check the box for the Appellate Defender.

An order of appellate entries also identifies the hearings that will be transcribed for the appeal, assigns a court reporter to prepare the transcripts, directs the clerk to send a copy of the complete trial division court file to the juvenile's appellate attorney, and assigns a translator to the appeal if a translator is needed. If counsel does not prepare the order of appellate entries, counsel should ensure that the order of appellate entries lists all of the hearing dates and that section five, which concerns a translator, identifies the juvenile's native language if the juvenile needs a translator. If all of the relevant hearing dates are not listed, the appellate attorney will have to identify the hearings, file a motion to have the hearings transcribed, and coordinate with the court reporter to prepare transcripts of the hearings, which will delay the appeal. Additionally, if the order of appellate entries does not appoint a translator when one is needed, the appellate attorney will be required to file a motion to appoint a translator, which will delay communication with the juvenile while the motion is ruled on by the court and the appellate attorney coordinates with the translator.

A blank order of appellate entries is available on the Administrative Office of the Courts website. *See* Form AOC-J-470 (Appellate Entries in Delinquency Proceeding) (June 2015). Although the order of appellate entries includes a notation that the juvenile entered notice of appeal, the order is *not* a substitute for giving proper notice of appeal. *State v. Blue*, 115 N.C. App. 108, 113 (1994).

B. Timeliness of the Transfer

Currently, there is no deadline under the Rules of Appellate Procedure for the trial court to enter an order of appellate entries. In part because of the lack of any deadline, there is usually a delay between the filing of the notice of appeal and the appointment of the Appellate Defender. In some cases, the delay lasts several weeks, which in turn delays the appeal. One of the purposes of the Juvenile Code is to provide "swift" dispositions in juvenile delinquency cases. G.S. 7B-1500(2)a. Counsel therefore should take the following steps to reduce delays that may occur in district court after notice of appeal is filed.

First, counsel should talk to the juvenile before the dispositional hearing about whether the juvenile intends to appeal. Although G.S. 7B-2602 gives the juvenile 10 days to enter notice of appeal, giving notice of appeal when disposition is entered will prevent delays at the outset of the appeal. *See supra* § 16.2, Notice of Appeal (discussing giving oral notice of appeal).

Second, counsel should fill out the order of appellate entries and submit it to the judge after giving oral notice of appeal or filing written notice of appeal. Although the order of appellate entries is often prepared by the clerk, there is no rule preventing counsel from completing the form. If counsel prepares the order of appellate entries and presents it to the judge, counsel can reduce any delays that might result from the clerk completing the order. Counsel should ensure that the originals of a written notice of appeal and order of appellate entries are filed with the clerk.

Third, counsel should work with the clerk to ensure that a court reporter is assigned to the appeal in a timely manner. Generally, the first deadline in an appeal is for the preparation of the transcript. *See* N.C. R. APP. P. 7 (stating that the court reporter has 60 days to prepare the transcript in civil appeals). In some counties, the clerk knows which court reporter to assign to a juvenile delinquency appeal. In other counties, the clerk does not immediately know who to assign and must identify a court reporter, which delays commencement of the initial deadline for the transcript. If the clerk is unsure which court reporter to assign, counsel should contact the Court Reporting Manager for the Administrative Office of the Courts (AOC). David Jester, the current Court Reporting Manager, will assist the clerk in identifying a court reporter for the juvenile's appeal. He can be reached by phone at (919) 831-5974 or by email at David.E.Jester@nccourts.org. Counsel should also check that the clerk completes the "Tracking and Receipt" section on the second page of the order of appellate entries as the date that the recording of the hearing is transmitted to the court reporter starts the initial 60-day period that the court reporter has to prepare the transcript.

Fourth, counsel should ensure that the clerk sends a copy of the order of appellate entries to the Office of the Appellate Defender in a timely manner. According to Rule 3.2(c) of the Rules of the Office of Indigent Defense Services for Providing Legal Representation in Non-Capital Criminal Appeals and Non-Criminal Appeals (May 2015), the clerk "shall immediately" send the judgment and order of appellate entries to the Office of the Appellate Defender once the order of appellate entries is filed. If there is any question of whether the order has been sent, counsel may contact the Office of the Appellate Defender and advise the office of the appeal. The Office of the Appellate Defender will follow up with the clerk or counsel if there is a delay in receiving the order of appellate entries.

16.5 Disposition Pending Appeal

If the juvenile is placed in custody at the conclusion of the dispositional hearing and the juvenile gives notice of appeal, counsel should seek the juvenile's release while the appeal is pending. Counsel should argue that the juvenile should be released under G.S. 7B-2605. According to the statute, the juvenile must be released, with or without conditions, unless the court enters a temporary order affecting custody or placement. Such an order must be in writing and must state "compelling reasons" that the placement or custody is in the best interests of the juvenile or the State. *In re G.C.*, 230 N.C. App. 511, 519 (2013) (remanding order denying release where the court failed to provide a written statement of compelling reasons for denying the juvenile's release); *In re J.J.D.L.*, 189 N.C. App. 777, 781 (2008) (no error in denying motion for release from custody pending appeal where the trial court found as a compelling reason that the juvenile had committed first degree sex offenses with a child); *In re K.T.L.*, 177 N.C. App. 365 (2006) (order placing juvenile in custody of Department of Social Services satisfied G.S. 7B-2605 because it was in writing and provided compelling reasons for placement); *In re W.H.*, 166 N.C. App. 643, 648 (2004) (although issue was moot, stating that conclusions in dispositional order would have provided compelling reasons for continued custody of the juvenile if the court had entered a separate order under G.S. 7B-2605).

A sample motion and order for the juvenile's release under G.S. 7B-2605 are available on the Juvenile Defender website. Sections 2 and 3 on the first page of the AOC form for the order of appellate entries also provide the court with space to address the question of the juvenile's release. *See* Form AOC-J-470 (Appellate Entries in Delinquency Proceeding) (June 2015).

G.S. 7B-2605 permits the juvenile's release regardless of the type of custody. For instance, depending on the offense classification and the juvenile's delinquency history level, the court can place the juvenile in intermittent confinement under G.S. 7B-2506(12), confinement at a juvenile detention facility under G.S. 7B-2506(20), or confinement at a Youth Development Center under G.S. 7B-2506(24). If the court orders any of these types of custody, counsel should seek the juvenile's release under G.S. 7B-2605.

If the court orders probation or other dispositional alternatives that do not involve custody, counsel should consider filing a motion to stay the dispositional alternatives. A sample motion to stay disposition pending the appeal is available on the Juvenile Defender website. Although the Juvenile Code does not address whether the trial court may grant a stay, stays are authorized under Rule 8 of the N.C. Rules of Appellate Procedure. Counsel should advise the juvenile that the juvenile will still be required to comply with the dispositional alternatives if the adjudication or dispositional orders are upheld on appeal.

16.6   Disposition Following Resolution of Appeal

If the appellate court upholds the adjudicatory or dispositional order, the juvenile court has authority to modify the original order of adjudication or disposition. The court may make changes found to be in the best interest of the juvenile "to reflect any adjustment made by the juvenile or change in circumstances during the period of time the appeal was pending." G.S. 7B-2606. The statute makes provision for this order to be entered ex parte, with notice given to interested parties to show cause within 10 days why the modifying order should be vacated or altered.

Several due process issues are raised by this statute, and it is therefore unlikely to be used. Counsel should object to a modification that imposes a more onerous disposition absent a subsequent adjudication and should request an opportunity to be heard. The statute provides counsel opportunity to inform the court of progress made by the juvenile during the appellate process that warrants a more favorable adjudication or disposition.

16.7   Cost of Appeal

A juvenile has the right to appointed counsel on appeal in delinquency proceedings. The juvenile is presumed to be indigent. G.S. 7B-2000. In some circumstances, the court may order reimbursement of appointed attorney's fees, including those of the appellate defender, from a parent, guardian, or trustee in possession of funds or property for the benefit of the juvenile. *See* G.S. 7B-2002; G.S. 7A-450.1, 7A-450.2, 7A-450.3. Although a parent or guardian who may be ordered to pay the cost of appeal might exert pressure on a juvenile not to appeal, the decision to appeal is the juvenile's. Counsel has a duty to be a zealous advocate for the juvenile, which includes filing an appeal on request of the juvenile.

Chapter 17
Expunction of Juvenile Records

17.1   Expunction

Expunction is a statutory process that allows a former juvenile respondent to file a petition to have the court records of the juvenile proceeding, as well as any law enforcement records and records maintained by the Division of Adult Correction and Juvenile Justice, destroyed. After expunction of juvenile records, the former juvenile respondent may generally proceed as if the juvenile proceeding never occurred. This will protect the former juvenile respondent from certain collateral consequences, as well as prevent an adjudication from being used in certain criminal proceedings. *See infra* § 17.5, Effect of Expunction.

Statutory criteria must be met; not all adjudications or records can be expunged. This chapter discusses the requirements and procedures for expunction of juvenile court records relating to a dismissed petition alleging delinquency or to an adjudication of delinquency. Procedures for expunction of records relating to cases involving undisciplined juveniles are not included in this discussion.

The former respondent in a juvenile delinquency proceeding will ordinarily become eligible for expunction of records after the involvement of appointed counsel has ended. Counsel should provide information to a juvenile client who may be eligible to have records expunged so that the client can pursue expunction independently or through hired counsel at the appropriate time. For a "reminder card" that you can provide your juvenile client and other information on expunctions of juvenile court records, see the Expunction Toolkit, a collection of materials on juvenile court expunctions prepared by the Office of the Juvenile Defender. *See also* Expunction of Delinquency Matters in John Rubin, Relief from a Criminal Conviction: A Digital Guide to Expunctions, Certificates of Relief, and Other Procedures in North Carolina (UNC School of Government 2016).

17.2   Expunction of Juvenile Court Records: Adjudication of Delinquency

A. Criteria

Age. A person must be at least 18 years of age to file a petition for expunction of juvenile court records relating to an adjudication of delinquency. G.S. 7B-3200(a).

Adjudications that may be expunged. An adjudication for an offense other than one that would have been a Class A, B1, B2, C, D, or E felony if committed by an adult is eligible for expunction. G.S. 7B-3200(b)(1). The excluded offenses cannot be expunged.

When to file. A petition for expunction of an eligible adjudication can be filed if at least 18 months have elapsed since the person was released from juvenile court jurisdiction and the person has not subsequently been adjudicated delinquent or convicted of any felony or misdemeanor other than a "traffic violation," a term that is not defined. G.S. 7B-3200(b)(2); *see also* Frequently Asked Questions about Expunctions and Other Relief (discussing meaning of traffic violations in adult context) in Relief from a Criminal Conviction: A Digital Guide to Expunctions, Certificates of Relief, and Other Procedures in North Carolina (UNC School of Government 2016).

B. Petition

The petition for expunction must be filed in the court where the person was adjudicated delinquent. G.S. 7B-3200(b). Pursuant to G.S. 7B-3200(c), a petition must contain the following:

- an affidavit by the petitioner stating that the petitioner has been of good behavior since the adjudication and has not subsequently been adjudicated delinquent or convicted of any felony or misdemeanor other than a traffic violation,
- verified affidavits of two people not related to the petitioner or to each other by blood or marriage stating that they know the character and reputation of the petitioner in the community in which the petitioner lives and that the petitioner's character and reputation are good, and
- a statement that the petition is a motion in the cause in the case in which the petitioner was adjudicated delinquent.

See Form AOC-J-903M (Petition and Motion in the Cause for Expunction of Juvenile Record) (Mar. 2002), and Form AOC-J-904M (Affidavit of Good Character (Expunction of Juvenile Record)) (Mar. 2002). The Administrative Office of the Courts (AOC) forms do not specifically include requests and orders for the Division of Adult Correction and Juvenile Justice to destroy its records, including those maintained on the North Carolina Juvenile Online Information Network (NC-JOIN); for the juvenile court counselors to destroy their records; or for the AOC to destroy its records, including those maintained on JWise, the automated information management system for juvenile courts. These requests must be added to the forms, or counsel must draft an appropriate petition and order. A sample "Petition and Order to Expunge Juvenile Record" is available on the Office of the Juvenile Defender website.

C. Service of Petition and Notice

The petitioner must serve the petition on the prosecutor in the district where the adjudication occurred. Notice of the date of the hearing must be given to the prosecutor. G.S. 7B-3200(c). The statute does not state who must give notice of the hearing, but it appears that the clerk sends notice of the hearing date to the petitioner and to the prosecutor.

D. Objection by Prosecutor

Within 10 days of receipt of the petition, the prosecutor may file an objection. G.S. 7B-3200(c). The prosecutor is presumably allowed to present evidence and argue against granting the petition at the hearing although this is not specified by statute.

E. Hearing

A hearing must be held at which the court will consider whether the petitioner has met the criteria for expunction, listed *supra* § 17.2A, Criteria. The statute provides no procedures for conducting the hearing.

F. Order

If the court finds that the petitioner has met the criteria for expunction, it must enter an order directing the clerk of superior court and all law enforcement agencies to expunge records concerning the adjudication. The clerk must forward a certified copy of the order to the sheriff, chief of police, or other law enforcement agency. G.S. 7B-3200(e). Records that must be expunged include all records containing references to arrests, complaints, referrals, petitions, and orders. G.S. 7B-3200(d); *see* Form AOC-J-905 (Order for Expunction of Juvenile Record) (Oct. 2016). Because the AOC form order does not identify all the necessary agencies that have juvenile records, these should be added or a separate order drafted. *See supra* § 17.2B, Petition.

17.3   Expunction of Juvenile Court Records: Dismissed Petition

A. Criteria

A person who is at least 16 years of age may file a petition for expunction of juvenile court records relating to a petition alleging delinquency that was dismissed without an adjudication of delinquency. G.S. 7B-3200(h). It appears that records of a dismissed petition may be expunged even if the person has other adjudications of delinquency or criminal convictions.

B. Petition

The petition must be filed in the court in which the person was alleged to be delinquent. G.S. 7B-3200(h). There are no provisions in the statute specifying what the petition must allege. It appears that the petition need allege only that a petition alleging delinquency was filed, that it was dismissed, and that the petitioner is at least 16 years of age. *See* Form AOC-J-909M (Petition/Order/Notice Expunction of Juvenile Records upon Dismissal) (Mar. 2002).

C. Service of Petition and Notice

A petition for expunction of juvenile court records regarding a dismissed petition must be served on the chief juvenile court counselor in the district where the petition was filed. If the chief court counselor files an objection to the petition, a hearing must be scheduled and notice given to the chief court counselor. G.S. 7B-3200(h).

D. Objection by Chief Court Counselor

The chief court counselor has 10 days from receipt of service of the petition to file an objection. If an objection is filed, the court must hold a hearing on the petition. G.S. 7B-3200(h). It appears that the only ground for filing an objection is if the petition was not, in fact, dismissed.

E. Hearing

A hearing must be held if the chief court counselor files an objection or if the court directs that a hearing be held. The court must consider whether the criteria discussed *supra* in § 17.2A, Criteria, have been met. G.S. 7B-3200(h). The statute provides no procedures for conducting the hearing.

If no objection to the petition is filed, the court has discretion to grant the petition without holding a hearing. *Id.*

F. Order

If the court finds that the petitioner has met the criteria for expunction, it must enter an order directing the clerk and all law enforcement agencies to expunge their records concerning the dismissed petition. Records that must be expunged include all records containing references to arrests, complaints, referrals, juvenile petitions, and orders. G.S. 7B-3200(h); *see* Form AOC-J-905 (Order for Expunction of Juvenile Record) (Oct. 2016); *see also supra* § 17.2B, Petition (discussing other records that counsel should request be expunged).

The clerk must forward a certified copy of the order to the sheriff, chief of police, or other appropriate law enforcement agency and to the chief court counselor. These officials must immediately destroy all records relating to the allegations that the juvenile was delinquent. G.S. 7B-3200(h).

17.4 Notice of Expunction Procedures and Expunction

When a court enters disposition in a juvenile delinquency case, it must provide the juvenile with information either orally in court or in writing on the procedures under G.S. 7B-3200 for expunging juvenile records. G.S. 7B-2512(b). Based on G.S. 7B-2512(b), the AOC forms for Level 1 and Level 2 dispositions now contain boxes prompting courts to inform juveniles of expunction procedures. *See* Form AOC-J-461 (Juvenile Level 1 Disposition Order) (Oct. 2016); Form AOC-J-475 (Juvenile Level 2 Disposition Order) (Oct. 2016).

After the court enters an order granting expunction of the juvenile's records and the records have been expunged, the clerk must send written notice to the petitioner at the petitioner's last known address that the juvenile record has been expunged. Pursuant to G.S. 7B-3202, the notice must inform the petitioner that with respect to the matter in the record, the petitioner: may not be held thereafter under any provision of any laws to be guilty of perjury or otherwise giving a false statement by reason of the juvenile's failure to recite or acknowledge such record or response to any inquiry made of the juvenile for any purpose except that upon testifying in a delinquency proceeding, the juvenile may be required by a court to disclose that the juvenile was adjudicated delinquent. *See* Form AOC-J-906M (Notice of Expunction of Juvenile Record) (Mar. 2002).

17.5　Effect of Expunction

A.　Generally

Expunction allows the person who was the subject of the expunged juvenile proceeding to go forward as if the proceeding had never occurred. G.S. 7B-3201(a) provides that the person and the person's parents may not be held guilty of perjury or of giving a false statement "by reason of the person's failure to recite or acknowledge such record or response to any inquiry made of the person for any purpose." An exception is that in a delinquency proceeding, a juvenile "defendant" who chooses to testify or a juvenile witness may be ordered to testify regarding past adjudications regardless of expunction. G.S. 7B-3201(b); *In re S.S.T.*, 165 N.C. App. 533, 534–35 (2004).

B.　School Records

When a petition is filed alleging that the juvenile committed a felony, the juvenile court counselor must provide written notification to the principal of the juvenile's school. G.S. 7B-3101(a). If a court later grants the juvenile's petition for expunction, the principal must "shred, burn, or otherwise destroy" any documents the school received involving the petition. G.S. 115C-404(a).

C.　Fingerprint and Photograph Exception

Fingerprints and photographs taken after the juvenile is taken into custody are not eligible for expunction. G.S. 7B-2102(d). They must be destroyed, however, if a juvenile petition is not filed within one year of the fingerprinting and photographing, the court does not find probable cause, or the juvenile is not adjudicated delinquent of any offense that would be a felony or misdemeanor if committed by an adult. G.S. 7B-2102(e); *see supra* "Destruction of fingerprints and photographs" in § 2.8E, Nontestimonial Identification Records. Counsel should file a motion to destroy the juvenile's fingerprints and photographs if any one of the criteria in G.S. 7B-2102(e) are met. Although there is no provision in G.S. 7B-2101 permitting officers to take fingerprints and photographs of a juvenile facing a divertible offense, it is possible that officers might do so anyway. If officers take fingerprints and photographs under these circumstances, counsel should file a motion to destroy the fingerprints and photographs on the ground that they are not permitted under G.S. 7B-2102.

D.　Adult Criminal Proceedings

Expunction of juvenile delinquency records may affect decisions involving pretrial release, plea agreements, and probation if the juvenile is involved in later adult criminal proceedings. If the defendant in a criminal proceeding involving a Class A1 misdemeanor or a felony was less than 21 years of age at the time of the offense, the juvenile's record of an adjudication of delinquency for a Class A1 misdemeanor or a felony that occurred after the defendant reached 13 years of age may be used by law enforcement officers, magistrates, courts, and prosecutors for pretrial release, plea negotiation decisions, and plea acceptance decisions. G.S. 7B-3000(e). In addition, G.S. 7B-3000(e1) permits a probation officer assigned to supervise an adult defendant sentenced to probation for an offense committed while the person was less than 25 years of age to examine the defendant's juvenile records involving cases in which the defendant was adjudicated delinquent for felonies. If the juvenile successfully expunges his or her juvenile court records, the records should not adversely affect the juvenile in these matters.

E. Impact on Expunctions in Adult Court

Juvenile expunctions should not be a bar to receiving an adult expunction because the adult expunction statutes do not make a prior expunction of a delinquency matter a bar. As a practical matter, however, they might affect a court's consideration of a petition for expunction in adult court. Under G.S. 7B-3200(i), the clerk of superior court is required to file with the AOC the names of people who are granted expunctions under the Juvenile Code. Apparently, when a person requests an expunction of an adult matter, the AOC reports all prior expunctions, including expunctions of delinquency matters, to the court. A court might take this information into account even though the adult expunction statutes do not make a juvenile expunction a consideration.

Two adult expunction statutes state generally that a prior expunction is a bar. Thus, a court is authorized to grant an expunction of a nonviolent felony conviction based on an offense committed before the defendant was 18 if, among other things, a "search of the confidential records of expunctions conducted by the Administrative Office of the Courts shows that the petitioner has not been previously granted an expunction." G.S. 15A-145.4(e)(7). Similar language appears in G.S. 15A-145.6 for expunction of convictions for prostitution. Although this general language might suggest that a juvenile expunction could prevent a court from granting these types of expunction in adult court, it seems unlikely that the General Assembly intended this result. When a court reviews a petition for expunction under G.S. 15A-145.4, it *may* consider "the petitioner's juvenile record." The statute does not prohibit the court from granting an expunction if the petitioner has a juvenile record. It would seem contradictory if the statute permitted a court to grant an expunction to an adult with a juvenile record while barring an expunction for an adult who no longer had a juvenile record. *See State v. Barksdale*, 181 N.C. 621, 625 (1921) ("[W]here a literal interpretation of the language of a statute will lead to absurd results or contravene the manifest purpose of the Legislature, as otherwise expressed, the reason and purpose of the law shall control and the strict letter thereof shall be disregarded.").

In light of the above, counsel should discuss with the juvenile the potential impact of a juvenile expunction on future expunctions in adult court.

F. Other Consequences

Although access to juvenile delinquency records are limited under G.S. 7B-3000 and 7B-3001, requests regarding juvenile delinquency records are not uncommon and may affect the juvenile's educational, housing, and employment opportunities. *See* Riya Saha Shah

& Jean Strout, *Future Interrupted: The Collateral Damage Caused by Proliferation of Juvenile Records* (Feb. 2016) (providing an overview of how juvenile court records are disclosed through background checks), and Juvenile Law Center, *New Study Reveals Majority of U.S. States Fail to Protect Juvenile Records*, Pursuing Justice (Nov. 13, 2014). Counsel should advise the juvenile that expunging juvenile court records could help the juvenile avoid adverse consequences that might result from disclosure of the records.

North Carolina Commission on Indigent Defense Services

Performance Guidelines for Appointed Counsel in Juvenile Delinquency Proceedings at the Trial Level

Adopted December 14, 2007

North Carolina Commission on Indigent Defense Services

Performance Guidelines for Appointed Counsel in Juvenile Delinquency Proceedings at the Trial Level

Commission on Indigent Defense Services
Juvenile Delinquency Performance Guidelines
Adopted December 14, 2007

Acknowledgments

The development of these Performance Guidelines for Appointed Counsel in Juvenile Delinquency Proceedings at the Trial Level was overseen by the North Carolina Juvenile Defender, Eric J. Zogry. The Commission on Indigent Defense Services ("IDS Commission") and Office of Indigent Defense Services ("IDS Office") are grateful to the following committee members and consultants, who generously gave their time and expertise to this project:

- Rhoda Billings, Retired Professor of Law, Wake Forest University, Winston-Salem, and IDS Commissioner
- Tamar Birckhead, Assistant Professor of Law, University of North Carolina, Chapel Hill
- Cameron Bush, Assistant Public Defender, Lumberton
- John Cox, Attorney at Law, Graham
- Caitlin Fenhagen, Assistant Public Defender, Chapel Hill
- Samuel Spagnola, Attorney at Law, Greensboro

Preface

The primary goal of the Commission on Indigent Defense Services ("IDS Commission") is to ensure that indigent persons in North Carolina who are entitled to counsel at state expense are afforded high quality legal representation. *See* G.S. 7A-498.1(2). To further that goal, the Indigent Defense Services Act of 2000 directs the Commission to establish "[s]tandards for the performance of public defenders and appointed counsel." G.S. 7A-498.5(c)(4).

These performance guidelines are based largely on the "Performance Guidelines for Indigent Defense Representation in Non-Capital Criminal Cases at the Trial Level" that have been promulgated by the IDS Commission, as well as a review of standards and guidelines in Georgia and Kentucky and the Juvenile Defender Delinquency Notebook published by the National Juvenile Defender Center. For several months, a Juvenile Delinquency Performance Guidelines Committee reviewed drafts of these guidelines and revised them to fit the nuances of North Carolina law and practice. Once a final proposed draft was complete, it was distributed to all private appointed counsel and assistant public defenders who handle delinquency proceedings, as well as all district court judges and other interested persons, for their comments and feedback. Based on the comments that were received, the Committee made a number of improvements to the guidelines. The full IDS Commission then adopted the attached performance guidelines on December 14, 2007.

These performance guidelines cover all juvenile delinquency cases in North Carolina. The guidelines are intended to identify issues that may arise at each stage of a delinquency proceeding and to recommend effective approaches to resolving those issues. Because all provisions will not be applicable in all cases, the guidelines direct counsel to use his or her best professional judgment in determining what steps to undertake in specific cases. The Commission hopes these guidelines will be useful as a training tool and resource for new and experienced juvenile defense attorneys, as well as a tool for potential systemic reform in some areas. The guidelines are not intended to serve as a benchmark for ineffective assistance of counsel claims or attorney disciplinary proceedings.

The IDS Commission believes that providing high quality juvenile defense representation is a difficult and challenging endeavor, which requires great skill and dedication. That skill and dedication is demonstrated by juvenile defense counsel across North Carolina on a daily basis, and the Commission commends those counsel. The Commission recognizes that the goals embodied in these guidelines will not be attainable without sufficient funding and resources and hopes the North Carolina General Assembly will continue its support of both quality indigent defense services and appropriate dispositional options for juveniles.

The IDS Commission thanks all of the juvenile defense attorneys who zealously represent juveniles across the state. In addition, the Commission thanks everyone who assisted in drafting these performance guidelines and who offered comments. The Commission plans to review and revise the guidelines on a regular basis to ensure that they continue to comply with North Carolina law and reflect quality performance, and it invites ongoing feedback from the defense bar and juvenile defense community.

North Carolina Commission On Indigent Defense Services

Performance Guidelines For Appointed Counsel in Juvenile Delinquency Proceedings at the Trial Level

SECTION 1: GENERAL PROVISIONS

Guideline 1.1 Function of the Performance Guidelines

(a) The Commission on Indigent Defense Services hereby adopts these performance guidelines to promote one of the purposes of the Indigent Defense Services Act of 2000—improving the quality of indigent defense representation in North Carolina—and pursuant to G.S. 7A-498.5(c)(4).

(b) These guidelines are intended to serve as a guide for counsel's performance in juvenile delinquency proceedings at the district court level and to contain a set of considerations and recommendations to assist appointed counsel in providing quality representation for juveniles. The guidelines also may be used as a training tool.

(c) These are performance guidelines, not standards. The steps covered in these guidelines are not to be undertaken automatically in every case. Instead, the steps actually taken should be tailored to the requirements of a particular case. In deciding what steps are appropriate, counsel should use his or her best professional judgment.

Guideline 1.2 Definitions

(a) *Juvenile*: Any person under the age of eighteen who is not married, emancipated, or a member of the armed forces of the United States, or any person who is 18 to 20 years of age and has been adjudicated delinquent and committed to a youth development center.

(b) *Juvenile delinquent or delinquent juvenile*: A juvenile who has been adjudicated delinquent of an offense that would be a crime if committed by an adult.

(c) *Appointed counsel*: An attorney appointed to represent a juvenile in a juvenile delinquency proceeding.

(d) *Expressed interests*: The stated desires of the juvenile client about the direction and objectives of the case.

SECTION 2: ROLE, QUALIFICATIONS, AND DUTIES OF DEFENSE COUNSEL

Guideline 2.1 Role of Defense Counsel

(a) An attorney in a juvenile delinquency proceeding is the juvenile's voice to the court, representing the expressed interests of the juvenile at every stage of the proceedings. The attorney owes the same duties to the juvenile under the North Carolina Rules of Professional Conduct, including the duties of loyalty and confidentiality, as an attorney owes to a client who is an adult criminal defendant.

(b) The attorney for a juvenile is bound to advocate the expressed interests of the juvenile. In addition, the attorney has a responsibility to counsel the juvenile, recommend to the juvenile actions consistent with the juvenile's interests, and advise the juvenile as to potential outcomes of various courses of action.

(c) An attorney in a juvenile delinquency proceeding should be familiar with the "Role of Defense Counsel in Delinquency Proceedings" approved by the Commission on Indigent Defense Services, available at www.ncids.org under the "Juvenile Defender" link.

Guideline 2.2 Education, Training, and Experience of Defense Counsel

(a) To provide quality representation, counsel must be familiar with the Juvenile Code and the substantive criminal law and procedure in North Carolina. Counsel should also be familiar with any applicable local rules of the judicial district, which can be obtained in the local clerk's office and may be available at www.nccourts.org, as well as the practices of the specific judge before whom a case is pending.

(b) Counsel has an ongoing obligation to stay abreast of changes and developments in juvenile law and procedure and criminal law and procedure and to continue his or her legal education, skills training, and professional development.

(c) Before accepting appointment to a juvenile delinquency case, counsel should have sufficient experience, knowledge, skill, and training in areas such as communication techniques with children and adolescents, adolescent brain development, motions practice, detention advocacy, pre-adjudication preparation, and adjudication, disposition and post-disposition advocacy to provide quality representation. Counsel should have knowledge and understanding of the practice and procedures of the local court counselor's office and the role and functions of other court actors. If appropriate, counsel is encouraged to consult with other attorneys to acquire pertinent additional knowledge and information, including information about the practices of judges, prosecutors, and other court personnel.

Guideline 2.3 General Duties of Defense Counsel

(a) Before accepting appointment to a juvenile delinquency case, counsel has an obligation to ensure that he or she has sufficient time, resources, knowledge, and experience to provide quality representation to the juvenile. If it later appears that counsel is unable to provide quality representation, counsel should move to withdraw. If counsel is allowed to withdraw, he or she should cooperate with new counsel to the extent that such cooperation is in accord with the North Carolina Rules of Professional Conduct.

(b) Counsel must be alert to all actual and potential conflicts of interest that would impair his or her ability to represent a juvenile client. If counsel identifies a potential conflict of interest, counsel should fully disclose the conflict to all affected persons and, if appropriate, obtain informed consent to proceed on behalf of the juvenile or move to withdraw. Counsel may seek an advisory opinion on any potential conflicts from the North Carolina State Bar. Mere tactical disagreements between counsel and a juvenile ordinarily do not justify withdrawal from a case. If it is necessary for counsel to withdraw, counsel should do so in a way that protects the juvenile's rights and interests and does not violate counsel's ethical duties to the juvenile.

(c) Counsel has an obligation to maintain regular contact with his or her juvenile client and to keep the juvenile informed of the progress of the case. Counsel should promptly comply with any reasonable request by the juvenile for information and reply to correspondence and telephone calls from the juvenile.

(d) Counsel should maintain a relationship with the juvenile client's parent or guardian, but should not allow that relationship to interfere with counsel's duties to the juvenile or the expressed interests of the juvenile.

(e) Counsel should appear on time for all scheduled court hearings in a juvenile's case. If scheduling conflicts arise, counsel should resolve them in accordance with Rule 3.1 of the General Rules of Practice and any applicable local rules.

(f) Counsel should never give preference to retained clients over juveniles for whom counsel has been appointed.

SECTION 3: INTERVIEWING THE JUVENILE

Guideline 3.1 Preparation for the Initial Interview

(a) Counsel should arrange for an initial interview with the juvenile as soon as practicable after being assigned to the juvenile's case. Absent exceptional circumstances, if the juvenile is in detention, the initial interview should take place within three business days after counsel receives notice of assignment to the juvenile's case. If necessary, counsel may arrange for a designee to conduct the initial interview.

(b) Before conducting the initial interview, the attorney should, if possible:

(1) be familiar with the charges against the juvenile and the elements of and potential dispositions for each charged offense;

(2) obtain copies of all relevant documents that are available, including copies of any petitions and related documents, recommendations and reports made by the court counselor's office, and law enforcement reports; and

(3) if the juvenile is detained:

(A) be familiar with the legal criteria governing the circumstances under which the court may order release and the procedures that will be followed in setting those conditions;

(B) be familiar with the different types of pre-adjudication release conditions the court may set, any written policies of the judicial district, and whether any person or agency is available to act as a custodian for the juvenile's release; and

(C) be familiar with any procedures available for reviewing the trial judge's determination to continue custody.

Guideline 3.2 The Initial Interview

(a) The purposes of the initial interview are to acquire information from the juvenile concerning the facts of the case and to provide the juvenile with information concerning the case.

If the juvenile remains in secure custody, counsel should also acquire information from the juvenile concerning pre-adjudication release.

(b) Counsel should communicate with the juvenile in a manner that will be effective, considering the juvenile's maturity, intellectual ability, language, educational level, special education needs, cultural background, gender, and physical, mental, and emotional health. If appropriate, counsel should file a motion to have a foreign language or sign language interpreter appointed by the court and present at the initial interview.

(c) Information about the juvenile that counsel should attempt to acquire during the initial interview includes, but is not limited to:

(1) the juvenile's current living arrangements, family relationships, and ties to the community, including the length of time his or her family has lived at the current and former addresses, as well as the juvenile's supervision when at home;

(2) the immigration status of the juvenile and his or her family members, if applicable;

(3) the juvenile's educational history, including current grade level and attendance and any disciplinary history;

(4) the juvenile's physical and mental health, including any impairing conditions such as substance abuse or learning disabilities, and any prescribed medications and other immediate needs;

(5) the juvenile's delinquency history, if any, including arrests, detentions, diversions, adjudications, and failures to appear in court;

(6) whether there are any other pending charges against the juvenile and the identity of any other appointed or retained counsel;

(7) whether the juvenile is on probation or post-release supervision and, if so, the name of his or her court counselor and the juvenile's past or present performance under supervision;

(8) the options available to the juvenile for release if the juvenile is in secure custody; and

(9) the names of individuals or other sources that counsel can contact to verify the information provided by the juvenile, and the permission of the juvenile to contact those sources.

(d) Information about the specific juvenile delinquency matter that counsel should attempt to acquire from the juvenile includes, but is not limited to:

(1) the facts surrounding the juvenile delinquency matter;

(2) any evidence of improper police or other governmental conduct, including interrogation procedures, that may affect the juvenile's rights;

(3) any possible witnesses and where they may be located;

(4) any evidence that should be preserved; and

(5) evidence of the juvenile's capacity to stand trial and mental state at the time of the offense.

(e) When appropriate, counsel should be prepared at the initial interview to ask the juvenile to sign a release authorizing counsel to access confidential information, such as school records and medical or mental health records.

(f) Information counsel should provide to the juvenile during the initial interview includes, but is not limited to:

(1) an explanation of the procedures that will be followed in setting the conditions of pre-adjudication release if the juvenile remains in secure custody;

(2) an explanation of the type of information that will be requested in any future interview that may be conducted by a court counselor, and an explanation that the juvenile is not required to and should not make statements concerning the offense;

(3) an explanation of the attorney-client privilege and instructions not to talk to anyone about the facts of the case without first consulting counsel;

(4) the nature of the charges and potential penalties;

(5) a general procedural overview of the progression of the case, where possible;

(6) how counsel can be reached and when counsel plans to have contact with the juvenile next;

(7) the date and time of the next scheduled court proceeding in the case;

(8) realistic answers, where possible, to the juvenile's questions; and

(9) what arrangements will be made or attempted for the satisfaction of the juvenile's most pressing needs, such as medical or mental health attention, and contact with family members.

SECTION 4: PROCEEDINGS BEFORE THE ADJUDICATORY HEARING

Guideline 4.1 General Obligations of Counsel Regarding Pre-Adjudication Release

(a) Unless contrary to the expressed interests of the juvenile, counsel has an obligation to attempt to secure the prompt pre-adjudication release of the juvenile under the conditions most favorable to the juvenile.

(b) While hearings in delinquency proceedings are open pursuant to G.S. 7B-2402, counsel should consider moving the court to close any initial proceedings, including secure custody, first appearance, probable cause, and transfer hearings. Factors counsel should consider when making this request include the age of the juvenile, the nature of the charges, and any information that may be discussed during the hearing that could harm the juvenile. If requested by the juvenile, counsel should move to close the proceedings.

(c) If the juvenile is detained, counsel should try to ensure, prior to any initial court hearing, that the juvenile does not appear before the judge in inappropriate clothing or in shackles or handcuffs. If a detained juvenile is brought before the judge in detention clothing, shackles, or handcuffs, counsel should object and seek relief from the court pursuant to G.S. 7B-2402.1.

Guideline 4.2 Secure Custody Hearings

(a) Counsel should make all reasonable efforts to interview the juvenile prior to the initial secure custody hearing.

(b) At a secure custody hearing, counsel should be prepared to present to the court a statement of the factual circumstances and factors supporting release and to propose conditions of release, including those in G.S. 7B-1906(f). Counsel should consider preparing for the court a proposed release order that includes conditions of release. Counsel should consider the potential consequences of statements made by the juvenile at any secure custody hearing and advise the juvenile accordingly.

(c) If the juvenile is released, counsel should fully explain the conditions of release to the juvenile and advise him or her of the potential consequences of a violation of those conditions.

(d) If the juvenile remains in detention, counsel should alert the detention facility in writing and, if appropriate, the court, to any special medical, psychiatric, or educational needs of the juvenile that are known to counsel.

Guideline 4.3 First Appearance in Felony Cases

(a) Counsel should be aware of all statutory time limits for first appearance hearings in felony cases and should make any appropriate objections and motions.

(b) If counsel has not met with the juvenile before the first appearance hearing, counsel should meet with the juvenile as soon as possible after the first appearance and before the next hearing.

Guideline 4.4 Probable Cause Hearing in Felony Cases

(a) Counsel should be aware of all statutory time limits for probable cause hearings in felony cases involving a juvenile who is at least 13 years of age and should make any appropriate objections and motions.

(b) Counsel should discuss with the juvenile the meaning of probable cause and the procedural aspects surrounding a probable cause determination. Counsel should consider any concessions the prosecution might make if the juvenile waives, or does not oppose a continuance of, a probable cause hearing. Before waiving a probable cause hearing, counsel should consider the possible benefits of a hearing, including the potential for discovery and the development of impeachment evidence. Counsel also should be aware of all consequences if the juvenile waives a probable cause hearing, including the effect of waiver on the outcome of a transfer hearing. Counsel should be aware of local customs with respect to probable case hearings, including whether or not waiver of probable cause ensures that the juvenile's case will remain in delinquency court.

(c) In preparing for a probable cause hearing, counsel should be familiar with Article 22 of the Juvenile Code and should specifically consider:

(1) the elements of each of the offenses alleged;

(2) the law for establishing probable cause;

(3) the procedure for conducting a probable cause hearing under G.S. 7B-2202;

(4) factual information that is available concerning the existence or lack of probable cause;

(5) tactical considerations for whether to conduct cross-examination, full or partial, of prosecution witnesses;

(6) whether additional factual information and impeachment evidence could be discovered by counsel during the hearing;

(7) any continuing need to pursue release of the juvenile if the juvenile is in custody; and

(8) that counsel should not call the juvenile or defense witnesses to testify at the probable cause hearing unless there are sound tactical reasons for doing so.

(d) Counsel should make reasonable efforts to ensure that the probable cause hearing is recorded and, with permission of the court, should consider utilizing a personal recording device in case the court recording device fails.

Guideline 4.5 Transfer Hearings in Felony Cases

(a) Counsel should be aware of all statutory time limits for transfer hearings in felony cases involving a juvenile who is at least 13 years of age and should make any appropriate objections and motions.

(b) Counsel should prepare for a transfer hearing to the same degree as for an adjudicatory hearing and should be aware that the decision to transfer a juvenile to adult court may only be reversed upon a finding of abuse of discretion by the superior court.

(c) In preparation for the transfer hearing, counsel should be familiar with the procedures of a transfer hearing, with a particular focus on the eight factors the court must consider pursuant to G.S. 7B-2203.

(d) At the transfer hearing, counsel should review all information provided to the court by the prosecution and should be prepared to cross-examine any witnesses the prosecution presents.

(e) Unless the juvenile directs otherwise, counsel should present any evidence to the court that counsel believes will support a decision not to transfer. Evidence may include, but is not limited to, the juvenile's record, performance on court supervision, educational history, mental and emotional state, intellectual functioning, developmental issues, and family history. Counsel should be prepared to present testimony to prevent transfer, including testimony by people who can provide helpful insight into the juvenile's character, such as teachers, counselors, psychologists, community members, probation officers, religious affiliates, family members, friends, employers, or other persons with a positive personal or professional view of the juvenile.

(f) Counsel should make reasonable efforts to ensure that the transfer hearing is recorded and, with permission of the court, should consider utilizing a personal recording device in case the court recording device fails.

(g) If the court orders transfer of jurisdiction to adult court, counsel should consider appealing the matter to superior court to request remand to district court and to preserve the issue for possible review in the appellate division.

SECTION 5: INCRIMINATING EVIDENCE AND CAPACITY TO PROCEED

Guideline 5.1 Search Warrants, Interrogations, and Prosecution Requests for Non-Testimonial Evidence

(a) Counsel should be familiar with the law governing search warrants under G.S. 15A-24 *et seq.* and applicable case law, including the requirements for a search warrant application, the basis for issuing a warrant, the required form and content of a warrant, the execution and service of a warrant, and the permissible scope of the search.

(b) Counsel should be familiar with the law governing a juvenile's protection against self-incrimination, including G.S. 7B-2101 and applicable case law.

(c) Counsel should be familiar with the law governing the prosecution's power to require a juvenile to provide non-testimonial evidence (such as participation in an in-person lineup, handwriting exemplars, and physical specimens), the potential consequences if a juvenile refuses to comply with a non-testimonial identification order issued pursuant to G.S. 7B-2103 *et seq.*, and the extent to which counsel may participate in or observe the proceedings.

Guideline 5.2 Juvenile's Capacity to Proceed

(a) When defense counsel has a good faith doubt as to the juvenile's capacity to proceed in a delinquency case, counsel should consider consulting the capacity to proceed sections in the North Carolina Civil Commitment Manual and the North Carolina Defender Manual, available at www.ncids.org, and should:

(1) file an *ex parte* motion to obtain the services of a mental health expert and thereby determine whether to raise the juvenile's capacity to proceed; or

(2) file a motion questioning the juvenile's capacity to proceed or enter an admission under G.S. 7B-2401, G.S. 15A-1001(a), and applicable case law, in which case the court may order a mental health examination at a state facility or by the appropriate local forensic examiner.

(b) Although the juvenile's expressed interests ordinarily control, counsel may question capacity to proceed without the juvenile's assent or over the juvenile's objection, if necessary.

(c) After counsel receives and reviews the report from any court-ordered examination, counsel should consider whether to file a motion requesting a formal hearing on the juvenile's capacity to proceed.

(d) If capacity to proceed is at issue, counsel still has a duty to continue to prepare the case for all anticipated court proceedings.

(e) If the court enters an order finding the juvenile incapable of proceeding and orders involuntary commitment proceedings to be initiated, defense counsel ordinarily will not represent the juvenile at those proceedings but should cooperate with the commitment attorney upon request.

SECTION 6: CASE REVIEW, PREPARATION, AND DISCOVERY

Guideline 6.1 Charging Language in Delinquency Petition

(a) Counsel should review the delinquency petition in all cases and determine whether there are any defects, such as:

(1) the petition does not list all of the essential elements of the charged offense;

(2) the petition contains more than one charge in a single count; and/or

(3) the petition does not allege a crime for which the juvenile may be charged.

If there are defects, counsel should determine whether to move to dismiss the petition after considering all relevant factors, including but not limited to the type of defect, the likelihood of obtaining a favorable ruling, and the likelihood that the charge will be refiled. Counsel also should be aware of all potential consequences of a motion to dismiss, including alerting the prosecution to defects in the charging language.

(b) Even if the petition adequately charges an offense that would be a crime if committed by an adult, counsel should be sufficiently familiar with the language of the petition to recognize a fatal variance at trial and move to dismiss the charge if the evidence is insufficient to support the charge as pled.

(c) Counsel should be aware of all time limits under G.S. 7B-1703 that are applicable to the filing of a delinquency petition and should consider moving to dismiss the petition if the statutory time limits are not followed.

Guideline 6.2 Case Review, Investigation, and Preparation

(a) Counsel has a duty to conduct an independent case review and investigation. The juvenile's admissions of responsibility or other statements to counsel do not necessarily obviate the need for independent review and investigation. The review and investigation should be conducted as promptly as possible.

(b) Counsel should be aware that under G.S. 7B-2408, no statement made to the intake court counselor is admissible prior to the dispositional hearing.

(c) Sources of review and investigative information may include the following:

(1) *Petitions, Statutes, and Case Law.* Counsel should obtain and examine copies of all petitions in the case to determine the specific charges that have been brought against the juvenile. The relevant statutes and precedents should be examined to identify:

(A) the elements of the offense(s) with which the juvenile is charged;

(B) the defenses, ordinary and affirmative, that may be available, as well as the proper manner for asserting any available defenses; and

(C) any defects in the petitions, constitutional or otherwise, such as statute of limitations, double jeopardy, or others.

(2) *The Juvenile.* Counsel should conduct an in-depth interview or interviews of the juvenile as outlined in Section 3, *supra*.

(3) *Potential Witnesses.* Counsel should consider whether to interview potential witnesses, including any complaining witnesses and others adverse to the juvenile. If counsel conducts interviews of potential witnesses, he or she should attempt to do so in the presence of a third person who will be available, if necessary, to testify as a defense witness at the adjudicatory hearing. Alternatively, counsel should have an investigator conduct the interviews.

(4) *The Police and Prosecution.* Counsel should utilize available discovery procedures to secure information in the possession of the prosecution or law enforcement authorities, including police reports, unless sound tactical reasons exist for not doing so (*e.g.*, defense obligations under G.S. 7B-2301). *See* Guideline 6.3, *infra*.

(5) *The Courts.* If possible, counsel should request and review tapes or transcripts from any previous hearings in the case. Counsel should also review the juvenile's prior court file(s) and request that the court counselor provide the juvenile's prior court history from North Carolina Juvenile Online Information Network (NCJOIN).

(6) *Information in the Possession of Third Parties.* When appropriate, counsel should seek a release or court order to obtain necessary confidential information about the juvenile, co-juvenile(s), witness(es), or victim(s) that is in the possession of third parties. Counsel should be aware of privacy laws and other requirements governing disclosure of the type of confidential information being sought.

(7) *Physical Evidence.* When appropriate, counsel should make a prompt request to the police or investigative agency for any physical evidence or expert reports relevant to the offense or sentencing. Counsel should view the physical evidence consistent with case needs.

(8) *The Scene.* When appropriate, counsel or an investigator should view the scene of the alleged offense. This should be done under circumstances as similar as possible to those existing at the time of the alleged incident (*e.g.*, weather, time of day, lighting conditions, and seasonal changes). Counsel should consider taking photographs and creating diagrams or charts of the actual scene of the alleged offense.

(9) *Assistance from Experts, Investigators, and Interpreters.* Counsel should consider whether expert or investigative assistance, including consultation and testimony, is necessary or appropriate to:

(A) prepare a defense;

(B) adequately understand the prosecution's case;

(C) rebut the prosecution's case; or

(D) investigate the juvenile's capacity to proceed, mental state at the time of the offense, and capacity to make a knowing and intelligent waiver of constitutional rights.

If counsel determines that expert or investigative assistance is necessary and appropriate, counsel should file an *ex parte* motion setting forth the particularized showing of necessity required by *Ake v. Oklahoma*, 470 U.S. 68, 105 S. Ct. 1087 (1985), *State v. Ballard*, 333 N.C. 515, 428 S.E.2d 178 (1993), and their progeny. If appropriate, counsel should also file a motion to have a foreign language or sign language interpreter appointed by the court. Counsel should preserve for appeal any denial of expert, investigative, or interpreter funding by making all proper objections and motions on the record.

(d) During case preparation and throughout the adjudicatory hearing, counsel should identify potential legal issues and the corresponding objections. Counsel should consider the strategy of making objections, including the proper timing and method. Counsel should also consider how best to respond to objections that could be raised by the prosecution.

Guideline 6.3 Discovery

(a) Counsel has a duty to pursue discovery procedures provided by the applicable rules of criminal procedure and the Juvenile Code (G.S. 7B-2300 *et seq.*) and to pursue such informal discovery methods as may be available to supplement the factual investigation of the case.

(b) Before filing a formal motion with the court, counsel must serve the prosecutor with a written request for voluntary disclosure, unless counsel and the prosecutor agree in writing to comply voluntarily with G.S. 7B-2300 *et seq.* Counsel must file a motion to compel discovery if the prosecution's response is unsatisfactory or delayed. Regardless of the prosecution's response, counsel should file a motion to compel discovery if the case is proceeding to an adjudicatory hearing.

(c) In exceptional cases, counsel should consider not making a discovery request or signing a written agreement under G.S. 7B-2300 on the ground that it will trigger a defense obligation to disclose evidence under G.S. 7B-2301.

(d) Unless there are sound tactical reasons for not requesting discovery or signing a written agreement under G.S. 7B-2300 (*e.g.*, defense obligations under G.S. 7B-2301), counsel should seek discovery to the broadest extent permitted under federal and state law, including but not limited to the following items:

(1) all information to which the juvenile is entitled under G.S. 7B-2300;

(2) all potential exculpatory information and evidence to which the defense is entitled under *Brady v. Maryland*, 373 U.S. 83, 83 S. Ct. 1194 (1963) and its progeny, including but not limited to:

(A) impeachment evidence, such as a witness's prior adjudications or convictions, misconduct, or juvenile court record; bias of a witness; a witness's capacity to observe, perceive, or recollect; and psychiatric evaluations of a witness;

(B) evidence discrediting police investigation and credibility;

(C) evidence undermining the identification of the juvenile;

(D) evidence tending to show the guilt or responsibility of another;

(E) the identity of favorable witnesses; and

(F) exculpatory physical evidence; and

(3) to the extent not provided under statutory discovery, any other information necessary to the defense of the case, including but not limited to:

(A) the names, addresses, and availability of prosecution witnesses;

(B) the details of the circumstances under which any oral or written statements by the accused or a co-juvenile were made;

(C) any evidence of prior bad acts that the prosecution may intend to use against the juvenile;

(D) the data underlying any expert reports; and

(E) any evidence necessary to enable counsel to determine whether to file a motion to suppress evidence.

(e) Counsel should seek the timely production and preservation of discoverable evidence. If the prosecution fails to disclose or belatedly discloses discoverable evidence, counsel should consider requesting one or more sanctions, akin to those provided by G.S. 15A-910.

(f) If counsel believes the prosecution may destroy or consume in testing evidence that is significant to the case (*e.g.*, rough notes of law enforcement interviews, 911 tapes, drugs, or blood samples), counsel should file a motion to preserve the evidence in the event that it is discoverable.

(g) Counsel should timely comply with all of the requirements in G.S. 7B-2301 governing disclosure of evidence by the juvenile and notice of defenses and expert witnesses.

Guideline 6.4 Theory of the Case

During case review, investigation, and preparation for the adjudicatory hearing, counsel should develop and continually reassess a theory of the case. A theory of the case is one central theory that organizes the facts, emotions, and legal basis for a finding of not responsible or adjudication of a lesser offense, while also telling the juvenile's story of innocence, reduced culpability, or unfairness. The theory of the case furnishes the basic position from which counsel determines all actions in a case.

SECTION 7: PRE-ADJUDICATION MOTIONS

Guideline 7.1 The Decision to File Pre-Adjudication Motions

(a) Counsel should consider filing appropriate pre-adjudication motions whenever there exists a good faith reason to believe that the applicable law may entitle the juvenile to relief which the court has authority to grant.

(b) Counsel should consult the local rules of the judicial district to determine whether they establish deadlines for pre-adjudication motions and should comply with any such rules.

(c) The decision to file pre-adjudication motions should be made after thorough investigation and after considering the applicable law in light of the circumstances of each case, as well as the need to preserve issues for appellate review. Among the issues that counsel should consider addressing in pre-adjudication motions are:

(1) the constitutionality of the implicated statute(s);

(2) the sufficiency of the petition under all applicable statutory and constitutional provisions;

(3) the dismissal of a charge on double jeopardy grounds;

(4) the propriety and prejudice of any joinder or severance of charges or juveniles;

(5) the statutory and constitutional discovery obligations of the prosecution;

(6) the suppression of evidence gathered as the result of violations of the North Carolina Constitution, the United States Constitution, and applicable federal and state statutes, including:

(A) the fruits of any illegal searches or seizures;

(B) any statements or confessions obtained in violation of the juvenile's right to counsel, privilege against self-incrimination, or rights protected under G.S. 7B-2101; and

(C) the fruits of any unconstitutional identification procedures;

(7) whether there are grounds to prevent discovery or testimony or other evidence based on privilege;

(8) access to necessary support or investigative resources or experts;

(9) the need for a change of venue;

(10) the juvenile's calendaring rights under the Juvenile Code;

(11) the juvenile's right to a continuance in order adequately to prepare his or her case;

(12) matters of trial evidence that may be appropriately litigated by means of a pre-adjudication motion *in limine*, including exclusion of any pre-adjudication statements the juvenile may have made at intake;

(13) recusal of the trial judge;

(14) the full recordation of all proceedings;

(15) matters of courtroom procedure; and

(16) notice of affirmative defenses.

Guideline 7.2 Filing and Arguing Pre-Adjudication Motions

(a) Motions should be filed in a timely manner, comport with the formal requirements of statute and court rules, and succinctly inform the court of the authority relied upon.

(b) When a hearing on a motion requires the taking of evidence, counsel's preparation for the evidentiary hearing should include:

(1) investigation, discovery, and research relevant to the claim(s) advanced;

(2) subpoenaing of all helpful evidence, and subpoenaing and preparation of all helpful witnesses;

(3) full understanding of the burdens of proof, evidentiary principles, and procedures applicable to the hearing, including the potential advantages and disadvantages of having the juvenile and other defense witnesses testify;

(4) obtaining the assistance of an expert witness when appropriate; and

(5) preparation and submission of a memorandum of law when appropriate.

(c) Unless there are sound tactical reasons for not doing so, counsel should request that the court rule on all previously filed defense motions prior to the adjudicatory hearing.

(d) If a hearing on a pre-adjudication motion is held in advance of an adjudicatory hearing, counsel should attempt to obtain the transcript of the hearing for use at the adjudicatory hearing, if appropriate.

Guideline 7.3 Subsequent Filing and Renewal of Pre-Adjudication Motions

(a) Counsel should be prepared to raise during the adjudication proceedings any issue that is appropriately raised pre-adjudication, but could not have been so raised because the facts supporting the motion were unknown or not reasonably available.

(b) Counsel should be prepared to renew pre-adjudication motions or file additional motions at any subsequent stage of the proceedings if new supporting information is later disclosed or made available. Counsel should also renew pre-adjudication motions and object to the admission of challenged evidence at the adjudicatory hearing to preserve the motions and objections for appellate review pursuant to Rule 10(b) of the North Carolina Rules of Appellate Procedure and *State v. Tutt*, 171 N.C. App. 518, 615 S.E.2d 688 (2005).

SECTION 8: PLEAS

Guideline 8.1 Advising the Juvenile About Pleas

(a) Counsel should explain to the juvenile that certain decisions concerning a possible plea ultimately must be made by the juvenile, as well as the advantages and disadvantages inherent in those choices. The decisions that must be made by the juvenile include whether to admit or deny the allegations of the petition, whether to accept a plea agreement, and whether to testify at a plea hearing.

(b) After appropriate investigation and case review, counsel should explore with the juvenile the possibility and desirability of negotiating a plea to the charges rather than proceeding to an adjudicatory hearing. In doing so, counsel should fully explain to the juvenile the rights that would be waived by a decision to enter a plea and not proceed to the adjudicatory hearing, including the fact that an admission of the allegations of the petition is the same as an adjudication, and the impact of the decision on the juvenile's right to appeal.

Guideline 8.2 Preparation for Plea Negotiations

(a) In preparing for plea negotiations, counsel should attempt to become familiar with any practices and policies of the particular district, judge, prosecuting attorney and, when applicable, court counselor's office, which may affect the content and likely results of a negotiated plea bargain.

(b) Counsel should be familiar with:

(1) the various types of pleas that may be agreed to, including an admission of responsibility, a plea of no contest, a conditional admission in which the juvenile retains the right to appeal the denial of a suppression motion, a plea in which the juvenile is not required personally to acknowledge his or her involvement (*Alford* plea), and a plea to dismiss the case after adjudication under G.S. 7B-2501(d);

(2) the advantages and disadvantages of each available plea according to the circumstances of the case; and

(3) whether a proposed plea agreement is binding on the court.

(c) To develop an overall negotiation plan, counsel should be fully aware and advise the juvenile of the possible results of an adjudication, including:

(1) the maximum term of confinement for the offense;

(2) any requirements for registration such as sex offender registration, and for being fingerprinted and photographed;

(3) the possibility that an adjudication or admission of the offense could be used for cross-examination or sentence enhancement in the event of future criminal cases;

(4) the availability of appropriate dispositional options; and

(5) the potential collateral consequences of entering a plea, such as deportation or other effects on immigration status; effects on motor vehicle or other licensing; educational notifications; distribution of fingerprint and photographic information; and the potential exposure to or impact on any federal charges.

(d) In developing a negotiation strategy, counsel should be completely familiar with:

(1) concessions that the juvenile might offer the prosecution as part of a negotiated agreement, such as:

(A) waiving the probable cause hearing;

(B) declining to assert the right to proceed to the adjudicatory hearing on the merits of the charge;

(C) refraining from asserting or litigating a particular pre-adjudication motion;

(D) agreeing to fulfill specified restitution conditions or to participate in community work or service programs or other dispositional options;

(E) assisting the prosecution in investigating the present case or other alleged delinquent activity; and

(F) waiving a challenge to the validity or proof of a prior adjudication;

(2) benefits the juvenile might obtain from a negotiated agreement, such as:

(A) that the prosecution will not seek transfer;

(B) that the juvenile may enter an admission and preserve the right to litigate and contest the denial of a suppression motion;

(C) dismissal or reduction of one or more of the charged offenses, either immediately or upon completion of conditions of a deferred adjudication;

(D) that the juvenile will not be subject to further investigation or prosecution for uncharged alleged delinquent conduct;

(E) that the prosecution will not oppose the juvenile's release pending disposition or appeal;

(F) that the juvenile will receive, with the agreement of the court, a specified disposition;

(G) that at the disposition hearing, the prosecution will take, or refrain from taking, a specified position with respect to the sanction to be imposed on the juvenile by the court; and

(H) that at the disposition hearing, the prosecution will not present certain information;

(3) information favorable to the juvenile concerning matters such as the offense, mitigating factors and relative culpability, prior offenses, personal background, familial status, and educational and other relevant social information;

(4) information that would support a disposition other than confinement, such as the potential for rehabilitation or the nonviolent nature of the crime; and

(5) information concerning the availability of dispositional options, such as treatment programs, community treatment facilities, and community service work opportunities.

Guideline 8.3 Ongoing Preparation During Plea Negotiations

(a) Notwithstanding plea negotiations with the prosecution, counsel should continue to prepare and investigate the case to the extent necessary to protect the juvenile's rights and interests in the event that plea negotiations fail.

(b) Counsel should keep the juvenile fully informed of any plea discussions and negotiations and convey to the juvenile any offers made by the prosecution for a negotiated agreement.

Guideline 8.4 The Decision to Enter a Plea

(a) If counsel and the prosecution reach a tentative negotiated agreement, counsel should explain to the juvenile the full content of the agreement, including its advantages, disadvantages, and potential consequences. Counsel should also inform the juvenile that any plea agreement may be rejected by the court and the consequences of a rejection.

(b) Counsel should again advise the juvenile of the possible results of an adjudication as set forth in Guideline 8.2(c), *supra*.

(c) Counsel may not accept or reject a plea agreement without the juvenile's express authorization. Although the decision to accept or reject a plea agreement ultimately rests with the juvenile, if counsel believes the juvenile's decisions are not in his or her best legal interests, counsel should make every effort to ensure that the juvenile understands all of the potential consequences before the juvenile makes a final decision.

Guideline 8.5 Preparing the Juvenile for Entry of Plea

If the juvenile agrees to a negotiated plea, prior to the entry of a plea, counsel should:

(1) fully explain to the juvenile the nature of the plea hearing and the meaning of the questions on the transcript of admission;

(2) fully explain to the juvenile the conditions and limits of the plea agreement and the maximum punishment, sanctions, and other consequences the juvenile will be exposed to by entering a plea; and

(3) fully explain to the juvenile the plea hearing process, the role he or she may play in the hearing, including answering questions of the judge, the need to speak clearly and audibly before the court, and the need to behave appropriately and respond in a respectful manner to the court.

Guideline 8.6 Entry of Plea

(a) Counsel should not allow a juvenile to plead responsible based on oral conditions that are not disclosed to the court.

(b) When the juvenile enters a plea, counsel should ensure that the full content and conditions of the plea agreement between the prosecution and defense are legibly recorded on the transcript of admission.

(c) Subsequent to the acceptance of a plea by the court, counsel should review and explain the plea proceedings to the juvenile and respond to any questions and concerns of the juvenile.

SECTION 9: THE ADJUDICATORY HEARING

Guideline 9.1 General Adjudicatory Hearing Preparation

(a) Counsel should explain to the juvenile that, although it is the juvenile's decision whether to deny the allegations of the petition and proceed to an adjudicatory hearing, decisions concerning adjudication strategy are ordinarily to be made by counsel, after consultation with the juvenile and investigation of the applicable facts and law. However, counsel should be aware that, under the North Carolina Rules of Professional Conduct, if counsel and a fully informed competent juvenile reach an absolute impasse as to tactical decisions, the juvenile's wishes may control.

(b) Throughout preparation and adjudication, counsel should develop a theory of the defense and ensure that counsel's decisions and actions are consistent with that theory.

(c) In advance of the adjudicatory hearing, counsel should take all steps necessary to complete thorough investigation, discovery, and research. Among the steps counsel should take in preparation are:

(1) interviewing and subpoenaing all potentially helpful witnesses;

(2) subpoenaing any potentially helpful physical or documentary evidence;

(3) filing applicable pre-trial motions, with supporting briefs, memorandum, case law, and other supporting documentation, if appropriate;

(4) when appropriate, obtaining funds for defense investigators and experts and arranging for defense experts to consult and/or testify on issues that are potentially helpful;

(5) obtaining and reading transcripts of any prior proceedings in the case or related proceedings; and

(6) obtaining photographs or preparing charts, maps, diagrams, or other visual aids of any scenes, persons, objects, or information that may aid the court in understanding the juvenile's defense.

(d) When appropriate, counsel should have the following relevant information and materials available at the time of the adjudicatory hearing:

(1) copies of all documents filed in the case;

(2) documents prepared by investigators;

(3) reports, test results, and other materials disclosed by the prosecution pursuant to G.S. 7B-2300 *et seq.*;

(4) a plan, outline, or draft of an opening statement, if appropriate;

(5) cross-examination plans for all possible prosecution witnesses;

(6) direct-examination plans for all prospective defense witnesses;

(7) copies of defense subpoenas;

(8) any prior statements of all prosecution witnesses (*e.g.*, transcripts and police reports);

(9) any prior statements of all defense witnesses;

(10) reports from defense experts;

(11) a list of all defense exhibits and the witnesses through whom they will be introduced;

(12) originals and copies of all defense documentary exhibits;

(13) copies of statutes and cases; and

(14) a plan, outline, or draft of the closing argument.

(e) Counsel should be familiar with the rules of evidence that apply in adjudicatory proceedings, the law relating to all stages of the adjudicatory process, including the standards of proof in each proceeding, and the legal and evidentiary issues that reasonably can be anticipated to arise during the adjudicatory hearing.

(f) Counsel should decide if it is beneficial to obtain an advance ruling on issues likely to arise at the adjudicatory hearing (*e.g.*, use of prior adjudications to impeach the juvenile) and, if appropriate, prepare motions and memoranda for such advance rulings.

(g) Counsel should arrange with court personnel and/or the sheriff's office for counsel to be able to confer with the juvenile in a confidential setting during the adjudicatory hearing.

(h) Counsel should consider moving the court under G.S. 7B-2402 to close any initial proceedings. Factors counsel should consider when making this request include the age of the juvenile, the nature of the charges, and any information that may be discussed during the hearing that could harm the juvenile. If requested by the juvenile, counsel should move to close the proceedings.

(i) Throughout preparation and adjudication, counsel should consider the potential effects that particular actions may have upon disposition if there is a finding of delinquency.

(j) Counsel should consider moving the court to sequester any witnesses who may be called to testify at the adjudicatory hearing.

Guideline 9.2 Juvenile Dress and Demeanor at the Adjudicatory Hearing

(a) When appropriate, counsel should advise the juvenile as to suitable courtroom dress and demeanor.

(b) If the juvenile is detained, counsel should try to ensure, prior to the court hearing, that the juvenile does not appear before the judge in inappropriate clothing or in shackles or handcuffs. If a detained juvenile is brought before the judge in detention clothing, shackles, or handcuffs, counsel should object and seek appropriate relief from the court pursuant to G.S. 7B-2402.1.

Guideline 9.3 Preserving the Record on Appeal

Throughout the adjudicatory process, counsel should establish a proper record for appellate review, including making reasonable efforts to ensure that the adjudicatory hearing is recorded. If a relevant and important non-verbal event occurs during the adjudicatory hearing, counsel should ask to have the record reflect what happened. With permission of the court, counsel should also consider utilizing a personal recording device in case the court recording device fails.

Guideline 9.4 Opening Statement

(a) Though an opening statement is not always presented at a bench hearing, counsel should consider the potential benefits of making an opening statement. If counsel decides to make an opening statement, counsel should consider whether to ask for sequestration of witnesses before the statement.

(b) Counsel should be familiar with North Carolina law and the individual trial judge's practices regarding the permissible content of an opening statement. If appropriate, counsel should ask the court to instruct the prosecution not to mention in opening statement contested evidence for which the court has not determined admissibility.

(c) Counsel should consider the strategic advantages and disadvantages of disclosure of particular information during opening statement.

(d) Counsel should have a clear understanding of his or her objectives in making an opening statement. Appropriate objectives include:

(1) introducing the theory of the defense case;

(2) providing an overview of the defense case;

(3) identifying the weaknesses of the prosecution's case;

(4) emphasizing the prosecution's burden of proof; and

(5) preparing the court for the juvenile's testimony or decision not to testify.

(e) Whenever the prosecutor oversteps the bounds of a proper opening statement, counsel should consider objecting, requesting a mistrial, or seeking cautionary instructions, unless sound tactical considerations weigh against any such objections or requests. Such tactical considerations may include, but are not limited to:

(1) the significance of the prosecutor's error; and

(2) the possibility that an objection might enhance the significance of the information in the court's mind, or otherwise negatively affect the court.

Guideline 9.5 Preparing for and Confronting the Prosecution's Case

(a) Counsel should anticipate weaknesses in the prosecution's proof, and research and prepare to argue corresponding motions for judgment of dismissal or not delinquent.

(b) Counsel should consider the advantages and disadvantages of entering into stipulations concerning the prosecution's case.

(c) Unless sound tactical reasons exist for not doing so, counsel should make timely objections and motions to strike improper prosecution evidence and assert all possible statutory and constitutional grounds for exclusion of the evidence. If evidence offered by the prosecution is admissible only for a limited purpose, counsel generally should request that the court limit consideration to the proper purpose.

(d) Counsel should seek to ensure that any statements made by the juvenile to the court counselor during the preliminary hearing and evaluation process be excluded from the adjudicatory hearing pursuant to G.S. 7B-2408.

(e) In preparing for cross-examination, counsel should:

(1) be familiar with North Carolina law and procedures concerning cross-examination and impeachment of witnesses;

(2) be prepared to question witnesses as to the existence and content of prior statements;

(3) consider the need to integrate cross-examination, the theory of the defense, and closing argument;

(4) determine what counsel expects to accomplish by cross-examination of each witness and avoid asking questions that are unnecessary or might elicit responses harmful to the defense case;

(5) anticipate witnesses the prosecution might call in its case-in-chief or in rebuttal, and consider a cross-examination plan for each of the anticipated witnesses;

(6) be alert to inconsistencies, variations, and contradictions within each witness's testimony;

(7) be alert to inconsistencies, variations, and contradictions between different witnesses' testimony;

(8) review any prior statements and prior relevant testimony of the prospective witnesses;

(9) when appropriate, review relevant statutes and local police regulations for possible use in cross-examining police witnesses; and

(10) be alert to issues relating to witness credibility, including bias and motive for testifying.

(f) Counsel should consider conducting a *voir dire* examination of potential prosecution witnesses who may not be competent to give particular testimony, including expert witnesses and younger witnesses. Counsel should be aware of the law concerning competency of witnesses in general, and admission of expert testimony in particular, to be able to raise appropriate objections.

(g) Before beginning cross-examination, counsel should ascertain whether the prosecutor provided copies of all prior statements of prosecution witnesses as required by G.S. 7B-2300. If disclosure was not properly made, counsel should request appropriate relief similar to that found in G.S. 15A-910, including:

(1) adequate time to review the documents or investigate and prepare further before commencing cross-examination, including a continuance or recess if necessary;

(2) exclusion of the witness's testimony and all evidence affected by that testimony;

(3) a mistrial;

(4) dismissal of the case; and/or

(5) any other sanctions counsel believes would remedy the violation.

(h) At the close of the prosecution's case, counsel should move for a judgment of dismissal on each count charged. Where appropriate, counsel should be prepared with supporting case law.

Guideline 9.6 Presenting the Defense Case

(a) In consultation with the juvenile, counsel should develop an overall defense strategy. In deciding on defense strategy, counsel should consider whether the juvenile's interests are best served by not presenting defense evidence and relying instead on the evidence and inferences, or lack thereof, from the prosecution's case.

(b) Counsel should discuss with the juvenile all of the considerations relevant to the juvenile's decision to testify, including the likelihood of cross-examination and impeachment concerning prior adjudications and prior bad acts that affect credibility.

(c) Counsel should be aware of the elements of any affirmative defense(s) and know whether the defense bears a burden of persuasion or production.

(d) In preparing for presentation of the defense case, counsel should, where appropriate:

(1) develop a plan for direct examination of each potential defense witness;

(2) determine the effect that the order of witnesses may have on the defense case;

(3) consider the possible use of character witnesses and any negative consequences that may flow from such testimony;

(4) consider the need for expert witnesses;

(5) consider the use of demonstrative evidence and the most effective order of exhibits; and

(6) be fully familiar with North Carolina statutory and case law on objections, motions to strike, offers of proof, and preserving the record on appeal.

(e) In developing and presenting the defense case, counsel should consider the implications it may have for rebuttal by the prosecution.

(f) Counsel should prepare all defense witnesses for direct examination and possible cross-examination. When appropriate, counsel should also advise witnesses of suitable courtroom dress and demeanor.

(g) If a prosecution objection to a proper question is sustained or defense evidence is improperly excluded, counsel should rephrase the question or make an offer of proof.

(h) Counsel should conduct redirect examination as appropriate.

(i) At the close of all of the evidence, counsel should renew the motion for judgment of dismissal on each charged count.

Guideline 9.7 Closing Argument

(a) In developing a closing argument, counsel should review the proceedings to determine what aspects can be used in support of defense summation and should:

(1) highlight any weaknesses in the prosecution's case;

(2) point out favorable inferences to be drawn from the evidence;

(3) incorporate into the argument:

(A) the theory of the defense case;

(B) helpful testimony from direct and cross-examinations;

(C) responses to anticipated prosecution arguments; and

(D) any relevant visual aids and exhibits; and

(4) consider the effects of the defense argument on the prosecution's rebuttal argument.

(b) Whenever the prosecutor exceeds the scope of permissible argument, counsel should object or request a mistrial unless sound tactical considerations suggest otherwise. Such tactical considerations may include, but are not limited to:

(1) the significance of the prosecution's error;

(2) the possibility that an objection might enhance the significance of the information in the court's mind;

(3) whether, with respect to a motion for mistrial, counsel believes that the case will result in a favorable decision for the juvenile; and

(4) the need to preserve the objection for appellate review.

SECTION 10: THE DISPOSITIONAL HEARING

Guideline 10.1 Dispositional Procedures

Counsel should be familiar with applicable dispositional procedures, including:

(1) the effect that plea negotiations may have on the dispositional discretion of the court;

(2) the procedural operation of disposition;

(3) the practices of the court counselor's office in preparation of the pre-dispositional report, and the juvenile's rights in that process;

(4) the right of access by counsel and the juvenile to the pre-dispositional report;

(5) the defense dispositional presentation and/or memorandum;

(6) the opportunity to challenge information presented to the court for disposition;

(7) the availability of an evidentiary hearing to challenge information, and the applicable rules of evidence and burden of proof at such a hearing; and

(8) the participation that victims and prosecution or defense witnesses may have in the dispositional proceedings.

Guideline 10.2 Advising the Juvenile About Disposition

(a) If the juvenile enters a plea or is found delinquent, counsel should be familiar with and advise the juvenile of the dispositional requirements, options, and alternatives applicable to the offense, including:

(1) the applicable disposition laws, including the dispositional chart, calculation of the juvenile's delinquency history, and exposure to commitment to a youth development center;

(2) disposition continued;

(3) probation or suspension of confinement and mandatory and permissible conditions of probation;

(4) any mandatory requirements for registration, such as sex offender registration, or for fingerprinting and photographing; and

(5) the possibility of expunction and sealing of records.

(b) Counsel should be familiar with and advise the juvenile of the direct and collateral consequences of the adjudication and disposition including, as appropriate:

(1) credit for pre-adjudication detention;

(2) the likelihood that the adjudication could be used for sentence enhancement in the event of future criminal cases; and

(3) if applicable, other potential collateral consequences of the adjudication and disposition, such as deportation or other effects on immigration status; effects on motor vehicle or other licensing; and the potential exposure to or impact on any federal charges, educational notification, and distribution of fingerprint and photographic information.

Guideline 10.3 Preparation for Disposition

In preparing for disposition, counsel should:

(1) be aware and inform the juvenile of the judge's practices and procedures, if possible;

(2) maintain regular contact with the juvenile prior to the dispositional hearing, and inform the juvenile and his or her parent or guardian of the steps being taken in preparation for disposition and what to expect at the dispositional hearing;

(3) obtain from the juvenile relevant information concerning such subjects as his or her background and personal history, prior record, educational history, mental health history and condition, and employment history, if any, and obtain from the juvenile sources through which the information provided can be corroborated;

(4) utilize dispositional experts, including mental health, developmental, or educational professionals, if applicable;

(5) inform the juvenile of his or her right to speak at the dispositional proceeding, and assist the juvenile in preparing the statement, if any, to be made to the court, after considering the possible consequences that any admission or other statement may have on an appeal, subsequent adjudicatory hearing, adjudication on other offenses, or other judicial proceedings, such as collateral or restitution proceedings;

(6) inform the juvenile if counsel will ask the court to consider a particular disposition;

(7) collect and present documents and affidavits to support the defense position and, when relevant, prepare and present witnesses to testify at the dispositional hearing;

(8) prepare any expert or other witnesses to address the court;

(9) consult with any child and family treatment team, if appropriate and possible; and

(10) unless there are sound tactical reasons for not doing so, attempt to determine whether the prosecution will advocate that a particular type or length of confinement be imposed.

Guideline 10.4 The Pre-Dispositional Report

(a) Counsel should be familiar with the procedures concerning the preparation and submission of a pre-dispositional report by the court counselor's office.

(b) If a pre-dispositional report is prepared, counsel should:

(1) provide to the court counselor preparing the report relevant information favorable to the juvenile, including, where appropriate, the juvenile's version of the offense;

(2) prepare the juvenile to be interviewed by the court counselor preparing the report, if the juvenile has not already been interviewed;

(3) make reasonable efforts to review the completed report and discuss it with the juvenile before going to court;

(4) try to ensure the juvenile has adequate time to examine the report, unless directed by the court not to disclose information in the report pursuant to G.S. 7B-2413; and

(5) take appropriate steps to ensure that erroneous or misleading information that may harm the juvenile is challenged or deleted from the report.

Guideline 10.5 The Defense Dispositional Plan

Counsel should prepare a defense dispositional plan and, where appropriate, a dispositional memorandum. Among the topics counsel may wish to include in the dispositional presentation or memorandum are:

(1) information favorable to the juvenile concerning such matters as the offense, mitigating factors and relative culpability, prior adjudications, personal background, educational history, employment record and opportunities, and familial and financial status;

(2) information that would support a disposition other than confinement, such as the potential for rehabilitation or the nonviolent nature of the crime;

(3) information concerning the availability of treatment programs, community treatment facilities, and community service work opportunities;

(4) challenges to incorrect or incomplete information and inappropriate inferences and characterizations that are before the court; and

(5) a defense confinement proposal, if necessary.

Guideline 10.6 The Dispositional Hearing

(a) At the dispositional hearing, counsel should take the steps necessary to advocate fully for the requested disposition and to protect the juvenile's legal rights and interests.

(b) If appropriate, counsel should present supporting evidence, including testimony of the juvenile and witnesses, affidavits, letters, and public records to establish the facts favorable to the juvenile. Counsel should also try to ensure that the juvenile is not harmed by inaccurate information or information that is not properly before the court in determining the disposition to be imposed.

(c) If the court has the authority to do so, counsel should request specific orders or recommendations from the court concerning the place of confinement and any psychiatric treatment or drug rehabilitation, and against deportation or exclusion of the juvenile, if applicable.

(d) Counsel should identify and preserve potential issues for appeal, including making reasonable efforts to ensure that the dispositional hearing is recorded. With permission of the court, counsel should also consider utilizing a personal recording device in case the court recording device fails.

SECTION 11: POST-DISPOSITION OBLIGATIONS AND APPEALS

Guideline 11.1 Explaining the Disposition to the Juvenile

After the dispositional hearing is complete, counsel should fully explain to the juvenile the terms of the disposition, including any conditions of probation and implications of violating probation.

Guideline 11.2 Motion to Modify or Vacate

Counsel should be familiar with the procedures available under G.S. 7B-2600 to seek relief from the dispositional order and should utilize those procedures when appropriate.

Guideline 11.3 Right to Appeal to the Appellate Division

(a) Counsel should inform the juvenile of his or her right to appeal the judgment of the court to the appellate division, the action that must be taken to perfect an appeal, and the possible outcomes of a decision to appeal.

(b) If the juvenile has a right to appeal and wants to appeal, the attorney should enter notice of appeal in accordance with the procedures and timelines set forth in G.S. 7B-2602 *et seq.* and the Rules of Appellate Procedure, and should consider offering to the court a completed form appellate entries (AOC-J-470) appointing the Office of the Appellate Defender. Pursuant to Rule 33(a) of the North Carolina Rules of Appellate Procedure and Rules 1.7(a) and 3.2(a) of the Rules of the Commission on Indigent Defense Services, the entry of notice of appeal does not constitute a general appearance as counsel of record in the appellate division.

(c) If the juvenile does not have a right to appeal and counsel believes there is a meritorious issue in the case that might be raised in the appellate division by means of a petition for writ of *certiorari*, counsel should inform the juvenile of his or her opinion and consult with the Office of the Appellate Defender about the appropriate procedure.

(d) Where the juvenile takes an appeal, trial counsel should cooperate in providing information to appellate counsel concerning the proceedings in the trial court and should timely respond to reasonable requests from appellate counsel for additional information about the case.

Guideline 11.4 Disposition Pending Appeal

(a) If a juvenile decides to appeal the adjudication or disposition of the court, counsel should inform the juvenile of any right that may exist under G.S. 7B-2605 to be released pending disposition of the appeal and, prior to the appointment of appellate counsel, make such a motion when appropriate. Counsel should also consult with the juvenile as to the possible outcomes of such a motion.

(b) If an appeal is taken and appellate counsel is appointed, trial counsel should cooperate with appellate counsel in providing information if appellate counsel pursues a request for release.

Guideline 11.5 Post-Disposition Obligations

Even after counsel's representation in a case is complete, counsel should comply with a juvenile's reasonable requests for information and materials that are part of counsel's file. Counsel should also take reasonable steps to correct clerical or other errors in court documents.

Chapter 19
Raise the Age Legislation

19.1   Overview

In June 2017, the General Assembly enacted the Juvenile Justice Reinvestment Act, which raised the age of criminal responsibility to 18. The Act ends the century-long practice of prosecuting 16 and 17-year-olds in criminal court. As a result of this change, there are no jurisdictions in the country that automatically prosecute juveniles as young as 16 years old in criminal court.

The Act does not completely eliminate prosecution of juveniles as adults. For example, under the Act, 16 and 17-year-olds charged with motor vehicle offenses must still be prosecuted in criminal court. Similarly, transfer to superior court is mandatory for any case involving a Class A through G felony committed by a 16 or 17-year-old in which an indictment has been filed or a juvenile court judge has found probable cause.

Some of the changes required by the Act take effect in 2017, described below. Most of the changes, however, do not take effect until December 1, 2019. Whether those changes apply to individual juveniles depends on the offense date in the case. Thus, a 16 or 17-year-old charged with a crime in 2018 could not hold the case open until December 1, 2019, in order to be prosecuted in juvenile court. If a crime was committed by a 16 or 17-year old before December 1, 2019, the juvenile would still be prosecuted in criminal court. If the offense date is on or after December 1, 2019, the new provisions apply. For a discussion of those changes, see LaToya Powell, 2017 Juvenile Justice Reinvestment Act.

19.2   Changes Effective in 2017

A.   Effective October 1, 2017 and Applicable to Complaints Filed on or after that Date

Victim's rights. Before enactment of the Juvenile Justice Reinvestment Act, a juvenile court counselor was only required to provide written notification of a decision not to file a complaint as a juvenile petition to the complainant, who was typically a law enforcement officer. The Act now requires the court counselor to notify both the complainant and the alleged victim of this decision and to inform complainants and victims of their right to request review by a prosecutor of the decision. The Act also requires prosecutors to hold conferences with the complainant, court counselor, and victim about filing a petition. Previously, the prosecutor was only required to hold conferences with the complainant and the court counselor.

B. Effective October 1, 2017

Law enforcement access to information. The juvenile court counselor's record for juveniles must include the juvenile's delinquency record as well as consultations with law enforcement officers that do not result in the filing of a complaint. A consultation occurs, for example, when an officer refers a juvenile to the Division of Adult Correction and Juvenile Justice, but the juvenile is released without further action.

If a law enforcement officer is investigating an incident that could result in the filing of a complaint and requests information about a juvenile, the court counselor must share information related to prior law enforcement consultations regarding the juvenile and the juvenile's delinquency record. The officer may not obtain copies of juvenile records and must maintain the confidentiality of any information received.

C. Effective July 1, 2017

Electronic records. By July 1, 2018, the Administrative Office of the Courts (AOC) must expand access to the electronic records management system for juvenile courts, JWise, to include prosecutors and juvenile defense attorneys. Prosecutors and juvenile defense attorneys may only be permitted to access electronic records involving juvenile delinquency and not any records pertaining to cases involving abuse, neglect, and dependency or termination of parental rights. The AOC must also modify JWise so that users may access juvenile records from across the state and not solely juvenile records from individual counties.

School-justice partnerships to reduce school-based referrals to juvenile courts. The General Assembly enacted a new statute, G.S. 7A-343, that authorizes the Director of the AOC to develop plans for chief district court judges to establish partnerships with local law enforcement agencies, local boards of education, and local school administrative units. Any school-justice partnerships created under the plans must operate with the goal of reducing in-school arrests, out-of-school suspensions, and expulsions.

Juvenile Jurisdiction Advisory Committee. In light of the changes enacted by the Juvenile Justice Reinvestment Act, the General Assembly established a 21-member Juvenile Jurisdiction Advisory Committee to develop a plan for implementation of the Act. The committee will be comprised of stakeholders in the juvenile justice system, including court counselors, judges, prosecutors, juvenile defense attorneys, and victim advocates. The committee will be located in the Division of Adult Correction and

Juvenile Justice and must submit periodic reports to the General Assembly until January 15, 2023.

Juvenile justice training for law enforcement officers. The minimum standards for entry-level employment for law enforcement officers must now include: (1) handling and processing of juvenile matters for referrals, diversion, arrests, and detention; (2) best practices for handling incidents involving juveniles; (3) adolescent development and psychology; and (4) promoting relationship building with youth as a key to delinquency prevention.

Appendix A
Juvenile Justice and Medicaid*

I.   Introduction

Medicaid is the publicly-funded insurance program that covers health care services for millions of low-income Americans, including 29 million children and teenagers. The majority of children who are involved in the juvenile justice system have incomes low enough to qualify them for Medicaid. In addition, many have significant unmet physical and mental health needs. Medicaid-covered services can greatly benefit this population when their health problems and alleged offenses are interrelated. But, while many children meet Medicaid eligibility requirements, they may not be enrolled in Medicaid or may have difficulty accessing the services to which they are entitled. Unfortunately, their families may be unaware of their potential eligibility for Medicaid and the services to which they could have access. Moreover, many juvenile defenders and others who work with justice-involved children may not be aware of the full range of services available under the program. An understanding of the Medicaid program can therefore help juvenile defenders better assist the clients they serve.

Medicaid covers basic and specialized physical health services, as well as a wide array of mental, behavioral, and substance abuse treatment. It does not pay for services for most individuals who are incarcerated, including children who are placed in Youth Development Centers. Yet, it can play a central role in keeping children out of custody by, for example, funding community-based treatment alternatives and providing support for children transitioning back into the community.

Unfortunately, the complexity of Medicaid laws, policies, and administrative procedures can prevent potential beneficiaries from obtaining the services they need and confound advocates trying to assist them. This appendix to the North Carolina Juvenile Defender Manual is intended to help defenders understand the program and its potential benefits for children by providing an overview of North Carolina's Medicaid Program. It describes the structure of the Medicaid program, basic eligibility requirements, services covered, and rights to notice and opportunity to appeal denials of, and eligibility for, services. It concludes with a guide to sources of Medicaid rules and legal precedent, and a glossary of terms and acronyms.

II.   Medicaid Program Administration

Medicaid is a cooperative federal-state program designed to assist certain categories of low-income individuals—pregnant women, children under age 19 and their caretakers, people over age 65, and those with disabilities—with the cost of medical care. The program is cooperative in several important ways. Each state's Medicaid program is overseen by both federal and state agencies. Both federal and state statutes, regulations, and policies govern each Medicaid program. Moreover, as long as states comply with federal requirements, a portion of

---

*Authored by Sarah Somers, Joe McLean, and Ian McDonald, <u>National Health Law Program (NHeLP)</u>, Carrboro, North Carolina.

their Medicaid expenses will be covered by federal funds. The federal share of Medicaid costs is known as federal financial participation (FFP). In North Carolina in 2017 and 2018, federal funds cover approximately 67 percent of Medicaid services. 80 Fed. Reg. 73779 (Nov. 25, 2015); 81 Fed. Reg. 80078 (Nov. 15, 2016).

At the national level, Medicaid is administered by the Centers for Medicare and Medicaid Services (CMS), an agency within the U.S. Department of Health and Human Services (USDHHS). CMS provides interpretations of, and guidance on, the requirements of federal Medicaid law. Every state must make a Medicaid plan, which sets forth the specific characteristics of its Medicaid program, including who is eligible and what services are covered. CMS approves the state's Medicaid plan if it meets federal requirements.

Federal law requires each state to administer its Medicaid program through a single state agency. In North Carolina, it is the Department of Health and Human Services (DHHS). N.C. GEN. STAT. § 143-516. DHHS includes multiple separate divisions, including the Divisions of Medical Assistance (DMA), Social Services (DSS), and Mental Health, Developmental Disabilities and Substance Abuse Services (DMH/DD/SAS), each of which plays an important role in the Medicaid program.

DHHS has delegated primary responsibility for overseeing and managing the Medicaid program to DMA. DMA also provides training and technical assistance to county DSS offices, which determine Medicaid eligibility and administer the program at the local level. DMH/DD/SAS is responsible for managing behavioral health care for Medicaid enrollees. The division contracts with local management entities (LMEs), which are public, community-based care management entities that provide oversight for mental health, developmental disabilities and substance abuse services. Each is responsible for Medicaid beneficiaries in a designated geographic region or "catchment area." N.C. GEN. STAT. § 122C-115.4. LMEs conduct initial assessments, then contract with and refer consumers to private providers. Information for the LMEs can be found on the DMH/DD/SAS website (*see infra* Attachment A).

All LMEs are licensed and operate as Managed Care Organizations (MCOs). These MCOs can restrict the providers from whom Medicaid enrollees obtain services. In addition, they receive payments from the Medicaid agency based on the number of people enrolled. If the services they provide cost more than the payment they received from the state, the MCOs incur a loss. If services provided cost less, they may use the funds for other purposes.

North Carolina is scheduled to transition to a statewide managed care program for Medicaid in 2019. *See* 2015 N.C. Sess. Laws 245. Under this system, Prepaid Health Plans (PHPs) will manage all Medicaid services and receive monthly payments based on enrollment. For more information, see the state's website for resources on Medicaid transitions. In order to make this legislatively mandated change, in 2016 DHHS applied for permission to operate a demonstration project to implement its proposed managed care program This type of waiver is authorized under Section 1115 of the Medicaid Act. 42 U.S.C. § 1315. In addition, the Department amended this request in 2017 to request permission to expand coverage to many low-income adults. DHHS, NC Medicaid Transformations.

III.   Eligibility

A.   Background

Low income alone does not qualify an individual for Medicaid. Under current law, applicants must also be a resident of the state in which they are applying, be a citizen or a qualified alien, and fit into a specific category—generally, certain groups of children, caretaker relatives, pregnant women, people over age 65, and people with disabilities.

The federal health reform law, the Affordable Care Act (ACA), known colloquially as Obamacare, required states to expand Medicaid coverage to include nearly all individuals who have incomes below 133 percent of the Federal Poverty Level (FPL). 42 U.S.C. § 1396a(a)(10)(A)(i)(VIII). In 2012, the U.S. Supreme Court held that the USDHHS could not penalize states that refused to participate in the Medicaid expansion by withholding their federal Medicaid funds, effectively meaning that the ACA expansion was optional. *Nat'l Fed'n of Indep. Bus. v. Sebelius,* 567 U.S. 519 (2012). As of December 2017, North Carolina was one of the 18 states that chose not expand Medicaid to this population, although DHHS has requested permission from CMS to do so, as discussed above. The eligibility expansion would need to be approved by the state legislature to be officially submitted to CMS. After legislative approval, it would still need to be approved by CMS in order to go into effect.

Generally, individuals who are inmates of public institutions are not eligible for North Carolina Medicaid. This includes most incarcerated or detained children, with some important exceptions discussed below.

B.   Residency

To qualify for North Carolina Medicaid, a child must live in North Carolina. Her residence is generally that of her parent or legal guardian. 42 C.F.R. § 435.403(i)(2)(ii); 10A N.C. ADMIN. CODE 23E.0103(a). She cannot be denied Medicaid because she has not resided in the state for a specific period of time, nor can she be denied eligibility because she does not have a permanent or fixed address. Family and Children's Medicaid Manual MA-3205.IV.A.6; 42 U.S.C. § 1396a(b)(2). If the Medicaid agency places a child in an out-of-state setting, such as a residential treatment facility, the child will, under most circumstances, still be a North Carolina Medicaid enrollee.

C.   Citizenship

In order to qualify for Medicaid, a child must be a U.S. citizen or a "qualified alien." 8 U.S.C. §§ 1611, 1641; 10A N.C. ADMIN. CODE 23E.0102(b). A child is a U.S. citizen if he was born in the U.S., even if his parents are undocumented immigrants. "Qualified aliens" include refugees, asylees, children of veterans or active military personnel, American Indians born in Canada, Cuban or Haitian entrants, and Amerasian immigrants. DHHS, Integrated Eligibility Manual 15140. A child does not have to disclose the immigration status of his parents in order to apply for Medicaid. U.S. Dep't of Health & Human Servs., *Dear State Health & Welfare Officials,* (Jan. 21, 2003).

There is an exception for emergency services. Emergency services and treatment are covered for labor and delivery, and for conditions that have a sudden onset and manifest by acute symptoms of sufficient severity that the lack of immediate medical attention could seriously jeopardize health, seriously impair bodily functions, or cause serious dysfunction of organs or body parts. If an individual meets all eligibility requirements for Medicaid other than citizenship, services to treat such emergency conditions are covered. 10A N.C. ADMIN. CODE 23E.0102(c); Integrated Eligibility Manual 15190, 15190.20.

D.   Financial Eligibility

To qualify for Medicaid, applicants' income—and sometimes resources—must be below certain thresholds that vary depending on the specific eligibility category. Income is money received, including earnings, investment income, and some cash benefits from government programs or pensions. It may also be "in-kind" income, such as food and shelter. Resources may be cash or property that can be liquidated or converted to cash. Income and resources are considered automatically available, or "deemed" from a parent to a child. Therefore, custodial parents' income and resources are usually counted when determining a child's eligibility for Medicaid. Family & Children's Medicaid Manual MA 3305.IV.E.1. Grandparents and stepparents are generally not financially responsible for children living with them, so their income and resources are generally not counted. 10A N.C. ADMIN. CODE 23E.0203(b)(4); Family & Children's Medicaid Manual MA 3305.IV.E.2.b-d.

E.   Specific Categories of Eligibility

There are a number of eligibility categories through which children may qualify for Medicaid. Generally, children who have incomes below 210 percent of the Federal Poverty Level—about $52,000 for a family of four—will qualify for either Medicaid or for insurance through NC Health Choice. *See* Division of Medical Assistance, Basic Medicaid Eligibility (Mar. 10, 2017).

1.   Low-Income Children

The ACA extended mandatory Medicaid coverage to children younger than age 19 in families at or below 133 percent of the FPL. 42 U.S.C. § 1396a(a)(10)(A)(i)(VIII). Most non-citizen children are still excluded. The Medicaid expansion for children was not affected by the Supreme Court's decision in *National Federation of Independent Business v. Sebelius*.

As of 2014, states now use Modified Adjusted Gross Income (MAGI) to determine Medicaid eligibility for most of these children. For income, MAGI is based largely on adjusted gross income as reported for federal income tax purposes. Under these rules, there is no resource limit; in other words, regardless of the value of houses, cars, or other property that a family owns, if their income is below the necessary level, their child still may qualify for Medicaid. 42 U.S.C. § 1396a(e)(14).

North Carolina has opted to provide Medicaid coverage to all children under age 6 if their income is below 210 percent of the FPL, or about $52,000 per year for a family of four. As required by the ACA, children ages 6 and older, but under age 19, are eligible for Medicaid if their household income is below 133 percent of the FPL, or about $33,000 per year for a family of four. Division of Medical Assistance, Basic Medicaid Eligibility.

2.   Families with Dependent Children

Traditionally, Medicaid eligibility was linked to eligibility for the federal Aid to Families with Dependent Children (AFDC). When Congress repealed that program in 1996 and replaced it with Temporary Assistance for Needy Families (TANF), it required states to cover families who would have been eligible as AFDC existed in 1996. 42 U.S.C. § 1396u-1(a).

Today, TANF is what most people refer to as "welfare," i.e., cash payments. In North Carolina, individuals who receive benefits through North Carolina's version of TANF, called Work First Family Assistance (WFFA), automatically qualify for Medicaid. WFFA applies only to families with children, and the income eligibility level for WFFA is extremely low—no more than about $7,100 per year for a family of four. Families also must have resources worth less than $3,000 to qualify. MA-3320.I.

3.   Adopted and Foster Children

Any child with a federal Title IV-E adoption or foster care agreement is automatically eligible for Medicaid. Family and Children's Medicaid Manual MA-3230.VI.A. An adopted child who does not have a Title IV-E adoption agreement but has special medical or rehabilitative needs is also eligible for Medicaid. *Id.*, 3230.V.B. The eligibility of these children is determined based on their own income and resources, not the income and resources of the adoptive parents. *Id.*, 3230.V.B.3(f)(2).

Adolescents who were in foster care on their 18th birthday are eligible for Medicaid, regardless of their resources or income, until they turn 21. *Id.*, 3230.X.

4.   Pregnant Adolescents

If an adolescent is pregnant, she is eligible for Medicaid if she has an income up to 196 percent of the FPL. *See* Division of Medical Assistance, Basic Medicaid Eligibility. In 2017, this is a monthly income of around $2,650 for the pregnant adolescent and her unborn child. 82 Fed. Reg. 8831 (Jan. 26, 2017); Family and Children's Medicaid Manual MA-3310.I.A. The income of her parents or others she is living with is not counted, even if they are supporting her. Family and Children's Medicaid Manual MA-3310.III.B-C. If they give her actual cash money it will, however, count toward her income. Regardless of changes in her income, she remains eligible for 60 days postpartum. 10A N.C. ADMIN. CODE 23D.0101(7).

5.   SSI Recipients

Supplemental Security Income (SSI) is the federal cash assistance program for low-income people with disabilities whose disabilities or age prevent them from engaging in substantial gainful activity. 42 U.S.C. § 1382c(a)(3)(B). All recipients of SSI qualify for Medicaid, including individuals who receive SSI pending a final determination of blindness or disability or who receive SSI conditionally pending disposal of excess resources. 10A N.C. ADMIN. CODE 23D.0101(9); *see also* 42 C.F.R. § 435.120.

6. Medically Needy

Individuals who otherwise qualify for Medicaid but have income that exceeds the eligibility limits may still be eligible as "medically needy." Such individuals may apply medical expenses to their income and "spend down" to a certain set level, called the medically needy income level (MNIL). 42 U.S.C. § 1396a(a)(10)(C). In North Carolina, this is known as meeting a "deductible." To meet it, an individual must show that he has incurred, but not necessarily paid, medical expenses equal to the deductible within the previous six months. The MNIL is very low in North Carolina, so a significant amount of expenses must be incurred before an individual can qualify in this category. *See generally* 10A N.C. ADMIN. CODE 23E.0209; Adult Medicaid Manual MA-2360.I-III; Family and Children's Medicaid Manual MA-3315.II-III.

7. Health Choice (Children's Health Insurance Program)

Some children with low incomes may not qualify for Medicaid, but may instead qualify for North Carolina Health Choice (NCHC), which is the state's program under the federal Children's Health Insurance Program (CHIP). This program serves uninsured children who do not qualify for Medicaid and have family income under 211 percent of the FPL. N.C. GEN. STAT. § 108A-70.21; Family and Children's Medicaid Manual MA-3255.II. NCHC, like Medicaid, has used MAGI income calculations since 2014. 42 U.S.C. § 1397bb(1)(B)(v). For most children, NCHC covers a less comprehensive set of services than Medicaid and, unlike Medicaid, enrollment can be frozen and wait lists imposed if the program reaches capacity. It may still, however, provide important health care services for children who do not qualify for Medicaid.

F. Eligibility Rules for Inmates of Public Institutions

Federal law does not link eligibility to incarceration status but does provide that federal funds cannot cover Medicaid services for anyone who is an "inmate of a public institution." 42 U.S.C. § 1396d(a)(A); *see also* 42 C.F.R. §§ 435.1009(a)(1), 441.13(a)(1). Nothing in federal law prohibits inmates from being eligible for Medicaid, but states may not receive federal Medicaid reimbursement for services provided to them while they are incarcerated. The federal government does not, however, *prevent* states from terminating Medicaid eligibility for inmates. Predictably, therefore, many states—including North Carolina—do terminate Medicaid eligibility for most individuals when they enter prison, jail, or detention. Thus, in North Carolina, inmates, including children, are not eligible for Medicaid. Adult Medicaid Manual MA-2510.II.A; Family and Children's Medicaid Manual MA-3360.II.A.

Federal guidance explains that an individual is an inmate "when serving time for a criminal offense or confined involuntarily in State or Federal prisons, jails, detention facilities, or other penal facilities." U.S. Dep't of Health & Human Servs., HCFA Program Issuance Transmittal Notice Region IV (Mar. 6, 1998). A public institution is one that "is the responsibility of a governmental unit or over which a governmental unit exercises administrative control." 42 C.F.R. § 435.1010. It does not include, however, intermediate care facility services for people with intellectual disabilities, such as the Murdoch Developmental Center, which are covered by Medicaid. Nor does it include Psychiatric Residential Treatment Facilities or Level I-III group homes, which are also coverable under Medicaid. *See generally* 42 U.S.C. § 1396d(a); Family and Children's Medicaid Manual MA-3360.II.D-E.

North Carolina policy provides that a child is not eligible for Medicaid if she is committed to a federal prison, state juvenile justice facility, county or local jail, forestry camp, or other facility "operated primarily for the detention of children who are determined by the court to be delinquent." Adult Medicaid Admin. Letters, DMA Administrative Letter No: 09-08 (Aug. 27, 2008); Family and Children's Medicaid Manual MA-3360 II.A.3. This includes when she is transferred from such a setting to another facility, such as a hospital, to receive care.

Significantly, a child is not considered an inmate for Medicaid purposes if she is on house arrest, probation, or parole. Family and Children's Medicaid Manual MA-3360.II.A.1.

1.   Temporary Detention

The federal prohibition on using federal Medicaid funds to cover services for inmates does not apply when an individual is in an institution for "a temporary period pending other arrangements appropriate to his needs." 42 C.F.R. § 435.1010(b). In North Carolina, if a child is placed in a detention setting prior to adjudication, he may be eligible for Medicaid depending on his final placement. If his final placement is the Youth Development Center (YDC) or other public institution, the child is considered to have been an inmate since he was initially detained and therefore not eligible for Medicaid during that time. If the child's final placement is any place other than a penal institution (placed with a relative or in a residential treatment center, for example) the child is considered to have never been an inmate of a penal institution, even during the period he was in the YDC. Family and Children's Medicaid Manual MA-3360.II.A.4.a. This means that services a child may have received during such temporary detention can be covered by Medicaid.

Notably, inmates who are in the custody of Department of Corrections (unlike most children who are inmates and are in the custody of Division of Juvenile Justice) have Medicaid suspended rather than terminated. Adult Medicaid Admin. Letters, DMA Administrative Letter No: 09-08, Medicaid Suspension Addendum 1 (Sept. 9, 2010), *superseded in part by* Medicaid Suspension Addendum 2 (Apr. 7, 2011).

2.   Eligibility Determinations While in a Public Institution

For children who are not eligible for Medicaid when they are detained in public institutions, Medicaid applications may be accepted during detention. But if the child remains detained at the end of the application processing period—either because she has been committed to a YDC or because she has not yet been given a final placement—the application will be denied. If the final placement is not in a detention setting, the application will be re-opened and processed. Family and Children's Medicaid Manual MA-3360.II.A.4.b(1).

It is important to note, however, that in practice, there is likely to be considerable variation throughout the state in procedures and policies for terminating Medicaid for children who are inmates, depending on the county in which the child lives. It is possible that a child who is an inmate will not have her Medicaid terminated, especially if she is confined for a relatively short period of time and her eligibility re-determination does not occur until she has been released.

IV.   Services

A.   Background

Federal law requires states to cover certain "mandatory" services in their Medicaid plans, including physician, hospital, clinic, nursing home, and family planning services. States also may cover certain "optional" services, including rehabilitative, dental, and personal care services; and physical, occupational or speech therapy. 42 U.S.C. §§ 1396a(a)(10), 1396d(a). If a state chooses to cover optional services, they must indicate this in their state Medicaid plan. As explained below, because of Medicaid's Early Periodic Screening, Diagnostic, and Treatment (EPSDT) requirements, there is no such thing as an optional service for children.

B.   Early and Periodic Screening, Diagnostic, and Treatment Services (EPSDT)

1.   EPSDT Basics

States must cover EPSDT for children up to age 21 who are enrolled in Medicaid. Family and Children's Medicaid Manual MA-3540.XXXVIII; N.C. Dept. of Health & Human Servs., Division of Medical Assistance, *EPSDT Policy Instructions Update* (January 11, 2010), (*DMA EPSDT Policy Instructions*); *see also* 42 U.S.C. §§ 1396a(a)(10)(A), 1396a(a)(43), 1396d(a)(4)(B), 1396d(r). Unlike adults, for whom Medicaid coverage is subject to more limits, children under age 21 who qualify for Medicaid are entitled to a consistent and expansive set of covered services. Family and Children's Medicaid Manual MA-3540.XXXVIII B; *DMA EPSDT Policy Instructions*; 42 U.S.C. §1396a(a)(10)(A).

EPSDT, known as Health Check in North Carolina, is a set of services consisting of screening, immunizations, laboratory tests, and health education. Significantly, EPSDT includes all services that fit within the mandatory and optional service categories in the Medicaid Act that are "necessary to correct or ameliorate" physical and mental conditions. 42 U.S.C. §§ 1396a(a)(43)(C), 1396d(r)(5); 42 C.F.R. §§ 441.50-441.62. This means that North Carolina must cover all medically necessary Medicaid services that can be covered under federal Medicaid law *even if the state chooses not to cover the service for adults*. For example, a Medicaid agency can choose not to provide dental services to adults, but under EPSDT it must provide them to children. *DMA EPSDT Policy Instructions*, p. 3, 12 (listing required services for EPSDT).

EPSDT requires states to do more than merely offer to cover services. States are obligated to actively arrange for treatment, either by providing the service itself or through referral to appropriate agencies, organizations, or individuals, and by assisting with scheduling and transportation. The Medicaid agency must make available a variety of individual and group providers qualified and willing to provide EPSDT services. 42 U.S.C. § 1396a(a)(43)(A); 42 C.F.R. §§ 441.50-441.62

Thus, the Medicaid program must ensure that all Medicaid enrollees under age 21, including those involved in the juvenile justice system, have access to the services needed to correct a health problem, improve the problem, prevent it from getting worse, or help the child function with the problem.

2.   Periodic and Interperiodic Screens

Medicaid must cover periodic examinations, or "screens," that measure a child's medical, vision, hearing, and dental status. They must be performed at regular intervals, as determined by "periodicity schedules" that meet the standards of pediatric and adolescent medical and dental practice. Medical screens must provide a health and developmental history, a physical examination, immunizations, laboratory tests, and health education.

In addition, EPSDT covers visits to health care providers outside of the periodicity schedule if needed to determine whether a child has a condition that needs further care. 42 U.S.C. §§ 1396d(r)(1)-(4). These are called "interperiodic screens." Persons outside the health care system (for instance, a parent, court counselor, or juvenile defender) can make this determination and refer a child for an interperiodic screen. Centers for Medicare and Medicaid Services, *EPSDT—A Guide for States: Coverage in the Medicaid Benefit for Children and Adolescents* (June 2014), at 5 (citing example of interperiodic screening requirement when school nurse and teacher suspect a child may have a vision problem and recommend to child's parent that child see an optometrist). Following referral, "[a]ny qualified provider operating within the scope of his or her practice, as defined by state law, can provide a screening service," including providers not otherwise participating in Medicaid. *Id.* at 6.

3.   EPSDT's Broad Treatment Mandate

Medicaid must cover any service that fits within the broad categories described in the federal Medicaid statute, if necessary to "correct or ameliorate" an illness or condition detected during a periodic or interperiodic screen. 42 U.S.C. § 1396d(r)(5). Even if the service will not cure a condition, it must be covered if the service is necessary to improve or maintain a child's functioning or symptoms. The service requested must also be safe, effective, generally recognized as an accepted method of medical practice or treatment, and must not be experimental. 42 C.F.R. §§ 440.1-440.170.

North Carolina has adopted a detailed policy implementing the federal EPSDT requirements. The policy instruction is posted on the DMA and DMH/DD/SAS websites, and is included in the state's training materials for Medicaid providers. *DMA EPSDT Policy Instructions Update* (Jan. 11, 2010), https://www2.ncdhhs.gov/dma/epsdt/epsdtpolicyinstructions.pdf. These instructions reiterate and expand on the federal Medicaid statutory EPSDT requirements, and provide that there can be:

- *No waiting list for services.* Although hospitals or clinics may have waiting lists to schedule appointments or medical procedures, the Medicaid program itself cannot impose any waiting list for eligibility or service coverage.

- *No cap on the total cost of medically necessary services.*

- *No upper limit on the number of hours or units of medically necessary services covered.*

- *No limit on the number of visits to a physician, therapist, dentist, or other licensed clinician* (other than medical necessity).

- *No set list that specifies when or what EPSDT services or equipment may be covered.* Services need only fit within the general categories in the Medicaid statute at 42 U.S.C. § 1396d(a). For example, a service that fits within the category of "rehabilitative services" can be covered even if the specific service itself is not listed in DMA clinical policies or service definitions.

- *No co-payment or other out-of-pocket cost may be charged to the recipient.*

Id. at 2-3.

The policy reiterates the statutory requirement that services may be covered for Medicaid enrollees under EPSDT even if such services are never covered for adults over 21 or not listed in the state Medicaid plan. It also includes a list of categories of services that are covered under Medicaid, directly from the federal statute. This list is attached *infra* as Attachment C.

4.   Behavioral Health Services

Mental health and substance abuse services available under EPSDT are of particular importance for justice involved children. Although the federal law lists a number of specific mandatory services, such as inpatient psychiatric treatment, the general list of covered categories of services is not exhaustive. Under EPSDT, children have the right to virtually any home or community-based mental health service that a practitioner determines is medically necessary, as long as it fits within one of the categories of covered services. Some of the services covered through EPSDT that may be most useful to juvenile justice involved children are briefly described below. A detailed list of these service definitions can be found in the Division of Medical Assistance, Clinical Coverage, Policy No. 8-A, Attachment D (rev'd Apr. 1, 2017), at 26.

- *Mobile Crisis Management.* A crisis response that is available 24 hours a day, 365 days a year, when a child is actively experiencing a crisis. Mobile Crisis Management provides immediate evaluation, triage, and access to acute mental health, developmental disability and substance abuse services.

- *Intensive in-home services.* A short-term clinical care and counseling program for children and their families within the home or community setting.

- *Multisystemic Therapy* (MST). A program designed for children who have antisocial, aggressive/violent behaviors and are at risk of out-of-home placement. Specialized therapeutic and rehabilitative interventions are available to address special areas such as substance abuse, sexual abuse, sex offending, and domestic violence.

- *Assertive Community Treatment Team.* A multidisciplinary team treatment that provides psychiatric treatment in a community setting to persons with serious and persistent mental illness.

- *Child and Adolescent Day Treatment.* Services provided in a licensed facility for children or adolescents.

- *Substance Abuse Comprehensive Outpatient Program.* An intensive, structured, short-term substance abuse treatment program.

- *Ambulatory Detoxification.* A program designed to safely detoxify individuals from drugs and alcohol without a hospital admission.

- *Medically Supervised Detoxification/Crisis Stabilization.* A medically supervised evaluation and withdrawal management service that occurs in a permanent facility with inpatient beds.

- *Opioid Treatment.* A service that uses methadone or other drugs approved for the treatment of opiate addiction in conjunction with the provision of rehabilitation and medical services.

Notably, some of these service definitions contain limits on services that are not consistent with EPSDT requirements or North Carolina's EPSDT policy. In order to be consistent with EPSDT's prohibition on automatic hourly limits that are unrelated to medical necessity, this policy contains a special provision related to EPSDT, providing that:

> Service limitations on scope, amount, duration, frequency, location of service, and/or other specific criteria described in clinical coverage policies may be exceeded or may not apply as long as the provider's documentation shows that the requested service is medically necessary "to correct or ameliorate a defect, physical or mental illness, or a condition" [health problem]; that is, provider documentation shows how the service, product, or procedure will correct or improve or maintain the recipient's health in the best condition possible, compensate for a health problem, prevent it from worsening, or prevent the development of additional health problems.

DMA, Clinical Coverage Policy 8-A, at 3.

North Carolina authorizes a type of provider, Critical Access Behavioral Health Agencies (CABHAs), which are responsible for providing some mental health and substance abuse services. CABHAs have specific staffing requirements, and are the only approved provider for certain types of behavioral health services (Day Treatment, Intensive In-Home, or Community Support Team).

V.   Community Alternative Programs (CAPs)

A.   Home and Community-Based Services for People with Disabilities

Federal law allows states to cover home and community-based services for people with disabilities through programs known as waivers. These programs provide services for individuals who require the level of care provided in an institution (hospital, intermediate care facility, or skilled nursing facility) and who, but for waiver services, would be institutionalized. 42 U.S.C. § 1396n(c). They are called waivers because they allow states to waive certain otherwise mandatory federal Medicaid requirements in order to target certain populations for these services. Waivers must be "cost neutral," meaning that it must cost less for a state to provide community based waiver services to individuals in the waiver than it would to cover institutional care for those individuals.

Waivers can serve individuals who would not otherwise be eligible due to income because waivers apply the same income eligibility rules that apply to institutionalized individuals. Typically, when determining eligibility, the Medicaid agency must consider the income and resources of an applicant's parent. If, however, an individual is in an institution or meets the criteria for a waiver, only the income and resources of the child, not the parent, are considered. This means that children generally are able to meet the income eligibility requirements and qualify for the waiver if they meet other eligibility criteria such as severity of disability. It is important to emphasize that children may receive both waiver and EPSDT services as waiver services are supposed to complement EPSDT services.

North Carolina's waiver program for people with intellectual and developmental disabilities is the NC Innovations Waiver. The waivers cover services for people with developmental disabilities that could not otherwise be covered by Medicaid, such as respite, home modifications, and habilitation. Habilitation services are "designed to assist individuals in acquiring, retaining, and improving the self-help, socialization and adaptive skills necessary to reside successfully" in community settings. 42 U.S.C. § 1396n(c)(5)(A); *see also* Disability Rights North Carolina, *Innovation Waivers*.

Some behavioral health services, notably, applied behavioral analysis (ABA) and other therapies for children with autism, have traditionally been considered habilitative and, therefore, only covered under the Innovations Waiver. In 2014, however, the federal government clarified that ABA can be covered under EPSDT. If a service fits into a Medicaid service category, such as rehabilitative or preventative services and meets other Medicaid requirements like medical necessity, it should be covered under EPSDT. For more information on this topic, *see* Disability Rights North Carolina, *Autism Related Services in North Carolina*.

VI.   Due Process

All Medicaid enrollees, including children, have rights to written notice and the opportunity for an administrative hearing when the Medicaid agency takes an adverse action against them. These rights are based on the Medicaid statute and regulations, North Carolina statutes and regulations, and guaranteed by the North Carolina and U.S. Constitutions. 10A N.C.

ADMIN. CODE 22H .0101; N.C. GEN. STAT. §§ 108A-70.9A, B, 108A-79; 42 U.S.C. § 1396a(a)(3); 42 C.F.R. §§ 431.200-431.250. Medicaid due process rights are also clarified and memorialized in a settlement of a North Carolina Medicaid case, *McCartney ex rel. McCartney v. Cansler*, 608 F. Supp. 2d 694 (E.D.N.C. 2009), *aff'd sub nom., D.T.M. ex rel. McCartney v. Cansler*, 382 F. App'x 334 (4th Cir. 2010). These rights are discussed in detail in this section.

A. Actions Triggering Due Process Rights

Individuals are entitled to notice and opportunity for hearing when the Medicaid agency or its contractor denies eligibility; denies requests for, terminates, or reduces services; or fails to determine eligibility or approve service requests within a reasonable time. N.C. GEN. STAT. § 108A-70.9A(d)(a); 10A N.C. ADMIN. CODE 22H.0101(a); Adult Medicaid Manual MA-2420.II.B; Family and Children's Medicaid MA-3430.II. Notice of adverse decisions must be made in writing and mailed to the appropriate person. Generally, the notice must be mailed to the custodial parent of the child. If, however, the child has a legal guardian or is in the custody of DSS, the notice must be mailed to them. Family and Children's Medicaid MA-3430.III.A.

Notices must provide the specific reason for the adverse action, cite the specific legal authority for the action, and, where applicable, provide an explanation of the right to continued benefits. The notices of action must also contain a Medicaid Services Hearing Request Form. N.C. GEN. STAT. § 108A-70.9A(e), 108A-79(c); 10A N.C. ADMIN. CODE 22H.0101, 71P.0102(3). Medicaid regulations provide that there is no right to a hearing if the sole reason is a change in law or policy, but Medicaid beneficiaries are still entitled to a hearing if such a change gives rise to a legitimate factual dispute, such as whether the change applies to that individual. 42 C.F.R. § 431.220(b).

B. Hearings

There are two different types of hearing systems available for Medicaid issues—one for issues related to determinations of eligibility for the Medicaid program and a second for those related to denial, suspension, or reduction of services.

DSS handles appeals related to eligibility. Adult Medicaid Manual MA-2420; Family and Children's Medicaid MA-3430. A claimant must first have a local hearing before the county DSS director. A state-level hearing is then available if the individual is dissatisfied with the result. N.C. GEN. STAT. § 108A-79(g). State level hearings may also be requested in the first instance by individuals disputing a determination that they are not disabled. Adult Medicaid Manual MA-2420.V.B.4.; Family and Children's Medicaid MA-3430.V.B.4. Hearings may be requested orally or in writing and must be requested within 60 days of the adverse action. N.C. GEN. STAT. § 108A-79(c).

DSS hears appeals of eligibility determinations at the state level. An appeal of a local hearing to a DSS state-level hearing must be made within 15 days of the local hearing decision. N.C. GEN. STAT. § 108A-79(g).

The Office of Administrative Hearings (OAH) hears appeals of reductions, suspensions, terminations, or denials of requests for services. N.C. GEN. STAT. §§ 108A-70.9A, B. All claimants also have to the right to participate in no-cost, optional mediation services before a hearing.

The procedure varies depending on where the individual lives and which services are involved. In some counties, Medicaid recipients must enroll in MCOs to receive behavioral health services. Individuals who are enrolled in MCOs must first exhaust an internal MCO grievance system. The timelines and other aspects of the grievance systems will be determined by the MCO's contract. This information must be provided to MCO enrollees at the time of enrollment and when a notice of action is provided.

A request for a formal OAH hearing must be made within 30 days of the notice of action, or the decision from an MCO internal grievance. N.C. GEN. STAT. § 108A-70.9A(d). Additional information about OAH hearings can be found at Hearings Division – Medicaid.

Requests for hearings to contest transfer or discharge from a facility must be made within eleven days of the action. 10A N.C. ADMIN. CODE 22H.0203.

Issue	Eligibility	Services
Local Hearing	DSS (mandatory, except for disability determination)	None
Time to request	60 days after notice mailed/given	11 days after notice mailed/given
State-level hearing	DSS	Office of Administrative Hearings
Time to request	15 days after mailing local decision	30 days after action
Right to petition for judicial review	Yes	Yes

If a hearing request is made before the effective date of the adverse action, generally within ten days of the date of the notice, the claimant must continue to receive benefits pending the result of the hearing. N.C. GEN. STAT. §§ 108A-70.9A(c)(7), 108A-79(c)(6).

C.   Rights at Hearings

The hearing must be conducted at a reasonable time, date, and place by an impartial hearing official who did not take part in the initial decision. N.C. GEN. STAT. § 108A-79(d). All administrative hearings must be *de novo* and the hearing officer must be permitted to consider evidence that was not available to the agency at the time of the agency's original decision. *Robinson ex rel. Robinson v. N.C. Dep't of Health and Human Servs.*, 715 S.E.2d 569 (N.C. App. 2011). At the hearing, the claimant must be able to present witnesses, establish facts, present argument without undue interference, and cross-examine witnesses. N.C. GEN. STAT. § 108A-79(e).

D.   Post-hearing action

If the decision is favorable to the child, corrective payments must be made retroactive to the date that the incorrect action was taken, if the payments were not made during the pendency of the appeal. 10A N.C. ADMIN. CODE 23G.0203. If the decision is not favorable to the child, the state may institute an action to recover any costs of the continued services during the appeals process. 10A N.C. ADMIN. CODE 22H.0104(d).

The final agency decision may be appealed by filing a petition in Superior Court within 30 days of receiving notice of the decision. N.C. GEN. STAT. §§ 150B-43 – 150B-45.

VII.   Conclusion

Medicaid is a crucial resource for justice-involved and at risk children. Working knowledge of the program can help juvenile defenders better represent these children and, perhaps, avoid commitment. The program is, however, complex, dense, and ever-evolving. Additional resources are available to help navigate Medicaid, including advocates who represent children in Medicaid appeals. Some of these sources and agencies are described in the attachments that follow.

Attachment A: Sources of Medicaid Law, Policy, and Information

Federal Law:
42 U.S.C §§ 1396-1396w-5.
42 C.F.R. §§ 430-456.725.

Federal Policy:
Centers for Medicare and Medicaid Services (CMS)
- State Medicaid Manual (sub-regulatory policy statements)
  - www.cms.gov/Regulations-and-Guidance/Guidance/Manuals/Paper-Based-Manuals-Items/CMS021927.html
- Dear State Medicaid Director Letters
  - www.medicaid.gov/Federal-Policy-Guidance/Federal-Policy-Guidance.html

North Carolina Law:
N.C. General Statutes 108a-54 et seq.
10 N.C. Administrative Code. Chapters 26 and 50

North Carolina Medicaid Policy:
- Adult Medicaid Manual
  - https://www2.ncdhhs.gov/info/olm/manuals/dma/abd/man
- Family and Children's Medicaid Manual
  - https://www2.ncdhhs.gov/info/olm/manuals/dma/fcm/man

Federal Agencies:
- **Department of Health & Human Services, Centers for Medicare & Medicaid Services (CMS)**
  - www.cms.gov
  - www.medicaid.gov (information about Medicaid)
  - www.healthcare.gov (information about enrolling in public insurance coverage)

North Carolina State Governmental Entities:
- **Division of Medical Assistance**
  - www.ncdhhs.gov/dma
  - EPSDT information - www.ncdhhs.gov/dma/provider/epsdthealthcheck.htm

- **Division of Mental Health/Developmental Disabilities/Substance Abuse Services**
  - www.ncdhhs.gov/mhddsas
  - Listing of LMEs - www.ncdhhs.gov/mhddsas/lmeonblue.htm
- Mental health and substance abuse service definitions - https://files.nc.gov/ncdma/documents/files/8A_1.pdf

- **Department of Social Services**
  - www.ncdhhs.gov/dss
- **Office of Administrative Hearings**
  - www.ncoah.com

Medicaid Advocacy Organizations:

These organizations may be able to assist children who have been denied Medicaid services.

- Disability Rights North Carolina – www.disabilityrightsnc.org
- Legal Aid of North Carolina – www.legalaidnc.org
- Advocates for Children's Services – www.legalaidnc.org/Pages/about-us/projects/Advocates-for-Childrens-Services.aspx
- Charlotte Center for Legal Advocacy (formerly Legal Services of the Southern Piedmont) – www.lssp.org (Charlotte area)
- Council for Children's Rights – www.cfcrights.org (Charlotte area)

Attachment B: Glossary of Acronyms

AFDC
Aid to Families with Dependent Children
> *Former federal cash assistance program for children deprived of parental support.*

CABHA
Critical Access Behavioral Health Agency
> *Behavioral health entity that supplies Community Support Teams, Intensive In-Home Services, and Day Treatment.*

CAP
Community Alternatives Programs
> *Medicaid program for individuals with disabilities that provides services in the community to prevent institutionalization.*

CAP I/DD
Community Alternatives Program for Intellectual or Developmental Disabilities
> *CAP program for people who need the level of care provided in an intermediate care facility for people with intellectual or developmental disabilities (including state developmental centers).*

CHIP
Children's Health Insurance Program
> *Federal-state program for uninsured children with incomes too high to qualify for Medicaid.*

CMS
Centers for Medicare & Medicaid Services
> *Federal agency responsible for administering Medicaid and Medicare.*

DMA
Division of Medical Assistance
> *North Carolina's state Medicaid agency.*

DMHDDSAS
Division of Mental Health, Developmental Disabilities, and Substance Abuse Services
> *North Carolina's agency serving people with people with one of these disabilities.*

EPSDT
Early and Periodic Screening, Diagnosis and Treatment

FFP
Federal financial participation
> *Federal funding provided to the state to match its state Medicaid expenditures.*

FPL
Federal poverty level
>   *Federally established income level denoting the official poverty level, linked to eligibility for many programs.*

HCFA
Health Care Financing Agency
>   *Former name of CMS, name changed in 2001.*

LME
Local management entity
>   *Local agency (private or public) that oversees and administers mental health, developmental disability, and substance abuse services.*

MCO
Managed Care Organization

OAH
North Carolina's Office of Administrative Hearings

PBH
Piedmont Behavioral Health

TANF
Temporary Assistance to Needy Families
>   *Federal program of cash assistance to low income families.*

WFFA
Work First Family Assistance
>   *North Carolina's TANF program.*

Attachment C: Covered EPSDT Services

- Inpatient hospital services (other than services in an institution for mental disease)
- Outpatient hospital services
- Rural health clinic services (including home visits for homebound individuals)
- Federally-qualified health center services
- Other laboratory and X-ray services (in an office or similar facility)
- Family planning services and supplies
- Physician services (in office, recipient's home, hospital, nursing facility, or elsewhere)
- Medical and surgical services furnished by a dentist
- Home health care services (nursing services; home health aides; medical supplies, equipment, and appliances suitable for use in the home; physical therapy, occupation therapy, speech pathology, audiology services provided by a home health agency or by a facility licensed by the State to provide medical rehabilitation services)
- Private duty nursing services
- Clinic services (including services outside of clinic for eligible homeless individuals)
- Dental services
- Physical therapy, occupational therapy, and services for individuals with speech, hearing, and language disorders
- Prescribed drugs
- Dentures
- Prosthetic devices
- Eyeglasses
- Services in an intermediate care facility for the mentally retarded
- Medical care, or any other type of remedial care recognized under State law, furnished by licensed practitioners within the scope of their practice as defined by State law, specified by the Secretary (also includes transportation by a provider to whom a direct vendor payment can appropriately be made)
- Other diagnostic, screening, preventive, and rehabilitative services, including any medical or remedial services (provided in a facility, a home, or other setting) recommended by a physician or other licensed practitioner of the healing arts within the scope of their practice under State law, for the maximum reduction of physical or mental disability and restoration of an individual to the best possible functional level
- Inpatient psychiatric hospital services for individuals under age 21
- Services furnished by a midwife, which the nurse-midwife is legally authorized to perform under state law, without regard to whether the nurse-midwife is under the supervision of, or associated with, a physician or other health care provider throughout the maternity cycle
- Hospice care
- Case-management services
- TB-related services
- Respiratory care services
- Services furnished by a certified pediatric nurse practitioner or certified family nurse practitioner, which the practitioner is legally authorized to perform under state law

- Personal care services (in a home or other location) furnished to an individual who is not an inpatient or resident of a hospital, nursing facility, intermediate care facility for the mentally retarded, or institution for mental disease
- Primary care case management services

Source: 42 U.S.C. § 1396d(a); *DMA EPSDT Policy Instructions Update* (Jan. 11, 2010), https://www2.ncdhhs.gov/dma/epsdt/epsdtpolicyinstructions.pdf